**Procedural Due Process:** • Paul v Davis: mugshot
• Roth - 1 yr contract teacher, not a bilateral expect
  so yes bilateral • Cleveland b of ed v Loudermill -
• Goldberg v Kelly - Food stamps, import
• Mathews - disability benefits • Hamdi
★ Mathews factors → 1. value of private int  2. risk of error + secured by new proc
  3. Gov interest + costs of new process       notice → evidentiary → Jury
                                                          hearing

## Standing: • Lujan animals
1. Injury in fact
   A. Concrete + particularized
   B. Actual or Imminent
      not conjectural/hypo
2. Causal connection
   w/ Def actions NOT 3rd
   party actions
3. Redressability
   ★ can be granted by
   congress

**2022-2023 CASE SUPPLEMENT**
*for*
**MODERN CONSTITUTIONAL LAW**
*(Second Edition)*

Friedman

## Anti-Commandeering
• NY nuclear waste
• San Ant Transit
  labor laws
• Printz gun bg check

Congress can regulate
states when acting
privately. NOT when
doing state things
OR treat as person
Police force

## Political Questions
1. Textually demonstrable constitutional commitment to another branch
2. lack of discoverable and manageable test
3. cannot be decided w/o Policy determination by someone else
4. due respect to other branches
5. unquestioning adherence to already made political decision
6. Ew... embarrassing

## Religion ~~Strict Scrutiny~~  • Employment div v Smith - Peyote, fac N + Gen App
• Cuomo - Covid  • Kennedy - Coach
1. Facially Neutral + Generally Applicable → rational basis
2. Not F. Neutral or G. App → Strict Scrutiny
3. religion gets lowest restrict if multiple

Establishment → Compulsion or Coercion, hard to prove w/o social pressure

**Note: Always do State action + Standing + PQ**

**2022-2023 CASE** ~~~~~~~ **NT**

**MODE**~~~~~~~~~~~~~~~~

> Don't Panic! Type outline!
> ~~Passss~~
> ID: 81071
> Ph: 9D87E743

RHW Press ✦ Boston, MA

2022-2023 CASE SUPPLEMENT
for
MODERN CONSTITUTIONAL LAW
(Second Edition)

© Lawrence Friedman | November 30, 2022

All rights reserved. Published in the United States by RHW Press, Boston, MA. No part of this publication may be reproduced or transmitted in any form or by any means without written permission.

*Table of Contents*

**Chapter 1:**
**The Constitution and How Constitutional Law Works,** 7

**Chapter 2:**
**Separation of Powers: the Legislative Power,** 75

**Chapter 3:**
**Separation of Powers: the Executive Power,** 87

**Chapter 5:**
**The State Action Doctrine,** 127

**Chapter 7:**
**Substantive Due Process,** 135

**Chapter 9:**
**The Religion Clauses,** 257

**Chapter 10:**
**Justiciability,** 311

This supplement includes major constitutional decisions from the U.S. Supreme Court through July 2022.

# Chapter 1
# The Constitution and
# How Constitutional Law Works

"We must never forget that it is a constitution we are expounding."
— *Chief Justice John Marshall, McCulloch v. Maryland (1819)*

This book is at heart a guide to American constitutional law — and really only a few slivers of it. For example, the book does not cover in any great detail criminal procedure, which is primarily based in the Fourth, Fifth, and Sixth Amendments to the U.S. Constitution and is the subject of its own course. Nor does the book cover the esoteric issues surrounding some of the more obscure provisions of the Constitution, issues most lawyers in practice are unlikely to encounter. Rather, this book seeks to provide you an overview of how constitutional law works, by reviewing basic separation of powers concepts, and by providing in-depth treatment of individual rights issues under the First and Fourteenth Amendments.

Unlike other constitutional law casebooks (and courses), this book proposes no grand unifying theory of constitutional law — an area of law, you will see, that is undeniably messy and complicated. To the competing philosophies and theories of constitutional law, moreover, this book will devote relatively little attention; while debates between and among scholars and jurists about constitutional interpretation can be fascinating (not to mention frustrating), the federal district court or state trial court judge before whom you are likely to be arguing the merits of a constitutional claim will be more interested in having you help them figure out how settled doctrine should be properly applied in the case at hand. And that task is no small matter — for one thing, your clients are depending upon you to know the doctrine and how to apply it. That is why they hired you in the first place.

At bottom, then, this book is a resource. Its aims are to help you to understand how constitutional law works in practice, and to help you to develop your ability to make sound constitutional arguments. This chapter will discuss the first question, while the second is essentially the focus of the rest of the book.

## A. How Constitutional Law Works

Contrary to popular belief, the constitutional law upon which most lawyers rely in their everyday practices is not found in the document itself. Rather, it is found in the decisions of the United States Supreme Court in which the Court interprets the various provisions of the Constitution and articulates the doctrinal frameworks — the judicial tests — that should be used in future cases by the lower federal and state courts to determine whether a constitutional violation of some sort has occurred. That said, it all begins with the text, and it is important to have some understanding of the government and the rights that the document itself establishes.

Accordingly, it is to the text that we first turn.

Following the preamble, Article I of the U.S. Constitution enumerates the powers of Congress. Sovereignty lies with the people of the United States; in ratifying the Constitution the people took from the states certain powers and responsibilities and gave them to Congress, while at the same time establishing that the enumeration of legislative powers in Article I represents the entirety of what Congress can do. And what Congress can do is quite a bit, but far from everything; all other powers remain with the states, which have primary responsibility for regulating the health, safety, and welfare of their citizens — that is, the people of the United States. Such local control enables those elected representatives closer to the people themselves to create and enforce the rules by which the people will be governed. Our concern in this book is with a handful of Congress's powers under Article I: the commerce power, the taxing power, the spending power, the treaty power, and the necessary and proper power.

Article II details the powers of the President. As you may have noticed in reading the text of the Constitution, these are fewer in number than the powers delegated to Congress, but potentially broader in scope. The President has all the executive power and the obligation to execute the laws faithfully. In our modern world, most federal regulation comes from administrative agencies that are lodged in (or around) the executive branch. These agencies act on the direction of Congress through enabling statutes that dictate the terms upon which the agencies will regulate various subject matters. Similar agencies (and many others) exist at the state level; indeed, despite the proliferation of federal agencies since the Second World War, it is still the case that most regulation that affects Americans in their daily lives may be traced to state governmental action.

In Article III, the Constitution establishes the Supreme Court and spells out some of the details of the judicial branch; it also empowers Congress to create and maintain the other courts in the federal judicial system. Article IV concerns the full faith and credit states must give to one another's laws, controls the admission of new states into the union, and guarantees a republican form of government — a guarantee that is a subject of one of the last cases in this book, *Baker v. Carr* (1962). Article V outlines the means by which the Constitution can be amended — either by a two-thirds vote of both houses and the agreement of three-quarters of the states, which has been accomplished some 27 times; or by constitutional convention, which has not been attempted — and the Supremacy Clause, which puts federal law above state and local laws.

There is no express separation of powers provision in the Constitution (unlike some state constitutions); rather, the boundaries of the branches and their separation from one another may be inferred from the structure of the government the Constitution establishes, with distinct departments devoted to the legislative, executive, and judicial functions. This is a horizontal separation; the Constitution also establishes a vertical separation of powers, between the federal government and the states.

These separations, all a part of what is known as "federalism," serve important purposes: to prevent any one person or group in one branch from getting away with too much, or exercising the power of another branch, and by requiring cooperation between Congress and the President in order for a policy idea to become the law of the land. The distinct departments at the federal level also provide for different perspectives on issues of policy at different times — there is a temporal element to separation of powers. In a real sense, much of constitutional law could be reduced to a separation of powers analysis, for it often falls to the courts ultimately to determine who gets to decide an issue — Congress, the President, the states, or perhaps the judiciary itself.

To illustrate how horizontal federalism in our constitutional system works, consider the appointment process under Article II, Section 2, which grants the President the power to nominate and appoint executive officers with the advice and consent of the Senate. Imagine you are counsel to the Senate Judiciary Committee and asked by your clients (the various senators on the committee) to address the constitutionality of a proposal whereby judicial vacancies would be filled through a binding national referendum. This, the Senators believe, would avoid protracted and potentially pointless confirmation hearings that serve more as an opportunity for senators to grandstand than an effort to determine whether judicial nominees are genuinely qualified to serve as judges for life in the federal system.

The question for you is: would such a proposal violate Article II, Section 2? To answer that question, you need to determine what the Constitution requires. The text of Section 2 seems to reflect the separation of powers principles discussed above: the President selects nominees to the federal courts, but those individuals cannot assume their judgeships absent approval by one house of the legislature, the Senate. In this way, the power to appoint judges cannot be exercised by one branch acting alone: the President chooses while the Senate vets and ultimately approves. From the institutional relationship established by the text, we can derive a rule: at a minimum, once the President nominates an individual to a judicial post, the Senate must do something. In other words, the Constitution contemplates the Senate taking some independent action in respect to judicial nominees; it does not appear to contemplate the Senate offloading the entirety of its constitutional responsibility to give its advice and consent onto the American people through a binding referendum. With just the text and a sense of how separation of powers operates under the Constitution, you can see a doctrine begin to emerge — a test unstated by the text itself, but which can be plausibly inferred from the text and which lawyers, lawmakers, and judges could apply consistently in like cases to determine whether the Constitution has been violated. That test — relatively unformed though it may be at this point — and not the constitutional text, will be the basis for arguments in subsequent cases raising similar issues.

How constitutional law works, then, is through decision-making by the Supreme Court about what the text means and how it should be applied — not the literal text (well, almost never), but, rather, the doctrine derived from the text, which allows lawyers and judges to test the Constitution's limits in future cases. A hallmark of the rule of law is consistency — a consistency that allows the law to be predictably and not arbitrarily applied by the courts. The constitutional doctrines articulated by the Supreme Court provide the means by which the Constitution can be consistently and predictably applied over time (until such time as the test is abandoned and replaced with another). Knowing the doctrine and how to apply it are critical skills in constitutional litigation.

This is not to say that all constitutional doctrines are perfectly formed — far from it. Many doctrines may have obvious flaws, or ignore all kinds of considerations that the framers might have thought important, or reflect little regard for the current wishes of the American people. But, even given such defects, these doctrinal tests give us sets of rules that will channel subsequent judicial decision-making, so that the rulings in particular cases reflect the application of reason and not arbitrary or result-oriented preferences. And this commitment to principle — to consistency and predictability — is no small thing: it is the basis not just for constitutional decision-making, but the common law and much statutory interpretation as well. Whether you consider doctrine to be more like a code or a formula, identifying it and applying it are the tasks with which much of the first year of law school is centrally concerned.

## B. Constitutional Doctrines: Free Speech and the Right to Bear Arms

Now, let's consider what constitutional law looks like in two specific contexts — the guarantee of freedom of speech, under the First Amendment; and the right to bear arms in self-defense, under the Second Amendment. These discussions should serve to help you to understand how constitutional law works in practice—and give you some sense about how the doctrines that the Court has developed in each of these areas should be applied.

### 1. Freedom of Speech

The First Amendment states, among other things, that "Congress shall make no law . . . abridging the freedom of speech." The Supreme Court has applied the First Amendment to the states via the Fourteenth Amendment, through a process known as "incorporation." You don't need to know the details of how incorporation works at this point, and we will look at it more closely later in the course, when we study the Fourteenth Amendment's due process clause.

What follows are First Amendment decisions about whether the government can prohibit individuals from speaking in various ways — for example, by burning a selective service card, though music, or by burning an American flag. Pay close attention in each case to how the Supreme Court interprets the free speech protection, and how the doctrinal principles the Court elaborates help to guide it to the determination that the governing laws at issue in each case do or do not violate the Constitution.

Here are some basic questions to keep in mind as you read these and all the cases in this book:

- What is the essential issue? How does that issue spring from a government-created regulation?
- What is the doctrinal test the court applies? Is there more than one test, depending upon the issue? Is there a test to determine which doctrinal test the court will employ?
- How does the court apply the doctrinal tests to the facts? How does it rely upon precedent as it does so?
- Is your understanding of the doctrinal test — the "black-letter law" — different now that we have seen it applied in the particular contexts of these cases?
- In the end, who gets to decide how speech may be regulated?

## United States v. O'Brien
### 391 U.S. 367 (1968)

Mr. Chief Justice Warren delivered the opinion of the Court.

On the morning of March 31, 1966, David Paul O'Brien and three companions burned their Selective Service registration certificates on the steps of the South Boston Courthouse. . . .

For this act, O'Brien was indicted, tried, convicted, and sentenced in the United States District Court for the District of Massachusetts. He did not contest the fact that he had burned the certificate. He stated in argument to the jury that he burned the certificate publicly to influence others to adopt his anti-war beliefs. . . . The indictment upon which he was tried charged that he "willfully and knowingly did mutilate, destroy, and change by burning . . . [his] Registration Certificate (Selective Service System Form No. 2); in violation of Title 50, App. United States Code, Section 462(b)." Section 462(b) is part of the Universal Military Training and Service Act of 1948. Section 462(b)(3) . . . was amended by Congress in 1965 (adding the words italicized below), so that, at the time O'Brien burned his certificate, an offense was committed by any person, "who forges, alters, *knowingly destroys, knowingly mutilates*, or in any manner changes any such certificate. . . ." (Italics supplied.) . . .

. . . We hold that the 1965 Amendment is constitutional both as enacted and as applied. We therefore vacate the judgment of the Court of Appeals and reinstate the judgment and sentence of the District Court. . . .

When a male reaches the age of 18, he is required by the Universal Military Training and Service Act to register with a local draft board. He is assigned a Selective Service number, and within five days he is issued a registration certificate. Subsequently, and based on a questionnaire completed by the registrant, he is assigned a classification denoting his eligibility for induction, and, "[a]s soon as practicable" thereafter, he is issued a Notice of Classification. This initial classification is not necessarily permanent, and if, in the interim before induction, the registrant's status changes in some relevant way, he may be reclassified. After such a reclassification, the local board, "as soon as practicable," issues to the registrant a new Notice of Classification.

Both the registration and classification certificates are small white cards, approximately 2 by 3 inches. The registration certificate specifies the name of the registrant, the date of registration, and the number and address of the local board with which he is registered. Also inscribed upon it are the date and place of the registrant's birth, his residence at registration, his physical description, his signature, and his Selective Service number. . . .

The classification certificate shows the registrant's name, Selective Service number, signature, and eligibility classification. It specifies whether he was so classified by his local board, an appeal board, or the President. It contains the address of his local board and the date the certificate was mailed.

Both the registration and classification certificates bear notices that the registrant must notify his local board in writing of every change in address, physical condition, and occupational, marital, family, dependency, and military status, and of any other fact which might change his classification. . . .

By the 1965 Amendment, Congress added to § 12(b)(3) of the 1948 Act the provision here at issue, subjecting to criminal liability not only one who "forges, alters, or in any manner changes," but also one who "knowingly destroys, [or] knowingly mutilates" a certificate. We note at the outset that the 1965 Amendment plainly does not abridge free speech on its face, and we do not understand O'Brien to argue otherwise. . . . It prohibits the knowing destruction of certificates issued by the Selective Service System, and there is nothing necessarily expressive about such conduct. The Amendment does not distinguish between public and private destruction, and it does not punish only destruction engaged in for the purpose of expressing views. A law prohibiting destruction of Selective Service certificates no more abridges free speech on its face than a motor vehicle law prohibiting the destruction of drivers' licenses, or a tax law prohibiting the destruction of books and records.

O'Brien . . . argues that the 1965 Amendment is unconstitutional as applied to him because his act of burning his registration certificate was protected "symbolic speech" within the First Amendment. His argument is that the freedom of expression which the First Amendment guarantees includes all modes of "communication of ideas by conduct," and that his conduct is within this definition because he did it in "demonstration against the war and against the draft."

We cannot accept the view that an apparently limitless variety of conduct can be labeled "speech" whenever the person engaging in the conduct intends thereby to express an idea. However, even on the assumption that the alleged communicative element in O'Brien's conduct is sufficient to bring into play the First Amendment, it does not necessarily follow that the destruction of a registration certificate is constitutionally protected activity. This Court has held that, when "speech" and "nonspeech" elements are combined in the same course of conduct, a sufficiently important governmental interest in regulating the nonspeech element can justify incidental limitations on First Amendment freedoms. To characterize the quality of the governmental interest which must appear, the Court has employed a variety of descriptive terms: compelling; substantial; subordinating; paramount; cogent; strong. Whatever imprecision inheres in these terms, we think it clear that a government regulation is sufficiently justified if it is within the constitutional power of the Government; if it furthers an important or substantial governmental interest; if the governmental interest is unrelated to the suppression of free expression, and if the incidental restriction on alleged First Amendment freedoms is no greater than is essential to the furtherance of that interest. We find that the 1965 Amendment to § 12(b)(3) of the Universal Military Training and Service Act meets all of these requirements, and consequently that O'Brien can be constitutionally convicted for violating it.

The constitutional power of Congress to raise and support armies and to make all laws necessary and proper to that end is broad and sweeping. Lichter v. United States (1948). The power of Congress to classify and conscript manpower for military service is "beyond question." *Lichter*. Pursuant to this power, Congress may establish a system of registration for individuals liable for training and service, and may require such individuals, within reason, to cooperate in the registration system. The issuance of certificates indicating the registration and eligibility classification of individuals is a legitimate and substantial administrative aid in the functioning of this system. And legislation to insure the continuing availability of issued certificates serves a legitimate and substantial purpose in the system's administration.

O'Brien's argument to the contrary is necessarily premised upon his unrealistic characterization of Selective Service certificates. He essentially adopts the position that such certificates are so many pieces of paper designed to notify registrants of their registration or classification, to be retained or tossed in the wastebasket according to the convenience or taste of the registrant. Once the registrant has received notification, according to this view, there is no reason for him to retain the certificates. O'Brien notes that most of the information on a registration certificate serves no notification purpose at all; the registrant hardly needs to be told his address and physical characteristics. We agree that the registration certificate contains much information of which the registrant needs no notification. This circumstance, however, does not lead to the conclusion that the certificate serves no purpose, but that, like the classification certificate, it serves purposes in addition to initial notification. Many of these purposes would be defeated by the certificates' destruction or mutilation. Among these are:

1. The registration certificate serves as proof that the individual

described thereon has registered for the draft. The classification certificate shows the eligibility classification of a named but undescribed individual. Voluntarily displaying the two certificates is an easy and painless way for a young man to dispel a question as to whether he might be delinquent in his Selective Service obligations. Correspondingly, the availability of the certificates for such display relieves the Selective Service System of the administrative burden it would otherwise have in verifying the registration and classification of all suspected delinquents. Further, since both certificates are in the nature of "receipts" attesting that the registrant has done what the law requires, it is in the interest of the just and efficient administration of the system that they be continually available, in the event, for example, of a mix-up in the registrant's file. Additionally, in a time of national crisis, reasonable availability to each registrant of the two small cards assures a rapid and uncomplicated means for determining his fitness for immediate induction, no matter how distant in our mobile society he may be from his local board.

2. The information supplied on the certificates facilitates communication between registrants and local boards, simplifying the system and benefiting all concerned. To begin with, each certificate bears the address of the registrant's local board, an item unlikely to be committed to memory. Further, each card bears the registrant's Selective Service number, and a registrant who has his number readily available so that he can communicate it to his local board when he supplies or requests information can make simpler the board's task in locating his file. Finally, a registrant's inquiry, particularly through a local board other than his own, concerning his eligibility status is frequently answerable simply on the basis of his classification certificate; whereas, if the certificate were not reasonably available and the registrant were uncertain of his classification, the task of answering his questions would be considerably complicated.

3. Both certificates carry continual reminders that the registrant must notify his local board of any change of address, and other specified changes in his status. The smooth functioning of the system requires that local boards be continually aware of the status and whereabouts of registrants, and the destruction of certificates deprives the system of a potentially useful notice device.

4. The regulatory scheme involving Selective Service certificates includes clearly valid prohibitions against the alteration, forgery, or similar deceptive misuse of certificates.

The destruction or mutilation of certificates obviously increases the difficulty of detecting and tracing abuses such as these. Further, a mutilated certificate might itself be used for deceptive purposes.

The many functions performed by Selective Service certificates establish beyond doubt that Congress has a legitimate and substantial interest in preventing their wanton and unrestrained destruction and assuring their continuing availability by punishing people who knowingly and willfully destroy or mutilate them. . . .

We think it apparent that the continuing availability to each registrant of his Selective Service certificates substantially furthers the smooth and proper functioning of the system that Congress has established to raise armies. We think it also apparent that the Nation has a vital interest in having a system for raising armies that functions with maximum efficiency and is capable of easily and quickly responding to continually changing circumstances. For these reasons, the Government has a substantial interest in assuring the continuing availability of issued Selective Service certificates.

It is equally clear that the 1965 Amendment specifically protects this substantial governmental interest. We perceive no alternative means that would more precisely and narrowly assure the continuing availability of issued Selective Service certificates than a law which prohibits their willful mutilation or destruction. The 1965 Amendment prohibits such conduct and does nothing more. In other words, both the governmental interest and the operation of the 1965 Amendment are limited to the noncommunicative aspect of O'Brien's conduct. The governmental interest and the scope of the 1965 Amendment are limited to preventing harm to the smooth and efficient functioning of the Selective Service System. When O'Brien deliberately rendered unavailable his registration certificate, he willfully frustrated this governmental interest. For this noncommunicative impact of his conduct, and for nothing else, he was convicted.

The case at bar is therefore unlike one where the alleged governmental interest in regulating conduct arises in some measure because the communication allegedly integral to the conduct is itself thought to be harmful. In *Stromberg v. California* (1931), for example, this Court struck down a statutory phrase which punished people who expressed their "opposition to organized government" by displaying "any flag, badge, banner, or device." Since the statute there was aimed at suppressing communication it could not be sustained as a regulation of noncommunicative conduct.

In conclusion, we find that, because of the Government's substantial interest in assuring the continuing availability of issued Selective Service certificates, because amended § 462(b) is an appropriately narrow means of protecting this interest and condemns only the independent noncommunicative impact of conduct within its reach, and because the noncommunicative impact of O'Brien's act of burning his registration certificate frustrated the Government's interest, a sufficient governmental interest has been shown to justify O'Brien's conviction.

[T]he Court of Appeals should have affirmed the judgment of conviction entered by the District Court. Accordingly, we vacate the judgment of the Court of Appeals, and reinstate the judgment and sentence of the District Court. . . .

It is so ordered.

Mr. Justice Marshall took no part in the consideration or decision of these cases.

[Concurring opinions omitted.]

**NOTES AND QUESTIONS**

1. *O'Brien* confirms what you likely suspected before you came

to law school — that the First Amendment's command that "no law" abridge the "freedom of speech" does not actually mean no law. Rather, the Supreme Court has interpreted the First Amendment to allow restrictions on speech in certain instances. *O'Brien* represents one of those instances: the government has more freedom to regulate conduct, so long as its interest in regulation is "unrelated to the suppression of free expression" and any "incidental restriction on alleged First Amendment freedoms is no greater than is essential to the furtherance of that interest."

2. Think about it this way: the regulation itself did not prohibit speech — rather, it prohibited destruction of Selective Service documents. But O'Brien sought by his destruction of one of those documents to send a message. The question then becomes: does prosecuting him for violating this regulation abridge his right to freedom of speech?

3. The answer in this case is "no" according to the test the Court develops to address governmental regulations that do not have as their aim the abridgment of speech — in other words, the test used by the courts to address the many, many regulations that might, in their enforcement, have some incidental effect on speech interests. Consider the application of the test in the next case, which does not involve symbolic speech, as in *O'Brien*.

## Ward v. Rock Against Racism
### 491 U.S. 781 (1989)

Justice Kennedy delivered the opinion of the Court.

Rock Against Racism, respondent in this case, is an unincorporated association which, in its own words, is "dedicated to the espousal and promotion of antiracist views." Each year from 1979 through 1986, RAR has sponsored a program of speeches and rock music at the bandshell. RAR has furnished the sound equipment and sound technician used by the various performing groups at these annual events.

Over the years, the city received numerous complaints about excessive sound amplification at respondent's concerts from park users and residents of areas adjacent to the park. . . .

The city . . . undertook to develop comprehensive New York City Parks Department Use Guidelines for the Naumberg Bandshell. A principal problem to be addressed by the guidelines was controlling the volume of amplified sound at bandshell events. A major concern was that at some bandshell performances the event sponsors had been unable to "provide the amplification levels required and 'crowds unhappy with the sound became disappointed or unruly.' " The city found that this problem had several causes, including inadequate sound equipment, sound technicians who were either unskilled at mixing sound outdoors or unfamiliar with the acoustics of the bandshell and its surroundings, and the like. Because some performers compensated for poor sound mix by raising volume, these factors tended to exacerbate the problem of excess noise.

[T]he city concluded that the most effective way to achieve adequate but not excessive sound amplification would be for the city to furnish high quality sound equipment and retain an independent, experienced sound technician for all performances at the bandshell. After an extensive search the city hired a private sound company capable of meeting the needs of all the varied users of the bandshell.

The Use Guidelines were promulgated on March 21, 1986. After learning that it would be expected to comply with the guidelines at its upcoming annual concert in May 1986, respondent . . . filed a motion for an injunction against the enforcement of certain aspects of the guidelines. The District Court preliminarily enjoined enforcement of the sound-amplification rule on May 1, 1986. Under the protection of the injunction, and alone among users of the bandshell in the 1986 season, RAR was permitted to use its own sound equipment and technician, just as it had done in prior years. RAR's 1986 concert again generated complaints about excessive noise from park users and nearby residents.

After the concert, respondent amended its complaint to seek damages and a declaratory judgment striking down the guidelines as facially invalid. After hearing five days of testimony about various aspects of the guidelines, the District Court issued its decision upholding the sound-amplification guideline. . . . The Court of Appeals reversed. . . . [That] court . . . concluded that the sound-amplification guideline was invalid because the city had failed to prove that its regulation "was the least intrusive means of regulating the volume."

We granted certiorari to clarify the legal standard applicable to governmental regulation of the time, place, or manner of protected speech. Because the Court of Appeals erred in requiring the city to prove that its regulation was the least intrusive means of furthering its legitimate governmental interests, and because the ordinance is valid on its face, we now reverse.

## II

[E]ven in a public forum the government may impose reasonable restrictions on the time, place, or manner of protected speech, provided the restrictions "are justified without reference to the content of the regulated speech, that they are narrowly tailored to serve a significant governmental interest, and that they leave open ample alternative channels for communication of the information." *Clark v. Community for Creative Non-Violence* (1984). We consider these requirements in turn.

### A

The principal inquiry in determining content neutrality, in speech cases generally and in time, place, or manner cases in particular, is whether the government has adopted a regulation of speech because of disagreement with the message it conveys. The government's purpose is the controlling consideration. A regulation that serves purposes unrelated to the content of expression is deemed neutral, even if it has an incidental effect on some speakers or messages but not others. Government regulation of expressive activity is content neutral so long as it is "justified without reference to the content of the regulated speech." *Community for Creative Non-Violence* (emphasis added).

The principal justification for the sound-amplification guideline is the city's desire to control noise levels at bandshell events, in order to retain the character of the Sheep Meadow and its more sedate activities, and to avoid undue intrusion into residential areas and other areas of the park. This justification for the guideline "ha[s] nothing to do with content," *Boos v. Barry* (1988), and it satisfies the requirement that time, place, or manner regulations be content neutral.

The only other justification offered below was the city's interest in "ensur[ing] the quality of sound at Bandshell events." Respondent urges that this justification is not content neutral because it is based upon the quality, and thus the content, of the speech being regulated. In respondent's view, the city is seeking to assert artistic control over performers at the bandshell by enforcing a bureaucratically determined, value-laden conception of good sound. . . .

While respondent's arguments that the government may not interfere with artistic judgment may have much force in other contexts, they are inapplicable to the facts of this case. The city has disclaimed in express terms any interest in imposing its own view of appropriate sound mix on performers. To the contrary, as the District Court found, the city requires its sound technician to defer to the wishes of event sponsors concerning sound mix. On this record, the city's concern with sound quality extends only to the clearly content-neutral goals of ensuring adequate sound amplification and avoiding the volume problems associated with inadequate sound mix. . . .

**B**

The city's regulation is also "narrowly tailored to serve a significant governmental interest." *Community for Creative Non-Violence*. Despite respondent's protestations to the contrary, it can no longer be doubted that government "ha[s] a substantial interest in protecting its citizens from unwelcome noise." *City Council of Los Angeles v. Taxpayers for Vincent* (1984). This interest is perhaps at its greatest when government seeks to protect "the well-being, tranquility, and privacy of the home," *Frisby v. Schultz* (1988) [quotation omitted], but it is by no means limited to that context, for the government may act to protect even such traditional public forums as city streets and parks from excessive noise.

We think it also apparent that the city's interest in ensuring the sufficiency of sound amplification at bandshell events is a substantial one. The record indicates that inadequate sound amplification has had an adverse effect on the ability of some audiences to hear and enjoy performances at the bandshell. The city enjoys a substantial interest in ensuring the ability of its citizens to enjoy whatever benefits the city parks have to offer, from amplified music to silent meditation.

The Court of Appeals recognized the city's substantial interest in limiting the sound emanating from the bandshell. The court concluded, however, that the city's sound-amplification guideline was not narrowly tailored to further this interest, because "it has not [been] shown . . . that the requirement of the use of the city's sound system and technician was the least intrusive means of regulating the volume." (emphasis added). In the court's judgment, there were several alternative methods of achieving the desired end that would have been less restrictive of respondent's First Amendment rights.

The Court of Appeals erred in sifting through all the available or imagined alternative means of regulating sound volume in order to determine whether the city's solution was "the least intrusive means" of achieving the desired end. [But] our cases quite clearly hold that restrictions on the time, place, or manner of protected speech are not invalid "simply because there is some imaginable alternative that might be less burdensome on speech." *United States v. Albertini* (1985).

The Court of Appeals apparently drew its least-intrusive-means requirement from *United States v. O'Brien* (1968), the case in which we established the standard for judging the validity of restrictions on expressive conduct. The court's reliance was misplaced, however, for we have held that the O'Brien test "in the last analysis is little, if any, different from the standard applied to time, place, or manner restrictions." *Community for Creative Non-Violence.* . . .

Lest any confusion on the point remain, we reaffirm today that a regulation of the time, place, or manner of protected speech must be narrowly tailored to serve the government's legitimate, content-neutral interests but that it need not be the least restrictive or least intrusive means of doing so. Rather, the requirement of narrow tailoring is satisfied "so long as the . . . regulation promotes a substantial government interest that would be achieved less effectively absent the regulation." Albertini. To be sure, this standard does not mean that a time, place, or manner regulation may burden substantially more speech than is necessary to further the government's legitimate interests. Government may not regulate expression in such a manner that a substantial portion of the burden on speech does not serve to advance its goals. So long as the means chosen are not substantially broader than necessary to achieve the government's interest, however, the regulation will not be invalid simply because a court concludes that the government's interest could be adequately served by some less-speech-restrictive alternative. . . .

It is undeniable that the city's substantial interest in limiting sound volume is served in a direct and effective way by the requirement that the city's sound technician control the mixing board during performances. Absent this requirement, the city's interest would have been served less well, as is evidenced by the complaints about excessive volume generated by respondent's past concerts. The alternative regulatory methods hypothesized by the Court of Appeals reflect nothing more than a disagreement with the city over how much control of volume is appropriate or how that level of control is to be achieved. The Court of Appeals erred in failing to defer to the city's reasonable determination that its interest in controlling volume would be best served by requiring bandshell performers to utilize the city's sound technician.

The city's second content-neutral justification for the guideline, that of ensuring "that the sound amplification [is] sufficient to reach all listeners within the defined concert-ground," also supports the city's choice of regulatory methods. By providing competent sound technicians and adequate amplification equipment, the city eliminated the problems of inexperienced technicians and insufficient sound volume that had plagued some bandshell performers in the past. No doubt this concern is not applicable to respondent's concerts, which apparently were characterized by more-than-adequate sound amplification. But that fact is beside the point, for the validity of the regulation depends on the relation it bears to the overall problem the government seeks to correct, not on the extent to which it furthers the government's interests in an individual case. Here, the regulation's effectiveness must be judged by considering all the varied groups that use the bandshell, and it is valid so long as the city could reasonably have determined that its interests overall would be served less effectively without the sound-amplification guideline than with it. Considering these proffered justifications together, therefore, it is apparent that the guideline directly furthers the city's legitimate governmental interests and that those interests would have been less well served in the absence of the sound-amplification guideline.

Respondent nonetheless argues that the sound-amplification guideline is not narrowly tailored because, by placing control of sound mix in the hands of the city's technician, the guideline sweeps far more broadly than is necessary to further the city's legitimate concern with sound volume. . . .

If the city's regulatory scheme had a substantial deleterious effect on the ability of bandshell performers to achieve the quality of sound they desired, respondent's concerns would have considerable force. The District Court . . . squarely rejected respondent's claim that the city's "technician is not able properly to implement a sponsor's instructions as to sound quality or mix," finding that "[n]o evidence to that effect was offered at trial; as noted, the evidence is to the contrary." In view of these findings, which were not disturbed by the Court of Appeals, we must conclude that the city's guideline has no material impact on any performer's ability to exercise complete artistic control over sound quality. Since the guideline allows the city to control volume without interfering with the performer's desired sound mix, it is not "substantially broader than necessary" to achieve the city's legitimate ends, City Council of Los Angeles, and thus it satisfies the requirement of narrow tailoring.

C

The final requirement, that the guideline leave open ample alternative channels of communication, is easily met. Indeed, in this respect the guideline is far less restrictive than regulations we have upheld in other cases, for it does not attempt to ban any particular manner or type of expression at a given place or time. Rather, the guideline continues to permit expressive activity in the bandshell, and has no effect on the quantity or content of that expression beyond regulating the extent of amplification. That the city's limitations on volume may reduce to some degree the potential audience for respondent's speech is of no consequence, for there has been no showing that the remaining avenues of communication are inadequate.

## III

The city's sound-amplification guideline is narrowly tailored to serve the substantial and content-neutral governmental interests of avoiding excessive sound volume and providing sufficient amplification within the bandshell concert ground, and the guideline leaves open ample channels of communication. Accordingly, it is valid under the First Amendment as a reasonable regulation of the place and manner of expression. The judgment of the Court of Appeals is

Reversed.

Justice Blackmun concurs in the result.

[Dissenting opinion of Justice Marshall omitted.]

### NOTES AND QUESTIONS

**1.** Does it seem that *O'Brien* and *Ward* appear to permit the government a fairly broad canvas upon which it can enact valid regulations that may have some incidental impact on free speech rights? The answer is "yes."

**2.** *O'Brien* and *Ward* represent just one doctrinal path under the First Amendment's protection of free speech — a path that is implicated only when a regulation is content-neutral — that is, when a regulation that is not aimed at speech and, indeed, has only an incidental effect on speech. The *Ward* court mentioned the typical example of such a regulation, what are commonly referred to as "time, place, or manner" restrictions — that is, regulations that dictate the conditions under which individuals may speak, without regard to the content of that speech. Under *O'Brien* and *Ward*, so long as the governmental purpose is not to restrict speech, and the regulation is narrowly tailored to effectuate the government's ends, it likely will be upheld.

**3.** But there is another analytical path a court may follow — the one concerned with regulations that are directed at the content of speech. The next case sets out that path, and spells out which of the two paths lawyers and courts must follow when faced with particular facts.

### Texas v. Johnson
### 491 U.S. 397 (1989)

Brennan, J.

After publicly burning an American flag as a means of political protest, Gregory Lee Johnson was convicted of desecrating a flag in violation of Texas law. This case presents the question whether his conviction is consistent with the First Amendment. We hold that it is not.

I

While the Republican National Convention was taking place in Dallas in 1984, respondent Johnson participated in a political demonstration dubbed the "Republican War Chest Tour." . . . The demonstrators marched through the Dallas streets, chanting political slogans and stopping at several corporate locations to stage "die-ins" intended to dramatize the consequences of nuclear war. On several occasions they spray-painted the walls of buildings and overturned potted plants, but Johnson himself took no part in such activities. He did, however, accept an American flag handed to him by a fellow protestor who had taken it from a flagpole outside one of the targeted buildings.

The demonstration ended in front of Dallas City Hall, where Johnson unfurled the American flag, doused it with kerosene, and set it on fire. . . . After the demonstrators dispersed, a witness to the flag burning collected the flag's remains and buried them in his backyard. No one was physically injured or threatened with injury, though several witnesses testified that they had been seriously offended by the flag burning.

Of the approximately 100 demonstrators, Johnson alone was charged with a crime. The only criminal offense with which he was charged was the desecration of a venerated object in violation of Tex. Penal Code Ann. § 42.09(a)(3) (1989).* After a trial, he was convicted, sentenced to one year in prison, and fined $2,000. The Court of Appeals for the Fifth District of Texas at Dallas affirmed Johnson's conviction. But the Texas Court of Criminal Appeals reversed, holding that the State could not, consistent with the First Amendment, punish Johnson for burning the flag in these circumstances.

To justify Johnson's conviction for engaging in symbolic speech, the State asserted two interests: preserving the flag as a symbol of national unity and preventing breaches of the peace. The Court of Criminal Appeals held that neither interest supported his conviction.

II

Johnson was convicted of flag desecration for burning the flag rather than for uttering insulting words. This fact somewhat complicates our consideration of his conviction under the First Amendment. We must first determine whether Johnson's burning of the flag constituted expressive conduct, permitting him to invoke the First Amendment in challenging his conviction. If his conduct was expressive, we next decide whether the State's regulation is related to the suppression of free expression. If the State's regulation is not related to expression, then the less stringent standard we announced in *United States v. O'Brien* (1968) for regulations of noncommunicative conduct controls. If it is, then we are outside of *O'Brien*'s test, and we must ask whether this interest justifies Johnson's conviction under a more demanding standard.

The First Amendment literally forbids the abridgment only of "speech," but we have long recognized that its protection does not end at the spoken or written word. While we have rejected "the view that an apparently limitless variety of conduct can be labeled 'speech' whenever the person engaging in the conduct intends thereby to express an idea," we have acknowledged that conduct may be "sufficiently imbued with elements of communication to fall within the scope of the First and Fourteenth Amendments."

In deciding whether particular conduct possesses sufficient communicative elements to bring the First Amendment into play, we have asked whether "[a]n intent to convey a particularized message was present, and [whether] the likelihood was great that the message would be understood by those who viewed it." *Spence v. Washington* (1974). Hence, we have recognized the expressive nature of students' wearing of black armbands to protest American military involvement in Vietnam; of a sit-in by blacks in a "whites only" area to protest segregation; of the wearing of American military uniforms in a dramatic presentation criticizing American involvement in Vietnam; and of picketing about a wide variety of causes.

Especially pertinent to this case are our decisions recognizing the communicative nature of conduct relating to flags. Attaching a peace sign to the flag, refusing to salute the flag, and displaying a red flag, we have held, all may find shelter under the First Amendment. That we have had little difficulty identifying an expressive element in conduct relating to flags should not be surprising. The very purpose of a national flag is to serve as a symbol of our country; it is, one might say, "the one visible manifestation of two hundred years of nationhood." . . . Pregnant with expressive content, the flag as readily signifies this Nation as does the combination of letters found in "America."

We have not automatically concluded, however, that any action taken with respect to our flag is expressive. Instead, in characterizing such action for First Amendment purposes, we have considered the context in which it occurred. . . .

The State of Texas conceded for purposes of its oral argument in this case that Johnson's conduct was expressive conduct. . . . Johnson burned an American flag as part — indeed, as the culmination — of a political demonstration that coincided with the convening of the Republican Party and its renomination of Ronald Reagan for President. The expressive, overtly political nature of this conduct was both intentional and overwhelmingly apparent. . . . In these circumstances, Johnson's burning of the flag was conduct "sufficiently imbued with elements of communication," to implicate the First Amendment.

### III

The government generally has a freer hand in restricting expressive conduct than it has in restricting the written or spoken word. It may not, however, proscribe particular conduct because it has expressive elements. "[W]hat might be termed the more generalized guarantee of freedom of expression makes the communicative nature of conduct an inadequate basis for singling out that conduct for proscription. A law directed at the communicative nature of conduct must, like a law directed at speech itself, be justified by the substantial showing of need that the First Amendment requires."

It is, in short, not simply the verbal or nonverbal nature of the expression, but the governmental interest at stake, that helps to determine whether a restriction on that expression is valid.

Thus, . . . we have limited the applicability of *O'Brien*'s relatively lenient standard to those cases in which "the governmental interest is unrelated to the suppression of free expression." Id. In stating, moreover, that *O'Brien*'s test "in the last analysis is little, if any, different from the standard applied to time, place, or manner restrictions," *Clark v. Community for Creative Nonviolence* (1984), we have highlighted the requirement that the governmental interest in question be unconnected to expression in order to come under *O'Brien*'s less demanding rule.

In order to decide whether *O'Brien*'s test applies here, therefore, we must decide whether Texas has asserted an interest in support of Johnson's conviction that is unrelated to the suppression of expression. If we find that an interest asserted by the State is simply not implicated on the facts before us, we need not ask whether *O'Brien*'s test applies. The State offers two separate interests to justify this conviction: preventing breaches of the peace and preserving the flag as a symbol of nationhood and national unity. We hold that the first interest is not implicated on this record and that the second is related to the suppression of expression.

A

Texas claims that its interest in preventing breaches of the peace justifies Johnson's conviction for flag desecration. However, no disturbance of the peace actually occurred or threatened to occur because of Johnson's burning of the flag. [The State] admits that "no actual breach of the peace occurred at the time of the flagburning or in response to the flagburning." . . . The only evidence offered by the State at trial to show the reaction to Johnson's actions was the testimony of several persons who had been seriously offended by the flag burning.

The State's position, therefore, amounts to a claim that an audience that takes serious offense at particular expression is necessarily likely to disturb the peace and that the expression may be prohibited on this basis. Our precedents do not countenance such a presumption. On the contrary, they recognize that a principal "function of free speech under our system of government is to invite dispute. It may indeed best serve its high purpose when it induces a condition of unrest, creates dissatisfaction with conditions as they are, or even stirs people to anger." *Terminiello v. Chicago* (1949). It would be odd indeed to conclude both that "if it is the speaker's opinion that gives offense, that consequence is a reason for according it constitutional protection," *FCC v. Pacifica Foundation* (1978) (opinion of Stevens, J.), and that the government may ban the expression of certain disagreeable ideas on the unsupported presumption that their very disagreeableness will provoke violence.

[We conclude] that the State's interest in maintaining order is not implicated on these facts. The State need not worry that our holding will disable it from preserving the peace. We do not suggest that the First Amendment forbids a State to prevent "imminent lawless action." *Brandenburg v. Ohio* (1969). And, in fact, Texas already has a statute specifically prohibiting breaches of the peace, which tends to confirm that Texas need not punish this flag desecration in order to keep the peace.

**B**

The State also asserts an interest in preserving the flag as a symbol of nationhood and national unity. In *Spence*, we acknowledged that the government's interest in preserving the flag's special symbolic value "is directly related to expression in the context of activity" such as affixing a peace symbol to a flag. We are equally persuaded that this interest is related to expression in the case of Johnson's burning of the flag. The State, apparently, is concerned that such conduct will lead people to believe either that the flag does not stand for nationhood and national unity, but instead reflects other, less positive concepts, or that the concepts reflected in the flag do not in fact exist, that is, that we do not enjoy unity as a Nation. These concerns blossom only when a person's treatment of the flag communicates some message, and thus are related "to the suppression of free expression" within the meaning of *O'Brien*. We are thus outside of *O'Brien*'s test altogether.

**IV**

It remains to consider whether the State's interest in preserving the flag as a symbol of nationhood and national unity justifies Johnson's conviction. As in Spence, "[w]e are confronted with a case of prosecution for the expression of an idea through activity," and "[a]ccordingly, we must examine with particular care the interests advanced by [petitioner] to support its prosecution." Johnson was not, we add, prosecuted for the expression of just any idea; he was prosecuted for his expression of dissatisfaction with the policies of this country, expression situated at the core of our First Amendment values.

Moreover, Johnson was prosecuted because he knew that his politically charged expression would cause "serious offense." If he had burned the flag as a means of disposing of it because it was dirty or torn, he would not have been convicted of flag desecration under this Texas law: federal law designates burning as the preferred means of disposing of a flag "when it is in such condition that it is no longer a fitting emblem for display," and Texas has no quarrel with this means of disposal. The Texas law is thus not aimed at protecting the physical integrity of the flag in all circumstances, but is designed instead to protect it only against impairments that would cause serious offense to others. Texas concedes as much.

Whether Johnson's treatment of the flag violated Texas law thus depended on the likely communicative impact of his expressive conduct. Our decision in *Boos v. Barry* (1988) tells us that this restriction on Johnson's expression is content based. In Boos, we considered the constitutionality of a law prohibiting "the display of any sign within 500 feet of a foreign embassy if that sign tends to bring that foreign government into 'public odium' or 'public disrepute.' " Rejecting the argument that the law was content neutral because it was justified by "our international law obligation to shield diplomats from speech that offends their dignity," we held that "[t]he emotive impact of speech on its audience is not a 'secondary effect' " unrelated to the content of the expression itself.

According to the principles announced in *Boos*, Johnson's political expression was restricted because of the content of the message he conveyed. We must therefore subject the State's asserted interest in preserving the special symbolic character of the flag to "the most exacting scrutiny." *Boos*.

Texas argues that its interest in preserving the flag as a symbol of nationhood and national unity survives this close analysis. . . . [T]he State's claim is that it has an interest in preserving the flag as a symbol of nationhood and national unity, a symbol with a determinate range of meanings. According to Texas, if one physically treats the flag in a way that would tend to cast doubt on either the idea that nationhood and national unity are the flag's referents or that national unity actually exists, the message conveyed thereby is a harmful one and therefore may be prohibited.

If there is a bedrock principle underlying the First Amendment, it is that the government may not prohibit the expression of an idea simply because society finds the idea itself offensive or disagreeable. . . . In holding in *West Virginia State Board of Education v. Barnette* (1943) that the Constitution did not leave this course open to the government, Justice Jackson described one of our society's defining principles in words deserving of their frequent repetition: "If there is any fixed star in our constitutional constellation, it is that no official, high or petty, can prescribe what shall be orthodox in politics, nationalism, religion, or other matters of opinion or force citizens to confess by word or act their faith therein." . . .

In short, nothing in our precedents suggests that a State may foster its own view of the flag by prohibiting expressive conduct relating to it. To bring its argument outside our precedents, Texas attempts to convince us that even if its interest in preserving the flag's symbolic role does not allow it to prohibit words or some expressive conduct critical of the flag, it does permit it to forbid the outright destruction of the flag. The State's argument cannot depend here on the distinction between written or spoken words and nonverbal conduct. That distinction, we have shown, is of no moment where the nonverbal conduct is expressive, as it is here, and where the regulation of that conduct is related to expression, as it is here. In addition, both *Barnette* and *Spence* involved expressive conduct, not only verbal communication, and both found that conduct protected.

Texas' focus on the precise nature of Johnson's expression, moreover, misses the point of our prior decisions: their enduring lesson, that the government may not prohibit expression simply because it disagrees with its message, is not dependent on the particular mode in which one chooses to express an idea. If we were to hold that a State may forbid flag burning wherever it is likely to endanger the flag's symbolic role, but allow it wherever burning a flag promotes that role — as where, for example, a person ceremoniously burns a dirty flag — we would be saying that when it comes to impairing the flag's physical integrity, the flag itself may be used as a symbol — as a substitute for the written or spoken word or a "short cut from mind to mind" — only in one direction. We would be permitting a State to "prescribe what shall be orthodox" by saying that one may burn the flag to convey one's attitude toward it and its referents only if one does not endanger the flag's representation of nationhood and national unity.

. . . To conclude that the government may permit designated symbols to be used to communicate only a limited set of messages would be to enter territory having no discernible or defensible boundaries. Could the government, on this theory, prohibit the burning of state flags? Of copies of the Presidential seal? Of the Constitution? In evaluating these choices under the First Amendment, how would we decide which symbols were sufficiently special to warrant this unique status? To do so, we would be forced to consult our own political preferences, and impose them on the citizenry, in the very way that the First Amendment forbids us to do.

There is, moreover, no indication — either in the text of the Constitution or in our cases interpreting it — that a separate juridical category exists for the American flag alone. Indeed, we would not be surprised to learn that the persons who framed our Constitution and wrote the Amendment that we now construe were not known for their reverence for the Union Jack. The First Amendment does not guarantee that other concepts virtually sacred to our Nation as a whole — such as the principle that discrimination on the basis of race is odious and destructive — will go unquestioned in the marketplace of ideas. We decline, therefore, to create for the flag an exception to the joust of principles protected by the First Amendment.

It is not the State's ends, but its means, to which we object. [W]e do not doubt that the government has a legitimate interest in making efforts to "preserv[e] the national flag as an unalloyed symbol of our country." *Spence v. Washington* (1974). . . . To say that the government has an interest in encouraging proper treatment of the flag, however, is not to say that it may criminally punish a person for burning a flag as a means of political protest. "National unity as an end which officials may foster by persuasion and example is not in question. The problem is whether under our Constitution compulsion as here employed is a permissible means for its achievement." *Barnette*.

. . . Our decision is a reaffirmation of the principles of freedom and inclusiveness that the flag best reflects, and of the conviction that our toleration of criticism such as Johnson's is a sign and source of our strength. Indeed, one of the proudest images of our flag, the one immortalized in our own national anthem, is of the bombardment it survived at Fort McHenry. It is the Nation's resilience, not its rigidity, that Texas sees reflected in the flag — and it is that resilience that we reassert today.

The way to preserve the flag's special role is not to punish those who feel differently about these matters. It is to persuade them that they are wrong. . . . We do not consecrate the flag by punishing its desecration, for in doing so we dilute the freedom that this cherished emblem represents.

V

Johnson was convicted for engaging in expressive conduct. The State's interest in preventing breaches of the peace does not support his conviction because Johnson's conduct did not threaten to disturb the peace. Nor does the State's interest in preserving the flag as a symbol of nationhood and national unity justify his criminal conviction for engaging in political expression. The judgment of the Texas Court of Criminal Appeals is therefore

Affirmed.

Justice Kennedy, concurring.

I write not to qualify the words Justice Brennan chooses so well, for he says with power all that is necessary to explain our ruling. I join his opinion without reservation, but with a keen sense that this case, like others before us from time to time, exacts its personal toll. This prompts me to add to our pages these few remarks.

The case before us illustrates better than most that the judicial power is often difficult in its exercise. We cannot here ask another Branch to share responsibility, as when the argument is made that a statute is flawed or incomplete. For we are presented with a clear and simple statute to be judged against a pure command of the Constitution. The outcome can be laid at no door but ours.

The hard fact is that sometimes we must make decisions we do not like. We make them because they are right, right in the sense that the law and the Constitution, as we see them, compel the result. And so great is our commitment to the process that, except in the rare case, we do not pause to express distaste for the result, perhaps for fear of undermining a valued principle that dictates the decision. This is one of those rare cases.

Our colleagues in dissent advance powerful arguments why respondent may be convicted for his expression, reminding us that among those who will be dismayed by our holding will be some who have had the singular honor of carrying the flag in battle. And I agree that the flag holds a lonely place of honor in an age when absolutes are distrusted and simple truths are burdened by unneeded apologetics.

With all respect to those views, I do not believe the Constitution gives us the right to rule as the dissenting Members of the Court urge, however painful this judgment is to announce. Though symbols often are what we ourselves make of them, the flag is constant in expressing beliefs Americans share, beliefs in law and peace and that freedom which sustains the human spirit. The case here today forces recognition of the costs to which those beliefs commit us. It is poignant but fundamental that the flag protects those who hold it in contempt.

For all the record shows, this respondent was not a philosopher and perhaps did not even possess the ability to comprehend how repellent his statements must be to the Republic itself. But whether or not he could appreciate the enormity of the offense he gave, the fact remains that his acts were speech, in both the technical and the fundamental meaning of the Constitution. So I agree with the Court that he must go free.

Chief Justice Rehnquist, dissenting.

[T]he public burning of the American flag by Johnson was no essential part of any exposition of ideas, and at the same time it had a tendency to incite a breach of the peace. Johnson was free to make any verbal denunciation of the flag that he wished; indeed, he was free to burn the flag in private. He could publicly burn other symbols of the Government or effigies of political leaders. He did lead a march through the streets of Dallas, and conducted a rally in front of the Dallas City Hall. He engaged in a "die-in" to protest nuclear weapons. He shouted out various slogans during the march, including: "Reagan, Mondale which will it be? Either one means World War III"; "Ronald Reagan, killer of the hour, Perfect example of U.S. power"; and "red, white and blue, we spit on you, you stand for plunder, you will go under." For none of these acts was he arrested or prosecuted; it was only when he proceeded to burn publicly an American flag stolen from its rightful owner that he violated the Texas statute.

. . . The Texas statute deprived Johnson of only one rather inarticulate symbolic form of protest — a form of protest that was profoundly offensive to many — and left him with a full panoply of other symbols and every conceivable form of verbal expression to express his deep disapproval of national policy. Thus, in no way can it be said that Texas is punishing him because his hearers — or any other group of people — were profoundly opposed to the message that he sought to convey. Such opposition is no proper basis for restricting speech or expression under the First Amendment. It was Johnson's use of this particular symbol, and not the idea that he sought to convey by it or by his many other expressions, for which he was punished.

[Dissenting opinion of Justice Stevens omitted.]

## NOTES AND QUESTIONS

**1.** Justice Brennan set out the basic free speech framework in Johnson, and you should by this point be able to identify the initial doctrinal test the Court used to determine whether a particular instance of conduct qualifies for protection under the First Amendment. If conduct contains no expressive component, of course, it is not entitled to any protection under the First Amendment. Did the Court engage in this analysis in *O'Brien* — or, in that case, did it appear to assume the defendant's conduct was expressive? Note that, in most cases, there will be no controversy as to whether an individual was engaged in speech — as in Ward, for example, which involved speech in the form of music.

**2.** Having identified a particular instance of conduct as speech, we are faced with two different analytical paths that may guide judicial review of a regulation that allegedly infringes free speech: one for when the government's regulation is aimed at the content of the speech, another for when it is unrelated to speech. How do the elements of the two doctrinal paths differ? How did the Court determine which doctrinal path should be pursued in Johnson — how, in other words, did Justice Brennan distinguish the case from *O'Brien*?

**3.** The differing doctrinal paths lead to different kinds of judicial review — less intense scrutiny by the court of government regulations that do not have the suppression of speech as their aim, as in *Ward* and *O'Brien*, and more intense scrutiny of those that do, as in *Johnson*. The formulae articulate, for lower courts and state courts and the federal and state political branches and attorneys who need to advise clients, what level of justification by the government is necessary for a law restricting speech to survive judicial scrutiny.

**4.** Within each doctrinal path, too, there are multiple components. In the case of a regulation aimed directly at speech, as in Johnson, a court will first test the quality of the government's justification for the regulation, and then test the relative fit between the government's ends (assuming they are legitimate) and the means it has chosen to achieve those ends. How close a fit must there be when the regulation is aimed at the content of speech? In Johnson, what did the state of Texas assert in respect to each part of the test? What did the Court make of those arguments?

**5.** Johnson was not the end of the matter where flag-burning is concerned; in *United States v. Eichmann*, 496 U.S. 310 (1990), the Court addressed a congressional effort to overturn the Supreme Court's ruling in Johnson. This effort failed. The Court struck down the federal law, too, reasoning that:

> Although the Flag Protection Act contains no explicit content-based limitation on the scope of prohibited conduct, it is nevertheless clear that the Government's asserted interest is "related to the suppression of free expression," and concerned with the content of such expression. The Government's interest in protecting the "physical integrity" of a privately owned flag rests upon a perceived need to preserve the flag's status as a symbol of our Nation and certain national ideals. But the mere destruction or disfigurement of a particular physical manifestation of the symbol, without more, does not diminish or otherwise affect the symbol itself in any way. For example, the secret destruction of a flag in one's own basement would not threaten the flag's recognized meaning. Rather, the Government's desire to preserve the flag as a symbol for certain national ideals is implicated "only when a person's treatment of the flag communicates [a] message" to others that is inconsistent with those ideals.
>
> Moreover, the precise language of the Act's prohibitions confirms Congress' interest in the communicative impact of

flag destruction. The Act criminalizes the conduct of anyone who "knowingly mutilates, defaces, physically defiles, burns, maintains on the floor or ground, or tramples upon any flag." Each of the specified terms — with the possible exception of "burns" — unmistakably connotes disrespectful treatment of the flag and suggests a focus on those acts likely to damage the flag's symbolic value. And the explicit exemption for disposal of "worn or soiled" flags protects certain acts traditionally associated with patriotic respect for the flag.

Although Congress cast the Flag Protection Act of 1989 in somewhat broader terms than the Texas statute at issue in Johnson, the Act still suffers from the same fundamental flaw: It suppresses expression out of concern for its likely communicative impact. Despite the Act's wider scope, its restriction on expression cannot be "justified without reference to the content of the regulated speech." The Act therefore must be subjected to "the most exacting scrutiny," and for the reasons stated in Johnson, the Government's interest cannot justify its infringement on First Amendment rights. We decline the Government's invitation to reassess this conclusion in light of Congress' recent recognition of a purported "national consensus" favoring a prohibition on flag burning. Even assuming such a consensus exists, any suggestion that the Government's interest in suppressing speech becomes more weighty as popular opposition to that speech grows is foreign to the First Amendment.

### Expressions Hair Design v. Schneiderman
### 581 U.S.___ (2017)

Chief Justice Roberts delivered the opinion of the Court.

Each time a customer pays for an item with a credit card, the merchant selling that item must pay a transaction fee to the credit card issuer. Some merchants balk at paying the fees and want to discourage the use of credit cards, or at least pass on the fees to customers who use them. One method of achieving those ends is through differential pricing — charging credit card users more than customers using cash. Merchants who wish to employ differential pricing may do so in two ways relevant here: impose a surcharge for the use of a credit card, or offer a discount for the use of cash. In N.Y. Gen. Bus. Law § 518, New York has banned the former practice. The question presented is whether § 518 regulates merchants' speech and — if so — whether the statute violates the First Amendment. . . .

I

[Passed in 1984, N. Y. Gen. Bus. Law § 518 (provides) that "[n]o seller in any sales transaction may impose a surcharge on a holder who elects to use a credit card in lieu of payment by cash, check, or similar means."] Petitioners, five New York businesses and their owners, wish to impose surcharges on customers who use credit cards. Each time one of their customers pays with a credit card, these merchants must pay some transaction fee to the company that issued the credit card. The fee is generally two to three percent of the purchase price. Those fees add up, and the merchants allege that they pay tens of thousands of dollars every year to credit card companies. Rather than increase prices across the board to absorb those costs, the merchants want to pass the fees along only to their customers who choose to use credit cards. They also want to make clear that they are not the bad guys — that the credit card companies, not the merchants, are responsible for the higher prices. The merchants believe that surcharges for credit are more effective than discounts for cash in accomplishing these goals.

In 2013, after several major credit card issuers agreed to drop their contractual surcharge prohibitions, the merchants filed suit against the New York Attorney General and three New York District Attorneys to challenge § 518 — the only remaining obstacle to their charging surcharges for credit card use. As relevant here, they argued that the law violated the First Amendment by regulating how they communicated their prices, and that it was unconstitutionally vague because liability under the law "turn[ed] on the blurry difference" between surcharges and discounts.

The District Court ruled in favor of the merchants. . . . The Court of Appeals for the Second Circuit vacated the judgment of the District Court with instructions to dismiss the merchants' claims. It began by considering single-sticker pricing, where merchants post one price and would like to charge more to customers who pay by credit card. All the law did in this context, the Court of Appeals explained, was regulate a relationship between two prices — the sticker price and the price charged to a credit card user — by requiring that the two prices be equal. Relying on our precedent holding that price regulation alone regulates conduct, not speech, the Court of Appeals concluded that § 518 did not violate the First Amendment.

## II

[There is a question as to] what precise application of the law [plaintiffs] seek to challenge. Although the merchants have presented a wide array of hypothetical pricing regimes, they have expressly identified only one pricing scheme that they seek to employ: posting a cash price and an additional credit card surcharge, expressed either as a percentage surcharge or a "dollars-and-cents" additional amount. Under this pricing approach, petitioner Expressions Hair Design might, for example, post a sign outside its salon reading "Haircuts $10 (we add a 3% surcharge if you pay by credit card)." Or, petitioner Brooklyn Farmacy & Soda Fountain might list one of the sundaes on its menu as costing "$10 (with a $0.30 surcharge for credit card users)." We take petitioners at their word and limit our review to the question whether § 518 is unconstitutional as applied to this particular pricing practice.

## III

The next question is whether § 518 prohibits the pricing regime petitioners wish to employ. The Court of Appeals concluded that it does. The court read "surcharge" in § 518 to mean "an additional amount above the seller's regular price," and found it "basically self-evident" how § 518 applies to sellers who post a single sticker price: "the sticker price is the 'regular' price, so sellers may not charge credit-card customers an additional amount above the sticker price that is not also charged to cash customers." Under this interpretation, signs of the kind that the merchants wish to post — "$10, with a $0.30 surcharge for credit card users" — violate § 518 because they identify one sticker price — $10 — and indicate that credit card users are charged more than that amount.

. . . Where a seller posts a single sticker price, it is reasonable to treat that sticker price as the "usual or normal amount" and conclude, as the court below did, that a merchant imposes a surcharge when he charges a credit card user more than that sticker price. . . .

**IV**

Having concluded that § 518 bars the pricing regime petitioners wish to employ, we turn to their constitutional arguments. . . .

The Court of Appeals concluded that § 518 posed no First Amendment problem because the law regulated conduct, not speech. In reaching this conclusion, the Court of Appeals began with the premise that price controls regulate conduct alone. Section 518 regulates the relationship between "(1) the seller's sticker price and (2) the price the seller charges to credit card customers," requiring that these two amounts be equal. A law regulating the relationship between two prices regulates speech no more than a law regulating a single price. The Court of Appeals concluded that § 518 was therefore simply a conduct regulation.

But § 518 is not like a typical price regulation. Such a regulation — for example, a law requiring all New York delis to charge $10 for their sandwiches — would simply regulate the amount that a store could collect. In other words, it would regulate the sandwich seller's conduct. To be sure, in order to actually collect that money, a store would likely have to put "$10" on its menus or have its employees tell customers that price. Those written or oral communications would be speech, and the law—by determining the amount charged — would indirectly dictate the content of that speech. But the law's effect on speech would be only incidental to its primary effect on conduct, and "it has never been deemed an abridgment of freedom of speech or press to make a course of conduct illegal merely because the conduct was in part initiated, evidenced, or carried out by means of language, either spoken, written, or printed." *Rumsfeld v. Forum for Academic and Institutional Rights, Inc.* (2006) (quotation omitted).

Section 518 is different. The law tells merchants nothing about the amount they are allowed to collect from a cash or credit card payer. Sellers are free to charge $10 for cash and $9.70, $10, $10.30, or any other amount for credit. What the law does regulate is how sellers may communicate their prices. A merchant who wants to charge $10 for cash and $10.30 for credit may not convey that price any way he pleases. He is not free to say "$10, with a 3% credit card surcharge" or "$10, plus $0.30 for credit" because both of those displays identify a single sticker price — $10—that is less than the amount credit card users will be charged. Instead, if the merchant wishes to post a single sticker price, he must display $10.30 as his sticker price. Accordingly, while we agree with the Court of Appeals that § 518 regulates a relationship between a sticker price and the price charged to credit card users, we cannot accept its conclusion that § 518 is nothing more than a mine-run price regulation. In regulating the communication of prices rather than prices themselves, § 518 regulates speech.

Because it concluded otherwise, the Court of Appeals had no occasion to conduct a further inquiry into whether § 518, as a speech regulation, survived First Amendment scrutiny. On that question, the parties dispute whether § 518 is a valid commercial speech regulation . . . and whether the law can be upheld as a valid disclosure requirement. . . .

. . . [W]e decline to consider those questions in the first instance. Instead, we remand for the Court of Appeals to analyze § 518 as a speech regulation. . . .

It is so ordered.

Justice Breyer, concurring in the judgment.

I agree with the Court that New York's statute regulates speech. But that is because virtually all government regulation affects speech. Human relations take place through speech. And human relations include community activities of all kinds — commercial and otherwise.

When the government seeks to regulate those activities, it is often wiser not to try to distinguish between "speech" and "conduct." Instead, we can, and normally do, simply ask whether, or how, a challenged statute, rule, or regulation affects an interest that the First Amendment protects. If, for example, a challenged government regulation negatively affects the processes through which political discourse or public opinion is formed or expressed (interests close to the First Amendment's protective core), courts normally scrutinize that regulation with great care. If the challenged regulation restricts the informational function provided by truthful commercial speech, courts will apply a "lesser" (but still elevated) form of scrutiny. If, however, a challenged regulation simply requires a commercial speaker to disclose purely factual and uncontroversial information, courts will apply a more permissive standard of review. Because that kind of regulation normally has only a minimal effect on First Amendment interests, it normally need only be "reasonably related to the State's interest in preventing deception of consumers." *Zauderer v. Office of Disciplinary Counsel of Supreme Court of Ohio* (1985). Courts apply a similarly permissive standard of review to "regulatory legislation affecting ordinary commercial transactions." *United States v. Carolene Products* (1938). Since that legislation normally does not significantly affect the interests that the First Amendment protects, we normally look only for assurance that the legislation "rests upon some rational basis." Id.

I repeat these well-known general standards or judicial approaches both because I believe that determining the proper approach is typically more important than trying to distinguish "speech" from "conduct," see *Sorrell v. IMS Health Inc.* (2011) (Breyer, J., dissenting), and because the parties here differ as to which approach applies. That difference reflects the fact that it is not clear just what New York's law does. On its face, the law seems simply to tell merchants that they cannot charge higher prices to credit-card users. If so, then it is an ordinary piece of commercial legislation subject to rational basis review. It may, however, make more sense to interpret the statute as [requiring] a merchant, who posts prices and who wants to charge a higher credit-card price, simply to disclose that credit-card price. In that case, though affecting the merchant's "speech," it would not hinder the transmission of information to the public; the merchant would remain free to say whatever it wanted so long as it also revealed its credit-card price to customers. Accordingly, the law would still receive a deferential form of review.

Nonetheless, petitioners suggest that the statute does more. Because the statute's operation is unclear and because its interpretation is a matter of state law, I agree with the majority that we should remand the case to the Second Circuit. . . .

[Concurring opinion of Justice Sotomayor omitted.]

### NOTES AND QUESTIONS

**1.** The cases and Notes thus far have explored the doctrinal paths a court might follow depending upon the kind of regulation at issue: is the regulation aimed at expression, or is its effect on expression incidental? When dealing with conduct, of course, there is a preliminary determination to be made: is the conduct sufficiently expressive to count as speech? You saw the Johnson Court undertake this inquiry in the context of flag burning. That activity might be easily classified as conduct, but in other cases the line between pure speech (words, written or spoken) and conduct (activity that may be expressive) is not so clear, and this is the question that bedeviled the Second Circuit Court of Appeals in *Expressions Hair Design*.

**2.** Having stated the issue, how did the Court of Appeals go about concluding that the New York law regulated pure conduct and not speech? Why have the courts traditionally considered price regulations to concern conduct and not speech? Where in its analysis did the Court of Appeals err, according to Chief Justice Roberts, writing for a majority of the Supreme Court?

**3.** Chief Justice Roberts may be one of the finest writers on the Court — his opinions are clear and, to the extent they are clear, appear to provide useful guidance to lower court judges, lawmakers, and lawyers. But in his concurring opinion, Justice Breyer suggests that the line between speech and conduct is a bit more slippery than the Chief Justice's opinion acknowledges, and that the Court cannot make judgments about where to draw the line between conduct and speech without considering the particular expressive interests affected by the law in question. Does this approach complicate the doctrinal analysis unnecessarily? Or is Justice Breyer suggesting that a subtler test may work to deter courts from interpreting the First Amendment too broadly, by equating mere conduct with protected speech? Keep these questions in mind later in the course, when we explore substantive due process and its intersection with free speech in *Sorrell v. IMS Health Inc.*, 564 U.S. ___ (2011).

**4.** Returning to the question of which doctrinal path a court should follow, to which Justice Breyer refers in his concurring opinion, it's worth noting that, in some cases, the trigger for a less-deferential free speech analysis is not the content neutrality of the regulation but the nature of the speech being regulated. The Court has said, for example, that certain kinds of speech are deserving of virtually no protection under the First Amendment; these categorical exclusions from the First Amendment include defamation, obscenity, and something called "fighting words," which is the subject of the next case.

### R.A.V. v. City of St. Paul
### 505 U.S. 377 (1992)

Justice Scalia delivered the opinion of the Court.

In the predawn hours of June 21, 1990, petitioner and several other teenagers allegedly assembled a crudely made cross by taping together broken chair legs. They then allegedly burned the cross inside the fenced yard of a black family that lived across the street from the house where petitioner was staying. Although this conduct could have been punished under any of a number of laws, one of the two provisions under which respondent city of St. Paul chose to charge petitioner (then a juvenile) was the St. Paul Bias-Motivated Crime Ordinance, St. Paul, Minn., which provides: "Whoever places on public or private property a symbol, object, appellation, characterization or graffiti, including, but not limited to, a burning cross or Nazi swastika, which one knows or has reasonable grounds to know arouses anger, alarm or resentment in others on the basis of race, color, creed, religion or gender commits disorderly conduct and shall be guilty of a misdemeanor."

Petitioner moved to dismiss this count on the ground that the St. Paul ordinance was substantially overbroad and impermissibly content based and therefore facially invalid under the First Amendment. The trial court granted this motion, but the Minnesota Supreme Court reversed. . . . We granted certiorari.

**I**

In construing the St. Paul ordinance, we are bound by the construction given to it by the Minnesota court. Accordingly, we accept the Minnesota Supreme Court's authoritative statement that the ordinance reaches only those expressions that constitute "fighting words" within the meaning of *Chaplinsky v. New Hampshire* (1942). . . . Assuming, arguendo, that all of the expression reached by the ordinance is proscribable under the "fighting words" doctrine, we nonetheless conclude that the ordinance is facially unconstitutional in that it prohibits otherwise permitted speech solely on the basis of the subjects the speech addresses.

The First Amendment generally prevents government from

proscribing speech, or even expressive conduct, because of disapproval of the ideas expressed. Content-based regulations are presumptively invalid. From 1791 to the present, however, our society, like other free but civilized societies, has permitted restrictions upon the content of speech in a few limited areas, which are "of such slight social value as a step to truth that any benefit that may be derived from them is clearly outweighed by the social interest in order and morality." *Chaplinsky*. ...

[These] areas of speech can, consistently with the First Amendment, be regulated because of their constitutionally proscribable content (obscenity, defamation, etc.) — not [because] they are categories of speech entirely invisible to the Constitution, [which] may be made the vehicles for content discrimination unrelated to their distinctively proscribable content. Thus, the government may proscribe libel; but it may not make the further content discrimination of proscribing only libel critical of the government. . . .

Our cases surely do not establish the proposition that the First Amendment imposes no obstacle whatsoever to regulation of particular instances of such proscribable expression. . . . That would mean that a city council could enact an ordinance prohibiting only those legally obscene works that contain criticism of the city government or, indeed, that do not include endorsement of the city government. ... It is not true that "fighting words" have at most a "de minimis" expressive content, or that their content is in all respects "worthless and undeserving of constitutional protection," (White, J., concurring in the judgment); sometimes they are quite expressive indeed. We have not said that they constitute "no part of the expression of ideas," but only that they constitute "no essential part of any exposition of ideas." *Chaplinksy* (emphasis added).

The proposition that a particular instance of speech can be proscribable on the basis of one feature (e.g., obscenity) but not on the basis of another (e.g., opposition to the city government) is commonplace and has found application in many contexts. We have long held, for example, that nonverbal expressive activity can be banned because of the action it entails, but not because of the ideas it expresses — so that burning a flag in violation of an ordinance against outdoor fires could be punishable, whereas burning a flag in violation of an ordinance against dishonoring the flag is not. Similarly, we have upheld reasonable "time, place, or manner" restrictions, but only if they are "justified without reference to the content of the regulated speech." *Ward v. Rock Against Racism* (1989) (internal quotation marks omitted). And just as the power to proscribe particular speech on the basis of a noncontent element (e.g., noise) does not entail the power to proscribe the same speech on the basis of a content element; so also, the power to proscribe it on the basis of one content element (e.g., obscenity) does not entail the power to proscribe it on the basis of other content elements.

In other words, the exclusion of "fighting words" from the scope of the First Amendment simply means that, for purposes of that Amendment, the unprotected features of the words are, despite their verbal character, essentially a "nonspeech" element of communication. Fighting words are thus analogous to a noisy sound truck: Each is, as Justice Frankfurter recognized, a "mode of speech," *Niemotko v. Maryland* (1951) (opinion concurring in result); both can be used to convey an idea; but neither has, in and of itself, a claim upon the First Amendment. As with the sound truck, however, so also with fighting words: The government may not regulate use based on hostility — or favoritism — towards the underlying message expressed.

[The] First Amendment imposes . . . a "content discrimination" limitation upon a State's prohibition of proscribable speech. There is no problem whatever, for example, with a State's prohibiting obscenity (and other forms of proscribable expression) only in certain media or markets, for . . . that prohibition . . . would not discriminate on the basis of content. . . . When the basis for the content discrimination consists entirely of the very reason the entire class of speech at issue is proscribable, no significant danger of idea or viewpoint discrimination exists. Such a reason, having been adjudged neutral enough to support exclusion of the entire class of speech from First Amendment protection, is also neutral enough to form the basis of distinction within the class. To illustrate: A State might choose to prohibit only that obscenity which is the most patently offensive in its prurience — i.e., that which involves the most lascivious displays of sexual activity. But it may not prohibit, for example, only that obscenity which includes offensive political messages. . . .

Another valid basis for according differential treatment to even a content-defined subclass of proscribable speech is that the subclass happens to be associated with particular "secondary effects" of the speech, so that the regulation is "justified without reference to the content of the . . . speech," *Renton v. Playtime Theatres, Inc.* (1986) [quotation omitted]. A State could, for example, permit all obscene live performances except those involving minors. ... Where the government does not target conduct on the basis of its expressive content, acts are not shielded from regulation merely because they express a discriminatory idea or philosophy.

### II

Applying these principles to the St. Paul ordinance, we conclude that, even as narrowly construed by the Minnesota Supreme Court, the ordinance is facially unconstitutional. Although the phrase in the ordinance, "arouses anger, alarm or resentment in others," has been limited by the Minnesota Supreme Court's construction to reach only those symbols or displays that amount to "fighting words," the remaining, unmodified terms make clear that the ordinance applies only to "fighting words" that insult, or provoke violence, "on the basis of race, color, creed, religion or gender." Displays containing abusive invective, no matter how vicious or severe, are permissible unless they are addressed to one of the specified disfavored topics. Those who wish to use "fighting words" in connection with other ideas — to express hostility, for example, on the basis of political affiliation, union membership, or homosexuality — are not covered.

The First Amendment does not permit St. Paul to impose special prohibitions on those speakers who express views on disfavored subjects.

In its practical operation, moreover, the ordinance goes even beyond mere content discrimination, to actual viewpoint discrimination. Displays containing some words — odious racial epithets, for example — would be prohibited to proponents of all views. But "fighting words" that do not themselves invoke race, color, creed, religion, or gender — aspersions upon a person's mother, for example — would seemingly be usable ad libitum in the placards of those arguing in favor of racial, color, etc., tolerance and equality, but could not be used by those speakers' opponents. One could hold up a sign saying, for example, that all "anti-Catholic bigots" are misbegotten; but not that all "papists" are, for that would insult and provoke violence "on the basis of religion." St. Paul has no such authority to license one side of a debate to fight freestyle, while requiring the other to follow Marquis of Queensberry rules.

What we have here, it must be emphasized, is not a prohibition of fighting words that are directed at certain persons or groups (which would be facially valid if it met the requirements of the Equal Protection Clause); but rather, a prohibition of fighting words that contain (as the Minnesota Supreme Court repeatedly emphasized) messages of "bias-motivated" hatred and in particular, as applied to this case, messages "based on virulent notions of racial supremacy." One must wholeheartedly agree with the Minnesota Supreme Court that "[i]t is the responsibility, even the obligation, of diverse communities to confront such notions in whatever form they appear," but the manner of that confrontation cannot consist of selective limitations upon speech. St. Paul's brief asserts that a general "fighting words" law would not meet the city's needs because only a content- specific measure can communicate to minority groups that the "group hatred" aspect of such speech "is not condoned by the majority." The point of the First Amendment is that majority preferences must be expressed in some fashion other than silencing speech on the basis of its content.

[Further, the] content-based discrimination reflected in the St. Paul ordinance . . . assuredly does not fall within the exception for content discrimination based on the very reasons why the particular class of speech at issue (here, fighting words) is proscribable. As explained earlier, the reason why fighting words are categorically excluded from the protection of the First Amendment is not that their content communicates any particular idea, but that their content embodies a particularly intolerable (and socially unnecessary) mode of expressing whatever idea the speaker wishes to convey. St. Paul has not singled out an especially offensive mode of expression — it has not, for example, selected for prohibition only those fighting words that communicate ideas in a threatening (as opposed to a merely obnoxious) manner. Rather, it has proscribed fighting words of whatever manner that communicate messages of racial, gender, or religious intolerance. Selectivity of this sort creates the possibility that the city is seeking to handicap the expression of particular ideas. . . .

Finally, St. Paul and its amici defend the conclusion of the Minnesota Supreme Court that, even if the ordinance regulates expression based on hostility towards its protected ideological content, this discrimination is nonetheless justified because it is narrowly tailored to serve compelling state interests. Specifically, they assert that the ordinance helps to ensure the basic human rights of members of groups that have historically been subjected to discrimination, including the right of such group members to live in peace where they wish. We do not doubt that these interests are compelling, and that the ordinance can be said to promote them. But the "danger of censorship" presented by a facially content-based statute requires that that weapon be employed only where it is "necessary to serve the asserted [compelling] interest," *Burson v. Freeman* (1992) (plurality opinion) (emphasis added). The existence of adequate content- neutral alternatives thus "undercut[s] significantly" any defense of such a statute, Boos v. Barry (1988), casting considerable doubt on the government's protestations that "the asserted justification is in fact an accurate description of the purpose and effect of the law," *Burson* (Kennedy, J., concurring). The dispositive question in this case, therefore, is whether content discrimination is reasonably necessary to achieve St. Paul's compelling interests; it plainly is not. An ordinance not limited to the favored topics, for example, would have precisely the same beneficial effect. In fact the only interest distinctively served by the content limitation is that of displaying the city council's special hostility towards the particular biases thus singled out. That is precisely what the First Amendment forbids. The politicians of St. Paul are entitled to express that hostility — but not through the means of imposing unique limitations upon speakers who (however benightedly) disagree.

\* \* \*

Let there be no mistake about our belief that burning a cross in someone's front yard is reprehensible. But St. Paul has sufficient means at its disposal to prevent such behavior without adding the First Amendment to the fire.

The judgment of the Minnesota Supreme Court is reversed, and the case is remanded for proceedings not inconsistent with this opinion.

It is so ordered.

[Concurring opinion of Justice White omitted.]

[Concurring opinion of Justice Blackmun omitted.]

[Concurring opinion of Justice Stevens omitted.]

**NOTES AND QUESTIONS**

1. *R.A.V.* tells us something about the category of speech known as "fighting words" — which, as Justice Scalia reminds us, constitute "no essential part" of the exposition of ideas. But the case also tells us something more generally about content-based restrictions on speech — namely, that some regulations are problematical not just because

they focus on certain content, but because they reveal that the government has taken sides in a particular debate, amounting to what the Court has called "viewpoint discrimination." As one court succinctly put it: "The Constitution forbids the state to declare one perspective right and silence opponents." *American Booksellers Ass'n, Inc. v. Hudnut*, 771 F.2d 323 (7th Cir. 1985). How was the St. Paul ordinance in *R.A.V.* an example of such discrimination?

**2.** In addition to categories of speech that receive only the most minimal protection under the First Amendment, the Court has distinguished between laws that regulate political speech — such as speech on matters of public importance — and laws that regulate commercial speech — such as speech related to the marketing and selling of goods and services, as in Expressions Hair Design.

**3.** Finally, the Court has over time has accorded certain speech in certain places less protection under the First Amendment, including speech in the military, prisons, and, as discussed in the next case, schools.

## Mahonoy Area School District v. B.L.
### 594 U.S. ___ (2021)

Justice BREYER delivered the opinion of the Court.

A public high school student used, and transmitted to her Snapchat friends, vulgar language and gestures criticizing both the school and the school's cheerleading team. The student's speech took place outside of school hours and away from the school's campus. In response, the school suspended the student for a year from the cheerleading team. We must decide whether the Court of Appeals for the Third Circuit correctly held that the school's decision violated the First Amendment. Although we do not agree with the reasoning of the Third Circuit panel's majority, we do agree with its conclusion that the school's disciplinary action violated the First Amendment.

**I**

B. L. (who, together with her parents, is a respondent in this case) was a student at Mahanoy Area High School, a public school in Mahanoy City, Pennsylvania. At the end of her freshman year, B. L. tried out for a position on the school's varsity cheerleading squad and for right fielder on a private softball team. She did not make the varsity cheerleading team or get her preferred softball position, but she was offered a spot on the cheerleading squad's junior varsity team. B. L. did not accept the coach's decision with good grace, particularly because the squad coaches had placed an entering freshman on the varsity team.

That weekend, B. L. and a friend visited the Cocoa Hut, a local convenience store. There, B. L. used her smartphone to post two photos on Snapchat, a social media application that allows users to post photos and videos that disappear after a set period of time. B. L. posted the images to her Snapchat "story," a feature of the application that allows any person in the user's "friend" group (B. L. had about 250 "friends") to view the images for a 24 hour period.

The first image B. L. posted showed B. L. and a friend with middle fingers raised; it bore the caption: "Fuck school fuck softball fuck cheer fuck everything." The second image was blank but for a caption, which read: "Love how me and [another student] get told we need a year of jv before we make varsity but tha[t] doesn't matter to anyone else?" The caption also contained an upside-down smiley-face emoji.

B. L.'s Snapchat "friends" included other Mahanoy Area High School students, some of whom also belonged to the cheerleading squad. At least one of them, using a separate cellphone, took pictures of B. L.'s posts and shared them with other members of the cheerleading squad. One of the students who received these photos showed them to her mother (who was a cheerleading squad coach), and the images spread. That week, several cheerleaders and other students approached the cheerleading coaches "visibly upset" about B. L.'s posts. Questions about the posts persisted during an Algebra class taught by one of the two coaches.

After discussing the matter with the school principal, the coaches decided that because the posts used profanity in connection with a school extracurricular activity, they violated team and school rules. As a result, the coaches suspended B. L. from the junior varsity cheerleading squad for the upcoming year. B. L.'s subsequent apologies did not move school officials. The school's athletic director, principal, superintendent, and school board, all affirmed B. L.'s suspension from the team. In response, B. L., together with her parents, filed this lawsuit in Federal District Court.

The District Court found in B. L.'s favor. It first granted a temporary restraining order and a preliminary injunction ordering the school to reinstate B. L. to the cheerleading team. In granting B. L.'s subsequent motion for summary judgment, the District Court found that B. L.'s Snapchats had not caused substantial disruption at the school. Consequently, the District Court declared that B. L.'s punishment violated the First Amendment, and it awarded B. L. nominal damages and attorneys' fees and ordered the school to expunge her disciplinary record.

On appeal, a panel of the Third Circuit affirmed the District Court's conclusion. In so doing, the majority noted that this Court had previously held in *Tinker v. Des Moines Independent Community School Dist.* (1969) that a public high school could not constitutionally prohibit a peaceful student political demonstration consisting of "'pure speech'" on school property during the school day. In reaching its conclusion in Tinker, this Court emphasized that there was no evidence the student protest would "substantially interfere with the work of the school or impinge upon the rights of other students." But the Court also said that: "[C]onduct by [a] student, in class or out of it, which for any reason—whether it stems from time, place, or type of behavior—materially disrupts classwork or involves substantial disorder or invasion of the rights of others is ... not immunized by the constitutional guarantee of freedom of speech."

Many courts have taken this statement as setting a standard—a standard that allows schools considerable freedom on campus to discipline students for conduct that the First Amendment might otherwise protect. But here, the panel majority held that this additional freedom did "not apply to off-campus speech," which it defined as "speech that is outside school-owned, -operated, or -supervised channels and that is not reasonably interpreted as bearing the school's imprimatur." Because B. L.'s speech took place off campus, the panel concluded that the Tinker standard did not apply and the school consequently could not discipline B. L. for engaging in a form of pure speech.

The school district filed a petition for certiorari in this Court, asking us to decide "[w]hether [Tinker], which holds that public school officials may regulate speech that would materially and substantially disrupt the work and discipline of the school, applies to student speech that occurs off campus." We granted the petition.

## II

We have made clear that students do not "shed their constitutional rights to freedom of speech or expression," even "at the school house gate." Tinker. But we have also made clear that courts must apply the First Amendment "in light of the special characteristics of the school environment." *Hazelwood School Dist. v. Kuhlmeier* (1988) (internal quotation mark omitted). One such characteristic, which we have stressed, is the fact that schools at times stand in loco parentis, i.e., in the place of parents.

This Court has previously outlined three specific categories of student speech that schools may regulate in certain circumstances: (1) "indecent," "lewd," or "vulgar" speech uttered during a school assembly on school grounds; (2) speech, uttered during a class trip, that promotes "illegal drug use'; and (3) speech that others may reasonably perceive as "bear[ing] the imprimatur of the school," such as that appearing in a school-sponsored newspaper.

Finally, in *Tinker*, we said schools have a special interest in regulating speech that "materially disrupts classwork or involves substantial disorder or invasion of the rights of others." These special characteristics call for special leeway when schools regulate speech that occurs under its supervision.

Unlike the Third Circuit, we do not believe the special characteristics that give schools additional license to regulate student speech always disappear when a school regulates speech that takes place off campus. The school's regulatory interests remain significant in some off-campus circumstances. The parties' briefs, and those of amici, list several types of off-campus behavior that may call for school regulation. These include serious or severe bullying or harassment targeting particular individuals; threats aimed at teachers or other students; the failure to follow rules concerning lessons, the writing of papers, the use of computers, or participation in other online school activities; and breaches of school security devices, including material maintained within school computers.

[margin note: different threshold for off-cmpus behavior]

Even B. L. herself and the amici supporting her would redefine the Third Circuit's off-campus/on-campus distinction, treating as on campus: all times when the school is responsible for the student; the school's immediate surroundings; travel en route to and from the school; all speech taking place over school laptops or on a school's website; speech taking place during remote learning; activities taken for school credit; and communications to school e-mail accounts or phones. And it may be that speech related to extracurricular activities, such as team sports, would also receive special treatment under B. L.'s proposed rule.

We are uncertain as to the length or content of any such list of appropriate exceptions or carveouts to the Third Circuit majority's rule. That rule, basically, if not entirely, would deny the off-campus applicability of Tinker's highly general statement about the nature of a school's special interests. Particularly given the advent of computer-based learning, we hesitate to determine precisely which of many school-related off-campus activities belong on such a list. Neither do we now know how such a list might vary, depending upon a student's age, the nature of the school's off-campus activity, or the impact upon the school itself. Thus, we do not now set forth a broad, highly general First Amendment rule stating just what counts as "off campus" speech and whether or how ordinary First Amendment standards must give way off campus to a school's special need to prevent, e.g., substantial disruption of learning-related activities or the protection of those who make up a school community.

We can, however, mention three features of off-campus speech that often, even if not always, distinguish schools' efforts to regulate that speech from their efforts to regulate on-campus speech. Those features diminish the strength of the unique educational characteristics that might call for special First Amendment leeway.

First, a school, in relation to off-campus speech, will rarely stand in loco parentis. The doctrine of in loco parentis treats school administrators as standing in the place of students' parents under circumstances where the children's actual parents cannot protect, guide, and discipline them. Geographically speaking, off-campus speech will normally fall within the zone of parental, rather than school-related, responsibility.

Second, from the student speaker's perspective, regulations of off-campus speech, when coupled with regulations of on-campus speech, include all the speech a student utters during the full 24-hour day. That means courts must be more skeptical of a school's efforts to regulate off-campus speech, for doing so may mean the student cannot engage in that kind of speech at all. When it comes to political or religious speech that occurs outside school or a school program or activity, the school will have a heavy burden to justify intervention.

Third, the school itself has an interest in protecting a student's unpopular expression, especially when the expression takes place off campus. America's public schools are the nurseries of democracy. Our representative democracy only works if we protect the "marketplace of ideas." This free exchange facilitates an informed public opinion, which, when transmitted to lawmakers, helps produce laws that reflect the People's will. That protection must include the protection of unpopular ideas, for popular ideas have less need for protection. Thus, schools have a strong interest in ensuring that future generations understand the workings in practice of the well-known aphorism, "I disapprove of what you say, but I will defend to the death your right to say it." (Although this quote is often attributed to Voltaire, it was likely coined by an English writer, Evelyn Beatrice Hall.)

Given the many different kinds of off-campus speech, the different potential school-related and circumstance-specific justifications, and the differing extent to which those justifications may call for First Amendment leeway, we can, as a general matter, say little more than this: Taken together, these three features of much off-campus speech mean that the leeway the First Amendment grants to schools in light of their special characteristics is diminished. We leave for future cases to decide where, when, and how these features mean the speaker's off-campus location will make the critical difference. This case can, however, provide one example.

### III

Consider B. L.'s speech. Putting aside the vulgar language, the listener would hear criticism, of the team, the team's coaches, and the school—in a word or two, criticism of the rules of a community of which B. L. forms a part. This criticism did not involve features that would place it outside the First Amendment's ordinary protection. B. L.'s posts, while crude, did not amount to fighting words. And while B. L. used vulgarity, her speech was not obscene as this Court has understood that term. [To the contrary, B. L. uttered the kind of pure speech to which, were she an adult, the First Amendment would provide strong protection.]

Consider too when, where, and how B. L. spoke. Her posts appeared outside of school hours from a location outside the school. She did not identify the school in her posts or target any member of the school community with vulgar or abusive language. B. L. also transmitted her speech through a personal cellphone, to an audience consisting of her private circle of Snapchat friends. These features of her speech, while risking transmission to the school itself, nonetheless (for reasons we have just explained) diminish the school's interest in punishing B. L.'s utterance.

But what about the school's interest, here primarily an interest in prohibiting students from using vulgar language to criticize a school team or its coaches—at least when that criticism might well be transmitted to other students, team members, coaches, and faculty? We can break that general interest into three parts.

First, we consider the school's interest in teaching good manners and consequently in punishing the use of vulgar language aimed at part of the school community. The strength of this anti-vulgarity interest is weakened considerably by the fact that B. L. spoke outside the school on her own time.

B. L. spoke under circumstances where the school did not stand in loco parentis. And there is no reason to believe B. L.'s parents had delegated to school officials their own control of B. L.'s behavior at the Cocoa Hut. Moreover, the vulgarity in B. L.'s posts encompassed a message, an expression of B. L.'s irritation with, and criticism of, the school and cheerleading communities. Further, the school has presented no evidence of any general effort to prevent students from using vulgarity outside the classroom. Together, these facts convince us that the school's interest in teaching good manners is not sufficient, in this case, to overcome B. L.'s interest in free expression.

Second, the school argues that it was trying to prevent disruption, if not within the classroom, then within the bounds of a school-sponsored extracurricular activity. But we can find no evidence in the record of the sort of "substantial disruption" of a school activity or a threatened harm to the rights of others that might justify the school's action. Rather, the record shows that discussion of the matter took, at most, 5 to 10 minutes of an Algebra class "for just a couple of days" and that some members of the cheerleading team were "upset" about the content of B. L.'s Snapchats. But when one of B. L.'s coaches was asked directly if she had "any reason to think that this particular incident would disrupt class or school activities other than the fact that kids kept asking ... about it," she responded simply, "No." As we said in Tinker, "for the State in the person of school officials to justify prohibition of a particular expression of opinion, it must be able to show that its action was caused by something more than a mere desire to avoid the discomfort and unpleasantness that always accompany an unpopular viewpoint." The alleged disturbance here does not meet Tinker's demanding standard.

Third, the school presented some evidence that expresses (at least indirectly) a concern for team morale. One of the coaches testified that the school decided to suspend B. L., not because of any specific negative impact upon a particular member of the school community, but "based on the fact that there was negativity put out there that could impact students in the school." There is little else, however, that suggests any serious decline in team morale—to the point where it could create a substantial interference in, or disruption of, the school's efforts to maintain team cohesion. As we have previously said, simple "undifferentiated fear or apprehension ... is not enough to overcome the right to freedom of expression." Tinker.

It might be tempting to dismiss B. L.'s words as unworthy of the robust First Amendment protections discussed herein. But sometimes it is necessary to protect the superfluous in order to preserve the necessary. ...

* * *

Although we do not agree with the reasoning of the Third Circuit's panel majority, ... we nonetheless agree that the school violated B. L.'s First Amendment rights. The judgment of the Third Circuit is therefore affirmed.

It is so ordered.

[Concurring opinion of Justice ALITO omitted.]

[Dissenting opinion of Justice THOMAS omitted.]

## NOTES AND QUESTIONS

**1.** As you will see often with the modern court, this case raises more questions than it answers. That said, it does explain the background principle: while public school students do not "shed their constitutional rights to freedom of speech or expression," even "at the school house gate," *Tinker*, the court has made clear that the First Amendment applies in the public school context "in light of the special characteristics of the school environment." *Hazelwood School Dist. v. Kuhlmeier* (1988) (internal quotation mark omitted). Schools generally have a freer hand to regulate three specific categories of student speech: (1) speech that is "indecent," "lewd," or "vulgar" and spoken during a school assembly on school grounds; (2) speech that promotes illegal drug use and is spoken during a class trip; and (3) speech that third-parties reasonably might see as sponsored by the school, such as expression appearing in a school newspaper. In addition, the Court in *Tinker* held that schools have a special interest in regulating speech that "materially disrupts classwork or involves substantial disorder or invasion of the rights of others."

**2.** Why did the speech in this case not fall neatly into one of these categories? What distinguishes the speech at issue here from these other kinds of speech, which the Supreme Court has said can be regulated by a school?

**3.** What rule, if any, does the court establish regarding expression communicated by students through platforms the school itself does not control? What factors might the court consider in determining whether particular speech can be regulated by a school going forward?

**4.** It is important to understand that all legislative rules discriminate in some way — every federal, state, or local regulation draws lines between legal and illegal matters, between those individuals who operate within the law and those who operate without the law. The lines that trigger more intense judicial review are those that, in the First Amendment context, indicate governmental favoritism toward certain kinds of speech. As you will see, this kind of discrimination-based analysis informs other areas of constitutional law, including the Dormant Commerce Clause and Equal Protection, each of which is discussed later in this book.

**2. The Right to Bear Arms**

In all the ways that free speech doctrine under the First Amendment is relatively neat, orderly, and predictable, doctrine under the Second Amendment is not. The Second Amendment states: "A well regulated Militia, being necessary to the security of a free State, the right of the people to keep and bear Arms, shall not be infringed." As you will see, the Supreme Court in *District of Columbia v. Heller*, 554 U.S. 570 (2008), concluded that this provision affords individuals the right to use firearms in self-defense, a right that the Court subsequently expanded in a 2022 decision, *New York State Rifle & Pistol Association, Inc. v. Bruen*, 597 U.S. ___. In between these cases, the Supreme Court held that the Second Amendment applies to the states via the Fourteenth Amendment. See *McDonald v. City of Chicago*, 561 U.S. 742 (2010).

## District of Columbia v. Heller
## 554 U.S. 570 (2008)

Justice SCALIA delivered the opinion of the Court.

The District of Columbia generally prohibits the possession of handguns. It is a crime to carry an unregistered firearm, and the registration of handguns is prohibited. Wholly apart from that prohibition, no person may carry a handgun without a license, but the chief of police may issue licenses for 1-year periods. District of Columbia law also requires residents to keep their lawfully owned firearms, such as registered long guns, "unloaded and dissembled or bound by a trigger lock or similar device" unless they are located in a place of business or are being used for lawful recreational activities.

Respondent Dick Heller is a D.C. special police officer authorized to carry a handgun while on duty at the Thurgood Marshall Judiciary Building. He applied for a registration certificate for a handgun that he wished to keep at home, but the District refused. He thereafter filed a lawsuit in the Federal District Court for the District of Columbia seeking, on Second Amendment grounds, to enjoin the city from enforcing the bar on the registration of handguns, the licensing requirement insofar as it prohibits the carrying of a firearm in the home without a license, and the trigger-lock requirement insofar as it prohibits the use of "functional firearms within the home." The District Court dismissed respondent's complaint. The Court of Appeals for the District of Columbia Circuit, construing his complaint as seeking the right to render a firearm operable and carry it about his home in that condition only when necessary for self-defense, reversed. It held that the Second Amendment protects an individual right to possess firearms and that the city's total ban on handguns, as well as its requirement that firearms in the home be kept nonfunctional even when necessary for self-defense, violated that right. The Court of Appeals directed the District Court to enter summary judgment for respondent.

We granted certiorari.

## II

We turn first to the meaning of the Second Amendment.

The Second Amendment provides: "A well regulated Militia, being necessary to the security of a free State, the right of the people to keep and bear Arms, shall not be infringed." In interpreting this text, we are guided by the principle that "[t]he Constitution was written to be understood by the voters; its words and phrases were used in their normal and ordinary as distinguished from technical meaning." *United States v. Sprague* (1931). Normal meaning may of course include an idiomatic meaning, but it excludes secret or technical meanings that would not have been known to ordinary citizens in the founding generation.

The two sides in this case have set out very different interpretations of the Amendment. Petitioners and today's dissenting Justices believe that it protects only the right to possess and carry a firearm in connection with militia service. Respondent argues that it protects an individual right to possess a firearm unconnected with service in a militia, and to use that arm for traditionally lawful purposes, such as self-defense within the home.

The Second Amendment is naturally divided into two parts: its prefatory clause and its operative clause. The former does not limit the latter grammatically, but rather announces a purpose. ...

[A]part from [a] clarifying function, a prefatory clause does not limit or expand the scope of the operative clause. ... Therefore, while we will begin our textual analysis with the operative clause, we will return to the prefatory clause to ensure that our reading of the operative clause is consistent with the announced purpose.

**1. Operative Clause.**

a. "Right of the People." The first salient feature of the operative clause is that it codifies a "right of the people." The unamended Constitution and the Bill of Rights use the phrase "right of the people" two other times, in the First Amendment's Assembly-and-Petition Clause and in the Fourth Amendment's Search-and-Seizure Clause. The Ninth Amendment uses very similar terminology ("The enumeration in the Constitution, of certain rights, shall not be construed to deny or disparage others retained by the people"). All three of these instances unambiguously refer to individual rights, not "collective" rights, or rights that may be exercised only through participation in some corporate body.

Three provisions of the Constitution refer to "the people" in a context other than "rights"—the famous preamble ("We the people"), § 2 of Article I (providing that "the people" will choose members of the House), and the Tenth Amendment (providing that those powers not given the Federal Government remain with "the States" or "the people"). Those provisions arguably refer to "the people" acting collectively—but they deal with the exercise or reservation of powers, not rights. Nowhere else in the Constitution does a "right" attributed to "the people" refer to anything other than an individual right.

What is more, in all six other provisions of the Constitution that mention "the people," the term unambiguously refers to all members of the political community, not an unspecified subset. ...

This contrasts markedly with the phrase "the militia" in the prefatory clause. As we will describe below, the "militia" in colonial America consisted of a subset of "the people"—those who were male, able bodied, and within a certain age range. Reading the Second Amendment as protecting only the right to "keep and bear Arms" in an organized militia therefore fits poorly with the operative clause's description of the holder of that right as "the people."

We start therefore with a strong presumption that the Second Amendment right is exercised individually and belongs to all Americans.

b. "Keep and Bear Arms." We move now from the holder of the right—"the people"—to the substance of the right: "to keep and bear Arms."

Before addressing the verbs "keep" and "bear," we interpret their object: "Arms." The 18th-century meaning is no different from the meaning today. The 1773 edition of Samuel Johnson's dictionary defined "arms" as "[w]eapons of offence, or armour of defence." 1 Dictionary of the English Language 106 (4th ed.) (reprinted 1978) (hereinafter Johnson). Timothy Cunningham's important 1771 legal dictionary defined "arms" as "any thing that a man wears for his defence, or takes into his hands, or useth in wrath to cast at or strike another." 1 A New and Complete Law Dictionary.

The term was applied, then as now, to weapons that were not specifically designed for military use and were not employed in a military capacity. For instance, Cunningham's legal dictionary gave as an example of usage: "Servants and labourers shall use bows and arrows on Sundays, & c. and not bear other arms." Although one founding-era thesaurus limited "arms" (as opposed to "weapons") to "instruments of offence generally made use of in war," even that source stated that all firearms constituted "arms." 1 J. Trusler, The Distinction Between Words Esteemed Synonymous in the English Language 37 (3d ed. 1794) (emphasis added).

Some have made the argument, bordering on the frivolous, that only those arms in existence in the 18th century are protected by the Second Amendment. We do not interpret constitutional rights that way. Just as the First Amendment protects modern forms of communications, and the Fourth Amendment applies to modern forms of search, the Second Amendment extends, prima facie, to all instruments that constitute bearable arms, even those that were not in existence at the time of the founding.

We turn to the phrases "keep arms" and "bear arms." Johnson defined "keep" as, most relevantly, "[t]o retain; not to lose," and "[t]o have in custody." Webster defined it as "[t]o hold; to retain in one's power or possession." No party has apprised us of an idiomatic meaning of "keep Arms." Thus, the most natural reading of "keep Arms" in the Second Amendment is to "have weapons."

The phrase "keep arms" was not prevalent in the written documents of the founding period that we have found, but there are a few examples, all of which favor viewing the right to "keep Arms" as an individual right unconnected with militia service. William Blackstone, for example, wrote that Catholics convicted of not attending service in the Church of England suffered certain penalties, one of which was that they were not permitted to "keep arms in their houses." 4 Commentaries on the Laws of England 55 (1769) (hereinafter Blackstone). Petitioners point to militia laws of the founding period that required militia members to "keep" arms in connection with militia service, and they conclude from this that the phrase "keep Arms" has a militia-related connotation. This is rather like saying that, since there are many statutes that authorize aggrieved employees to "file complaints" with federal agencies, the phrase "file complaints" has an employment-related connotation. "Keep arms" was simply a common way of referring to possessing arms, for militiamen and everyone else.

At the time of the founding, as now, to "bear" meant to "carry." See Johnson 161; Webster; T. Sheridan, A Complete Dictionary of the English Language (1796); 2 Oxford English Dictionary 20 (2d ed. 1989) (hereinafter Oxford). When used with "arms," however, the term has a meaning that refers to carrying for a particular purpose—confrontation. In *Muscarello v. United States* (1998), in the course of analyzing the meaning of "carries a firearm" in a federal criminal statute, Justice GINSBURG wrote that "[s]urely a most familiar meaning is, as the Constitution's Second Amendment . . . indicate[s]: 'wear, bear, or carry . . . upon the person or in the clothing or in a pocket, for the purpose . . . of being armed and ready for offensive or defensive action in a case of conflict with another person.'" (dissenting opinion) (quoting Black's Law Dictionary 214 (6th ed.1990)). ... Although the phrase implies that the carrying of the weapon is for the purpose of "offensive or defensive action," it in no way connotes participation in a structured military organization.

From our review of founding-era sources, we conclude that this natural meaning was also the meaning that "bear arms" had in the 18th century. In numerous instances, "bear arms" was unambiguously used to refer to the carrying of weapons outside of an organized militia. The most prominent examples are those most relevant to the Second Amendment: nine state constitutional provisions written in the 18th century or the first two decades of the 19th, which enshrined a right of citizens to "bear arms in defense of themselves and the state" or "bear arms in defense of himself and the state." It is clear from those formulations that "bear arms" did not refer only to carrying a weapon in an organized military unit. Justice James Wilson interpreted the Pennsylvania Constitution's arms-bearing right, for example, as a recognition of the natural right of defense "of one's person or house"—what he called the law of "self preservation." 2 Collected Works of James Wilson 1142, and n. x (K. Hall & M. Hall eds.2007) (citing Pa. Const., Art. IX, § 21 (1790)). That was also the interpretation of those state constitutional provisions adopted by pre-Civil War state courts. These provisions demonstrate—again, in the most analogous linguistic context—that "bear arms" was not limited to the carrying of arms in a militia.

The phrase "bear Arms" also had at the time of the founding an idiomatic meaning that was significantly different from its natural meaning: "to serve as a soldier, do military service, fight" or "to wage war." But it unequivocally bore that idiomatic meaning only when followed by the preposition "against," which was in turn followed by the target of the hostilities. ...

Petitioners justify their limitation of "bear arms" to the military context by pointing out the unremarkable fact that it was often used in that context—the same mistake they made with respect to "keep arms." It is especially unremarkable that the phrase was often used in a military context in the federal legal sources (such as records of congressional debate) that have been the focus of petitioners' inquiry.

Those sources would have had little occasion to use it except in discussions about the standing army and the militia. And the phrases used primarily in those military discussions include not only "bear arms" but also "carry arms," "possess arms," and "have arms"—though no one thinks that those other phrases also had special military meanings. The common references to those "fit to bear arms" in congressional discussions about the militia are matched by use of the same phrase in the few nonmilitary federal contexts where the concept would be relevant. Other legal sources frequently used "bear arms" in nonmilitary contexts. Cunningham's legal dictionary, cited above, gave as an example of its usage a sentence unrelated to military affairs ("Servants and labourers shall use bows and arrows on Sundays, & c. and not bear other arms"). And if one looks beyond legal sources, "bear arms" was frequently used in nonmilitary contexts.

c. Meaning of the Operative Clause. Putting all of these textual elements together, we find that they guarantee the individual right to possess and carry weapons in case of confrontation. This meaning is strongly confirmed by the historical background of the Second Amendment. We look to this because it has always been widely understood that the Second Amendment, like the First and Fourth Amendments, codified a pre-existing right. The very text of the Second Amendment implicitly recognizes the pre-existence of the right and declares only that it "shall not be infringed."...

There seems to us no doubt, on the basis of both text and history, that the Second Amendment conferred an individual right to keep and bear arms. Of course the right was not unlimited, just as the First Amendment's right of free speech was not. Thus, we do not read the Second Amendment to protect the right of citizens to carry arms for any sort of confrontation, just as we do not read the First Amendment to protect the right of citizens to speak for any purpose. Before turning to limitations upon the individual right, however, we must determine whether the prefatory clause of the Second Amendment comports with our interpretation of the operative clause.

**2. Prefatory Clause.**

The prefatory clause reads: "A well regulated Militia, being necessary to the security of a free State. . . ."

a. "Well-Regulated Militia." In United States v. Miller (1939), we explained that "the Militia comprised all males physically capable of acting in concert for the common defense." That definition comports with founding-era sources.

Petitioners take a seemingly narrower view of the militia, stating that "[m]ilitias are the state- and congressionally-regulated military forces described in the Militia Clauses (art. I, § 8, cls. 15-16)." Although we agree with petitioners' interpretive assumption that "militia" means the same thing in Article I and the Second Amendment, we believe that petitioners identify the wrong thing, namely, the organized militia. Unlike armies and navies, which Congress is given the power to create ("to raise . . . Armies"; "to provide . . . a Navy," Art. I, § 8, cls. 12-13), the militia is assumed by

Article I already to be in existence. Congress is given the power to "provide for calling forth the Militia," § 8, cl. 15; and the power not to create, but to "organiz[e]" it—and not to organize "a" militia, which is what one would expect if the militia were to be a federal creation, but to organize "the" militia, connoting a body already in existence. This is fully consistent with the ordinary definition of the militia as all able-bodied men. From that pool, Congress has plenary power to organize the units that will make up an effective fighting force. That is what Congress did in the first Militia Act, which specified that "each and every free able-bodied white male citizen of the respective states, resident therein, who is or shall be of the age of eighteen years, and under the age of forty-five years (except as is herein after excepted) shall severally and respectively be enrolled in the militia." To be sure, Congress need not conscript every able-bodied man into the militia, because nothing in Article I suggests that in exercising its power to organize, discipline, and arm the militia, Congress must focus upon the entire body. Although the militia consists of all able-bodied men, the federally organized militia may consist of a subset of them.

Finally, the adjective "well-regulated" implies nothing more than the imposition of proper discipline and training.

b. "Security of a Free State." The phrase "security of a free State" meant "security of a free polity," not security of each of the several States.... It is true that the term "State" elsewhere in the Constitution refers to individual States, but the phrase "security of a free State" and close variations seem to have been terms of art in 18th-century political discourse, meaning a "free country" or free polity. Moreover, the other instances of "state" in the Constitution are typically accompanied by modifiers making clear that the reference is to the several States—"each state," "several states," "any state," "that state," "particular states," "one state," "no state." And the presence of the term "foreign state" in Article I and Article III shows that the word "state" did not have a single meaning in the Constitution.

There are many reasons why the militia was thought to be "necessary to the security of a free State." First, of course, it is useful in repelling invasions and suppressing insurrections. Second, it renders large standing armies unnecessary—an argument that Alexander Hamilton made in favor of federal control over the militia. Third, when the able-bodied men of a nation are trained in arms and organized, they are better able to resist tyranny.

**3. Relationship Between Prefatory Clause and Operative Clause.**

We reach the question, then: Does the preface fit with an operative clause that creates an individual right to keep and bear arms? It fits perfectly, once one knows the history that the founding generation knew and that we have described above. That history showed that the way tyrants had eliminated a militia consisting of all the able-bodied men was not by banning the militia but simply by taking away the people's arms, enabling a select militia or standing army to suppress political opponents. This is what had occurred in England that prompted codification of the right to have arms in the

English Bill of Rights.

The debate with respect to the right to keep and bear arms, as with other guarantees in the Bill of Rights, was not over whether it was desirable (all agreed that it was) but over whether it needed to be codified in the Constitution. During the 1788 ratification debates, the fear that the Federal Government would disarm the people in order to impose rule through a standing army or select militia was pervasive in Antifederalist rhetoric... Federalists responded that because Congress was given no power to abridge the ancient right of individuals to keep and bear arms, such a force could never oppress the people. It was understood across the political spectrum that the right helped to secure the ideal of a citizen militia, which might be necessary to oppose an oppressive military force if the constitutional order broke down.

It is therefore entirely sensible that the Second Amendment's prefatory clause announces the purpose for which the right was codified: to prevent elimination of the militia. The prefatory clause does not suggest that preserving the militia was the only reason Americans valued the ancient right; most undoubtedly thought it even more important for self-defense and hunting. But the threat that the new Federal Government would destroy the citizens' militia by taking away their arms was the reason that right—unlike some other English rights—was codified in a written Constitution. [Any] assertion that individual self-defense is merely a "subsidiary interest" of the right to keep and bear arms is profoundly mistaken. [S]elf-defense ... was the central component of the right itself.

If, as [petitioners] believe, the Second Amendment right is no more than the right to keep and use weapons as a member of an organized militia—if, that is, the organized militia is the sole institutional beneficiary of the Second Amendment's guarantee—it does not assure the existence of a "citizens' militia" as a safeguard against tyranny. For Congress retains plenary authority to organize the militia, which must include the authority to say who will belong to the organized force. That is why the first Militia Act's requirement that only whites enroll caused States to amend their militia laws to exclude free blacks. Thus, if petitioners are correct, the Second Amendment protects citizens' right to use a gun in an organization from which Congress has plenary authority to exclude them. It guarantees a select militia of the sort the Stuart kings found useful, but not the people's militia that was the concern of the founding generation.

### III

Like most rights, the right secured by the Second Amendment is not unlimited. From Blackstone through the 19th-century cases, commentators and courts routinely explained that the right was not a right to keep and carry any weapon whatsoever in any manner whatsoever and for whatever purpose. For example, the majority of the 19th-century courts to consider the question held that prohibitions on carrying concealed weapons were lawful under the Second Amendment or state analogues. [N]othing in our opinion should be taken to cast doubt on longstanding prohibitions on the possession of firearms by felons and the mentally ill, or laws forbidding the carrying of firearms in sensitive places such as schools and government buildings, or laws imposing conditions and qualifications on the commercial sale of arms.

We also recognize another important limitation on the right to keep and carry arms. [T]he sorts of weapons protected were those "in common use at the time." United States v. Miller (1939). We think that limitation is fairly supported by the historical tradition of prohibiting the carrying of "dangerous and unusual weapons." See 4 Blackstone 148-149 (1769).

It may be objected that if weapons that are most useful in military service—M-16 rifles and the like—may be banned, then the Second Amendment right is completely detached from the prefatory clause. But as we have said, the conception of the militia at the time of the Second Amendment's ratification was the body of all citizens capable of military service, who would bring the sorts of lawful weapons that they possessed at home to militia duty. It may well be true today that a militia, to be as effective as militias in the 18th century, would require sophisticated arms that are highly unusual in society at large. Indeed, it may be true that no amount of small arms could be useful against modern-day bombers and tanks. But the fact that modern developments have limited the degree of fit between the prefatory clause and the protected right cannot change our interpretation of the right.

**IV**

We turn finally to the law at issue here. As we have said, the law totally bans handgun possession in the home. It also requires that any lawful firearm in the home be disassembled or bound by a trigger lock at all times, rendering it inoperable.

[T]he inherent right of self-defense has been central to the Second Amendment right. The handgun ban amounts to a prohibition of an entire class of "arms" that is overwhelmingly chosen by American society for that lawful purpose. The prohibition extends, moreover, to the home, where the need for defense of self, family, and property is most acute. Under any of the standards of scrutiny that we have applied to enumerated constitutional rights, banning from the home "the most preferred firearm in the nation to 'keep' and use for protection of one's home and family," *Parker v. District of Columbia* (CADC 2007), would fail constitutional muster.

[T]he District's requirement (as applied to respondent's handgun) that firearms in the home be rendered and kept inoperable at all times ... makes it impossible for citizens to use them for the core lawful purpose of self-defense and is hence unconstitutional. The District argues that we should interpret this element of the statute to contain an exception for self-defense. But we think that is precluded by the unequivocal text, and by the presence of certain other enumerated exceptions: "Except for law enforcement personnel ..., each registrant shall keep any firearm in his possession unloaded and disassembled or bound by a trigger lock or similar device unless such firearm is kept at his place of business, or while being used for lawful recreational purposes within the District of Columbia." ...

In sum, we hold that the District's ban on handgun possession in the home violates the Second Amendment, as does its prohibition against rendering any lawful firearm in the home operable for the purpose of immediate self-defense. Assuming that Heller is not disqualified from the exercise of Second Amendment rights, the District must permit him to register his handgun and must issue him a license to carry it in the home.

* * *

We are aware of the problem of handgun violence in this country, and we take seriously the concerns raised by the many amici who believe that prohibition of handgun ownership is a solution. The Constitution leaves the District of Columbia a variety of tools for combating that problem, including some measures regulating handguns. But the enshrinement of constitutional rights necessarily takes certain policy choices off the table. These include the absolute prohibition of handguns held and used for self-defense in the home. Undoubtedly some think that the Second Amendment is outmoded in a society where our standing army is the pride of our Nation, where well-trained police forces provide personal security, and where gun violence is a serious problem. That is perhaps debatable, but what is not debatable is that it is not the role of this Court to pronounce the Second Amendment extinct.

We affirm the judgment of the Court of Appeals.

It is so ordered.

Justice STEVENS, with whom Justice SOUTER, Justice GINSBURG, and Justice BREYER join, dissenting.

The preamble to the Second Amendment makes three important points. It identifies the preservation of the militia as the Amendment's purpose; it explains that the militia is necessary to the security of a free State; and it recognizes that the militia must be "well regulated." In all three respects it is comparable to provisions in several State Declarations of Rights that were adopted roughly contemporaneously with the Declaration of Independence. Those state provisions highlight the importance members of the founding generation attached to the maintenance of state militias; they also underscore the profound fear shared by many in that era of the dangers posed by standing armies. While the need for state militias has not been a matter of significant public interest for almost two centuries, that fact should not obscure the contemporary concerns that animated the Framers.

The preamble thus both sets forth the object of the Amendment and informs the meaning of the remainder of its text. Such text should not be treated as mere surplusage, for "[i]t cannot be presumed that any clause in the constitution is intended to be without effect." *Marbury v. Madison* (1803).

The Court today tries to denigrate the importance of this clause of the Amendment by beginning its analysis with the Amendment's operative provision and returning to the preamble merely "to ensure that our reading of the operative clause is consistent with the announced purpose." That is not how this Court ordinarily reads such texts, and it is not how the preamble would have been viewed at the time the Amendment was adopted. While the Court makes the novel suggestion that it need only find some "logical connection" between the preamble and the operative provision, it does acknowledge that a prefatory clause may resolve an ambiguity in the text. Without identifying any language in the text that even mentions civilian uses of firearms, the Court proceeds to "find" its preferred reading in what is at best an ambiguous text, and then concludes that its reading is not foreclosed by the preamble. Perhaps the Court's approach to the text is acceptable advocacy, but it is surely an unusual approach for judges to follow.

When each word in the text is given full effect, the Amendment is most naturally read to secure to the people a right to use and possess arms in conjunction with service in a well-regulated militia. So far as appears, no more than that was contemplated by its drafters or is encompassed within its terms. Even if the meaning of the text were genuinely susceptible to more than one interpretation, the burden would remain on those advocating a departure from the purpose identified in the preamble and from settled law to come forward with persuasive new arguments or evidence. The textual analysis offered by respondent and embraced by the Court falls far short of sustaining that heavy burden. ...

## NOTES AND QUESTIONS

**1.** How does Justice Scalia, writing for the majority in Heller, reason his way to the conclusion that the Second Amendment, notwithstanding its prefatory clause, protects an individual right to bear arms in self-defense?

**2.** What are the dimensions of the right the Court announces in *Heller*? Does the Court suggest any limits? How does it seek to define those limits, if at all? What doctrinal test does the Court suggest lower courts employ when next they face a Second Amendment challenge to a firearms regulation?

**3.** These questions naturally flow from a decision that effectively announces a new understanding of a provision that, until the late twentieth century, pretty much everyone believed was confined to the bearing of arms in connection with militia membership. See *United States v. Miller*, 307 U.S. 174 (1939). But if you're struggling to answer them, you're in good company: from 2008, when the Court decided Heller, until the next case (decided in 2022), most lower courts adapted some form of the ends-means inquiry we saw in the First Amendment context for use in Second Amendment cases. Turns out that was wrong.

### New York State Rifle & Pistol Assoc., Inc. v. Bruen
### 597 U.S. ___ (2022)

Justice THOMAS delivered the opinion of the Court.

In *District of Columbia v. Heller* (2008) and *McDonald v.*

*Chicago* (2010), we recognized that the Second and Fourteenth Amendments protect the right of an ordinary, law-abiding citizen to possess a handgun in the home for self-defense. In this case, petitioners and respondents agree that ordinary, law-abiding citizens have a similar right to carry handguns publicly for their self-defense. We too agree, and now hold, consistent with *Heller* and *McDonald*, that the Second and Fourteenth Amendments protect an individual's right to carry a handgun for self-defense outside the home.

... Because the State of New York issues public-carry licenses only when an applicant demonstrates a special need for self-defense, we conclude that the State's licensing regime violates the Constitution.

**I**

New York State has regulated the public carry of handguns at least since the early 20th century. ... Today's licensing scheme largely tracks that of the early 1900s. It is a crime in New York to possess "any firearm" without a license, whether inside or outside the home, punishable by up to four years in prison or a $5,000 fine for a felony offense, and one year in prison or a $1,000 fine for a misdemeanor. Meanwhile, possessing a loaded firearm outside one's home or place of business without a license is a felony punishable by up to 15 years in prison.

A license applicant who wants to possess a firearm at home (or in his place of business) must convince a "licensing officer"—usually a judge or law enforcement officer—that, among other things, he is of good moral character, has no history of crime or mental illness, and that "no good cause exists for the denial of the license."). If he wants to carry a firearm outside his home or place of business for self-defense, the applicant must obtain an unrestricted license to "have and carry" a concealed "pistol or revolver." To secure that license, the applicant must prove that "proper cause exists" to issue it. If an applicant cannot make that showing, he can receive only a "restricted" license for public carry, which allows him to carry a firearm for a limited purpose, such as hunting, target shooting, or employment.

No New York statute defines "proper cause." But New York courts have held that an applicant shows proper cause only if he can "demonstrate a special need for self-protection distinguishable from that of the general community." E.g., *In re Klenosky* (N.Y. App. 1980). This "special need" standard is demanding. For example, living or working in an area "noted for criminal activity" does not suffice. *In re Bernstein* (N.Y. App. Div. 1981). Rather, New York courts generally require evidence "of particular threats, attacks or other extraordinary danger to personal safety." *In re Martinek* (N.Y. App. Div. 2002).

[T]he vast majority of States—43 by our count—are "shall issue" jurisdictions, where authorities must issue concealed-carry licenses whenever applicants satisfy certain threshold requirements, without granting licensing officials discretion to deny licenses based on a perceived lack of need or suitability. Meanwhile, only six States and the District of Columbia have "may issue" licensing laws, under which authorities have discretion to deny concealed-carry licenses even when the applicant satisfies the statutory criteria, usually because the applicant has not demonstrated cause or suitability for the relevant license. ...

As set forth in the pleadings below, petitioners Brandon Koch and Robert Nash are law-abiding, adult citizens of Rensselaer County, New York. Koch lives in Troy, while Nash lives in Averill Park. Petitioner New York State Rifle & Pistol Association, Inc., is a public-interest group organized to defend the Second Amendment rights of New Yorkers. Both Koch and Nash are members.

In 2014, Nash applied for an unrestricted license to carry a handgun in public. Nash did not claim any unique danger to his personal safety; he simply wanted to carry a handgun for self-defense. In early 2015, the State denied Nash's application for an unrestricted license but granted him a restricted license for hunting and target shooting only. In late 2016, Nash asked a licensing officer to remove the restrictions, citing a string of recent robberies in his neighborhood. After an informal hearing, the licensing officer denied the request. The officer reiterated that Nash's existing license permitted him "to carry concealed for purposes of off road back country, outdoor activities similar to hunting," such as "fishing, hiking & camping etc." But, at the same time, the officer emphasized that the restrictions were "intended to prohibit [Nash] from carrying concealed in ANY LOCATION typically open to and frequented by the general public."

Between 2008 and 2017, Koch was in the same position as Nash: He faced no special dangers, wanted a handgun for general self-defense, and had only a restricted license permitting him to carry a handgun outside the home for hunting and target shooting. In late 2017, Koch applied to a licensing officer to remove the restrictions on his license, citing his extensive experience in safely handling firearms. Like Nash's application, Koch's was denied, except that the officer permitted Koch to "carry to and from work."

Respondents are the superintendent of the New York State Police, who oversees the enforcement of the State's licensing laws, and a New York Supreme Court justice, who oversees the processing of licensing applications in Rensselaer County. Petitioners sued respondents for declaratory and injunctive relief alleging that respondents violated their Second and Fourteenth Amendment rights by denying their unrestricted-license applications on the basis that they had failed to show "proper cause," i.e., had failed to demonstrate a unique need for self-defense.

The District Court dismissed petitioners' complaint and the Court of Appeals affirmed. ... We granted certiorari to decide whether New York's denial of petitioners' license applications violated the Constitution.

II

In the years since [*Heller* and *McDonald*], the Courts of Appeals have coalesced around a "two-step" framework for analyzing Second

Amendment challenges that combines history with means-end scrutiny. [W]e decline to adopt that two-part approach [and] hold that when the Second Amendment's plain text covers an individual's conduct, the Constitution presumptively protects that conduct. To justify its regulation, the government may not simply posit that the regulation promotes an important interest. Rather, the government must demonstrate that the regulation is consistent with this Nation's historical tradition of firearm regulation. Only if a firearm regulation is consistent with this Nation's historical tradition may a court conclude that the individual's conduct falls outside the Second Amendment's "unqualified command." *Konigsberg v. State Bar of Cal.* (1961).

[T]he two-step test that Courts of Appeals have developed to assess Second Amendment claims proceeds as follows. At the first step, the government may justify its regulation by "establish[ing] that the challenged law regulates activity falling outside the scope of the right as originally understood." The Courts of Appeals then ascertain the original scope of the right based on its historical meaning. If the government can prove that the regulated conduct falls beyond the Amendment's original scope, "then the analysis can stop there; the regulated activity is categorically unprotected." *United States v. Greeno* (CA6 2012) (internal quotation marks omitted). But if the historical evidence at this step is "inconclusive or suggests that the regulated activity is not categorically unprotected," the courts generally proceed to step two. *Kanter v. Barr* (CA7 2019) (internal quotation marks omitted).

At the second step, courts often analyze "how close the law comes to the core of the Second Amendment right and the severity of the law's burden on that right." Id. (internal quotation marks omitted). The Courts of Appeals generally maintain "that the core Second Amendment right is limited to self-defense in the home." *Gould v. Morgan* (CA1 2018) (emphasis added). If a "core" Second Amendment right is burdened, courts apply "strict scrutiny" and ask whether the Government can prove that the law is "narrowly tailored to achieve a compelling governmental interest." *Kolbe v. Hogan* (CA4 2017) (internal quotation marks omitted). Otherwise, they apply intermediate scrutiny and consider whether the Government can show that the regulation is "substantially related to the achievement of an important governmental interest." *Kalchalsky v. County of Westchester* (CA2 2012). Both respondents and the United States largely agree with this consensus, arguing that intermediate scrutiny is appropriate when text and history are unclear in attempting to delineate the scope of the right.

Despite the popularity of this two-step approach, it is one step too many. Step one of the predominant framework is broadly consistent with *Heller*, which demands a test rooted in the Second Amendment's text, as informed by history. But *Heller* and *McDonald* do not support applying means-end scrutiny in the Second Amendment context. Instead, the government must affirmatively prove that its firearms regulation is part of the historical tradition that delimits the outer bounds of the right to keep and bear arms.

*Heller*'s methodology centered on constitutional text and history. Whether it came to defining the character of the right (individual or militia dependent), suggesting the outer limits of the right, or assessing the constitutionality of a particular regulation, Heller relied on text and history. It did not invoke any means-end test such as strict or intermediate scrutiny.

Moreover, [in *Heller*] we declined to engage in means-end scrutiny because "[t]he very enumeration of the right takes out of the hands of government—even the Third Branch of Government—the power to decide on a case-by-case basis whether the right is really worth insisting upon." We then concluded: "A constitutional guarantee subject to future judges' assessments of its usefulness is no constitutional guarantee at all."

[T]he Courts of Appeals' second step is inconsistent with *Heller*'s historical approach and its rejection of means-end scrutiny. We reiterate that the standard for applying the Second Amendment is as follows: When the Second Amendment's plain text covers an individual's conduct, the Constitution presumptively protects that conduct. The government must then justify its regulation by demonstrating that it is consistent with the Nation's historical tradition of firearm regulation. Only then may a court conclude that the individual's conduct falls outside the Second Amendment's "unqualified command."

This Second Amendment standard accords with how we protect other constitutional rights. Take, for instance, the freedom of speech in the First Amendment, to which *Heller* repeatedly compared the right to keep and bear arms. In that context, "[w]hen the Government restricts speech, the Government bears the burden of proving the constitutionality of its actions." *United States v. Playboy Entertainment Group, Inc.* (2000). In some cases, that burden includes showing whether the expressive conduct falls outside of the category of protected speech. And to carry that burden, the government must generally point to historical evidence about the reach of the First Amendment's protections.

[R]eliance on history to inform the meaning of constitutional text —especially text meant to codify a pre-existing right—is, in our view, more legitimate, and more administrable, than asking judges to "make difficult empirical judgments" about "the costs and benefits of firearms restrictions," especially given their "lack [of] expertise" in the field.

If the last decade of Second Amendment litigation has taught this Court anything, it is that federal courts tasked with making such difficult empirical judgments regarding firearm regulations under the banner of "intermediate scrutiny" often defer to the determinations of legislatures. But while that judicial deference to legislative interest balancing is understandable—and, elsewhere, appropriate—it is not deference that [applies] here. ...

The test that we set forth in *Heller* and apply today requires courts to assess whether modern firearms regulations are consistent with the Second Amendment's text and historical understanding. In some cases, that inquiry will be fairly straightforward. For instance, when a challenged regulation addresses a general societal problem that has persisted since the 18th century, the lack of a distinctly similar historical regulation addressing that problem is relevant evidence that the challenged regulation is inconsistent with the Second Amendment. Likewise, if earlier generations addressed the societal problem, but did so through materially different means, that also could be evidence that a modern regulation is unconstitutional. And if some jurisdictions actually attempted to enact analogous regulations during this timeframe, but those proposals were rejected on constitutional grounds, that rejection surely would provide some probative evidence of unconstitutionality.

*Heller* itself exemplifies this kind of straightforward historical inquiry. One of the District's regulations challenged in *Heller* "totally ban[ned] handgun possession in the home." The District in *Heller* addressed a perceived societal problem—firearm violence in densely populated communities—and it employed a regulation—a flat ban on the possession of handguns in the home—that the Founders themselves could have adopted to confront that problem. Accordingly, after considering "founding-era historical precedent," including "various restrictive laws in the colonial period," and finding that none was analogous to the District's ban, Heller concluded that the handgun ban was unconstitutional.

New York's proper-cause requirement concerns the same alleged societal problem addressed in *Heller*: "handgun violence," primarily in "urban area[s]." Following the course charted by *Heller*, we will consider whether "historical precedent" from before, during, and even after the founding evinces a comparable tradition of regulation. And, as we explain below, we find no such tradition in the historical materials that respondents and their amici have brought to bear on that question.

While the historical analogies here and in *Heller* are relatively simple to draw, other cases implicating unprecedented societal concerns or dramatic technological changes may require a more nuanced approach. [The regulatory challenges posed by firearms today are not always the same as those that preoccupied the Founders in 1791 or the Reconstruction generation in 1868.] ... Although its meaning is fixed according to the understandings of those who ratified it, the Constitution can, and must, apply to circumstances beyond those the Founders specifically anticipated.

 We have already recognized in Heller at least one way in which the Second Amendment's historically fixed meaning applies to new circumstances: Its reference to "arms" does not apply "only [to] those arms in existence in the 18th century." "Just as the First Amendment protects modern forms of communications, and the Fourth Amendment applies to modern forms of search, the Second Amendment extends, prima facie, to all instruments that constitute bearable arms, even those that were not in existence at the time of the founding." (citations omitted). Thus, even though the Second

Amendment's definition of "arms" is fixed according to its historical understanding, that general definition covers modern instruments that facilitate armed self-defense.

Much like we use history to determine which modern "arms" are protected by the Second Amendment, so too does history guide our consideration of modern regulations that were unimaginable at the founding. When confronting such present-day firearm regulations, this historical inquiry that courts must conduct will often involve reasoning by analogy—a commonplace task for any lawyer or judge. Like all analogical reasoning, determining whether a historical regulation is a proper analogue for a distinctly modern firearm regulation requires a determination of whether the two regulations are "relevantly similar." C. Sunstein, On Analogical Reasoning, 106 Harv. L. Rev. 741, 773 (1993). And because "[e]verything is similar in infinite ways to everything else," id., one needs "some metric enabling the analogizer to assess which similarities are important and which are not," F. Schauer & B. Spellman, Analogy, Expertise, and Experience, 84 U. Chi. L. Rev. 249, 254 (2017). For instance, a green truck and a green hat are relevantly similar if one's metric is "things that are green." They are not relevantly similar if the applicable metric is "things you can wear."

While we do not now provide an exhaustive survey of the features that render regulations relevantly similar under the Second Amendment, we do think that *Heller* and *McDonald* point toward at least two metrics: how and why the regulations burden a law-abiding citizen's right to armed self-defense. As we stated in *Heller* and repeated in *McDonald*, "individual self-defense is 'the central component' of the Second Amendment right." Therefore, whether modern and historical regulations impose a comparable burden on the right of armed self-defense and whether that burden is comparably justified are "central" considerations when engaging in an analogical inquiry. *McDonald* (quoting *Heller*).

To be clear, analogical reasoning under the Second Amendment is neither a regulatory straightjacket nor a regulatory blank check. [A]nalogical reasoning requires only that the government identify a well-established and representative historical analogue, not a historical twin. So even if a modern-day regulation is not a dead ringer for historical precursors, it still may be analogous enough to pass constitutional muster.

Consider, for example, *Heller*'s discussion of "longstanding" "laws forbidding the carrying of firearms in sensitive places such as schools and government buildings." Although the historical record yields relatively few 18th- and 19th-century "sensitive places" where weapons were altogether prohibited—e.g., legislative assemblies, polling places, and courthouses—we are also aware of no disputes regarding the lawfulness of such prohibitions. We therefore can assume it settled that these locations were "sensitive places" where arms carrying could be prohibited consistent with the Second Amendment. And courts can use analogies to those historical regulations of "sensitive places" to determine that modern regulations prohibiting the carry of firearms in new and analogous sensitive places are constitutionally permissible.

Although we have no occasion to comprehensively define "sensitive places" in this case, we do think respondents err in their attempt to characterize New York's proper-cause requirement as a "sensitive-place" law. In their view, "sensitive places" where the government may lawfully disarm law-abiding citizens include all "places where people typically congregate and where law-enforcement and other public-safety professionals are presumptively available." [E]xpanding the category of "sensitive places" simply to all places of public congregation that are not isolated from law enforcement defines the category of "sensitive places" far too broadly. Respondents' argument would in effect exempt cities from the Second Amendment and would eviscerate the general right to publicly carry arms for self-defense that we discuss in detail below....

**III**

We have little difficulty concluding that [the Second Amendment protects Koch's and Nash's proposed course of conduct—carrying handguns publicly for self-defense.] Respondents do not dispute this. Nor could they. Nothing in the Second Amendment's text draws a home/public distinction with respect to the right to keep and bear arms. As we explained in *Heller*, the "textual elements" of the Second Amendment's operative clause— "the right of the people to keep and bear Arms, shall not be infringed"—"guarantee the individual right to possess and carry weapons in case of confrontation." Heller further confirmed that the right to "bear arms" refers to the right to "wear, bear, or carry ... upon the person or in the clothing or in a pocket, for the purpose ... of being armed and ready for offensive or defensive action in a case of conflict with another person." Id. (quotation omitted).

This definition of "bear" naturally encompasses public carry. Most gun owners do not wear a holstered pistol at their hip in their bedroom or while sitting at the dinner table. Although individuals often "keep" firearms in their home, at the ready for self-defense, most do not "bear" (i.e., carry) them in the home beyond moments of actual confrontation. To confine the right to "bear" arms to the home would nullify half of the Second Amendment's operative protections.

Moreover, confining the right to "bear" arms to the home would make little sense given that self-defense is "the central component of the [Second Amendment] right itself." *Heller*. After all, the Second Amendment guarantees an "individual right to possess and carry weapons in case of confrontation," and confrontation can surely take place outside the home.

Although we remarked in *Heller* that the need for armed self-defense is perhaps "most acute" in the home, we did not suggest that the need was insignificant elsewhere. Many Americans hazard greater danger outside the home than in it. The text of the Second Amendment reflects that reality.

The Second Amendment's plain text thus presumptively guarantees petitioners Koch and Nash a right to "bear" arms in public for self-defense.

Conceding that the Second Amendment guarantees a general right to public carry, respondents instead claim that the Amendment "permits a State to condition handgun carrying in areas 'frequented by the general public' on a showing of a nonspeculative need for armed self-defense in those areas." To support that claim, the burden falls on respondents to show that New York's proper-cause requirement is consistent with this Nation's historical tradition of firearm regulation. Only if respondents carry that burden can they show that the pre-existing right codified in the Second Amendment, and made applicable to the States through the Fourteenth, does not protect petitioners' proposed course of conduct.

Respondents appeal to a variety of historical sources from the late 1200s to the early 1900s. We categorize these periods as follows: (1) medieval to early modern England; (2) the American Colonies and the early Republic; (3) antebellum America; (4) Reconstruction; and (5) the late-19th and early-20th centuries.

We categorize these historical sources because, when it comes to interpreting the Constitution, not all history is created equal. "Constitutional rights are enshrined with the scope they were understood to have when the people adopted them." *Heller* (emphasis added). The Second Amendment was adopted in 1791; the Fourteenth in 1868. Historical evidence that long predates either date may not illuminate the scope of the right if linguistic or legal conventions changed in the intervening years. ...

As with historical evidence generally, courts must be careful when assessing evidence concerning English common-law rights. The common law, of course, developed over time. And English common-law practices and understandings at any given time in history cannot be indiscriminately attributed to the Framers of our own Constitution. ... Sometimes, in interpreting our own Constitution, "it [is] better not to go too far back into antiquity for the best securities of our liberties," *Funk v. United States* (1933), unless evidence shows that medieval law survived to become our Founders' law. ...

Similarly, we must also guard against giving post-enactment history more weight than it can rightly bear. It is true that in *Heller* we reiterated that evidence of "how the Second Amendment was interpreted from immediately after its ratification through the end of the 19th century" represented a "critical tool of constitutional interpretation." We therefore examined "a variety of legal and other sources to determine the public understanding of [the Second Amendment] after its ... ratification." ... [W]e recognize that "where a governmental practice has been open, widespread, and unchallenged since the early days of the Republic, the practice should guide our interpretation of an ambiguous constitutional provision." *NLRB v. Noel Canning* (2014) (Scalia, J., concurring in judgment).

But to the extent later history contradicts what the text says, the text controls. ... Thus, "postratification adoption or acceptance of laws that are inconsistent with the original meaning of the constitutional text obviously cannot overcome or alter that text."

*Heller* (Kavanaugh, J., dissenting).

As we recognized in *Heller* itself, because post-Civil War discussions of the right to keep and bear arms "took place 75 years after the ratification of the Second Amendment, they do not provide as much insight into its original meaning as earlier sources." ... In other words, this 19th-century evidence was "treated as mere confirmation of what the Court thought had already been established."

* * *

With these principles in mind, we turn to respondents' historical evidence. Throughout modern Anglo-American history, the right to keep and bear arms in public has traditionally been subject to well-defined restrictions governing the intent for which one could carry arms, the manner of carry, or the exceptional circumstances under which one could not carry arms. But apart from a handful of late-19th-century jurisdictions, the historical record compiled by respondents does not demonstrate a tradition of broadly prohibiting the public carry of commonly used firearms for self-defense. Nor is there any such historical tradition limiting public carry only to those law-abiding citizens who demonstrate a special need for self-defense. We conclude that respondents have failed to meet their burden to identify an American tradition justifying New York's proper-cause requirement. Under Heller's text-and-history standard, the proper-cause requirement is therefore unconstitutional.

**IV**

The constitutional right to bear arms in public for self-defense is not "a second-class right, subject to an entirely different body of rules than the other Bill of Rights guarantees." *McDonald* (plurality opinion). We know of no other constitutional right that an individual may exercise only after demonstrating to government officers some special need. That is not how the First Amendment works when it comes to unpopular speech or the free exercise of religion. It is not how the Sixth Amendment works when it comes to a defendant's right to confront the witnesses against him. And it is not how the Second Amendment works when it comes to public carry for self-defense.

[We] reverse the judgment of the Court of Appeals and remand the case for further proceedings consistent with this opinion.

It is so ordered.

Justice ALITO, concurring.

*Heller* correctly recognized that the Second Amendment codifies the right of ordinary law-abiding Americans to protect themselves from lethal violence by possessing and, if necessary, using a gun. In 1791, when the Second Amendment was adopted, there were no police departments, and many families lived alone on isolated farms or on the frontiers. If these people were attacked, they were on their own. It is hard to imagine the furor that would have erupted if the Federal Government and the States had tried to take away the guns that these people needed for protection.

Today, unfortunately, many Americans have good reason to fear that they will be victimized if they are unable to protect themselves.

And today, no less than in 1791, the Second Amendment guarantees their right to do so.

[Concurring opinion of Justice KAVANAUGH omitted.]

[Concurring opinion of Justice BARRETT omitted.]

Justice BREYER, with whom Justice SOTOMAYOR and Justice KAGAN join, dissenting.

How does the Court justify striking down New York's law without first considering how it actually works on the ground and what purposes it serves? The Court does so by purporting to rely nearly exclusively on history [and refusing] to employ what it calls "means-end scrutiny." That is, it refuses to consider whether New York has a compelling interest in regulating the concealed carriage of handguns or whether New York's law is narrowly tailored to achieve that interest. Although I agree that history can often be a useful tool in determining the meaning and scope of constitutional provisions, I believe the Court's near-exclusive reliance on that single tool today goes much too far.

[E]very Court of Appeals to have addressed the question has [applied] a level of "means-ends" scrutiny "that is proportionate to the severity of the burden that the law imposes on the right": strict scrutiny if the burden is severe, and intermediate scrutiny if it is not.

The Court today replaces the Courts of Appeals' consensus framework with its own history-only approach. ... The Court attempts to justify its deviation from our normal practice by claiming that the Courts of Appeals' approach is inconsistent with *Heller*. In doing so, the Court implies that all 11 Courts of Appeals that have considered this question misread Heller.

To the contrary, it is this Court that misreads Heller. The opinion in Heller did focus primarily on "constitutional text and history," but it did not "rejec[t] ... means-end scrutiny," as the Court claims. Consider what the Heller Court actually said. True, the Court spent many pages in *Heller* discussing the text and historical context of the Second Amendment. But that is not surprising because the *Heller* Court was asked to answer the preliminary question whether the Second Amendment right to "bear Arms" encompasses an individual right to possess a firearm in the home for self-defense. The *Heller* Court concluded that the Second Amendment's text and history were sufficiently clear to resolve that question: The Second Amendment, it said, does include such an individual right. ...

But the *Heller* Court did not end its opinion with that preliminary question. After concluding that the Second Amendment protects an individual right to possess a firearm for self-defense, the *Heller* Court added that that right is "not unlimited." It thus had to determine whether the District of Columbia's law, which banned handgun possession in the home, was a permissible regulation of the right. In answering that second question, it said: "Under any of the standards of scrutiny that we have applied to enumerated constitutional rights, banning from the home 'the most preferred firearm in the nation to "keep" and use for protection of one's home and family' would fail constitutional muster." (emphasis added; footnote and citation omitted). That language makes clear that the *Heller* Court understood some form of means-end scrutiny to apply. It did not need to specify whether that scrutiny should be intermediate or strict because, in its view, the District's handgun ban was so "severe" that it would have failed either level of scrutiny.

[The] Court today is wrong when it says that its rejection of means-end scrutiny and near-exclusive focus on history "accords with how we protect other constitutional rights." As the Court points out, we do look to history in the First Amendment context to determine "whether the expressive conduct falls outside of the category of protected speech." But, if conduct falls within a category of protected speech, we then use means-end scrutiny to determine whether a challenged regulation unconstitutionally burdens that speech. And the degree of scrutiny we apply often depends on the type of speech burdened and the severity of the burden. See, e.g., *Arizona Free Enterprise Club's Freedom Club PAC v. Bennett* (2011) (applying strict scrutiny to laws that burden political speech); *Ward v. Rock Against Racism* (1989) (applying intermediate scrutiny to time, place, and manner restrictions).

[A]pplying means-end scrutiny to laws that regulate the Second Amendment right to bear arms would not create a constitutional anomaly. Rather, it is the Court's rejection of means-end scrutiny and adoption of a rigid history-only approach that is anomalous.

The Court's near-exclusive reliance on history is not only unnecessary, it is deeply impractical. It imposes a task on the lower courts that judges cannot easily accomplish. Judges understand well how to weigh a law's objectives (its "ends") against the methods used to achieve those objectives (its "means"). Judges are far less accustomed to resolving difficult historical questions. Courts are, after all, staffed by lawyers, not historians. Legal experts typically have little experience answering contested historical questions or applying those answers to resolve contemporary problems.

The Court's insistence that judges and lawyers rely nearly exclusively on history to interpret the Second Amendment thus raises a host of troubling questions. Consider, for example, the following. Do lower courts have the research resources necessary to conduct exhaustive historical analyses in every Second Amendment case? What historical regulations and decisions qualify as representative analogues to modern laws? How will judges determine which historians have the better view of close historical questions? Will the meaning of the Second Amendment change if or when new historical evidence becomes available? And, most importantly, will the Court's approach permit judges to reach the outcomes they prefer and then cloak those outcomes in the language of history?

Consider *Heller* itself. That case, fraught with difficult historical questions, illustrates the practical problems with expecting courts to decide important constitutional questions based solely on history. The majority in Heller undertook 40 pages of textual and historical analysis and concluded that the Second Amendment's protection of the right to "keep and bear Arms" historically encompassed an "individual right to possess and carry weapons in case of confrontation"—that is, for self-defense. Justice Stevens' dissent conducted an equally searching textual and historical inquiry and concluded, to the contrary, that the term "bear Arms" was an idiom that protected only the right "to use and possess arms in conjunction with service in a well-regulated militia." I do not intend to relitigate *Heller* here. I accept its holding as a matter of stare decisis. I refer to its historical analysis only to show the difficulties inherent in answering historical questions and to suggest that judges do not have the expertise needed to answer those questions accurately.

... In *Heller*, we attempted to determine the scope of the Second Amendment right to bear arms by conducting a historical analysis, and some of us arrived at very different conclusions based on the same historical sources. Many experts now tell us that the Court got it wrong in a number of ways. That is understandable given the difficulty of the inquiry that the Court attempted to undertake. The Court's past experience with historical analysis should serve as a warning against relying exclusively, or nearly exclusively, on this mode of analysis in the future.

Failing to heed that warning, the Court today does just that. Its near-exclusive reliance on history will pose a number of practical problems. First, the difficulties attendant to extensive historical analysis will be especially acute in the lower courts. The Court's historical analysis in this case is over 30 pages long and reviews numerous original sources from over 600 years of English and American history. Lower courts—especially district courts—typically have fewer research resources, less assistance from amici historians, and higher caseloads than we do. They are therefore ill equipped to conduct the type of searching historical surveys that the Court's approach requires. ... In contrast, lawyers and courts are well equipped to administer means-end scrutiny, which is regularly applied in a variety of constitutional contexts.

Second, the Court's opinion today compounds these problems, for it gives the lower courts precious little guidance regarding how to resolve modern constitutional questions based almost solely on history. ... [T]he Court offers little explanation of how stringently its test should be applied. Ironically, the only two "relevan[t]" metrics that the Court does identify are "how and why" a gun control regulation "burden[s the] right to armed self-defense." In other words, the Court believes that the most relevant metrics of comparison are a regulation's means (how) and ends (why)—even as it rejects the utility of means-end scrutiny.

What the Court offers instead is a laundry list of reasons to discount seemingly relevant historical evidence. The Court believes that some historical laws and decisions cannot justify upholding modern regulations because, it says, they were outliers. It explains that just two court decisions or three colonial laws are not enough to satisfy its test. But the Court does not say how many cases or laws would suffice "to show a tradition of public-carry regulation." Other laws are irrelevant, the Court claims, because they are too dissimilar from New York's concealed-carry licensing regime. But the Court does not say what "representative historical analogue," short of a "twin" or a "dead ringer," would suffice. (emphasis deleted). Indeed, the Court offers many and varied reasons to reject potential representative analogues, but very few reasons to accept them. At best, the numerous justifications that the Court finds for rejecting historical evidence give judges ample tools to pick their friends out of history's crowd. At worst, they create a one-way ratchet that will disqualify virtually any "representative historical analogue" and make it nearly impossible to sustain common-sense regulations necessary to our Nation's safety and security.

Third, even under ideal conditions, historical evidence will often fail to provide clear answers to difficult questions. As an initial matter, many aspects of the history of firearms and their regulation are ambiguous, contradictory, or disputed. Unsurprisingly, the extent to which colonial statutes enacted over 200 years ago were actually enforced, the basis for an acquittal in a 17th-century decision, and the interpretation of English laws from the Middle Ages (to name just a few examples) are often less than clear. And even historical experts may reach conflicting conclusions based on the same sources. As a result, history, as much as any other interpretive method, leaves ample discretion to "loo[k] over the heads of the [crowd] for one's friends." A. Scalia & B. Garner, Reading Law: The Interpretation of Legal Texts 377 (2012).

Fourth, I fear that history will be an especially inadequate tool when it comes to modern cases presenting modern problems. Consider the Court's apparent preference for founding-era regulation. Our country confronted profoundly different problems during that time period than it does today. Society at the founding was "predominantly rural." C. McKirdy, Misreading the Past: The Faulty Historical Basis Behind the Supreme Court's Decision in District of Columbia v. Heller, 45 Capital U. L. Rev. 107, 151 (2017). In 1790, most of America's relatively small population of just four million people lived on farms or in small towns. Even New York City, the largest American city then, as it is now, had a population of just 33,000 people. Small founding-era towns are unlikely to have faced the same degrees and types of risks from gun violence as major metropolitan areas do today, so the types of regulations they adopted are unlikely to address modern needs.

This problem is all the more acute when it comes to "modern-day circumstances that [the Framers] could not have anticipated." Heller (Breyer, J., dissenting). How can we expect laws and cases that are over a century old to dictate the legality of regulations targeting "ghost guns" constructed with the aid of a three-dimensional printer? Or modern laws requiring all gun shops to offer smart guns, which can only be fired by authorized users? Or laws imposing additional criminal penalties for the use of bullets capable of piercing body armor?

The Court's answer is that judges will simply have to employ "analogical reasoning." But, as I explained above, the Court does not provide clear guidance on how to apply such reasoning. Even seemingly straightforward historical restrictions on firearm use may prove surprisingly difficult to apply to modern circumstances. The Court affirms *Heller*'s recognition that States may forbid public carriage in "sensitive places." But what, in 21st-century New York City, may properly be considered a sensitive place? Presumably "legislative assemblies, polling places, and courthouses," which the Court tells us were among the "relatively few" places "where weapons were altogether prohibited" in the 18th and 19th centuries. On the other hand, the Court also tells us that "expanding the category of 'sensitive places' simply to all places of public congregation that are not isolated from law enforcement defines th[at] category ... far too broadly." So where does that leave the many locations in a modern city with no obvious 18th- or 19th-century analogue? What about subways, nightclubs, movie theaters, and sports stadiums? The Court does not say.

[Laws addressing] ancient weapons will be of little help to courts confronting modern problems. And as technological progress pushes our society ever further beyond the bounds of the Framers' imaginations, attempts at "analogical reasoning" will become increasingly tortured. In short, a standard that relies solely on history is unjustifiable and unworkable.

## NOTES AND QUESTIONS

1. What is the test that emerges from *Bruen*—what will those individuals who challenge firearms regulations have to show to prevail? In what ways does this differ, if at all, from free speech doctrine under the First Amendment (or, indeed, the doctrine associated with almost every other individual right under the U.S. Constitution)?

2. Justice Thomas, in his majority opinion, suggests that the analysis the Court adopts in *Bruen* is no different from that which the Court has deployed in respect to other individual rights. That claim is demonstrably untrue, as you will see. What practical problems with the analysis the majority proposes does Justice Breyer anticipate going forward? What values important to constitutional law – and the Court as an institution – might be diminished by the analysis *Bruen* endorses?

3. If nothing else, *Bruen* demonstrates the way in which the meaning of the Constitution depends to a great extent upon the Court's membership at a given point in time. One of the themes of this course is the extent to which the Supreme Court controls constitutional interpretation—and the fact that the people have little recourse when the Court errs in this task. Unlike in many states, U.S. Supreme Court justices are not directly accountable to an electorate. Unlike most state constitutions, it is extraordinarily difficult to amend the U.S. Constitution.

### C. Doctrine and Judicial Review

Setting aside the Second Amendment decisions, the free speech cases discussed in this chapter illustrate how doctrine is the engine of constitutional law. Doctrine, in other words, is the means by which courts have operationalized otherwise indefinite constitutional text so that it becomes an enforceable rule of constitutional law. The judicial tests for content-based and content-neutral laws, for example, allow courts to determine, in consistent and predictable ways, whether particular laws run afoul of the First Amendment's guarantee of freedom of speech.

Doctrine, though, is more than just the black-letter principles contained in hornbooks and treatises. To fully appreciate how doctrine works, you must read cases closely, to discover their nuances and subtleties, to locate the distinctions and intricacies, all to the end of applying judicial tests to help determine whether your client has a constitutional claim or defense. Indeed, a lawyer's knowledge of doctrine and the ability to determine how it applies in a particular case are the skills that separate those of us who went to law school from those who did not — they are the value in the service that the lawyer provides a client. Only in the context of a factual scenario is it possible to appreciate the full dimensions of a judicial doctrine. In constitutional cases, moreover, courts don't just identify and apply doctrinal tests, they discuss counter-arguments and use those counter-arguments to explain the limits of particular doctrines. Indeed, it is in these discussions, when a court is examining the way in which a seemingly straightforward doctrine applies, that we learn just how far a doctrinal test can be stretched.

Dissenting opinions also enhance our understanding of a court's doctrinal analysis. In Texas v. Johnson, for example, you can see that the dissent has a very different view of how the Court should approach the initial question — that is, whether flag-burning should even be considered protected speech. Consider whether the dissent proposes a doctrinal test that would be useful in any circumstance not involving flag desecration — and, if it does not, whether that explains the dissent's failure to garner a majority.

*O'Brien, Ward, Johnson,* and *R.A.V.* are examples of judicial review in action — of the Supreme Court exercising the power to determine whether a particular state or federal law runs afoul of the U.S. Constitution. In *Marbury v. Madison,* 5 U.S. (Cranch) 137 (1803), Chief Justice John Marshall confirmed the judiciary's authority to review federal law, and in *Martin v. Hunter's Lessee,* 14 U.S. (Wheat.) 304 (1816), Justice Joseph Story did the same in respect to decisions of the state courts regarding federal constitutional law. The propriety of judicial review is still today a contested issue among jurists and scholars, and particularly at hearings in which Senators question judicial nominees. But it remains, as these decisions show, that the modern Supreme Court is quite comfortable exercising the authority to determine whether federal or state governmental action is consistent with the Constitution, even in cases that raise emotionally charged issues, like flag-burning.

The business of extracting doctrinal principles and applying them in other factual instances — whether to acts of the state or federal governments — resembles the common law method from other courses, like Torts and Contracts. Constitutional law starts with the text of the U.S. Constitution, but the precedential cases reflect the development of constitutional doctrine over time, just like in those other courses. Constitutional law, in short, is simply the doctrines that the U.S. Supreme Court has determined shall be the means by which constitutional commands will be implemented.

And, as in those other courses, we find doctrine articulated in judicial decisions. Those decisions are, therefore, the focus of each of the topics that follow in this casebook — separation of powers, including a look at the various powers of the President and Congress; and the protection of individual rights under the Fourteenth Amendment, including procedural due process, substantive due process, and equal protection. In our discussion of the Fourteenth Amendment we will refer back to the free speech cases in this chapter because free speech doctrine, and the importance of free speech as an individual interest, provides a necessary benchmark with which to navigate certain aspects of due process. And we'll conclude our survey of the Constitution with a look at the religion clauses of the First Amendment before turning to the doctrines that control which individuals get to go to court and maintain a constitutional challenge against a particular law or governmental action — the doctrines of what is known as justiciability.

## Chapter 2
## Separation of Powers: The Legislative Power

**Add after Note 4 on page 164:**

**5.** As you've no doubt gathered, much of what Congress legislates falls squarely within its power to do what is necessary and proper to carry into execution one of its enumerated powers, like its power to regulate interstate commerce, for example. But Congress also has implicit authority to engage in those activities that are necessary predicates to the legislative process. As the Court explains in the next case, while "Congress has no enumerated constitutional power to conduct investigations or issue subpoenas," the Court has held that each House has the power

> "to secure needed information" in order to legislate. *McGrain* v. *Daugherty* (1927). This "power of inquiry—with process to enforce it—is an essential and appropriate auxiliary to the legislative function." *Id.* Without information, Congress would be shooting in the dark, unable to legislate "wisely or effectively." *Id.* The congressional power to obtain information is "broad" and "indispensable." *Watkins* v. *United States* (1957). It encompasses inquiries into the administration of existing laws, studies of proposed laws, and "surveys of defects in our social, economic or political system for the purpose of enabling the Congress to remedy them." *Id.*

*Mazars* concerns the scope and limits on Congress's power of inquiry.

### Trump v. Mazars USA, LLP
### 591 U.S. ___ (2020)

Chief Justice ROBERTS delivered the opinion of the Court.

Over the course of five days in April 2019, three committees of the U. S. House of Representatives issued four subpoenas seeking information about the finances of President Donald J. Trump, his children, and affiliated businesses. We have held that the House has authority under the Constitution to issue subpoenas to assist it in carrying out its legislative responsibilities. The House asserts that the financial information sought here—encompassing a decade's worth of transactions by the President and his family—will help guide legislative reform in areas ranging from money laundering and terrorism to foreign involvement in U. S. elections. The President contends that the House lacked a valid legislative aim and instead sought these records to harass him, expose personal matters, and conduct law enforcement activities beyond its authority. The question presented is whether the subpoenas exceed the authority of the House under the Constitution.

We have never addressed a congressional subpoena for the President's information. Two hundred years ago, it was established that Presidents may be subpoenaed during a federal criminal proceeding, *United States* v. *Burr* (CC Va. 1807) (Marshall, Cir. J.), and earlier today we extended that ruling to state criminal proceedings, *Trump* v. *Vance* (2020). Nearly fifty years ago, we held that a federal prosecutor could obtain information from a President despite assertions of executive privilege, *United States* v. *Nixon* (1974), and more recently we ruled that a private litigant could subject a President to a damages suit and appropriate discovery obligations in federal court, *Clinton* v. *Jones* (1997).

This case is different. Here the President's information is sought not by prosecutors or private parties in connection with a particular judicial proceeding, but by committees of Congress that have set forth broad legislative objectives. Congress and the President—the two political branches established by the Constitution—have an ongoing relationship that the Framers intended to feature both rivalry and reciprocity. That distinctive aspect necessarily informs our analysis of the question before us.

I

A

Each of the three committees sought overlapping sets of financial documents, but each supplied different justifications for the requests.

The House Committee on Financial Services issued two subpoenas, both on April 11, 2019. The first, issued to Deutsche Bank, seeks the financial information of the President, his children, their immediate family members, and several affiliated business entities. Specifically, the subpoena seeks any document related to account activity, due diligence, foreign transactions, business statements, debt schedules, statements of net worth, tax returns, and suspicious activity identified by Deutsche Bank. The second, issued to Capital One, demands similar financial information with respect to more than a dozen business entities associated with the President. The Deutsche Bank subpoena requests materials from "2010 through the present," and the Capital One subpoena covers "2016 through the present," but both subpoenas impose no time limitations for certain documents, such as those connected to account openings and due diligence.

According to the House, the Financial Services Committee issued these subpoenas pursuant to House Resolution 206, which called for "efforts to close loopholes that allow corruption, terrorism, and money laundering to infiltrate our country's financial system." H. Res. 206 (Mar. 13, 2019). Such loopholes, the resolution explained, had allowed "illicit money, including from Russian oligarchs," to flow into the United States through "anonymous shell companies" using investments such as "luxury high-end real estate." The House also invokes the oversight plan of the Financial Services Committee, which stated that the Committee intends to review banking regulation and "examine the implementation, effectiveness, and enforcement" of laws designed to prevent money laundering and the financing of terrorism. H. R. Rep. No. 116–40 (2019). The plan further provided that the Committee would "consider proposals to prevent the abuse of the financial system" and "address any vulnerabilities identified" in the real estate market.

On the same day as the Financial Services Committee, the Permanent Select Committee on Intelligence issued an identical subpoena to Deutsche Bank—albeit for different reasons. According to the House, the Intelligence Committee subpoenaed Deutsche Bank as part of an investigation into foreign efforts to undermine the U. S. political process. Committee Chairman Adam Schiff had described that investigation in a previous statement, explaining that the Committee was examining alleged attempts by Russia to influence the 2016 election; potential links between Russia and the President's campaign; and whether the President and his associates had been compromised by foreign actors or interests. Chairman Schiff added that the Committee planned "to develop legislation and policy reforms to ensure the U. S. government is better positioned to counter future efforts to undermine our political process and national security."

Four days after the Financial Services and Intelligence Committees, the House Committee on Oversight and Reform issued another subpoena, this time to the President's personal accounting firm, Mazars USA, LLP. The subpoena demanded information related to the President and several affiliated business entities from 2011 through 2018, including statements of financial condition, independent auditors' reports, financial reports, underlying source documents, and communications between Mazars and the President or his businesses. The subpoena also requested all engagement agreements and contracts "[w]ithout regard to time."

Chairman Elijah Cummings explained the basis for the subpoena in a memorandum to the Oversight Committee. According to the chairman, recent testimony by the President's former personal attorney Michael Cohen, along with several documents prepared by Mazars and supplied by Cohen, raised questions about whether the President had accurately represented his financial affairs. Chairman Cummings asserted that the Committee had "full authority to investigate" whether the President: (1) "may have engaged in illegal conduct before and during his tenure in office," (2) "has undisclosed conflicts of interest that may impair his ability to make impartial policy decisions," (3) "is complying with the Emoluments Clauses of the Constitution," and (4) "has accurately reported his finances to the Office of Government Ethics and other federal entities." "The Committee's interest in these matters," Chairman Cummings concluded, "informs its review of multiple laws and legislative proposals under our jurisdiction."

**B**

Petitioners—the President in his personal capacity, along with his children and affiliated businesses—filed two suits challenging the subpoenas. They contested the subpoena issued by the Oversight Committee in the District Court for the District of Columbia (*Mazars*), and the subpoenas issued by the Financial Services and Intelligence Committees in the Southern District of New York (*Deutsche Bank*). In both cases, petitioners contended that the subpoenas lacked a legitimate legislative purpose and violated the separation of powers. The President did not, however, resist the subpoenas by arguing that any of the requested records were protected by executive privilege. For relief, petitioners asked for declaratory judgments and injunctions preventing Mazars and the banks from complying with the subpoenas. Although named as defendants, Mazars and the banks took no positions on the legal issues in these cases, and the House committees intervened to defend the subpoenas.

Petitioners' challenges failed. In *Mazars*, the District Court granted judgment for the House, and the D. C. Circuit affirmed. In upholding the subpoena issued by the Oversight Committee to Mazars, the Court of Appeals found that the subpoena served a "valid legislative purpose" because the requested information was relevant to reforming financial disclosure requirements for Presidents and presidential candidates. (internal quotation marks omitted). ... The D. C. Circuit denied rehearing ...

In *Deutsche Bank*, the District Court denied a preliminary injunction, and the Second Circuit[, while] acknowledging that the subpoenas are "surely broad in scope," ... held that the Intelligence Committee properly issued its subpoena to Deutsche Bank as part of an investigation into alleged foreign influence over petitioners and Russian interference with the U. S. political process. That investigation, the court concluded, could inform legislation to combat foreign meddling and strengthen national security.

As to the subpoenas issued by the Financial Services Committee to Deutsche Bank and Capital One, the Court of Appeals concluded that they were adequately related to potential legislation on money laundering, terrorist financing, and the global movement of illicit funds through the real estate market. Rejecting the contention that the subpoenas improperly targeted the President, the court explained in part that the President's financial dealings with Deutsche Bank made it "appropriate" for the House to use him as a "case study" to determine "whether new legislation is needed." ...

We granted certiorari in both cases and stayed the judgments below pending our decision.

## II

### A

The question presented is whether the subpoenas exceed the authority of the House under the Constitution. Historically, disputes over congressional demands for presidential documents have not ended up in court. Instead, they have been hashed out in the "hurly-burly, the give-and-take of the political process between the legislative and the executive." Hearings on S. 2170 et al. before the Subcommittee on Intergovernmental Relations of the Senate Committee on Government Operations, 94th Cong., 1st Sess., 87 (1975) (A. Scalia, Assistant Attorney General, Office of Legal Counsel).

That practice began with George Washington and the early Congress. In 1792, a House committee requested Executive Branch documents pertaining to General St. Clair's campaign against the

Indians in the Northwest Territory, which had concluded in an utter rout of federal forces when they were caught by surprise near the present-day border between Ohio and Indiana. Since this was the first such request from Congress, President Washington called a Cabinet meeting, wishing to take care that his response "be rightly conducted" because it could "become a precedent." 1 Writings of Thomas Jefferson 189 (P. Ford ed. 1892).

The meeting, attended by the likes of Alexander Hamilton, Thomas Jefferson, Edmund Randolph, and Henry Knox, ended with the Cabinet of "one mind": The House had authority to "institute inquiries" and "call for papers" but the President could "exercise a discretion" over disclosures, "communicat[ing] such papers as the public good would permit" and "refus[ing]" the rest. *Id.* President Washington then dispatched Jefferson to speak to individual congressmen and "bring them by persuasion into the right channel." *Id.* The discussions were apparently fruitful, as the House later narrowed its request and the documents were supplied without recourse to the courts.

Jefferson, once he became President, followed Washington's precedent. In early 1807, after Jefferson had disclosed that "sundry persons" were conspiring to invade Spanish territory in North America with a private army, 16 Annals of Cong. 686–687, the House requested that the President produce any information in his possession touching on the conspiracy (except for information that would harm the public interest). Jefferson chose not to divulge the entire "voluminous" correspondence on the subject, explaining that much of it was "private" or mere "rumors" and "neither safety nor justice" permitted him to "expos[e] names" apart from identifying the conspiracy's "principal actor": Aaron Burr. *Id.* Instead of the entire correspondence, Jefferson sent Congress particular documents and a special message summarizing the conspiracy. *Id.* Neither Congress nor the President asked the Judiciary to intervene.

Ever since, congressional demands for the President's information have been resolved by the political branches without involving this Court. The Reagan and Clinton presidencies provide two modern examples:

During the Reagan administration, a House subcommittee subpoenaed all documents related to the Department of the Interior's decision whether to designate Canada a reciprocal country for purposes of the Mineral Lands Leasing Act. President Reagan directed that certain documents be withheld because they implicated his confidential relationship with subordinates. While withholding those documents, the administration made "repeated efforts" at accommodation through limited disclosures and testimony over a period of several months. 6 Op. of Office of Legal Counsel 751, 780 (1982). Unsatisfied, the subcommittee and its parent committee eventually voted to hold the Secretary of the Interior in contempt, and an innovative compromise soon followed: All documents were made available, but only for one day with no photocopying, minimal notetaking, and no participation by non-Members of Congress. *Id.*

In 1995, a Senate committee subpoenaed notes taken by a White House attorney at a meeting with President Clinton's personal lawyers concerning the Whitewater controversy. The President resisted the subpoena on the ground that the notes were protected by attorney-client privilege, leading to "long and protracted" negotiations and a Senate threat to seek judicial enforcement of the subpoena. S. Rep. No. 104–204 (1996). Eventually the parties reached an agreement, whereby President Clinton avoided the threatened suit, agreed to turn over the notes, and obtained the Senate's concession that he had not waived any privileges. *Id.*

Congress and the President maintained this tradition of negotiation and compromise—without the involvement of this Court—until the present dispute. Indeed, from President Washington until now, we have never considered a dispute over a congressional subpoena for the President's records. And, according to the parties, the appellate courts have addressed such a subpoena only once, when a Senate committee subpoenaed President Nixon during the Watergate scandal. In that case, the court refused to enforce the subpoena, and the Senate did not seek review by this Court.

This dispute therefore represents a significant departure from historical practice. Although the parties agree that this particular controversy is justiciable, we recognize that it is the first of its kind to reach this Court; that disputes of this sort can raise important issues concerning relations between the branches; that related disputes involving congressional efforts to seek official Executive Branch information recur on a regular basis, including in the context of deeply partisan controversy; and that Congress and the Executive have nonetheless managed for over two centuries to resolve such disputes among themselves without the benefit of guidance from us. Such longstanding practice "is a consideration of great weight" in cases concerning "the allocation of power between [the] two elected branches of Government," and it imposes on us a duty of care to ensure that we not needlessly disturb "the compromises and working arrangements that [those] branches . . . themselves have reached." *NLRB* v. *Noel Canning* (2014) (quoting *The Pocket Veto Case* (1929)). With that in mind, we turn to the question presented.

**B**

[Because Congress's power of inquiry] is "justified solely as an adjunct to the legislative process," it is subject to several limitations. *Id.* Most importantly, a congressional subpoena is valid only if it is "related to, and in furtherance of, a legitimate task of the Congress." *Id.* The subpoena must serve a "valid legislative purpose," *Quinn* v. *United States* (1955); it must "concern[ ] a subject on which legislation 'could be had,'" *Eastland* v. *United States Servicemen's Fund* (1975) (quoting *McGrain*).

Furthermore, Congress may not issue a subpoena for the purpose of "law enforcement," because "those powers are assigned under our Constitution to the Executive and the Judiciary." *Quinn*. Thus Congress may not use subpoenas to "try" someone "before [a] committee for any crime or wrongdoing." *McGrain*. Congress has no "'general' power to inquire into private affairs and compel disclosures," *id.*, and "there is no congressional power to expose for the sake of exposure," *Watkins*. "Investigations conducted solely for the personal aggrandizement of the investigators or to 'punish' those investigated are indefensible." *Id.*

Finally, recipients of legislative subpoenas retain their constitutional rights throughout the course of an investigation. And recipients have long been understood to retain common law and constitutional privileges with respect to certain materials, such as attorney-client communications and governmental communications protected by executive privilege.

C

The President contends, as does the Solicitor General appearing on behalf of the United States, that the usual rules for congressional subpoenas do not govern here because the President's papers are at issue. They argue for a more demanding standard based in large part on cases involving the Nixon tapes—recordings of conversations between President Nixon and close advisers discussing the break-in at the Democratic National Committee's headquarters at the Watergate complex. The tapes were subpoenaed by a Senate committee and the Special Prosecutor investigating the break-in, prompting President Nixon to invoke executive privilege and leading to two cases addressing the showing necessary to require the President to comply with the subpoenas.

Those cases, the President and the Solicitor General now contend, establish the standard that should govern the House subpoenas here. Quoting *Nixon*, the President asserts that the House must establish a "demonstrated, specific need" for the financial information, just as the Watergate special prosecutor was required to do in order to obtain the tapes. And drawing on *Senate Select Committee on Presidential Campaign Activities v. Nixon* (CADC 1974) (en banc)—the D. C. Circuit case refusing to enforce the Senate subpoena for the tapes—the President and the Solicitor General argue that the House must show that the financial information is "demonstrably critical" to its legislative purpose.

We disagree that these demanding standards apply here. Unlike the cases before us, *Nixon* and *Senate Select Committee* involved Oval Office communications over which the President asserted executive privilege. That privilege safeguards the public interest in candid, confidential deliberations within the Executive Branch; it is "fundamental to the operation of Government." *Nixon*. As a result, information subject to executive privilege deserves "the greatest protection consistent with the fair administration of justice." *Id.* We decline to transplant that protection root and branch to cases involving nonprivileged, private information, which by definition does not implicate sensitive Executive Branch deliberations.

The standards proposed by the President and the Solicitor General —if applied outside the context of privileged information—would risk seriously impeding Congress in carrying out its responsibilities. The President and the Solicitor General would apply the same exacting standards to *all* subpoenas for the President's information, without recognizing distinctions between privileged and nonprivileged information, between official and personal information, or between various legislative objectives. Such a categorical approach would represent a significant departure from the longstanding way of doing business between the branches, giving short shrift to Congress's important interests in conducting inquiries to obtain the information it needs to legislate effectively. Confounding the legislature in that effort would be contrary to the principle that:

> It is the proper duty of a representative body to look diligently into every affair of government and to talk much about what it sees. It is meant to be the eyes and the voice, and to embody the wisdom and will of its constituents. Unless Congress have and use every means of acquainting itself with the acts and the disposition of the administrative agents of the government, the country must be helpless to learn how it is being served.

*United States* v. *Rumely* (1953) (internal quotation marks omitted).

Legislative inquiries might involve the President in appropriate cases; as noted, Congress's responsibilities extend to "every affair of government." *Id.* (internal quotation marks omitted). Because the President's approach does not take adequate account of these significant congressional interests, we do not adopt it.

**D**

The House meanwhile would have us ignore that these suits involve the President. Invoking our precedents concerning investigations that did not target the President's papers, the House urges us to uphold its subpoenas because they "relate[ ] to a valid legislative purpose" or "concern[ ] a subject on which legislation could be had." That approach is appropriate, the House argues, because the cases before us are not "momentous separation-of-powers disputes."

[This approach] fails to take adequate account of the significant separation of powers issues raised by congressional subpoenas for the President's information. Congress and the President have an ongoing institutional relationship as the "opposite and rival" political branches established by the Constitution. The Federalist No. 51. As a result, congressional subpoenas directed at the President differ markedly from congressional subpoenas we have previously reviewed, and they bear little resemblance to criminal subpoenas issued to the President in the course of a specific investigation. Unlike those subpoenas, congressional subpoenas for the President's information unavoidably pit the political branches against one another.

Far from accounting for separation of powers concerns, the House's approach aggravates them by leaving essentially no limits on the congressional power to subpoena the President's personal records. Any personal paper possessed by a President could potentially "relate to" a conceivable subject of legislation, for Congress has broad legislative powers that touch a vast number of subjects. The President's financial records could relate to economic reform, medical records to health reform, school transcripts to education reform, and so on. Indeed, at argument, the House was unable to identify *any* type of information that lacks some relation to potential legislation.

Without limits on its subpoena powers, Congress could "exert an imperious controul" over the Executive Branch and aggrandize itself at the President's expense, just as the Framers feared. The Federalist No. 71 (A. Hamilton). And a limitless subpoena power would transform the "established practice" of the political branches. *Noel Canning* (internal quotation marks omitted). Instead of negotiating over information requests, Congress could simply walk away from the bargaining table and compel compliance in court.

The House and the courts below suggest that these separation of powers concerns are not fully implicated by the particular subpoenas here, but we disagree. We would have to be "blind" not to see what "[a]ll others can see and understand": that the subpoenas do not represent a run-of-the-mill legislative effort but rather a clash between rival branches of government over records of intense political interest for all involved. *Rumely* (quoting *Child Labor Tax Case* (1922) (Taft, C. J.)).

The interbranch conflict here does not vanish simply because the subpoenas seek personal papers or because the President sued in his personal capacity. The President is the only person who alone composes a branch of government. As a result, there is not always a clear line between his personal and official affairs. … Given the close connection between the Office of the President and its occupant, congressional demands for the President's papers can implicate the relationship between the branches regardless whether those papers are personal or official. Either way, a demand may aim to harass the President or render him "complaisan[t] to the humors of the Legislature." The Federalist No. 71. In fact, a subpoena for personal papers may pose a heightened risk of such impermissible purposes, precisely because of the documents' personal nature and their less evident connection to a legislative task. No one can say that the controversy here is less significant to the relationship between the branches simply because it involves personal papers. Quite the opposite. That appears to be what makes the matter of such great consequence to the President and Congress.

In addition, separation of powers concerns are no less palpable here simply because the subpoenas were issued to third parties. Congressional demands for the President's information present an interbranch conflict no matter where the information is held—it is, after all, the President's information. Were it otherwise, Congress could sidestep constitutional requirements any time a President's information is entrusted to a third party—as occurs with rapidly increasing frequency. Indeed, Congress could declare open season on the President's information held by schools, archives, internet service providers, e-mail clients, and financial institutions. The Constitution does not tolerate such ready evasion….

E

... For more than two centuries, the political branches have resolved information disputes using the wide variety of means that the Constitution puts at their disposal. The nature of such interactions would be transformed by judicial enforcement of either of the approaches suggested by the parties, eroding a "[d]eeply embedded traditional way[ ] of conducting government." *Youngstown Sheet & Tube Co.* v. *Sawyer* (1952) (Frankfurter, J., concurring).

A balanced approach is necessary, [and we] conclude that, in assessing whether a subpoena directed at the President's personal information is "related to, and in furtherance of, a legitimate task of the Congress," *Watkins*, courts must perform a careful analysis that takes adequate account of the separation of powers principles at stake, including both the significant legislative interests of Congress and the "unique position" of the President, *Clinton* (internal quotation marks omitted). Several special considerations inform this analysis.

First, courts should carefully assess whether the asserted legislative purpose warrants the significant step of involving the President and his papers. "'[O]ccasion[s] for constitutional confrontation between the two branches' should be avoided whenever possible." *Cheney* v. *United States Dist. Court for D. C.* (2004) (quoting *Nixon*). Congress may not rely on the President's information if other sources could reasonably provide Congress the information it needs in light of its particular legislative objective. The President's unique constitutional position means that Congress may not look to him as a "case study" for general legislation.

Unlike in criminal proceedings, where "[t]he very integrity of the judicial system" would be undermined without "full disclosure of all the facts," *Nixon*, efforts to craft legislation involve predictive policy judgments that are "not hamper[ed] . . . in quite the same way" when every scrap of potentially relevant evidence is not available. *Cheney*. While we certainly recognize Congress's important interests in obtaining information through appropriate inquiries, those interests are not sufficiently powerful to justify access to the President's personal papers when other sources could provide Congress the information it needs.

Second, to narrow the scope of possible conflict between the branches, courts should insist on a subpoena no broader than reasonably necessary to support Congress's legislative objective. The specificity of the subpoena's request "serves as an important safeguard against unnecessary intrusion into the operation of the Office of the President." *Cheney*.

Third, courts should be attentive to the nature of the evidence offered by Congress to establish that a subpoena advances a valid legislative purpose. The more detailed and substantial the evidence of Congress's legislative purpose, the better. That is particularly true when Congress contemplates legislation that raises sensitive constitutional issues, such as legislation concerning the Presidency. In such cases, it is "impossible" to conclude that a subpoena is designed to advance a valid legislative purpose unless Congress adequately identifies its aims and explains why the President's information will advance its consideration of the possible legislation. *Watkins*.

Fourth, courts should be careful to assess the burdens imposed on the President by a subpoena. We have held that burdens on the President's time and attention stemming from judicial process and litigation, without more, generally do not cross constitutional lines. But burdens imposed by a congressional subpoena should be carefully scrutinized, for they stem from a rival political branch that has an ongoing relationship with the President and incentives to use subpoenas for institutional advantage.

Other considerations may be pertinent as well; one case every two centuries does not afford enough experience for an exhaustive list.

When Congress seeks information "needed for intelligent legislative action," it "unquestionably" remains "the duty of *all* citizens to cooperate." *Watkins* (emphasis added). Congressional subpoenas for information from the President, however, implicate special concerns regarding the separation of powers. The courts below did not take adequate account of those concerns. The judgments of the Courts of Appeals for the D. C. Circuit and the Second Circuit are vacated, and the cases are remanded for further proceedings consistent with this opinion.

It is so ordered.

Justice THOMAS, dissenting.

Congress' legislative powers do not authorize it to engage in a nationwide inquisition with whatever resources it chooses to appropriate for itself. The majority's solution—a nonexhaustive four-factor test of uncertain origin—is better than nothing. But the power that Congress seeks to exercise here has even less basis in the Constitution than the majority supposes. I would reverse in full because the power to subpoena private, nonofficial documents is not a necessary implication of Congress' legislative powers. If Congress wishes to obtain these documents, it should proceed through the impeachment power. Accordingly, I respectfully dissent.

Justice ALITO, dissenting.

... I agree that the lower courts erred and that these cases must be remanded, but I do not think that the considerations outlined by the Court can be properly satisfied unless the House is required to show more than it has put forward to date.

Specifically, the House should provide a description of the type of legislation being considered, and while great specificity is not necessary, the description should be sufficient to permit a court to assess whether the particular records sought are of any special importance. The House should also spell out its constitutional authority to enact the type of legislation that it is contemplating, and it should justify the scope of the subpoenas in relation to the articulated legislative needs. In addition, it should explain why the subpoenaed information, as opposed to information available from other sources, is needed. Unless the House is required to make a showing along these lines, I would hold that enforcement of the subpoenas cannot be ordered. Because I find the terms of the Court's remand inadequate, I must respectfully dissent.

## NOTES AND QUESTIONS

1. What is the scope of the Congress's power of inquiry? Why has the question never been tested before this case?

2. What multi-factor test does the Court adopt for application by the lower courts when a congressional information request is opposed by the President? Does the Court allow the possibility that other factors might be relevant? In light of the factors the Court approves, where did the lower courts in this case go wrong—what, in other words, will be considered on remand?

3. To appreciate the parameters of the test the Court approves, it might be helpful to compare it to a test the Court did not—Justice Alito's insistence that "the House should provide a description of the type of legislation being considered, and while great specificity is not necessary, the description should be sufficient to permit a court to assess whether the particular records sought are of any special importance." How should a lower court evaluate what information is necessary for Congress to consider in contemplating new legislation? It is one thing for a court to decide what evidence is relevant to a jury determination in a civil trial, quite another to make that determination for a co-equal branch of government.

4. In his opinion in *NFIB v. Sebelius*, Chief Justice Roberts cites *Printz v. United States* (1997) to support the proposition that some means chosen by Congress may not be proper. Strictly speaking, *Printz* is not a case about the scope of the necessary and proper authority but, rather, one (of a relatively small number of cases) about the judicially enforceable federalism limits on Congress's otherwise valid authority to act under Article I. It is to these limits that we next turn.

# Chapter 3
# Separation of Powers: The Executive Power

**Add after Note 2 on page 238:**

3. The Court was not done after *Free Enterprise* in rethinking the scope of Congress's authority to condition presidential control over the administrative state, as you will see in the next case.

### Seila Law LLC v. Consumer Financial Protection Bureau
### 591 U.S. ___ (2020)

Chief Justice ROBERTS delivered the opinion of the Court with respect to Parts I, II, and III.

In the wake of the 2008 financial crisis, Congress established the Consumer Financial Protection Bureau (CFPB), an independent regulatory agency tasked with ensuring that consumer debt products are safe and transparent. ... Instead of placing the agency under the leadership of a board with multiple members, Congress provided that the CFPB would be led by a single Director, who serves for a longer term than the President and cannot be removed by the President except for inefficiency, neglect, or malfeasance. The CFPB Director has no boss, peers, or voters to report to. Yet the Director wields vast rulemaking, enforcement, and adjudicatory authority over a significant portion of the U. S. economy. The question before us is whether this arrangement violates the Constitution's separation of powers.

[I]n *Free Enterprise Fund v. Public Company Accounting Oversight Bd.* (2010), we reiterated that, "as a general matter," the Constitution gives the President "the authority to remove those who assist him in carrying out his duties," id. "Without such power, the President could not be held fully accountable for discharging his own responsibilities; the buck would stop somewhere else." Id.

The President's power to remove—and thus supervise—those who wield executive power on his behalf follows from the text of Article II, was settled by the First Congress, and was confirmed in the landmark decision Myers v. United States (1926). Our precedents have recognized only two exceptions to the President's unrestricted removal power. In *Humphrey's Executor v. United States* (1935), we held that Congress could create expert agencies led by a group of principal officers removable by the President only for good cause. And in *United States v. Perkins* (1886) and *Morrison v. Olson* (1988), we held that Congress could provide tenure protections to certain inferior officers with narrowly defined duties.

We are now asked to extend these precedents to a new configuration: an independent agency that wields significant executive power and is run by a single individual who cannot be removed by the President unless certain statutory criteria are met. We decline to take that step. While we need not and do not revisit our prior decisions allowing certain limitations on the President's removal power, there are compelling reasons not to extend those precedents to the novel context of an independent agency led by a single Director. Such an agency lacks a foundation in historical practice and clashes with constitutional structure by concentrating power in a unilateral actor insulated from Presidential control.

We therefore hold that the structure of the CFPB violates the separation of powers. We go on to hold that the CFPB Director's removal protection is severable from the other statutory provisions bearing on the CFPB's authority. The agency may therefore continue to operate, but its Director, in light of our decision, must be removable by the President at will.

I

A

[In 2010, Congress] created the Consumer Financial Protection Bureau (CFPB) as an independent financial regulator within the Federal Reserve System. [Under the Dodd-Frank Wall Street Reform and Consumer Protection Act (Dodd-Frank),] Congress tasked the CFPB with "implement[ing]" and "enforc[ing]" a large body of financial consumer protection laws to "ensur[e] that all consumers have access to markets for consumer financial products and services and that markets for consumer financial products and services are fair, transparent, and competitive." Congress transferred the administration of 18 existing federal statutes to the CFPB, including the Fair Credit Reporting Act, the Fair Debt Collection Practices Act, and the Truth in Lending Act. In addition, Congress enacted a new prohibition on "any unfair, deceptive, or abusive act or practice" by certain participants in the consumer-finance sector. Congress authorized the CFPB to implement that broad standard (and the 18 pre-existing statutes placed under the agency's purview) through binding regulations.

Congress also vested the CFPB with potent enforcement powers. The agency has the authority to conduct investigations, issue subpoenas and civil investigative demands, initiate administrative adjudications, and prosecute civil actions in federal court. To remedy violations of federal consumer financial law, the CFPB may seek restitution, disgorgement, and injunctive relief, as well as civil penalties of up to $1,000,000 (inflation adjusted) for each day that a violation occurs. ...

The CFPB's rulemaking and enforcement powers are coupled with extensive adjudicatory authority. The agency may conduct administrative proceedings to "ensure or enforce compliance with" the statutes and regulations it administers. When the CFPB acts as an adjudicator, it has "jurisdiction to grant any appropriate legal or equitable relief." The "hearing officer" who presides over the proceedings may issue subpoenas, order depositions, and resolve any motions filed by the parties. At the close of the proceedings, the hearing officer issues a "recommended decision," and the CFPB Director considers that recommendation and "issue[s] a final decision and order."

... Rather than create a traditional independent agency headed by a multimember board or commission, Congress elected to place the CFPB under the leadership of a single Director. The CFPB Director is appointed by the President with the advice and consent of the Senate. The Director serves for a term of five years, during which the President may remove the Director from office only for "inefficiency, neglect of duty, or malfeasance in office."

Unlike most other agencies, the CFPB does not rely on the annual appropriations process for funding. Instead, the CFPB receives funding directly from the Federal Reserve, which is itself funded outside the appropriations process through bank assessments. Each year, the CFPB requests an amount that the Director deems "reasonably necessary to carry out" the agency's duties, and the Federal Reserve grants that request so long as it does not exceed 12% of the total operating expenses of the Federal Reserve (inflation adjusted). In recent years, the CFPB's annual budget has exceeded half a billion dollars.

**B**

Seila Law LLC is a California-based law firm that provides debt-related legal services to clients. In 2017, the CFPB issued a civil investigative demand to Seila Law to determine whether the firm had "engag[ed] in unlawful acts or practices in the advertising, marketing, or sale of debt relief services." The demand (essentially a subpoena) directed Seila Law to produce information and documents related to its business practices.

Seila Law asked the CFPB to set aside the demand, objecting that the agency's leadership by a single Director removable only for cause violated the separation of powers. The CFPB declined to address that claim and directed Seila Law to comply with the demand.

When Seila Law refused, the CFPB filed a petition to enforce the demand in the District Court. In response, Seila Law renewed its defense that the demand was invalid and must be set aside because the CFPB's structure violated the Constitution. The District Court disagreed and ordered Seila Law to comply with the demand (with one modification not relevant here). ... Because [the Court of Appeals] found *Humphrey's Executor* and *Morrison* "controlling," it affirmed the District Court's order requiring compliance with the demand.

We granted certiorari to address the constitutionality of the CFPB's structure. We also requested argument on an additional question: whether, if the CFPB's structure violates the separation of powers, the CFPB Director's removal protection can be severed from the rest of the Dodd-Frank Act.

Because the Government agrees with petitioner on the merits of the constitutional question, we appointed Paul Clement to defend the judgment below as amicus curiae. He has ably discharged his responsibilities.

**III**

We hold that the CFPB's leadership by a single individual removable only for inefficiency, neglect, or malfeasance violates the separation of powers.

**A**

[The] "executive Power" belongs to the President alone. But because it would be "impossib[le]" for "one man" to "perform all the great business of the State," the Constitution assumes that lesser executive officers will "assist the supreme Magistrate in discharging the duties of his trust." 30 Writings of George Washington 334 (J. Fitzpatrick ed. 1939).

These lesser officers must remain accountable to the President, whose authority they wield. As Madison explained, "[I]f any power whatsoever is in its nature Executive, it is the power of appointing, overseeing, and controlling those who execute the laws." 1 Annals of Cong. 463 (1789). That power, in turn, generally includes the ability to remove executive officials, for it is "only the authority that can remove" such officials that they "must fear and, in the performance of [their] functions, obey." *Bowsher v. Synar* (1986) (internal quotation marks omitted).

[In *Myers v. United States* (1926), the Court] recognized the President's prerogative to remove executive officials.... Chief Justice Taft, writing for the Court, conducted an exhaustive examination of the First Congress's determination in 1789, the views of the Framers and their contemporaries, historical practice, and our precedents up until that point. He concluded that Article II "grants to the President" the "general administrative control of those executing the laws, including the power of appointment and removal of executive officers." Id. (emphasis added). Just as the President's "selection of administrative officers is essential to the execution of the laws by him, so must be his power of removing those for whom he cannot continue to be responsible." Id. "[T]o hold otherwise," the Court reasoned, "would make it impossible for the President . . . to take care that the laws be faithfully executed." Id.

We recently reiterated the President's general removal power in Free Enterprise Fund[, which] left in place two exceptions to the President's unrestricted removal power. First, in *Humphrey's Executor*, decided less than a decade after *Myers*, the Court upheld a statute that protected the Commissioners of the FTC from removal except for "inefficiency, neglect of duty, or malfeasance in office." (quoting 15 U. S. C. §41). In reaching that conclusion, the Court stressed that Congress's ability to impose such removal restrictions "will depend upon the character of the office."

Because the Court limited its holding "to officers of the kind here under consideration," id., the contours of the *Humphrey's Executor* exception depend upon the characteristics of the agency before the Court. Rightly or wrongly, the Court viewed the FTC (as it existed in 1935) as exercising "no part of the executive power." Id. Instead, it was "an administrative body" that performed "specified duties as a legislative or as a judicial aid." Id. It acted "as a legislative agency" in "making investigations and reports" to Congress and "as an agency of the judiciary" in making recommendations to courts as a master in chancery. Id. "To the extent that [the FTC] exercise[d] any executive function[,] as distinguished from executive power in the constitutional sense," it did so only in the discharge of its "quasi-legislative or quasi-judicial powers." Id. (emphasis added).

The Court identified several organizational features that helped explain its characterization of the FTC as non-executive. Composed of five members—no more than three from the same political party—the Board was designed to be "non-partisan" and to "act with entire impartiality." Id. The FTC's duties were "neither political nor executive," but instead called for "the trained judgment of a body of experts" "informed by experience." Id. (internal quotation marks omitted). And the Commissioners' staggered, seven-year terms enabled the agency to accumulate technical expertise and avoid a "complete change" in leadership "at any one time." Id.

In short, *Humphrey's Executor* permitted Congress to give for-cause removal protections to a multimember body of experts, balanced along partisan lines, that performed legislative and judicial functions and was said not to exercise any executive power. Consistent with that understanding, the Court later applied "[t]he philosophy of *Humphrey's Executor*" to uphold for-cause removal protections for the members of the War Claims Commission—a three-member "adjudicatory body" tasked with resolving claims for compensation arising from World War II. *Wiener v. United States* (1958).

While recognizing an exception for multimember bodies with "quasi-judicial" or "quasi-legislative" functions, Humphrey's Executor reaffirmed the core holding of Myers that the President has "unrestrictable power . . . to remove purely executive officers." The Court acknowledged that between purely executive officers on the one hand, and officers that closely resembled the FTC Commissioners on the other, there existed "a field of doubt" that the Court left "for future consideration." Id.

We have recognized a second exception for inferior officers in two cases, *United States v. Perkins* and *Morrison v. Olson*. In *Perkins*, we upheld tenure protections for a naval cadet-engineer. And, in Morrison, we upheld a provision granting good-cause tenure protection to an independent counsel appointed to investigate and prosecute particular alleged crimes by high-ranking Government officials. Backing away from the reliance in Humphrey's Executor on the concepts of "quasi-legislative" and "quasi-judicial" power, we viewed the ultimate question as whether a removal restriction is of "such a nature that [it] impede[s] the President's ability to perform his constitutional duty." Although the independent counsel was a single person and performed "law enforcement functions that typically have been undertaken by officials within the Executive Branch," we concluded that the removal protections did not unduly interfere with the functioning of the Executive Branch because "the independent counsel [was] an inferior officer under the Appointments Clause, with limited jurisdiction and tenure and lacking policymaking or significant administrative authority." Id. ...

## B

Neither *Humphrey's Executor* nor *Morrison* resolves whether the CFPB Director's insulation from removal is constitutional. Start with Humphrey's Executor. Unlike the New Deal-era FTC upheld there, the CFPB is led by a single Director who cannot be described as a "body of experts" and cannot be considered "non-partisan" in the same sense as a group of officials drawn from both sides of the aisle. Moreover, while the staggered terms of the FTC Commissioners prevented complete turnovers in agency leadership and guaranteed that there would always be some Commissioners who had accrued significant expertise, the CFPB's single-Director structure and five-year term guarantee abrupt shifts in agency leadership and with it the loss of accumulated expertise.

In addition, the CFPB Director is hardly a mere legislative or judicial aid. Instead of making reports and recommendations to Congress, as the 1935 FTC did, the Director possesses the authority to promulgate binding rules fleshing out 19 federal statutes, including a broad prohibition on unfair and deceptive practices in a major segment of the U. S. economy. And instead of submitting recommended dispositions to an Article III court, the Director may unilaterally issue final decisions awarding legal and equitable relief in administrative adjudications. Finally, the Director's enforcement authority includes the power to seek daunting monetary penalties against private parties on behalf of the United States in federal court —a quintessentially executive power not considered in Humphrey's Executor.

The logic of Morrison also does not apply. Everyone agrees the CFPB Director is not an inferior officer, and her duties are far from limited. Unlike the independent counsel, who lacked policymaking or administrative authority, the Director has the sole responsibility to administer 19 separate consumer-protection statutes that cover everything from credit cards and car payments to mortgages and student loans. It is true that the independent counsel in Morrison was empowered to initiate criminal investigations and prosecutions, and in that respect wielded core executive power. But that power, while significant, was trained inward to high-ranking Governmental actors identified by others, and was confined to a specified matter in which the Department of Justice had a potential conflict of interest. By contrast, the CFPB Director has the authority to bring the coercive power of the state to bear on millions of private citizens and businesses, imposing even billion-dollar penalties through administrative adjudications and civil actions.

In light of these differences, the constitutionality of the CFPB Director's insulation from removal cannot be settled by Humphrey's Executor or Morrison alone.

## C

The question instead is whether to extend those precedents to ... an independent agency led by a single Director and vested with significant executive power. We decline to do so. Such an agency has no basis in history and no place in our constitutional structure.

"Perhaps the most telling indication of [a] severe constitutional problem" with an executive entity "is [a] lack of historical precedent" to support it. Free Enterprise Fund (internal quotation marks omitted). An agency with a structure like that of the CFPB is almost wholly unprecedented.

After years of litigating the agency's constitutionality, the Courts of Appeals, parties, and amici have identified "only a handful of isolated" incidents in which Congress has provided good-cause tenure to principal officers who wield power alone rather than as members of a board or commission. Id. "[T]hese few scattered examples"—four to be exact—shed little light. *NLRB v. Noel Canning* (2014).

First, the CFPB's defenders point to the Comptroller of the Currency, who enjoyed removal protection for one year during the Civil War. That example has rightly been dismissed as an aberration. It was "adopted without discussion" during the heat of the Civil War and abandoned before it could be "tested by executive or judicial inquiry." Myers. (At the time, the Comptroller may also have been an inferior officer, given that he labored "under the general direction of the Secretary of the Treasury.")

Second, the supporters of the CFPB point to the Office of the Special Counsel (OSC), which has been headed by a single officer since 1978. But this first enduring single-leader office, created nearly 200 years after the Constitution was ratified, drew a contemporaneous constitutional objection from the Office of Legal Counsel under President Carter and a subsequent veto on constitutional grounds by President Reagan. In any event, the OSC exercises only limited jurisdiction to enforce certain rules governing Federal Government employers and employees. It does not bind private parties at all or wield regulatory authority comparable to the CFPB.

Third, the CFPB's defenders note that the Social Security Administration (SSA) has been run by a single Administrator since 1994. That example, too, is comparatively recent and controversial. President Clinton questioned the constitutionality of the SSA's new single-Director structure upon signing it into law. In addition, unlike the CFPB, the SSA lacks the authority to bring enforcement actions against private parties. Its role is largely limited to adjudicating claims for Social Security benefits.

The only remaining example is the Federal Housing Finance Agency (FHFA), created in 2008 to assume responsibility for Fannie Mae and Freddie Mac. That agency is essentially a companion of the CFPB, established in response to the same financial crisis. It regulates primarily Government-sponsored enterprises, not purely private actors. And its single-Director structure is a source of ongoing controversy. Indeed, it was recently held unconstitutional by the Fifth Circuit, sitting en banc.

With the exception of the one-year blip for the Comptroller of the Currency, these isolated examples are modern and contested. And they do not involve regulatory or enforcement authority remotely comparable to that exercised by the CFPB. The CFPB's single-

Director structure is an innovation with no foothold in history or tradition.

In addition to being a historical anomaly, the CFPB's single-Director configuration is incompatible with our constitutional structure. Aside from the sole exception of the Presidency, that structure scrupulously avoids concentrating power in the hands of any single individual.

"The Framers recognized that, in the long term, structural protections against abuse of power were critical to preserving liberty." Bowsher. Their solution to governmental power and its perils was simple: divide it. To prevent the "gradual concentration" of power in the same hands, they enabled "[a]mbition . . . to counteract ambition" at every turn. The Federalist No. 51, p. 349 (J. Cooke ed. 1961) (J. Madison). At the highest level, they "split the atom of sovereignty" itself into one Federal Government and the States. *Gamble v. United States* (2019) (internal quotation marks omitted). They then divided the "powers of the new Federal Government into three defined categories, Legislative, Executive, and Judicial." *INS v. Chadha* (1983).

They did not stop there. Most prominently, the Framers bifurcated the federal legislative power into two Chambers: the House of Representatives and the Senate, each composed of multiple Members and Senators. Art. I, §§2, 3.

The Executive Branch is a stark departure from all this division. The Framers viewed the legislative power as a special threat to individual liberty, so they divided that power to ensure that "differences of opinion" and the "jarrings of parties" would "promote deliberation and circumspection" and "check excesses in the majority." See The Federalist No. 70 (A. Hamilton); see also id., No. 51. By contrast, the Framers thought it necessary to secure the authority of the Executive so that he could carry out his unique responsibilities. See id., No. 70. As Madison put it, while "the weight of the legislative authority requires that it should be . . . divided, the weakness of the executive may require, on the other hand, that it should be fortified." Id., No. 51.

The Framers deemed an energetic executive essential to "the protection of the community against foreign attacks," "the steady administration of the laws," "the protection of property," and "the security of liberty." Id., No. 70. Accordingly, they chose not to bog the Executive down with the "habitual feebleness and dilatoriness" that comes with a "diversity of views and opinions." Id. Instead, they gave the Executive the "[d]ecision, activity, secrecy, and dispatch" that "characterise the proceedings of one man." Id.

To justify and check that authority—unique in our constitutional structure—the Framers made the President the most democratic and politically accountable official in Government. Only the President (along with the Vice President) is elected by the entire Nation. And the President's political accountability is enhanced by the solitary nature of the Executive Branch, which provides "a single object for the jealousy and watchfulness of the people." Id. ...

The resulting constitutional strategy is straightforward: divide power everywhere except for the Presidency, and render the President directly accountable to the people through regular elections. In that scheme, individual executive officials will still wield significant authority, but that authority remains subject to the ongoing supervision and control of the elected President. Through the President's oversight, "the chain of dependence [is] preserved," so that "the lowest officers, the middle grade, and the highest" all "depend, as they ought, on the President, and the President on the community." 1 Annals of Cong. 499 (J. Madison).

The CFPB's single-Director structure contravenes this carefully calibrated system by vesting significant governmental power in the hands of a single individual accountable to no one. The Director is neither elected by the people nor meaningfully controlled (through the threat of removal) by someone who is. The Director does not even depend on Congress for annual appropriations. Yet the Director may unilaterally, without meaningful supervision, issue final regulations, oversee adjudications, set enforcement priorities, initiate prosecutions, and determine what penalties to impose on private parties. With no colleagues to persuade, and no boss or electorate looking over her shoulder, the Director may dictate and enforce policy for a vital segment of the economy affecting millions of Americans.

The CFPB Director's insulation from removal by an accountable President is enough to render the agency's structure unconstitutional. But several other features of the CFPB combine to make the Director's removal protection even more problematic. In addition to lacking the most direct method of presidential control—removal at will—the agency's unique structure also forecloses certain indirect methods of Presidential control.

Because the CFPB is headed by a single Director with a five-year term, some Presidents may not have any opportunity to shape its leadership and thereby influence its activities. A President elected in 2020 would likely not appoint a CFPB Director until 2023, and a President elected in 2028 may never appoint one. That means an unlucky President might get elected on a consumer-protection platform and enter office only to find herself saddled with a holdover Director from a competing political party who is dead set against that agenda. To make matters worse, the agency's single-Director structure means the President will not have the opportunity to appoint any other leaders—such as a chair or fellow members of a Commission or Board—who can serve as a check on the Director's authority and help bring the agency in line with the President's preferred policies.

The CFPB's receipt of funds outside the appropriations process further aggravates the agency's threat to Presidential control. The President normally has the opportunity to recommend or veto spending bills that affect the operation of administrative agencies. And, for the past century, the President has annually submitted a proposed budget to Congress for approval. Presidents frequently use these budgetary tools "to influence the policies of independent agencies." *PHH* (Henderson, J., dissenting). But no similar opportunity exists for the President to influence the CFPB Director.

Instead, the Director receives over $500 million per year to fund the agency's chosen priorities. And the Director receives that money from the Federal Reserve, which is itself funded outside of the annual appropriations process. This financial freedom makes it even more likely that the agency will "slip from the Executive's control, and thus from that of the people." *Free Enterprise Fund.*

**IV**

Having concluded that the CFPB's leadership by a single independent Director violates the separation of powers, we now turn to the appropriate remedy. [There] is a live controversy over the question of severability. And that controversy is essential to our ability to provide petitioner the relief it seeks: If the removal restriction is not severable, then we must grant the relief requested, promptly rejecting the demand outright. If, on the other hand, the removal restriction is severable, we must instead remand for the Government to press its ratification arguments in further proceedings. Unlike the lingering ratification issue, severability presents a pure question of law that has been fully briefed and argued by the parties. We therefore proceed to address it.

It has long been settled that "one section of a statute may be repugnant to the Constitution without rendering the whole act void." *Loeb v. Columbia Township Trustees* (1900) (quoting *Treasurer of Fayette Cty. v. People's & Drovers' Bank* (Ohio 1890)).... When Congress has expressly provided a severability clause, our task is simplified. We will presume "that Congress did not intend the validity of the statute in question to depend on the validity of the constitutionally offensive provision . . . unless there is strong evidence that Congress intended otherwise." *Alaska Airlines, Inc. v. Brock* (1987).

The only constitutional defect we have identified in the CFPB's structure is the Director's insulation from removal. If the Director were removable at will by the President, the constitutional violation would disappear. We must therefore decide whether the removal provision can be severed from the other statutory provisions relating to the CFPB's powers and responsibilities.

[Here,] the provisions of the Dodd-Frank Act bearing on the CFPB's structure and duties remain fully operative without the offending tenure restriction. Those provisions are capable of functioning independently, and there is nothing in the text or history of the Dodd-Frank Act that demonstrates Congress would have preferred no CFPB to a CFPB supervised by the President. Quite the opposite. [T]he Dodd-Frank Act contains an express severability clause. There is no need to wonder what Congress would have wanted if "any provision of this Act" is "held to be unconstitutional" because it has told us: "the remainder of this Act" should "not be affected."

... We think it clear that Congress would prefer that we use a scalpel rather than a bulldozer in curing the constitutional defect we identify today. ...

As in every severability case, there may be means of remedying the defect in the CFPB's structure that the Court lacks the authority to provide. Our severability analysis does not foreclose Congress from pursuing alternative responses to the problem—for example, converting the CFPB into a multimember agency. ...

Because we find the Director's removal protection severable from the other provisions of Dodd-Frank that establish the CFPB, we remand for the Court of Appeals to consider whether the civil investigative demand was validly ratified.

* * *

A decade ago, we declined to extend Congress's authority to limit the President's removal power to a new situation, never before confronted by the Court. We do the same today. In our constitutional system, the executive power belongs to the President, and that power generally includes the ability to supervise and remove the agents who wield executive power in his stead. While we have previously upheld limits on the President's removal authority in certain contexts, we decline to do so when it comes to principal officers who, acting alone, wield significant executive power. The Constitution requires that such officials remain dependent on the President, who in turn is accountable to the people.

The judgment of the United States Court of Appeals for the Ninth Circuit is vacated, and the case is remanded for further proceedings consistent with this opinion.

*It is so ordered.*

[Dissenting opinion of Justice THOMAS omitted.]

Justice KAGAN, with whom Justice Ginsburg, Justice Breyer, and Justice Sotomayor join, concurring in the judgment with respect to severability and dissenting in part.

What does the Constitution say about the separation of powers—and particularly about the President's removal authority? (Spoiler alert: about the latter, nothing at all.)

The majority offers the civics class version of separation of powers—call it the Schoolhouse Rock definition of the phrase. The Constitution's first three articles, the majority recounts, "split the atom of sovereignty" among Congress, the President, and the courts. (internal quotation marks omitted). ...

There is nothing wrong with that as a beginning. ... It is of course true that the Framers lodged three different kinds of power in three different entities. And that they did so for a crucial purpose—because, as James Madison wrote, "there can be no liberty where the legislative and executive powers are united in the same person[ ] or body" or where "the power of judging [is] not separated from the legislative and executive powers." The Federalist No. 47 (J. Cooke ed. 1961) (quoting Baron de Montesquieu).

The problem lies in treating the beginning as an ending too—in failing to recognize that the separation of powers is, by design, neither rigid nor complete. [A]s James Madison stated, the creation of distinct branches "did not mean that these departments ought to have no partial agency in, or no controul over the acts of each other." The Federalist No. 47 (emphasis deleted). To the contrary, Madison explained, the drafters of the Constitution—like those of then-existing state constitutions—opted against keeping the branches of government "absolutely separate and distinct." Id. ...

One way the Constitution reflects that vision is by giving Congress broad authority to establish and organize the Executive Branch. Article II presumes the existence of "Officer[s]" in "executive Departments." §2, cl. 1. But it does not, as you might think from reading the majority opinion, give the President authority to decide what kinds of officers—in what departments, with what responsibilities—the Executive Branch requires. Instead, Article I's Necessary and Proper Clause puts those decisions in the legislature's hands. Congress has the power "[t]o make all Laws which shall be necessary and proper for carrying into Execution" not just its own enumerated powers but also "all other Powers vested by this Constitution in the Government of the United States, or in any Department or Officer thereof." §8, cl. 18. Similarly, the Appointments Clause reflects Congress's central role in structuring the Executive Branch. Yes, the President can appoint principal officers, but only as the legislature "shall . . . establish[ ] by Law" (and of course subject to the Senate's advice and consent). Art. II, §2, cl. 2. And Congress has plenary power to decide not only what inferior officers will exist but also who (the President or a head of department) will appoint them. So as Madison told the first Congress, the legislature gets to "create[ ] the office, define[ ] the powers, [and] limit[ ] its duration." 1 Annals of Cong. 582 (1789). The President, as to the construction of his own branch of government, can only try to work his will through the legislative process.

The majority relies for its contrary vision on Article II's Vesting Clause, but the provision can't carry all that weight. ...

Nor can the Take Care Clause come to the majority's rescue. That Clause cannot properly serve as a "placeholder for broad judicial judgments" about presidential control. To begin with, the provision —"he shall take Care that the Laws be faithfully executed"—speaks of duty, not power. Art. II, §3. [Further, as] this Court has held, a President can ensure "faithful execution' of the laws"—thereby satisfying his "take care" obligation—with a removal provision like the one here. *Morrison*. A for-cause standard gives him "ample authority to assure that [an official] is competently performing [his] statutory responsibilities in a manner that comports with the [relevant legislation's] provisions." Id.

Finally, recall the Constitution's telltale silence: Nowhere does the text say anything about the President's power to remove subordinate officials at will. The majority professes unconcern. After all, ..."neither is there a 'separation of powers clause' or a 'federalism clause.'" But those concepts are carved into the Constitution's text— the former in its first three articles separating powers, the latter in its enumeration of federal powers and its reservation of all else to the States. And anyway, at-will removal is hardly such a "foundational doctrine[ ]," id.: You won't find it on a civics class syllabus. That's because removal is a tool—one means among many, even if sometimes an important one, for a President to control executive officials. To find that authority hidden in the Constitution as a "general rule" is to discover what is nowhere there.

History no better serves the majority's cause. As Madison wrote, "a regular course of practice" can "liquidate & settle the meaning of" disputed or indeterminate constitutional provisions. Letter to Spencer Roane (Sept. 2, 1819), in 8 Writings of James Madison 450 (G. Hunt ed. 1908). The majority lays claim to that kind of record, asserting that its muscular view of "[t]he President's removal power has long been confirmed by history." But that is not so. The early history—including the fabled Decision of 1789—shows mostly debate and division about removal authority. And when a "settle[ment of] meaning" at last occurred, it was not on the majority's terms. Instead, it supports wide latitude for Congress to create spheres of administrative independence.

Begin with evidence from the Constitution's ratification. [T]he congressional debates revealed three main positions. Some shared Hamilton's Federalist No. 77 view: The Constitution required Senate consent for removal. At the opposite extreme, others claimed that the Constitution gave absolute removal power to the President. And a third faction maintained that the Constitution placed Congress in the driver's seat: The legislature could regulate, if it so chose, the President's authority to remove. In the end, Congress passed a bill saying nothing about removal, leaving the President free to fire the Secretary of Foreign Affairs at will. But the only one of the three views definitively rejected was Hamilton's theory of necessary Senate consent. As even strong proponents of executive power have shown, Congress never "endorse[d] the view that [it] lacked authority to modify" the President's removal authority when it wished to. The summer of 1789 thus ended without resolution of the critical question: Was the removal power "beyond the reach of congressional regulation?"

At the same time, the First Congress gave officials handling financial affairs—as compared to diplomatic and military ones—some independence from the President. The title and first section of the statutes creating the Departments of Foreign Affairs and War designated them "executive departments." Act of July 27, 1789, ch. 4; Act of Aug. 7, 1789, ch. 7. The law creating the Treasury Department conspicuously avoided doing so. That difference in nomenclature signaled others of substance. Congress left the organization of the Departments of Foreign Affairs and War skeletal, enabling the President to decide how he wanted to staff them. By contrast, Congress listed each of the offices within the Treasury Department, along with their functions. See id. Of the three initial Secretaries, only the Treasury's had an obligation to report to Congress when requested. And perhaps most notable, Congress soon deemed the Comptroller of the Treasury's settlements of public accounts "final and conclusive." Act of Mar. 3, 1795, ch. 48, §4. That decision, preventing presidential overrides, marked the Comptroller as exercising independent judgment. True enough, no statute shielded the Comptroller from discharge. But even James Madison, who at this point opposed most removal limits, told Congress that "there may be strong reasons why an officer of this kind should not hold his office at the pleasure" of the Secretary or President. 1 Annals of Cong. 612. ...

Contrary to the majority's view, then, the founding era closed without any agreement that Congress lacked the power to curb the President's removal authority. And as it kept that question open, Congress took the first steps—which would launch a tradition—of distinguishing financial regulators from diplomatic and military officers. The latter mainly helped the President carry out his own constitutional duties in foreign relations and war. The former chiefly carried out statutory duties, fulfilling functions Congress had assigned to their offices. In addressing the new Nation's finances, Congress had begun to use its powers under the Necessary and Proper Clause to design effective administrative institutions. And that included taking steps to insulate certain officers from political influence.

As the decades and centuries passed, those efforts picked up steam. Confronting new economic, technological, and social conditions, Congress—and often the President—saw new needs for pockets of independence within the federal bureaucracy. And that was especially so, again, when it came to financial regulation. I mention just a few highlights here—times when Congress decided that effective governance depended on shielding technical or expertise-based functions relating to the financial system from political pressure (or the moneyed interests that might lie behind it). Enacted under the Necessary and Proper Clause, those measures—creating some of the Nation's most enduring institutions—themselves helped settle the extent of Congress's power. "[A] regular course of practice," to use Madison's phrase, has "liquidate[d]" constitutional meaning about the permissibility of independent agencies.

... What is more, the Court's precedents before today have accepted the role of independent agencies in our governmental system. [W]e have repeatedly upheld provisions that prevent the President from firing regulatory officials except for such matters as neglect or malfeasance. In those decisions, we sounded a caution, insisting that Congress could not impede through removal restrictions the President's performance of his own constitutional duties. (So, to take the clearest example, Congress could not curb the President's power to remove his close military or diplomatic advisers.) But within that broad limit, this Court held, Congress could protect from at-will removal the officials it deemed to need some independence from political pressures. Nowhere do those precedents suggest what the majority announces today: that the President has an "unrestricted removal power" subject to two bounded exceptions.

The majority grounds its new approach in *Myers*, ignoring the way this Court has cabined that decision. *Myers*, the majority tells us, found an unrestrained removal power "essential to the [President's] execution of the laws." What the majority does not say is that within a decade the Court abandoned that view (much as later scholars rejected

Taft's one-sided history). In *Humphrey's Executor v. United States* (1935), the Court unceremoniously—and unanimously—confined *Myers* to its facts. "[T]he narrow point actually decided" there, Humphrey's stated, was that the President could "remove a postmaster of the first class, without the advice and consent of the Senate." Nothing else in Chief Justice Taft's prolix opinion "c[a]me within the rule of stare decisis." Id. (Indeed, the Court went on, everything in *Myers* "out of harmony" with Humphrey's was expressly "disapproved.") Half a century later, the Court was more generous. Two decisions read Myers as standing for the principle that Congress's own "participation in the removal of executive officers is unconstitutional." *Bowsher v. Synar* (1986). *Bowsher* made clear that Myers had nothing to say about Congress's power to enact a provision merely "limit[ing] the President's powers of removal" through a for-cause provision. That issue, the Court stated, was "not presented" in "the *Myers* case." Id. Instead, the relevant cite was *Humphrey's*.

And Humphrey's found constitutional a statute identical to the one here, providing that the President could remove FTC Commissioners for "inefficiency, neglect of duty, or malfeasance in office." The *Humphrey's* Court, as the majority notes, relied in substantial part on what kind of work the Commissioners performed. (By contrast, nothing in the decision turned—as the majority suggests—on any of the agency's organizational features.) According to *Humphrey's*, the Commissioners' primary work was to "carry into effect legislative policies"—"filling in and administering the details embodied by [a statute's] general standard." In addition, the Court noted, the Commissioners recommended dispositions in court cases, much as a special master does. Given those "quasi-legislative" and "quasi-judicial"—as opposed to "purely executive"—functions, Congress could limit the President's removal authority. Or said another way, Congress could give the FTC some "independen[ce from] executive control." Id.

About two decades later, an again-unanimous Court in *Wiener v. United States* (1958), reaffirmed *Humphrey's*. The question in Wiener was whether the President could dismiss without cause members of the War Claims Commission, an entity charged with compensating injuries arising from World War II. [R]elying on *Humphrey's*, the Court said he could not. The Court described as "short-lived" *Myers'* view that the President had "inherent constitutional power to remove officials, no matter what the relation of the executive to the discharge of their duties." Here, the Commissioners were not close agents of the President, who needed to be responsive to his preferences. Rather, they exercised adjudicatory responsibilities over legal claims. Congress, the Court found, had wanted the Commissioners to do so "free from [political] control or coercive influence." Id. (quoting *Humphrey's*). And that choice, as *Humphrey's* had held, was within Congress's power....

Another three decades on, *Morrison v. Olson* (1988) both extended *Humphrey's* domain and clarified the standard for addressing removal issues. [*Morrison*] upheld for-cause protections afforded to an independent counsel with power to investigate and prosecute crimes committed by high-ranking officials. The Court well understood that those law enforcement functions differed from the rulemaking and adjudicatory duties highlighted in *Humphrey's* and *Wiener*. But that difference did not resolve the issue. An official's functions, *Morrison* held, were relevant to but not dispositive of a removal limit's constitutionality. The key question in all the cases, *Morrison* saw, was whether such a restriction would "impede the President's ability to perform his constitutional duty." Only if it did so would it fall outside Congress's power. And the protection for the independent counsel, the Court found, did not. Even though the counsel's functions were "purely executive," the President's "need to control the exercise of [her] discretion" was not "so central to the functioning of the Executive Branch as to require" unrestricted removal authority. Id. True enough, the Court acknowledged, that the for-cause standard prevented the President from firing the counsel for discretionary decisions or judgment calls. But it preserved "ample authority" in the President "to assure that the counsel is competently performing" her "responsibilities in a manner that comports with" all legal requirements. Id. ...

The majority's description of *Morrison* is not true to the decision. ... First, *Morrison* is no "exception" to a broader rule from Myers. Morrison echoed all of Humphrey's criticism of the by-then infamous Myers "dicta." It again rejected the notion of an "all-inclusive" removal power. Id. It yet further confined Myers' reach, making clear that Congress could restrict the President's removal of officials carrying out even the most traditional executive functions. And the decision, with care, set out the governing rule—again, that removal restrictions are permissible so long as they do not impede the President's performance of his own constitutionally assigned duties. Second, as all that suggests, *Morrison* is not limited to inferior officers. In the eight pages addressing the removal issue, the Court constantly spoke of "officers" and "officials" in general. By contrast, the Court there used the word "inferior" in just one sentence (which of course the majority quotes), when applying its general standard to the case's facts. ...

Even *Free Enterprise Fund*, in which the Court recently held a removal provision invalid, operated within the framework of this precedent—and in so doing, left in place a removal provision just like the one here. ...

So caselaw joins text and history in establishing the general permissibility of for-cause provisions giving some independence to agencies. Contrary to the majority's view, those laws do not represent a suspicious departure from illimitable presidential control over administration. For almost a century, this Court has made clear that Congress has broad discretion to enact for-cause protections in pursuit of good governance.

[Here, no one] had a doubt that the [CFPB] should be independent. As explained already, Congress has historically given—with this Court's permission—a measure of independence to financial regulators like the Federal Reserve Board and the FTC. And agencies of that kind had administered most of the legislation whose enforcement the new statute transferred to the CFPB. The law thus included an ordinary for-cause provision—once again, that the President could fire the CFPB's Director only for "inefficiency, neglect of duty, or malfeasance in office." That standard would allow the President to discharge the Director for a failure to "faithfully execute[ ]" the law, as well as for basic incompetence. U. S. Const., Art. II, §3. But it would not permit removal for policy differences.

The question here, which by now you're well equipped to answer, is whether including that for-cause standard in the statute creating the CFPB violates the Constitution.

Applying our longstanding precedent, the answer is clear: It does not. This Court, as the majority acknowledges, has sustained the constitutionality of the FTC and similar independent agencies. The for-cause protections for the heads of those agencies, the Court has found, do not impede the President's ability to perform his own constitutional duties, and so do not breach the separation of powers. There is nothing different here. The CFPB wields the same kind of power as the FTC and similar agencies. And all of their heads receive the same kind of removal protection. No less than those other entities —by now part of the fabric of government—the CFPB is thus a permissible exercise of Congress's power under the Necessary and Proper Clause to structure administration.

... The CFPB Director exercises the same powers, and receives the same removal protections, as the heads of other, constitutionally permissible independent agencies. How could it be that this opinion is a dissent?

The majority focuses on one (it says sufficient) reason: The CFPB Director is singular, not plural. "Instead of placing the agency under the leadership of a board with multiple members," the majority protests, "Congress provided that the CFPB would be led by a single Director." And a solo CFPB Director does not fit within either of the majority's supposed exceptions. He is not an inferior officer, so (the majority says) Morrison does not apply; and he is not a multimember board, so (the majority says) neither does Humphrey's. Further, the majority argues, "[a]n agency with a [unitary] structure like that of the CFPB" is "novel"—or, if not quite that, "almost wholly unprecedented." Finally, the CFPB's organizational form violates the "constitutional structure" because it vests power in a "single individual" who is "insulated from Presidential control."

I'm tempted at this point just to say: No. All I've explained about constitutional text, history, and precedent invalidates the majority's thesis. But I'll set out here some more targeted points, taking step by step the majority's reasoning.

First, as I'm afraid you've heard before, the majority's "exceptions" (like its general rule) are made up. To begin with, our precedents reject the very idea of such exceptions. "The analysis contained in our removal cases," Morrison stated, shuns any attempt "to define rigid categories" of officials who may (or may not) have job protection. Still more, the contours of the majority's exceptions don't connect to our decisions' reasoning. The analysis in Morrison, as I've shown, extended far beyond inferior officers. And of course that analysis had to apply to individual officers: The independent counsel was very much a person, not a committee. So the idea that Morrison is in a separate box from this case doesn't hold up. Similarly, Humphrey's and later precedents give no support to the majority's view that the number of people at the apex of an agency matters to the constitutional issue. Those opinions mention the "groupness" of the agency head only in their background sections. The majority picks out that until-now-irrelevant fact to distinguish the CFPB, and constructs around it an until-now-unheard-of exception. So if the majority really wants to see something "novel," it need only look to its opinion.

By contrast, the CFPB's single-director structure has a fair bit of precedent behind it. The Comptroller of the Currency. The Office of the Special Counsel (OSC). The Social Security Administration (SSA). The Federal Housing Finance Agency (FHFA). Maybe four prior agencies is in the eye of the beholder, but it's hardly nothing. I've already explained why the earliest of those agencies—the Civil-War-era Comptroller—is not the blip the majority describes. The office is one in a long line, starting with the founding-era Comptroller of the Treasury (also one person), of financial regulators designed to do their jobs with some independence. As for the other three, the majority objects: too powerless and too contested. I think not. On power, the SSA runs the Nation's largest government program—among other things, deciding all claims brought by its 64 million beneficiaries; the FHFA plays a crucial role in overseeing the mortgage market, on which millions of Americans annually rely; and the OSC prosecutes misconduct in the two-million-person federal workforce. All different from the CFPB, no doubt; but the majority can't think those matters beneath a President's notice. (Consider: Would the President lose more votes from a malfunctioning SSA or CFPB?) And controversial? Well, yes, they are. Almost all independent agencies are controversial, no matter how many directors they have. Or at least controversial among Presidents and their lawyers. That's because whatever might be said in their favor, those agencies divest the President of some removal power. If signing statements and veto threats made independent agencies unconstitutional, quite a few wouldn't pass muster. Maybe that's what the majority really wants (I wouldn't know)—but it can't pretend the disputes surrounding these agencies had anything to do with whether their heads are singular or plural.

Still more important, novelty is not the test of constitutionality when it comes to structuring agencies. Congress regulates in that sphere under the Necessary and Proper Clause, not (as the majority seems to think) a Rinse and Repeat Clause. The Framers understood that new times would often require new measures, and exigencies often demand innovation. ...

And Congress's choice to put a single director, rather than a multimember commission, at the CFPB's head violates no principle of separation of powers. The purported constitutional problem here is that an official has "slip[ped] from the Executive's control" and "supervision"—that he has become unaccountable to the President. (internal quotation marks omitted). So to make sense on the majority's own terms, the distinction between singular and plural agency heads must rest on a theory about why the former more easily "slip" from the President's grasp. But the majority has nothing to offer. In fact, the opposite is more likely to be true: To the extent that such matters are measurable, individuals are easier than groups to supervise.

To begin with, trying to generalize about these matters is something of a fool's errand. Presidential control, as noted earlier, can operate through many means—removal to be sure, but also appointments, oversight devices (e.g., centralized review of rulemaking or litigating positions), budgetary processes, personal outreach, and more. The effectiveness of each of those control mechanisms, when present, can then depend on a multitude of agency-specific practices, norms, rules, and organizational features. In that complex stew, the difference between a singular and plural agency head will often make not a whit of difference. Or to make the point more concrete, a multimember commission may be harder to control than an individual director for a host of reasons unrelated to its plural character. That may be so when the two are subject to the same removal standard, or even when the individual director has greater formal job protection. Indeed, the very category of multimember commissions breaks apart under inspection, spoiling the majority's essential dichotomy. Some of those commissions have chairs appointed by the President; others do not. Some of those chairs are quite powerful; others are not. Partisan balance requirements, term length, voting rules, and more—all vary widely, in ways that make a significant difference to the ease of presidential control. Why, then, would anyone distinguish along a simple commission/single-director axis when deciding whether the Constitution requires at-will removal?

But if the demand is for generalization, then the majority's distinction cuts the opposite way: More powerful control mechanisms are needed (if anything) for commissions. Holding everything else equal, those are the agencies more likely to "slip from the Executive's control." Just consider your everyday experience: It's easier to get one person to do what you want than a gaggle. So too, you know exactly whom to blame when an individual—but not when a group—does a job badly. The same is true in bureaucracies. A multimember structure reduces accountability to the President because it's harder for him to oversee, to influence—or to remove, if necessary—a group of five or more commissioners than a single director. Indeed, that is why Congress so often resorts to hydra-headed agencies. "[M]ultiple membership," an influential Senate Report concluded, is "a buffer against Presidential control" (especially when combined, as it often is, with partisan-balance requirements). Senate Committee on Governmental Affairs, Study on Federal Regulation, S. Doc. No. 95-91, vol. 5 (1977). ... It is hard to know why Congress did not take [this] tack when creating the CFPB. But its choice brought the agency only closer to the President—more exposed to his view, more subject to his sway. In short, the majority gets the matter backward: Where presidential control is the object, better to have one than many.

Because it has no answer on that score, the majority slides to a different question: Assuming presidential control of any independent agency is vanishingly slim, is a single-head or a multi-head agency more capable of exercising power, and so of endangering liberty? The majority says a single head is the greater threat because he may wield power "unilaterally" and "[w]ith no colleagues to persuade." (emphasis in original). So the CFPB falls victim to what the majority sees as a constitutional anti-power-concentration principle (with an exception for the President).

If you've never heard of a statute being struck down on that ground, you're not alone. It is bad enough to "extrapolat[e]" from the "general constitutional language" of Article II's Vesting Clause an unrestricted removal power constraining Congress's ability to legislate under the Necessary and Proper Clause. Morrison. It is still worse to extrapolate from the Constitution's general structure (division of powers) and implicit values (liberty) a limit on Congress's express power to create administrative bodies. And more: to extrapolate from such sources a distinction as prosaic as that between the SEC and the CFPB—i.e., between a multi-headed and single-headed agency. ...

"While the Constitution diffuses power the better to secure liberty, it also contemplates that practice will integrate the dispersed powers into a workable government." *Youngstown Sheet & Tube Co. v. Sawyer* (1952) (Jackson, J., concurring). The Framers took pains to craft a document that would allow the structures of governance to change, as times and needs change. The Constitution says only a few words about administration. As Chief Justice Marshall wrote: Rather than prescribing "immutable rules," it enables Congress to choose "the means by which government should, in all future time, execute its powers." *McCulloch v. Maryland* (1819). It authorizes Congress to meet new exigencies with new devices. So Article II does not generally prohibit independent agencies. Nor do any supposed structural principles. Nor do any odors wafting from the document. Save for when those agencies impede the President's performance of his own constitutional duties, the matter is left up to Congress.

Our history has stayed true to the Framers' vision. Congress has accepted their invitation to experiment with administrative forms—nowhere more so than in the field of financial regulation. And this Court has mostly allowed it to do so. The result is a broad array of independent agencies, no two exactly alike but all with a measure of insulation from the President's removal power. The Federal Reserve Board; the FTC; the SEC; maybe some you've never heard of. As to each, Congress thought that formal job protection for policymaking would produce regulatory outcomes in greater accord with the long-term public interest. Congress may have been right; or it may have been wrong; or maybe it was some of both. No matter—the branches accountable to the people have decided how the people should be governed.

The CFPB should have joined the ranks. Maybe it will still do so, even under today's opinion: The majority tells Congress that it may "pursu[e] alternative responses" to the identified constitutional defect —"for example, converting the CFPB into a multimember agency." But there was no need to send Congress back to the drawing board. The Constitution does not distinguish between single-director and multimember independent agencies. It instructs Congress, not this Court, to decide on agency design. Because this Court ignores that sensible—indeed, that obvious—division of tasks, I respectfully dissent.

## NOTES AND QUESTIONS

1. How does the independence of the CFPB differ from the independence of the accounting board in *Free Enterprise Fund* in respect to the President's power to remove? Both bodies, in the Court's view, were constitutionally infirm. One difference of note, though, is that the upshot of striking down the tenure provisions for the board in *Free Enterprise Fund* did not change the removal power the President had over accounting board members—they remained exclusively under the control of the Securities Exchange Commission, whose members could be removed from the President only for cause. Thus it is the SEC's commissioners who are comparable to the director of CFPB, not the accounting board itself. Why, then, is the SEC—or any independent agency—constitutional by the majority's lights? Is it just because they have been around so long?

2. Your answer to the last two questions should refer to the rule Chief Justice Roberts extracts from the precedent cases in this area— that is, the rule that independent agencies, like the SEC, will only be deemed constitutional in the narrow circumstances the majority outlined in *Seila Law*.

3. The majority opinion dismisses out of hand the argument that nowhere in the text of the constitution is the President given unqualified removal power over federal officers—indeed, the Constitution makes no mention of removal at all. What is Justice Kagan's response? Who has the better of the argument—is she correct that the removal power can be distinguished from the concepts of separation of powers and federalism, neither of which the Constitution names?

4. Chief Justice Roberts offered one perspective on the historical understanding of the separation of powers and the dissent another. The dissent notes, for example, that at the time of the framing state constitutions were not understood to wall the departments of government off from one another, notwithstanding textual provisions to the contrary. The Massachusetts Constitution, for example, provides in Article 30 that:

> In the government of this commonwealth, the legislative department shall never exercise the executive and judicial powers, or either of them: the executive shall never exercise the legislative and judicial powers, or either of them: the judicial

shall never exercise the legislative and executive powers, or either of them: to the end it may be a government of laws and not of men.

As clear as this statement about the separation of powers appears to be, the Massachusetts Supreme Judicial Court has long held that the borders between the departments of government are in some respects permeable; as the court observed in a 1977 *Opinion of the Justices*, for example, for government to function, "an absolute division is neither possible nor always desirable." Indeed, this "functionalist" approach to the separation of powers animates many U.S. Supreme Court decisions on the separation of powers between Congress and the President, including much of modern Commerce Clause jurisprudence as well as rulings on the President's foreign affairs and national security powers. As a historical matter, the formalism embraced by the *Seila Law* majority is by no means the only way in which courts have approached constitutional separation of powers questions.

**5.** The Court's interest in the area of executive appointment and removal did not end with *Seila Law* but continued into the next term. In *Collins v. Yellen*, 594 U.S. ___ (2021), the Court (per Justice Alito) ruled unconstitutional the for-cause restrictions on the President's ability to remove the director of the Federal Housing Finance Agency. The Court found *Seila Law* to be "all but dispositive," as the constitution prohibits "even 'modest restrictions' on the President's power to remove the head of an agency with a single top officer." (quoting *Seila Law*). Notwithstanding her dissent in *Seila Law*, Justice Kagan agreed that Collins was indistinguishable.

**Add after Note 4 on page 292:**

### E. A JUDICIALLY ENFORCEABLE LIMIT ON EXECUTIVE POWER: THE MAJOR QUESTIONS DOCTRINE

Several cases in this chapter have mentioned the delegation doctrine—the judge-made rule that the Constitution does not allow Congress to make unduly broad and vague delegations of authority to the executive. As noted above, the delegation doctrine is still good law, though a majority of the Court has not relied on it in some time. More recently, the Court has been developing a related rule, now known as the "major questions doctrine," as discussed in the next case.

**National Federation of Independent Business v. Occupational Safety and Health Administration**
**595 U.S. ___ (2022)**

[shadow/orders docket]

*Per Curiam.*

The Secretary of Labor, acting through the Occupational Safety and Health Administration, ... enacted a vaccine mandate for much of the Nation's work force. ...

Many States, businesses, and nonprofit organizations challenged OSHA's rule in Courts of Appeals across the country. The Fifth Circuit initially entered a stay. But when the cases were consolidated before the Sixth Circuit, that court lifted the stay and allowed OSHA's rule to take effect. Applicants now seek emergency relief from this Court, arguing that OSHA's mandate exceeds its statutory authority and is otherwise unlawful. Agreeing that applicants are likely to prevail, we grant their applications and stay the rule.

I

Congress enacted the Occupational Safety and Health Act in 1970. The Act created the Occupational Safety and Health Administration (OSHA), which is part of the Department of Labor and under the supervision of its Secretary. As its name suggests, OSHA is tasked with ensuring occupational safety—that is, "safe and healthful working conditions." § 651(b). It does so by enforcing occupational safety and health standards promulgated by the Secretary. Such standards must be "reasonably necessary or appropriate to provide safe or healthful employment." (emphasis added). They must also be developed using a rigorous process that includes notice, comment, and an opportunity for a public hearing.

The Act contains an exception to those ordinary notice-and-comment procedures for "emergency temporary standards." Such standards may "take immediate effect upon publication in the Federal Register." They are permissible, however, only in the narrowest of circumstances: the Secretary must show (1) "that employees are exposed to grave danger from exposure to substances or agents determined to be toxic or physically harmful or from new hazards," and (2) that the "emergency standard is necessary to protect employees from such danger." ...

[In November 2021, the Department of Labor issued] an emergency rule requiring all employers with at least 100 employees "to ensure their workforces are fully vaccinated or show a negative test at least once a week." ... [The] rule applies to all who work for employers with 100 or more employees. There are narrow exemptions for employees who work remotely "100 percent of the time" or who "work exclusively outdoors," but those exemptions are largely illusory. The Secretary has estimated, for example, that only nine percent of landscapers and groundskeepers qualify as working exclusively outside. The regulation otherwise operates as a blunt instrument. It draws no distinctions based on industry or risk of exposure to COVID-19. Thus, most lifeguards and linemen face the same regulations as do medics and meatpackers. OSHA estimates that 84.2 million employees are subject to its mandate.

[Following OSHA's publication of the vaccine mandate on November 5, 2021, numerous parties—including States, businesses, trade groups, and nonprofit organizations—filed petitions for review, with at least one petition arriving in each regional Court of Appeals. The cases were consolidated in the Sixth Circuit. Prior to consolidation, the Fifth Circuit stayed OSHA's rule pending further judicial review. When the consolidated cases arrived at the Sixth Circuit, [a] three-judge panel then dissolved the Fifth Circuit's stay, holding that OSHA's mandate was likely consistent with the agency's statutory and constitutional authority.]

Various parties then filed applications in this Court requesting that we stay OSHA's emergency standard. We consolidated two of those applications—one from the National Federation of Independent Business, and one from a coalition of States—and heard expedited argument on January 7, 2022.

**II**

The Sixth Circuit concluded that a stay of the rule was not justified. We disagree.

Applicants are likely to succeed on the merits of their claim that the Secretary lacked authority to impose the mandate. Administrative agencies ... possess only the authority that Congress has provided. The Secretary has ordered 84 million Americans to either obtain a COVID-19 vaccine or undergo weekly medical testing at their own expense. This is ... a significant encroachment into the lives—and health— of a vast number of employees. "We expect Congress to speak clearly when authorizing an agency to exercise powers of vast economic and political significance." *Alabama Assn. of Realtors v. Department of Health and Human Servs.* (2021) (per curiam) (internal quotation marks omitted). There can be little doubt that OSHA's mandate qualifies as an exercise of such authority.

The question, then, is whether the Act plainly authorizes the Secretary's mandate. It does not. The Act empowers the Secretary to set workplace safety standards, not broad public health measures. See 29 U.S.C. § 655(b) (directing the Secretary to set "occupational safety and health standards" (emphasis added)); § 655(c)(1) (authorizing the Secretary to impose emergency temporary standards necessary to protect "employees" from grave danger in the workplace). Confirming the point, the Act's provisions typically speak to hazards that employees face at work. And no provision of the Act addresses public health more generally, which falls outside of OSHA's sphere of expertise.

The dissent protests that we are imposing "a limit found no place in the governing statute." Not so. It is the text of the agency's Organic Act that repeatedly makes clear that OSHA is charged with regulating "occupational" hazards and the safety and health of "employees."

The Solicitor General does not dispute that OSHA is limited to regulating "work-related dangers." She instead argues that the risk of contracting COVID-19 qualifies as such a danger. We cannot agree. [COVID-19] is not an occupational hazard. ... COVID-19 can and does spread at home, in schools, during sporting events, and everywhere else that people gather. That kind of universal risk is no different from the day-to-day dangers that all face from crime, air pollution, or any number of communicable diseases. Permitting OSHA to regulate the hazards of daily life—simply because most Americans have jobs and face those same risks while on the clock—would significantly expand OSHA's regulatory authority without clear congressional authorization.

[A] vaccine mandate is strikingly unlike the workplace regulations that OSHA has typically imposed. A vaccination, after all, "cannot be undone at the end of the workday." *In re MCP No. 165* (CA6 2021) (Sutton, C. J., dissenting). Contrary to the dissent's contention, imposing a vaccine mandate on 84 million Americans in response to a worldwide pandemic is simply not "part of what the agency was built for."

... OSHA's indiscriminate approach fails to account for [the] crucial distinction [] between occupational risk and risk more generally—and accordingly the mandate takes on the character of a general public health measure, rather than an "occupational safety or health standard." 29 U.S.C. § 655(b) (emphasis added).

In looking for legislative support for the vaccine mandate, the dissent turns to the American Rescue Plan Act of 2021. That legislation, signed into law on March 11, 2021, of course said nothing about OSHA's vaccine mandate, which was not announced until six months later. In fact, the most noteworthy action concerning the vaccine mandate by either House of Congress has been a majority vote of the Senate disapproving the regulation on December 8, 2021. S. J. Res. 29, 117th Cong., 1st Sess. (2021).

It is telling that OSHA, in its half century of existence, has never before adopted a broad public health regulation of this kind—addressing a threat that is untethered, in any causal sense, from the workplace. This "lack of historical precedent," coupled with the breadth of authority that the Secretary now claims, is a "telling indication" that the mandate extends beyond the agency's legitimate reach. *Free Enterprise Fund v. Public Company Accounting Oversight Bd.* (2010) (internal quotation marks omitted).

... Although Congress has indisputably given OSHA the power to regulate occupational dangers, it has not given that agency the power to regulate public health more broadly. Requiring the vaccination of 84 million Americans, selected simply because they work for employers with more than 100 employees, certainly falls in the latter category.

\* \* \*

The applications for stays presented to Justice KAVANAUGH and by him referred to the Court are granted.

*It is so ordered.*

Justice GORSUCH, with whom Justice THOMAS and Justice ALITO join, concurring.

[T]his Court has established [a] firm rule: "We expect Congress to speak clearly" if it wishes to assign to an executive agency decisions "of vast economic and political significance." *Alabama Assn. of Realtors v. Department of Health and Human Servs.* (2021)

(per curiam) (internal quotation marks omitted). We sometimes call this the major questions doctrine.

OSHA's mandate fails that doctrine's test. The agency claims the power to force 84 million Americans to receive a vaccine or undergo regular testing. By any measure, that is a claim of power to resolve a question of vast national significance. Yet Congress has nowhere clearly assigned so much power to OSHA. Approximately two years have passed since this pandemic began; vaccines have been available for more than a year. Over that span, Congress has adopted several major pieces of legislation aimed at combating COVID-19. But Congress has chosen not to afford OSHA—or any federal agency—the authority to issue a vaccine mandate. Indeed, a majority of the Senate even voted to disapprove OSHA's regulation. ...

What is OSHA's reply? It directs us to 29 U.S.C. § 655(c)(1). In that statutory subsection, Congress authorized OSHA to issue "emergency" regulations upon determining that "employees are exposed to grave danger from exposure to substances or agents determined to be toxic or physically harmful" and "that such emergency standard[s] [are] necessary to protect employees from such danger[s]." According to the agency, this provision supplies it with "almost unlimited discretion" to mandate new nationwide rules in response to the pandemic so long as those rules are "reasonably related" to workplace safety. 86 Fed. Reg. 61402, 61405 (2021) (internal quotation marks omitted).

The Court rightly applies the major questions doctrine and concludes that this lone statutory subsection does not clearly authorize OSHA's mandate. Section 655(c)(1) was not adopted in response to the pandemic, but some 50 years ago at the time of OSHA's creation. Since then, OSHA has relied on it to issue only comparatively modest rules addressing dangers uniquely prevalent inside the workplace, like asbestos and rare chemicals. [Yet the agency now seeks to] regulate not just what happens inside the workplace but induce individuals to undertake a medical procedure that affects their lives outside the workplace. Historically, such matters have been regulated at the state level by authorities who enjoy broader and more general governmental powers. Meanwhile, at the federal level, OSHA arguably is not even the agency most associated with public health regulation. And in the rare instances when Congress has sought to mandate vaccinations, it has done so expressly. We have nothing like that here.

Why does the major questions doctrine matter? It ensures that the national government's power to make the laws that govern us remains where Article I of the Constitution says it belongs—with the people's elected representatives. If administrative agencies seek to regulate the daily lives and liberties of millions of Americans, the doctrine says, they must at least be able to trace that power to a clear grant of authority from Congress.

[The major questions doctrine serves to guard] against unintentional, oblique, or otherwise unlikely delegations of the legislative power. Sometimes, Congress passes broadly worded statutes seeking to resolve important policy questions in a field while leaving an agency to work out the details of implementation. Later, the agency may seek to exploit some gap, ambiguity, or doubtful expression in Congress's statutes to assume responsibilities far beyond its initial assignment. The major questions doctrine guards against this possibility by recognizing that Congress does not usually "hide elephants in mouseholes." *Whitman v. American Trucking Assns., Inc.* (2001). ...

[Here,] OSHA claims the power to issue a nationwide mandate on a major question but cannot trace its authority to do so to any clear congressional mandate. ... Under OSHA's reading, the law would afford it almost unlimited discretion—and certainly impose no "specific restrictions" that "meaningfully constrai[n]" the agency. *Touby v. United States* (1991). OSHA would become little more than a "roving commission to inquire into evils and upon discovery correct them." *A. L. A. Schecter Poultry Corp. v. United States* (1935) (Cardozo, J., concurring). ...

Justice BREYER, Justice SOTOMAYOR, and Justice KAGAN, dissenting.

Every day, COVID-19 poses grave dangers to the citizens of this country—and particularly, to its workers. The disease has by now killed almost 1 million Americans and hospitalized almost 4 million. It spreads by person-to-person contact in confined indoor spaces, so causes harm in nearly all workplace environments. And in those environments, more than any others, individuals have little control, and therefore little capacity to mitigate risk. COVID-19, in short, is a menace in work settings. The proof is all around us: Since the disease's onset, most Americans have seen their workplaces transformed.

So the administrative agency charged with ensuring health and safety in workplaces did what Congress commanded it to: It took action to address COVID-19's continuing threat in those spaces. The Occupational Safety and Health Administration (OSHA) issued an emergency temporary standard (Standard), requiring either vaccination or masking and testing, to protect American workers. The Standard falls within the core of the agency's mission: to "protect employees" from "grave danger" that comes from "new hazards" or exposure to harmful agents. 29 U.S.C. § 655(c)(1). OSHA estimates—and there is no ground for disputing—that the Standard will save over 6,500 lives and prevent over 250,000 hospitalizations in six months' time.

Yet today the Court issues a stay that prevents the Standard from taking effect. In our view, the Court's order seriously misapplies the applicable legal standards. And in so doing, it stymies the Federal Government's ability to counter the unparalleled threat that COVID-19 poses to our Nation's workers. Acting outside of its competence and without legal basis, the Court displaces the judgments of the Government officials given the responsibility to respond to workplace health emergencies. We respectfully dissent.

[Here, the] applicants are not "likely to prevail" under any proper view of the law. OSHA's rule perfectly fits the language of the applicable statutory provision. Once again, that provision commands —not just enables, but commands—OSHA to issue an emergency temporary standard whenever it determines "(A) that employees are exposed to grave danger from exposure to substances or agents determined to be toxic or physically harmful or from new hazards, and (B) that such emergency standard is necessary to protect employees from such danger." 29 U.S.C. § 655(c)(1). Each and every part of that provision demands that, in the circumstances here, OSHA act to prevent workplace harm.

The virus that causes COVID-19 is a "new hazard" as well as a "physically harmful" "agent." Merriam-Webster's Collegiate Dictionary 572 (11th ed. 2005) (defining "hazard" as a "source of danger"); id., at 24 (defining "agent" as a "chemically, physically, or biologically active principle"); id., at 1397 (defining "virus" as "the causative agent of an infectious disease").

The virus also poses a "grave danger" to millions of employees. As of the time OSHA promulgated its rule, more than 725,000 Americans had died of COVID-19 and millions more had been hospitalized. Since then, the disease has continued to work its tragic toll. In the last week alone, it has caused, or helped to cause, more than 11,000 new deaths. And because the disease spreads in shared indoor spaces, it presents heightened dangers in most workplaces.

Finally, the Standard is "necessary" to address the danger of COVID-19. OSHA based its rule, requiring either testing and masking or vaccination, on a host of studies and government reports showing why those measures were of unparalleled use in limiting the threat of COVID-19 in most workplaces. The agency showed, in meticulous detail, that close contact between infected and uninfected individuals spreads the disease; that "[t]he science of transmission does not vary by industry or by type of workplace"; that testing, mask wearing, and vaccination are highly effective—indeed, essential—tools for reducing the risk of transmission, hospitalization, and death; and that unvaccinated employees of all ages face a substantially increased risk from COVID-19 as compared to their vaccinated peers. In short, OSHA showed that no lesser policy would prevent as much death and injury from COVID-19 as the Standard would.

… OSHA employs, in both its enforcement and health divisions, numerous scientists, doctors, and other experts in public health, especially as it relates to work environments. Their decisions, we have explained, should stand so long as they are supported by "such relevant evidence as a reasonable mind might accept as adequate to support a conclusion." *American Textile Mfrs. Institute, Inc. v. Donovan* (1981) [quotation omitted]. Given the extensive evidence in the record supporting OSHA's determinations about the risk of COVID-19 and the efficacy of masking, testing, and vaccination, a court could not conclude that the Standard fails substantial-evidence review.

[The] majority claims that the Act does not "plainly authorize[]" the Standard because it gives OSHA the power to "set workplace safety standards" and COVID-19 exists both inside and outside the workplace. In other words, the Court argues that OSHA cannot keep workplaces safe from COVID-19 because the agency (as it readily acknowledges) has no power to address the disease outside the work setting.

But nothing in the Act's text supports the majority's limitation on OSHA's regulatory authority. Of course, the majority is correct that OSHA is not a roving public health regulator: It has power only to protect employees from workplace hazards. But as just explained, that is exactly what the Standard does. And the Act requires nothing more: Contra the majority, it is indifferent to whether a hazard in the workplace is also found elsewhere. The statute generally charges OSHA with "assur[ing] so far as possible ... safe and healthful working conditions." 29 U.S.C. § 651(b). That provision authorizes regulation to protect employees from all hazards present in the workplace—or, at least, all hazards in part created by conditions there. It does not matter whether those hazards also exist beyond the workplace walls. The same is true of the provision at issue here demanding the issuance of temporary emergency standards. Once again, that provision kicks in when employees are exposed in the workplace to "new hazards" or "substances or agents" determined to be "physically harmful." § 655(c)(1). The statute does not require that employees are exposed to those dangers only while on the workplace clock. And that should settle the matter. [Today, the majority] impose[s] a limit found no place in the governing statute.

Consistent with Congress's directives, OSHA has long regulated risks that arise both inside and outside of the workplace. For example, OSHA has issued, and applied to nearly all workplaces, rules combating risks of fire, faulty electrical installations, and inadequate emergency exits— even though the dangers prevented by those rules arise not only in workplaces but in many physical facilities (e.g., stadiums, schools, hotels, even homes). Similarly, OSHA has regulated to reduce risks from excessive noise and unsafe drinking water—again, risks hardly confined to the workplace. A biological hazard—here, the virus causing COVID-19—is no different. Indeed, Congress just last year made this clear. It appropriated $100 million for OSHA "to carry out COVID-19 related worker protection activities" in work environments of all kinds. That legislation refutes the majority's view that workplace exposure to COVID-19 is somehow not a workplace hazard. Congress knew—and Congress said —that OSHA's responsibility to mitigate the harms of COVID-19 in the typical workplace do not diminish just because the disease also endangers people in other settings.

That is especially so because—as OSHA amply established — COVID-19 poses special risks in most workplaces, across the country and across industries. The majority ignores these findings, but they provide more-than-ample support for the Standard. OSHA determined that the virus causing COVID-19 is "readily transmissible in workplaces because they are areas where multiple people come into contact with one another, often for extended periods of time." In other words, COVID-19 spreads more widely in workplaces than in other venues because more people spend more time together there. And critically, employees usually have little or no control in those settings. "[D]uring the workday," OSHA explained, "workers may have little ability to limit contact with coworkers, clients, members of the public, patients, and others, any one of whom could represent a source of exposure to" the virus. The agency backed up its conclusions with hundreds of reports of workplace COVID-19 outbreaks—not just in cheek-by-jowl settings like factory assembly lines, but in retail stores, restaurants, medical facilities, construction areas, and standard offices. But still, OSHA took care to tailor the Standard. Where it could exempt work settings without exposing employees to grave danger, it did so. In sum, the agency did just what the Act told it to: It protected employees from a grave danger posed by a new virus as and where needed, and went no further. The majority, in overturning that action, substitutes judicial diktat for reasoned policymaking.

The result of its ruling is squarely at odds with the statutory scheme. As shown earlier, the Act's explicit terms authorize the Standard. Once again, OSHA must issue an emergency standard in response to new hazards in the workplace that expose employees to "grave danger." The entire point of that provision is to enable OSHA to deal with emergencies—to put into effect the new measures needed to cope with new workplace conditions. The enacting Congress of course did not tell the agency to issue this Standard in response to this COVID-19 pandemic—because that Congress could not predict the future. But that Congress did indeed want OSHA to have the tools needed to confront emerging dangers (including contagious diseases) in the workplace. We know that, first and foremost, from the breadth of the authority Congress granted to OSHA. And we know that because of how OSHA has used that authority from the statute's beginnings—in ways not dissimilar to the action here. OSHA has often issued rules applying to all or nearly all workplaces in the Nation, affecting at once many tens of millions of employees. It has previously regulated infectious disease, including by facilitating vaccinations. And it has in other contexts required medical examinations and face coverings for employees. In line with those prior actions, the Standard here requires employers to ensure testing and masking if they do not demand vaccination. Nothing about that measure is so out-of-the-ordinary as to demand a judicially created exception from Congress's command that OSHA protect employees from grave workplace harms.

If OSHA's Standard is far-reaching—applying to many millions of American workers—it no more than reflects the scope of the crisis. The Standard responds to a workplace health emergency unprecedented in the agency's history: an infectious disease that has already killed hundreds of thousands and sickened millions; that is most easily transmitted in the shared indoor spaces that are the hallmark of American working life; and that spreads mostly without regard to differences in occupation or industry. Over the past two years, COVID-19 has affected—indeed, transformed—virtually every workforce and workplace in the Nation. Employers and employees alike have recognized and responded to the special risks of transmission in work environments. It is perverse, given these circumstances, to read the Act's grant of emergency powers in the way the majority does—as constraining OSHA from addressing one of the gravest workplace hazards in the agency's history. The Standard protects untold numbers of employees from a danger especially prevalent in workplace conditions. It lies at the core of OSHA's authority. It is part of what the agency was built for.

[The dispute concerns] a single, simple question: Who decides how much protection, and of what kind, American workers need from COVID-19? An agency with expertise in workplace health and safety, acting as Congress and the President authorized? Or a court, lacking any knowledge of how to safeguard workplaces, and insulated from responsibility for any damage it causes?

Here, an agency charged by Congress with safeguarding employees from workplace dangers has decided that action is needed. The agency has thoroughly evaluated the risks that the disease poses to workers across all sectors of the economy. It has considered the extent to which various policies will mitigate those risks, and the costs those policies will entail. It has landed on an approach that encourages vaccination, but allows employers to use masking and testing instead. It has meticulously explained why it has reached its conclusions. And in doing all this, it has acted within the four corners of its statutory authorization—or actually here, its statutory mandate. OSHA, that is, has responded in the way necessary to alleviate the "grave danger" that workplace exposure to the "new hazard[]" of COVID-19 poses to employees across the Nation. The agency's Standard is informed by a half century of experience and expertise in handling workplace health and safety issues. The Standard also has the virtue of political accountability, for OSHA is responsible to the President, and the President is responsible to—and can be held to account by—the American public.

And then, there is this Court. Its Members are elected by, and accountable to, no one. And we "lack[] the background, competence, and expertise to assess" workplace health and safety issues. *South Bay United Pentecostal Church* (2020) (opinion of ROBERTS, C. J.). When we are wise, we know enough to defer on matters like this one. When we are wise, we know not to displace the judgments of experts, acting within the sphere Congress marked out and under Presidential control, to deal with emergency conditions. Today, we are not wise. In the face of a still-raging pandemic, this Court tells the agency charged with protecting worker safety that it may not do so in all the workplaces needed. As disease and death continue to mount, this Court tells the agency that it cannot respond in the most effective way possible. Without legal basis, the Court usurps a decision that rightfully belongs to others. It undercuts the capacity of the responsible federal officials, acting well within the scope of their authority, to protect American workers from grave danger.

**NOTES AND QUESTIONS**

1. The so-called "major questions" doctrine can be traced all the way back to 2000 and a case called *FDA v. Brown & Williamson Tobacco Corp.*, 529 U.S. 120, in which the Court concluded that there are "extraordinary cases" in which the "history and the breadth of the authority that [the agency] has asserted," and the "economic and political significance" of the agency's assertion, provide a "reason to hesitate before concluding that Congress" meant to confer upon the agency the authority it claims. In that case, the Court ruled that Congress had not given the Food & Drug Administration the authority to regulate tobacco products as either "drugs" or "devices."

2. On the last day of the 2021-2022 term, the Court decided *West Virginia v. Environmental Protection Agency*, 597 U.S. ___ (2022). There, the Court held that the Clean Air Act did not "empowers [the agency] to devise carbon emissions caps based on a generation shifting approach." While this may appear to have been a technical point, Justice Kagan, in her dissenting opinion, noted that the Court had essentially stripped the EPA of "the power Congress gave it to respond" to the effects of global climate change.

3. The question that remains after West Virginia is which grants of congressional authority should not be deemed sufficiently clear to allow an agency to address what the Court has deemed a "major question." Writing shortly after the release of the decision, Kristin E. Hickman suggested that judicial reliance on the doctrine will depend upon "(1) "the 'history and the breadth of the authority that [the agency] has asserted,'" (2) "the 'economic and political significance' of that assertion," and (3) the extent to which the agency is relying on "'modest words,' 'vague terms,' or 'subtle device[s]'" rather than more direct delegations from Congress." "Notice & Comment: Thoughts on *West Virginia v. EPA*," Yale J. on Regulation, July 5, 2022. In other words, the major questions doctrine will apply "to curtail agency discretion when an agency stretches the boundaries of statutory interpretation to claim new authority to address big problems that weren't obviously under the agency's jurisdiction previously." Id. Of course, it remains unclear by what standards court will assess the "economic and political significance" of a particular agency action.

4. Like the delegation doctrine, you'll likely explore the major questions doctrine more thoroughly when you take a course in administrative law.

**Add after Note 3 on page 308:**

4. In the next case, the Court looks at state efforts to involve the President in litigation.

### Trump v. Vance
### 591 U.S. ___ (2020)

Chief Justice ROBERTS delivered the opinion of the Court.

[So] far as we and the parties can tell[, this case involves] the first state criminal subpoena directed to a President. The President contends that the subpoena is unenforceable. We granted certiorari to decide whether Article II and the Supremacy Clause categorically preclude, or require a heightened standard for, the issuance of a state criminal subpoena to a sitting President.

I

In the summer of 2018, the New York County District Attorney's Office opened an investigation into what it opaquely describes as "business transactions involving multiple individuals whose conduct may have violated state law." A year later, the office—acting on behalf of a grand jury—served a subpoena duces tecum (essentially a request to produce evidence) on Mazars USA, LLP, the personal accounting firm of President Donald J. Trump. The subpoena directed Mazars to produce financial records relating to the President and business organizations affiliated with him, including "[t]ax returns and related schedules," from "2011 to the present."

The President, acting in his personal capacity, sued the district attorney and Mazars in Federal District Court to enjoin enforcement of the subpoena. He argued that, under Article II and the Supremacy Clause, a sitting President enjoys absolute immunity from state criminal process. He asked the court to issue a "declaratory judgment that the subpoena is invalid and unenforceable while the President is in office" and to permanently enjoin the district attorney "from taking any action to enforce the subpoena." Mazars, concluding that the dispute was between the President and the district attorney, took no position on the legal issues raised by the President.

The District Court ... ruled that the President was not entitled to injunctive relief. [T]he Court of Appeals concluded that "presidential immunity does not bar the enforcement of a state grand jury subpoena directing a third party to produce non-privileged material, even when the subject matter under investigation pertains to the President." ...

We granted certiorari.

III

[We] are confronted for the first time with a subpoena issued to the President by a local grand jury operating under the supervision of a state court.

In the President's view, that distinction makes all the difference. He argues that the Supremacy Clause gives a sitting President absolute immunity from state criminal subpoenas because compliance with those subpoenas would categorically impair a President's performance of his Article II functions. The Solicitor General, arguing on behalf of the United States, agrees with much of the President's reasoning but does not commit to his bottom line. Instead, the Solicitor General urges us to resolve this case by holding that a state grand jury subpoena for a sitting President's personal records must, at the very least, "satisfy a heightened standard of need," which the Solicitor General contends was not met here.

We begin with the question of absolute immunity. No one doubts that Article II guarantees the independence of the Executive Branch. As the head of that branch, the President "occupies a unique position in the constitutional scheme." *Nixon v. Fitzgerald* (1982). His duties, which range from faithfully executing the laws to commanding the Armed Forces, are of unrivaled gravity and breadth. Quite appropriately, those duties come with protections that safeguard the President's ability to perform his vital functions.

In addition, the Constitution guarantees "the entire independence of the General Government from any control by the respective States." *Farmers and Mechanics Sav. Bank of Minneapolis v. Minnesota* (1914). As we have often repeated, "States have no power ... to retard, impede, burden, or in any manner control the operations of the constitutional laws enacted by Congress." *McCullough v. Maryland* (1819). It follows that States also lack the power to impede the President's execution of those laws.

[The President] argues that state criminal subpoenas pose a unique threat of impairment [of federal executive functioning] and thus demand greater protection. To be clear, the President does not contend here that this subpoena, in particular, is impermissibly burdensome. Instead he makes a categorical argument about the burdens generally associated with state criminal subpoenas, focusing on three: diversion, stigma, and harassment. We address each in turn.

The President's primary contention, which the Solicitor General supports, is that complying with state criminal subpoenas would necessarily divert the Chief Executive from his duties. He grounds that concern in Nixon v. Fitzgerald, which recognized a President's "absolute immunity from damages liability predicated on his official acts." In explaining the basis for that immunity, this Court observed that the prospect of such liability could "distract a President from his public duties, to the detriment of not only the President and his office but also the Nation that the Presidency was designed to serve." Id. The President contends that the diversion occasioned by a state criminal subpoena imposes an equally intolerable burden on a President's ability to perform his Article II functions.

But Fitzgerald did not hold that distraction was sufficient to confer absolute immunity. We instead drew a careful analogy to the common law absolute immunity of judges and prosecutors, concluding that a President, like those officials, must "deal fearlessly and impartially with the duties of his office"—not be made "unduly cautious in the discharge of [those] duties" by the prospect of civil liability for official acts. Id. (internal quotation marks omitted). Indeed, we expressly rejected immunity based on distraction alone 15 years later in Clinton v. Jones. There, President Clinton argued that the risk of being "distracted by the need to participate in litigation" entitled a sitting President to absolute immunity from civil liability, not just for official acts, as in Fitzgerald, but for private conduct as well. We disagreed with that rationale, explaining that the "dominant concern" in Fitzgerald was not mere distraction but the distortion of the Executive's "decisionmaking process" with respect to official acts that would stem from "worry as to the possibility of damages." The Court recognized that Presidents constantly face myriad demands on their attention, "some private, some political, and some as a result of official duty." Id. But, the Court concluded, "[w]hile such distractions may be vexing to those subjected to them, they do not ordinarily implicate constitutional ... concerns." Id.

The same is true of criminal subpoenas. Just as a "properly managed" civil suit is generally "unlikely to occupy any substantial amount of" a President's time or attention, id., two centuries of experience confirm that a properly tailored criminal subpoena will not normally hamper the performance of the President's constitutional duties. If anything, we expect that in the mine run of cases, where a President is subpoenaed during a proceeding targeting someone else, as Jefferson was, the burden on a President will ordinarily be lighter than the burden of defending against a civil suit.

The President, however, believes the district attorney is investigating him and his businesses. In such a situation, he contends, the "toll that criminal process ... exacts from the President is even heavier" than the distraction at issue in Fitzgerald and Clinton, because "criminal litigation" poses unique burdens on the President's time and will generate a "considerable if not overwhelming degree of mental preoccupation."

But the President is not seeking immunity from the diversion occasioned by the prospect of future criminal liability. Instead he concedes—consistent with the position of the Department of Justice—that state grand juries are free to investigate a sitting President with an eye toward charging him after the completion of his term. The President's objection therefore must be limited to the additional distraction caused by the subpoena itself. But that argument runs up against the 200 years of precedent establishing that Presidents, and their official communications, are subject to judicial process, even when the President is under investigation.

The President next claims that the stigma of being subpoenaed will undermine his leadership at home and abroad. Notably, the Solicitor General does not endorse this argument, perhaps because we have twice denied absolute immunity claims by Presidents in cases involving allegations of serious misconduct. But even if a tarnished reputation were a cognizable impairment, there is nothing inherently stigmatizing about a President performing "the citizen's normal duty of ... furnishing information relevant" to a criminal investigation. *Branzburg v. Hayes* (1972). Nor can we accept that the risk of association with persons or activities under criminal investigation can absolve a President of such an important public duty. Prior Presidents have weathered these associations in federal cases, and there is no reason to think any attendant notoriety is necessarily greater in state court proceedings.

To be sure, the consequences for a President's public standing will likely increase if he is the one under investigation. But, again, the President concedes that such investigations are permitted under Article II and the Supremacy Clause, and receipt of a subpoena would not seem to categorically magnify the harm to the President's reputation.

Additionally, while the current suit has cast the Mazars subpoena into the spotlight, longstanding rules of grand jury secrecy aim to prevent the very stigma the President anticipates. Of course, disclosure restrictions are not perfect. But those who make unauthorized disclosures regarding a grand jury subpoena do so at their peril.

Finally, the President and the Solicitor General warn that subjecting Presidents to state criminal subpoenas will make them "easily identifiable target[s]" for harassment. Fitzgerald. But we rejected a nearly identical argument in Clinton, where then-President Clinton argued that permitting civil liability for unofficial acts would "generate a large volume of politically motivated harassing and frivolous litigation." The President and the Solicitor General nevertheless argue that state criminal subpoenas pose a heightened risk and could undermine the President's ability to "deal fearlessly and impartially" with the States. Fitzgerald (internal quotation marks omitted). They caution that, while federal prosecutors are accountable to and removable by the President, the 2,300 district attorneys in this country are responsive to local constituencies, local interests, and local prejudices, and might "use criminal process to register their dissatisfaction with" the President. What is more, we are told, the state courts supervising local grand juries may not exhibit the same respect that federal courts show to the President as a coordinate branch of Government.

We recognize, as does the district attorney, that harassing subpoenas could, under certain circumstances, threaten the independence or effectiveness of the Executive. Even so, in Clinton we found that the risk of harassment was not "serious" because federal courts have the tools to deter and, where necessary, dismiss vexatious civil suits. And, while we cannot ignore the possibility that state prosecutors may have political motivations, here again the law already seeks to protect against the predicted abuse.

First, grand juries are prohibited from engaging in "arbitrary fishing expeditions" and initiating investigations "out of malice or an intent to harass." *United States v. R. Enterprises, Inc.* (1991). These protections, as the district attorney himself puts it, "apply with special force to a President, in light of the office's unique position as the head of the Executive Branch." And, in the event of such harassment, a President would be entitled to the protection of federal courts. The policy against federal interference in state criminal proceedings, while strong, allows "intervention in those cases where the District Court properly finds that the state proceeding is motivated by a desire to harass or is conducted in bad faith." *Huffman v. Pursue, Ltd.* (1975).

Second, ... our holding does not allow States to "run roughshod over the functioning of [the Executive B]ranch." The Supremacy Clause prohibits state judges and prosecutors from interfering with a President's official duties. Any effort to manipulate a President's policy decisions or to "retaliat[e]" against a President for official acts through issuance of a subpoena would thus be an unconstitutional attempt to "influence" a superior sovereign "exempt" from such obstacles. ...

Given these safeguards and the Court's precedents, we cannot conclude that absolute immunity is necessary or appropriate under Article II or the Supremacy Clause. ... On that point the Court is unanimous.

We next consider whether a state grand jury subpoena seeking a President's private papers must satisfy a heightened need standard. The Solicitor General would require a threshold showing that the evidence sought is "critical" for "specific charging decisions" and that the subpoena is a "last resort," meaning the evidence is "not available from any other source" and is needed "now, rather than at the end of the President's term." ...

We disagree, for three reasons. First, such a heightened standard would extend protection designed for official documents to the President's private papers. As the Solicitor General and Justice ALITO acknowledge, their proposed test is derived from executive privilege cases that trace back to Burr. Marshall explained that if Jefferson invoked presidential privilege over executive communications, the court would not "proceed against the president as against an ordinary individual" but would instead require an affidavit from the defense that "would clearly show the paper to be essential to the justice of the case." Burr. The Solicitor General and Justice ALITO would have us apply a similar standard to a President's personal papers. But this argument does not account for the relevant passage from Burr : "If there be a paper in the possession of the executive, which is not of an official nature, he must stand, as respects that paper, in nearly the same situation with any other individual." Id. (emphasis added). And it is only "nearly"—and not "entirely"—because the President retains the right to assert privilege over documents that, while ostensibly private, "partake of the character of an official paper." Id.

Second, neither the Solicitor General nor Justice ALITO has established that heightened protection against state subpoenas is necessary for the Executive to fulfill his Article II functions. Beyond the risk of harassment, which we addressed above, the only justification they offer for the heightened standard is protecting Presidents from "unwarranted burdens." In effect, they argue that even if federal subpoenas to a President are warranted whenever evidence is material, state subpoenas are warranted "only when [the] evidence is essential." But that double standard has no basis in law. For if the state subpoena is not issued to manipulate, the documents themselves are not protected, and the Executive is not impaired, then nothing in Article II or the Supremacy Clause supports holding state subpoenas to a higher standard than their federal counterparts.

Finally, in the absence of a need to protect the Executive, the public interest in fair and effective law enforcement cuts in favor of comprehensive access to evidence. Requiring a state grand jury to meet a heightened standard of need would hobble the grand jury's ability to acquire "all information that might possibly bear on its investigation." R. Enterprises, Inc. And, even assuming the evidence withheld under that standard were preserved until the conclusion of a President's term, in the interim the State would be deprived of investigative leads that the evidence might yield, allowing memories to fade and documents to disappear. This could frustrate the identification, investigation, and indictment of third parties (for whom applicable statutes of limitations might lapse). More troubling, it could prejudice the innocent by depriving the grand jury of exculpatory evidence.

Rejecting a heightened need standard does not leave Presidents with "no real protection." (opinion of ALITO, J.). To start, a President may avail himself of the same protections available to every other citizen. These include the right to challenge the subpoena on any grounds permitted by state law, which usually include bad faith and undue burden or breadth. ...

Furthermore, although the Constitution does not entitle the Executive to absolute immunity or a heightened standard, he is not "relegate[d]" only to the challenges available to private citizens. (opinion of ALITO, J.). A President can raise subpoena-specific constitutional challenges, in either a state or federal forum. As previously noted, he can challenge the subpoena as an attempt to influence the performance of his official duties, in violation of the Supremacy Clause. ...

In addition, the Executive can—as the district attorney concedes—argue that compliance with a particular subpoena would impede his constitutional duties. Incidental to the functions confided in Article II is "the power to perform them, without obstruction or impediment." 3 J. Story, Commentaries on the Constitution of the United States § 1563, pp. 418–419 (1833). As a result, "once the President sets forth and explains a conflict between judicial proceeding and public duties," or shows that an order or subpoena would "significantly interfere with his efforts to carry out" those duties, "the matter changes." Clinton (opinion of BREYER, J.). At that point, a court should use its inherent authority to quash or modify the subpoena, if necessary to ensure that such "interference with the President's duties would not occur." Id. (opinion of the Court).

* * *

[N]o citizen, not even the President, is categorically above the common duty to produce evidence when called upon in a criminal proceeding. We reaffirm that principle today and hold that the President is neither absolutely immune from state criminal subpoenas seeking his private papers nor entitled to a heightened standard of need. ...

The arguments presented here and in the Court of Appeals were limited to absolute immunity and heightened need. The Court of Appeals, however, has directed that the case be returned to the District Court, where the President may raise further arguments as appropriate.

We affirm the judgment of the Court of Appeals and remand the case for further proceedings consistent with this opinion.

*It is so ordered.*

[Concurring opinion of Justice KAVANAUGH omitted.]

[Dissenting opinion of Justice THOMAS omitted.]

Justice ALITO, dissenting.

[A] subpoena like the one now before us should not be enforced unless it meets a test that takes into account the need to prevent interference with a President's discharge of the responsibilities of the office. I agree with the Court that not all such subpoenas should be barred. There may be situations in which there is an urgent and critical need for the subpoenaed information. [I]n a case like the one at hand, a subpoena should not be allowed unless a heightened standard is met.

[We] should not treat this subpoena like an ordinary grand jury subpoena and should not relegate a President to the meager defenses that are available when an ordinary grand jury subpoena is challenged. …

The Presidency deserves greater protection. Thus, in a case like this one, a prosecutor should be required (1) to provide at least a general description of the possible offenses that are under investigation, (2) to outline how the subpoenaed records relate to those offenses, and (3) to explain why it is important that the records be produced and why it is necessary for production to occur while the President is still in office.

In the present case, the district attorney made a brief proffer, but important questions were left hanging. It would not be unduly burdensome to insist on answers before enforcing the subpoena.

## NOTES AND QUESTIONS

1. Does the result in this case follow inevitably from Nixon and Clinton? On what basis did President Trump seek a different result here?

2. In many ways, this is a simple case: because the President sought to end the state prosecution based upon some kind of absolute immunity from such action meant that the Court would need to address only that question—and note the way in which Chief Justice Roberts, writing for the majority, makes perfectly clear what the Court is deciding, and what it is not. Such minimalism, as noted elsewhere, has become a hallmark of his jurisprudence.

3. What arguments might the President make going forward—and what arguments might future Presidents make in similar cases? If legal rules – of any kind – create incentives and disincentives for individuals to take or not take certain actions, what effect might this decision have on presidential candidate selection in the future?

# Chapter 5
# The State Action Doctrine

### Add after Note 2 on page 389:

3.  No state action case that you have read thus far has been overruled. There are different ways in which you might organize the cases — chronologically, as presented here, or based on the *kind* of state action asserted. Think about how he Court categorized the alleged state action in the next case.

### Manhattan Community Access Corporation v. Halleck
### 587 U.S. ___ (2019)

Justice KAVANAUGH delivered the opinion of the Court.

The Free Speech Clause of the First Amendment constrains governmental actors and protects private actors. To draw the line between governmental and private, this Court applies what is known as the state-action doctrine. Under that doctrine, as relevant here, a private entity may be considered a state actor when it exercises a function "traditionally exclusively reserved to the State." *Jackson v. Metropolitan Edison Co.* (1974).

This state-action case concerns the public access channels on Time Warner's cable system in Manhattan. Public access channels are available for private citizens to use. The public access channels on Time Warner's cable system in Manhattan are operated by a private nonprofit corporation known as MNN. The question here is whether MNN—even though it is a private entity—nonetheless is a state actor when it operates the public access channels. In other words, is operation of public access channels on a cable system a traditional, exclusive public function? If so, then the First Amendment would restrict MNN's exercise of editorial discretion over the speech and speakers on the public access channels.

Under the state-action doctrine as it has been articulated and applied by our precedents, ... MNN therefore is not subject to First Amendment constraints on its editorial discretion. We reverse in relevant part the judgment of the Second Circuit, and we remand the case for further proceedings consistent with this opinion.

I

The New York State Public Service Commission regulates cable franchising in New York State and requires cable operators in the State to set aside channels on their cable systems for public access. State law requires that use of the public access channels be free of charge and first-come, first-served. Under state law, the cable operator operates the public access channels unless the local government in the area chooses to itself operate the channels or designates a private entity to operate the channels.

Time Warner (now known as Charter) operates a cable system in Manhattan. Under state law, Time Warner must set aside some channels on its cable system for public access. New York City (the City) has designated a private nonprofit corporation named Manhattan Neighborhood Network, commonly referred to as MNN, to operate Time Warner's public access channels in Manhattan. This case involves a complaint against MNN regarding its management of the public access channels.

Because this case comes to us on a motion to dismiss, we accept the allegations in the complaint as true.

DeeDee Halleck and Jesus Papoleto Melendez produced public access programming in Manhattan. They made a film about MNN's alleged neglect of the East Harlem community. Halleck submitted the film to MNN for airing on MNN's public access channels, and MNN later televised the film. Afterwards, MNN fielded multiple complaints about the film's content. In response, MNN temporarily suspended Halleck from using the public access channels.

Halleck and Melendez soon became embroiled in another dispute with MNN staff. In the wake of that dispute, MNN ultimately suspended Halleck and Melendez from all MNN services and facilities.

Halleck and Melendez then sued MNN, among other parties, in Federal District Court. The two producers claimed that MNN violated their First Amendment free-speech rights when MNN restricted their access to the public access channels because of the content of their film.

MNN moved to dismiss the producers' First Amendment claim on the ground that MNN is not a state actor and therefore is not subject to First Amendment restrictions on its editorial discretion. The District Court agreed ... The Second Circuit reversed in relevant part[, stating] that the public access channels in Manhattan are a public forum for purposes of the First Amendment. Reasoning that "public forums are usually operated by governments," the court concluded that MNN is a state actor subject to First Amendment constraints. ...

We granted certiorari to resolve disagreement among the Courts of Appeals on the question whether private operators of public access cable channels are state actors subject to the First Amendment.

## II

[T]he Fourteenth Amendment makes the First Amendment's Free Speech Clause applicable against the States. [T]he Free Speech Clause prohibits only *governmental* abridgment of speech. The Free Speech Clause does not prohibit *private* abridgment of speech.

[T]his Court's state-action doctrine distinguishes the government from individuals and private entities. See *Brentwood Academy v. Tennessee Secondary School Athletic Assn.* (2001). ...

Here, the producers claim that MNN, a private entity, restricted their access to MNN's public access channels because of the content of the producers' film. The producers have advanced a First Amendment claim against MNN. The threshold problem with that First Amendment claim is a fundamental one: MNN is a private entity.

Relying on this Court's state-action precedents, the producers assert that MNN is nonetheless a state actor subject to First Amendment constraints on its editorial discretion. Under this Court's cases, a private entity can qualify as a state actor ... when the private entity performs a traditional, exclusive public function, see, *e.g.*, *Jackson*. [Here, the] producers contend that MNN exercises a traditional, exclusive public function when it operates the public access channels on Time Warner's cable system in Manhattan. We disagree.

**A**

[A] private entity may qualify as a state actor when it exercises "powers traditionally exclusively reserved to the State." *Jackson*. It is not enough that the federal, state, or local government exercised the function in the past, or still does. And it is not enough that the function serves the public good or the public interest in some way. Rather, to qualify as a traditional, exclusive public function within the meaning of our state-action precedents, the government must have traditionally *and* exclusively performed the function.

The Court has stressed that "very few" functions fall into that category. *Flagg Bros., Inc. v. Brooks* (1978). Under the Court's cases, those functions include, for example, running elections and operating a company town. The Court has ruled that a variety of functions do not fall into that category, including, for example: running sports associations and leagues, administering insurance payments, operating nursing homes, providing special education, representing indigent criminal defendants, resolving private disputes, and supplying electricity.

The relevant function in this case is operation of public access channels on a cable system. That function has not traditionally and exclusively been performed by government.

Since the 1970s, when public access channels became a regular feature on cable systems, a variety of private and public actors have operated public access channels, including: private cable operators; private nonprofit organizations; municipalities; and other public and private community organizations such as churches, schools, and libraries.

The history of public access channels in Manhattan further illustrates the point. In 1971, public access channels first started operating in Manhattan. Those early Manhattan public access channels were operated in large part by private cable operators, with some help from private nonprofit organizations. Those private cable operators continued to operate the public access channels until the early 1990s, when MNN (also a private entity) began to operate the public access channels.

In short, operating public access channels on a cable system is not a traditional, exclusive public function within the meaning of this Court's cases.

**B**

To avoid that conclusion, the producers widen the lens and contend that the relevant function here is not simply the operation of public access channels on a cable system, but rather is more generally the operation of a public forum for speech. And according to the producers, operation of a public forum for speech is a traditional, exclusive public function.

That analysis mistakenly ignores the threshold state-action question. When the government provides a forum for speech (known as a public forum), the government may be constrained by the First Amendment, meaning that the government ordinarily may not exclude speech or speakers from the forum on the basis of viewpoint, or sometimes even on the basis of content.

By contrast, when a private entity provides a forum for speech, the private entity is not ordinarily constrained by the First Amendment because the private entity is not a state actor. The private entity may thus exercise editorial discretion over the speech and speakers in the forum. This Court so ruled in its 1976 decision in *Hudgens* v. *NLRB*. There, the Court held that a shopping center owner is not a state actor subject to First Amendment requirements such as the public forum doctrine.

The *Hudgens* decision reflects a commonsense principle: Providing some kind of forum for speech is not an activity that only governmental entities have traditionally performed. Therefore, a private entity who provides a forum for speech is not transformed by that fact alone into a state actor. After all, private property owners and private lessees often open their property for speech. Grocery stores put up community bulletin boards. Comedy clubs host open mic nights. ...

In short, merely hosting speech by others is not a traditional, exclusive public function and does not alone transform private entities into state actors subject to First Amendment constraints.

If the rule were otherwise, all private property owners and private lessees who open their property for speech would be subject to First Amendment constraints and would lose the ability to exercise what they deem to be appropriate editorial discretion within that open forum. Private property owners and private lessees would face the unappetizing choice of allowing all comers or closing the platform altogether. ... The Constitution does not disable private property owners and private lessees from exercising editorial discretion over speech and speakers on their property.

C

[T]he producers retort that this case differs from *Hudgens* because New York City has designated MNN to operate the public access channels on Time Warner's cable system, and because New York State heavily regulates MNN with respect to the public access channels. Under this Court's cases, however, those facts do not establish that MNN is a state actor.

New York City's designation of MNN to operate the public access channels is analogous to a government license, a government contract, or a government-granted monopoly. But as the Court has long held, the fact that the government licenses, contracts with, or grants a monopoly to a private entity does not convert the private entity into a state actor—unless the private entity is performing a traditional, exclusive public function.

Numerous private entities in America obtain government licenses, government contracts, or government-granted monopolies. If those facts sufficed to transform a private entity into a state actor, a large swath of private entities in America would suddenly be turned into state actors and be subject to a variety of constitutional constraints on their activities. ...

So, too, New York State's extensive regulation of MNN's operation of the public access channels does not make MNN a state actor. Under the State's regulations, air time on the public access channels must be free, and programming must be aired on a first-come, first-served basis. Those regulations restrict MNN's editorial discretion and in effect require MNN to operate almost like a common carrier. But under this Court's cases, those restrictions do not render MNN a state actor.

In *Jackson v. Metropolitan Edison Co.*, the leading case on point, the Court stated that the "fact that a business is subject to state regulation does not by itself convert its action into that of the State." In that case, the Court held that "a heavily regulated, privately owned utility, enjoying at least a partial monopoly in the providing of electrical service within its territory," was not a state actor. The Court explained that the "mere existence" of a "regulatory scheme"—even if "extensive and detailed"—did not render the utility a state actor. Nor did it matter whether the State had authorized the utility to provide electric service to the community, or whether the utility was the only entity providing electric service to much of that community.

This case closely parallels *Jackson*. Like the electric utility in *Jackson*, MNN is "a heavily regulated, privately owned" entity. As in *Jackson*, the regulations do not transform the regulated private entity into a state actor.

Put simply, being regulated by the State does not make one a state actor. As the Court's cases have explained, the "being heavily regulated makes you a state actor" theory of state action is entirely circular and would significantly endanger individual liberty and private enterprise. The theory would be especially problematic in the speech context, because it could eviscerate certain private entities' rights to exercise editorial control over speech and speakers on their properties or platforms. ...

In sum, we conclude that MNN is not subject to First Amendment constraints on how it exercises its editorial discretion with respect to the public access channels. To be sure, MNN is subject to state-law constraints on its editorial discretion (assuming those state laws do not violate a federal statute or the Constitution). If MNN violates those state laws, or violates any applicable contracts, MNN could perhaps face state-law sanctions or liability of some kind. We of course take no position on any potential state-law questions. We simply conclude that MNN, as a private actor, is not subject to First Amendment constraints on how it exercises editorial discretion over the speech and speakers on its public access channels.

... We reverse in relevant part the judgment of the Second Circuit, and we remand the case for further proceedings consistent with this opinion.

*It is so ordered.*

Justice SOTOMAYOR, with whom Justice GINSBURG, Justice BREYER, and Justice KAGAN join, dissenting.

The majority focuses on Jackson v. Metropolitan Edison Co. (1974), which is a paradigmatic example of a line of cases that reject § 1983 liability for private actors that simply operate against a regulatory backdrop. *Jackson* emphasized that the "fact that a business is subject to state regulation does not by itself convert its action into that of the State." Thus, the fact that a utility company entered the marketplace did not make it a state actor, even if it was highly regulated. The same rule holds, of course, for private comedy clubs and grocery stores.

The *Jackson* line of cases is inapposite here. MNN is not a private entity that simply ventured into the marketplace. It occupies its role because it was asked to do so by the City, which secured the public-access channels in exchange for giving up public rights of way, opened those channels up (as required by the State) as a public forum, and then deputized MNN to administer them. That distinguishes MNN from a private entity that simply sets up shop against a regulatory backdrop. To say that MNN is nothing more than a private organization regulated by the government is like saying that a waiter at a restaurant is an independent food seller who just happens to be highly regulated by the restaurant's owners.

[While the] City, of course, had no constitutional obligation to award a cable franchise or to operate public-access channels[,] once [it] did award a cable franchise, New York law required the City to obtain public-access channels, and to open them up as a public forum. That is when the City's obligation to act in accordance with the First Amendment with respect to the channels arose. That is why, when the City handed the administration of that forum off to an agent, the Constitution followed.

The majority is surely correct that "when a private entity provides a forum for speech, the private entity is not ordinarily constrained by the First Amendment." That is because the majority is not talking about *constitutional* forums—it is talking about spaces where private entities have simply invited others to come speak. A comedy club can decide to open its doors as wide as it wants, but it cannot appoint itself as a government agent. The difference is between providing a service of one's own accord and being asked by the government to administer a constitutional responsibility (indeed, here, existing to do so) on the government's behalf.

To see more clearly the difference between the cases on which the majority fixates and the present case, leave aside the majority's private comedy club. Imagine instead that a state college runs a comedy showcase each year, renting out a local theater and, pursuant to state regulations mandating open access to certain kinds of student activities, allowing students to sign up to perform on a first-come, first-served basis. After a few years, the college decides that it is tired of running the show, so it hires a performing-arts nonprofit to do the job. The nonprofit prefers humor that makes fun of a certain political party, so it allows only student acts that share its views to participate. Does the majority believe that the nonprofit is indistinguishable, for purposes of state action, from a private comedy club opened by local entrepreneurs?

I hope not. But two dangers lurk here regardless. On the one hand, if the City's decision to outsource the channels to a private entity did render the First Amendment irrelevant, there would be substantial cause to worry about the potential abuses that could follow. Can a state university evade the First Amendment by hiring a nonprofit to apportion funding to student groups? Can a city do the same by appointing a corporation to run a municipal theater? What about its parks?

On the other hand, the majority hastens ... to cabin it to the specific facts of this case. Those are prudent limitations. Even so, the majority's focus on *Jackson* still risks sowing confusion among the lower courts about how and when government outsourcing will render any abuses that follow beyond the reach of the Constitution.

In any event, there should be no confusion here. MNN is not a private entity that ventured into the marketplace and found itself subject to government regulation. It was asked to do a job by the government and compensated accordingly. If it does not want to do that job anymore, it can stop (subject, like any other entity, to its contractual obligations). But as long as MNN continues to wield the power it was given by the government, it stands in the government's shoes and must abide by the First Amendment like any other government actor.

### NOTES AND QUESTIONS

1. If anything has become clear from your study of the state action doctrine, it should be that the cases are idiosyncratic, and that the modern court continues to insist that the state action doctrine has defined boundaries. But results in state action cases depend, first and foremost, upon which case-type the court chooses as the most analogous to the one at hand.

2. Here, Justice Kavanaugh, writing for the majority, sees *Jackson* as the closest fit. But are the facts of this case as straightforward as the majority makes it out to be? Aren't there legitimate distinctions between *Jackson* and this case, as explained by Justice Sonya Sotomayor in her dissent? If so, why does Kavanaugh choose to characterize this case as more like *Jackson*? And why, for that matter, does it choose *Jackson*, and not *Brentwood Academy*, as the case most closely analogous to this one? Don't the facts here also suggest that there is some kind of inter-relationship between government and a private actor?

**3.** No state action case that you have read thus far has been overruled. Which means all of these cases are potentially available to you when you face a potential state action question. Given that statutes now prohibit the kind of discrimination at issue in the Civil Rights Cases, the actions at issue today are more likely to concern such individual rights as due process and free speech—as in *Jackson* and *Manhattan Community Access Corporation*, respectively.

**4.** There are different ways in which you might organize the cases in this section. You could arrange them chronologically, as presented in your casebook. Or, you could arrange them based upon the kind of state action asserted—remembering that the kind of state action turns on factual distinctions. Indeed, you should try not to forget that factual variations appear to play an inordinately large role in resolving particular state action issues. It is not difficult to imagine a few slight factual variations in *Manhattan Community Access Corporation* leading the court to a different result.

# Chapter 7
# Substantive Due Process

In addition to procedural due process, the Fifth and Fourteenth Amendments of the U.S. Constitution guarantee individuals *substantive* due process — that is, they guarantee the constitutional protection of certain substantive interests. Individuals cannot be deprived of these interests no matter how much process the state affords them. But this is not to say that government cannot regulate these interests — rather, as you will see, there is a doctrinal framework governing such regulation, one that should look familiar to you from your study of free speech and speech regulation in the first chapter.

We begin with a notorious substantive due process case — *Lochner v. New York* (1905), in which the Supreme Court struck down a New York labor law regulating the number of hours bakery employees could work. As you read the case, think about the test the Court applied to the regulation and the test that the dissenters would have applied, and why the Court has since abandoned the majority's approach. This is a rare instance, by the way, in which we must read and understand a case that today has only historical value, in order to appreciate the way in which the law has developed since. *Lochner* remains a constitutional touchstone, and you will see it mentioned in cases throughout this chapter.

## A. Economic Interests

### Lochner v. New York
### 198 U.S. 45 (1905)

Mr. Justice Peckham . . . delivered the opinion of the court.

The indictment, it will be seen, charges that the plaintiff in error violated . . . the labor law of the State of New York, in that he wrongfully and unlawfully required and permitted an employee working for him to work more than sixty hours in one week. . . . It is not an act merely fixing the number of hours which shall constitute a legal day's work, but an absolute prohibition upon the employer, permitting, under any circumstances, more than ten hours work to be done in his establishment. The employee may desire to earn the extra money, which would arise from his working more than the prescribed time, but this statute forbids the employer from permitting the employee to earn it.

The statute necessarily interferes with the right of contract between the employer and employees, concerning the number of hours in which the latter may labor in the bakery of the employer. The general right to make a contract in relation to his business is part of the liberty of the individual protected by the Fourteenth Amendment of the Federal Constitution. Under that provision no State can deprive any person of life, liberty or property without due process of law. The right to purchase or to sell labor is part of the liberty protected by this amendment, unless there are circumstances which exclude the right. There are, however, certain powers, existing in the sovereignty of each State in the Union, somewhat vaguely termed police powers, the exact description and limitation of which have not been attempted by the courts. Those powers, broadly stated and without, at present, any attempt at a more specific limitation, relate to the safety, health, morals and general welfare of the public. Both property and liberty are held on such reasonable conditions as may be imposed by the governing power of the State in the exercise of those powers, and with such conditions the Fourteenth Amendment was not designed to interfere.

The State, therefore, has power to prevent the individual from making certain kinds of contracts, and in regard to them the Federal Constitution offers no protection. If the contract be one which the State, in the legitimate exercise of its police power, has the right to prohibit, it is not prevented from prohibiting it by the Fourteenth Amendment. . . . [W]hen the State, by its legislature, in the assumed exercise of its police powers, has passed an act which seriously limits the right to labor or the right of contract in regard to their means of livelihood between persons who are *sui juris* (both employer and employee), it becomes of great importance to determine which shall prevail — the right of the individual to labor for such time as he may choose, or the right of the State to prevent the individual from laboring or from entering into any contract to labor, beyond a certain time prescribed by the State.

This court has recognized the existence and upheld the exercise of the police powers of the States in many cases which might fairly be considered as border ones, and it has, in the course of its determination of questions regarding the asserted invalidity of such statutes, on the ground of their violation of the rights secured by the Federal Constitution, been guided by rules of a very liberal nature, the application of which has resulted, in numerous instances, in upholding the validity of state statutes thus assailed. Among the later cases where the state law has been upheld by this court is that of *Holden v. Hardy* (1898). A provision in the act of the legislature of Utah was there under consideration, the act limiting the employment of workmen in all underground mines or workings, to eight hours per day, "except in cases of emergency, where life or property is in imminent danger." It also limited the hours of labor in smelting and other institutions for the reduction or refining of ores or metals to eight hours per day, except in like cases of emergency. The act was held to be a valid exercise of the police powers of the State. . . . It was held that the kind of employment, mining, smelting, etc., and the character of the employees in such kinds of labor, were such as to make it reasonable and proper for the State to interfere to prevent the employees from being constrained by the rules laid down by the proprietors in regard to labor. . . . There is nothing in *Holden v. Hardy* which covers the case now before us. . . .

It must, of course, be conceded that there is a limit to the valid exercise of the police power by the State. There is no dispute concerning this general proposition. Otherwise the Fourteenth Amendment would have no efficacy and the legislatures of the States would have unbounded power, and it would be enough to say that any piece of legislation was enacted to conserve the morals, the health or the safety of the people; such legislation would be valid, no matter how absolutely without foundation the claim might be. The claim of the police power would be a mere pretext — become another and delusive name for the supreme sovereignty of the State to be exercised free from constitutional restraint. This is not contended for. In every case that comes before this court, therefore, where legislation of this character is concerned and where the protection of the Federal Constitution is sought, the question necessarily arises: Is this a fair, reasonable and appropriate exercise of the police power of the State, or is it an unreasonable, unnecessary and arbitrary interference with the right of the individual to his personal liberty or to enter into those contracts in relation to labor which may seem to him appropriate or necessary for the support of himself and his family? Of course the liberty of contract relating to labor includes both parties to it. The one has as much right to purchase as the other to sell labor.

This is not a question of substituting the judgment of the court for that of the legislature. If the act be within the power of the State it is valid, although the judgment of the court might be totally opposed to the enactment of such a law. But the question would still remain: Is it within the police power of the State? And that question must be answered by the court.

The question whether this act is valid as a labor law, pure and simple, may be dismissed in a few words. There is no reasonable ground for interfering with the liberty of person or the right of free contract, by determining the hours of labor, in the occupation of a baker. There is no contention that bakers as a class are not equal in intelligence and capacity to men in other trades or manual occupations, or that they are not able to assert their rights and care for themselves without the protecting arm of the State, interfering with their independence of judgment and of action. They are in no sense wards of the State. Viewed in the light of a purely labor law, with no reference whatever to the question of health, we think that a law like the one before us involves neither the safety, the morals nor the welfare of the public, and that the interest of the public is not in the slightest degree affected by such an act. The law must be upheld, if at all, as a law pertaining to the health of the individual engaged in the occupation of a baker. It does not affect any other portion of the public than those who are engaged in that occupation. Clean and wholesome bread does not depend upon whether the baker works but ten hours per day or only sixty hours a week. The limitation of the hours of labor does not come within the police power on that ground.

It is a question of which of two powers or rights shall prevail — the power of the State to legislate or the right of the individual to liberty of person and freedom of contract. The mere assertion that the subject relates though but in a remote degree to the public health does not necessarily render the enactment valid. The act must have a more direct relation, as a means to an end, and the end itself must be appropriate and legitimate, before an act can be held to be valid which interferes with the general right of an individual to be free in his person and in his power to contract in relation to his own labor.

[T]he limit of the police power has been reached and passed in this case. There is, in our judgment, no reasonable foundation for holding this to be necessary or appropriate as a health law to safeguard the public health or the health of the individuals who are following the trade of a baker. If this statute be valid, and if, therefore, a proper case is made out in which to deny the right of an individual, *sui juris*, as employer or employee, to make contracts for the labor of the latter under the protection of the provisions of the Federal Constitution, there would seem to be no length to which legislation of this nature might not go. . . .

We think that there can be no fair doubt that the trade of a baker, in and of itself, is not an unhealthy one to that degree which would authorize the legislature to interfere with the right to labor, and with the right of free contract on the part of the individual, either as employer or employee. In looking through statistics regarding all trades and occupations, it may be true that the trade of a baker does not appear to be as healthy as some other trades, and is also vastly more healthy than still others. To the common understanding the trade of a baker has never been regarded as an unhealthy one. Very likely physicians would not recommend the exercise of that or of any other trade as a remedy for ill health. Some occupations are more healthy than others, but we think there are none which might not come under the power of the legislature to supervise and control the hours of working therein, if the mere fact that the occupation is not absolutely and perfectly healthy is to confer that right upon the legislative department of the Government. It might be safely affirmed that almost all occupations more or less affect the health. There must be more than the mere fact of the possible existence of some small amount of unhealthiness to warrant legislative interference with liberty. It is unfortunately true that labor, even in any department, may possibly carry with it the seeds of unhealthiness. But are we all, on that account, at the mercy of legislative majorities? A printer, a tinsmith, a locksmith, a carpenter, a cabinetmaker, a dry goods clerk, a bank's, a lawyer's or a physician's clerk, or a clerk in almost any kind of business, would all come under the power of the legislature, on this assumption. No trade, no occupation, no mode of earning one's living, could escape this all-pervading power, and the acts of the legislature in limiting the hours of labor in all employments would be valid, although such limitation might seriously cripple the ability of the laborer to support himself and his family. . . .

[W]e think that such a law as this, although passed in the assumed exercise of the police power, and as relating to the public health, or the health of the employees named, is not within that power, and is invalid. The act is not, within any fair meaning of the term, a health law, but is an illegal interference with the rights of individuals, both employers and employees, to make contracts regarding labor upon such terms as they may think best, or which they may agree upon with the other parties to such contracts. Statutes of the nature of that under review, limiting the hours in which grown and intelligent men may labor to earn their living, are mere meddlesome interferences with the rights of the individual, and they are not saved from condemnation by the claim that they are passed in the exercise of the police power and upon the subject of the health of the individual whose rights are interfered with, unless there be some fair ground, reasonable in and of itself, to say that there is material danger to the public health or to the health of the employees, if the hours of labor are not curtailed. If this be not clearly the case the individuals, whose rights are thus made the subject of legislative interference, are under the protection of the Federal Constitution regarding their liberty of contract as well as of person; and the legislature of the State has no power to limit their right as proposed in this statute. All that it could properly do has been done by it with regard to the conduct of bakeries, as provided for in the other sections of the act, above set forth. These several sections provide for the inspection of the premises where the bakery is carried on, with regard to furnishing proper wash-rooms and water-closets, apart from the bakeroom, also with regard to providing proper drainage, plumbing and painting; the sections, in addition, provide for the height of the ceiling, the cementing or tiling of floors, where necessary in the opinion of the factory inspector, and for other things of that nature; alterations are also provided for and are to be made where necessary in the opinion of the inspector, in order to comply with the provisions of the statute. These various sections may be wise and valid regulations, and they certainly go to the full extent of providing for the cleanliness and the healthiness, so far as possible, of the quarters in which bakeries are to be conducted. Adding to all these requirements, a prohibition to enter into any contract of labor in a bakery for more than a certain number of hours a week, is, in our judgment, so wholly beside the matter of a proper, reasonable and fair provision, as to run counter to that liberty of person and of free contract provided for in the Federal Constitution.

It was further urged on the argument that restricting the hours of labor in the case of bakers was valid because it tended to cleanliness on the part of the workers, as a man was more apt to be cleanly when not overworked, and if cleanly then his "output" was also more likely to be so. What has already been said applies with equal force to this contention. We do not admit the reasoning to be sufficient to justify the claimed right of such interference. The State in that case would assume the position of a supervisor, or *pater familias*, over every act of the individual, and its right of governmental interference with his hours of labor, his hours of exercise, the character thereof, and the extent to which it shall be carried would be recognized and upheld. In our judgment it is not possible in fact to discover the connection between the number of hours a baker may work in the bakery and the healthful quality of the bread made by the workman. The connection, if any exists, is too shadowy and thin to build any argument for the interference of the legislature. If the man works ten hours a day it is all right, but if ten and a half or eleven his health is in danger and his bread may be unhealthful, and, therefore, he shall not be permitted to do it. This, we think, is unreasonable and entirely arbitrary. When assertions such as we have adverted to become necessary in order to give, if possible, a plausible foundation for the contention that the law is a "health law," it gives rise to at least a suspicion that there was some other motive dominating the legislature than the purpose to subserve the public health or welfare.

[T]he limitation of the hours of labor as provided for in this section of the statute under which the indictment was found, and the plaintiff in error convicted, has no such direct relation to and no such substantial effect upon the health of the employee, as to justify us in regarding the section as really a health law. It seems to us that the real object and purpose were simply to regulate the hours of labor between the master and his employees (all being men, *sui juris*), in a private business, not dangerous in any degree to morals or in any real and substantial degree, to the health of the employees. Under such circumstances the freedom of master and employee to contract with each other in relation to their employment, and in defining the same, cannot be prohibited or interfered with, without violating the Federal Constitution.

The judgment of the Court of Appeals of New York as well as that of the Supreme Court and of the County Court of Oneida County must be reversed and the case remanded to the County Court for further proceedings not inconsistent with this opinion.

*Reversed.*

Mr. Justice Harlan, with whom Mr. Justice White and Mr. Justice Day concurred, dissenting.

[W]hat is called the liberty of contract may, within certain limits, be subjected to regulations designed and calculated to promote the general welfare or to guard the public health, the public morals or the public safety. "The liberty secured by the Constitution of the United States to every person within its jurisdiction does not import," this court has recently said, "an absolute right in each person to be, at all times and in all circumstances, wholly freed from restraint. There are manifold restraints to which every person is necessarily subject for the common good." *Jacobson v. Massachusetts* (1905).

Granting then that there is a liberty of contract which cannot be violated even under the sanction of direct legislative enactment, but assuming, as according to settled law we may assume, that such liberty of contract is subject to such regulations as the State may reasonably prescribe for the common good and the well-being of society, what are the conditions under which the judiciary may declare such regulations to be in excess of legislative authority and void? Upon this point there is no room for dispute; for, the rule is universal that a legislative enactment, Federal or state, is never to be disregarded or held invalid unless it be, beyond question, plainly and palpably in excess of legislative power. . . . If the end which the legislature seeks to accomplish be one to which its power extends, and if the means employed to that end, although not the wisest or best, are yet not plainly and palpably unauthorized by law, then the court cannot interfere. In other words, when the validity of a statute is questioned, the burden of proof, so to speak, is upon those who assert it to be unconstitutional.

Let these principles be applied to the present case.... It is plain that this statute was enacted in order to protect the physical well-being of those who work in bakery and confectionery establishments. It may be that the statute had its origin, in part, in the belief that employers and employees in such establishments were not upon an equal footing, and that the necessities of the latter often compelled them to submit to such exactions as unduly taxed their strength. Be this as it may, the statute must be taken as expressing the belief of the people of New York that, as a general rule, and in the case of the average man, labor in excess of sixty hours during a week in such establishments may endanger the health of those who thus labor. Whether or not this be wise legislation it is not the province of the court to inquire. Under our systems of government the courts are not concerned with the wisdom or policy of legislation. So that in determining the question of power to interfere with liberty of contract, the court may inquire whether the means devised by the State are germane to an end which may be lawfully accomplished and have a real or substantial relation to the protection of health, as involved in the daily work of the persons, male and female, engaged in bakery and confectionery establishments. But when this inquiry is entered upon I find it impossible, in view of common experience, to say that there is here no real or substantial relation between the means employed by the State and the end sought to be accomplished by its legislation. Nor can I say that the statute has no appropriate or direct connection with that protection to health which each State owes to her citizens, or that it is not promotive of the health of the employees in question, or that the regulation prescribed by the State is utterly unreasonable and extravagant or wholly arbitrary. Still less can I say that the statute is, beyond question, a plain, palpable invasion of rights secured by the fundamental law. Therefore I submit that this court will transcend its functions if it assumes to annul the statute of New York....

We judicially know that the question of the number of hours during which a workman should continuously labor has been, for a long period, and is yet, a subject of serious consideration among civilized peoples, and by those having special knowledge of the laws of health.... It is enough for the determination of this case, and it is enough for this court to know, that the question is one about which there is room for debate and for an honest difference of opinion. There are many reasons of a weighty, substantial character, based upon the experience of mankind, in support of the theory that, all things considered, more than ten hours' steady work each day, from week to week, in a bakery or confectionery establishment, may endanger the health, and shorten the lives of the workmen, thereby diminishing their physical and mental capacity to serve the State, and to provide for those dependent upon them.

If such reasons exist that ought to be the end of this case, for the State is not amenable to the judiciary, in respect of its legislative enactments, unless such enactments are plainly, palpably, beyond all question, inconsistent with the Constitution of the United States. We are not to presume that the State of New York has acted in bad faith. Nor can we assume that its legislature acted without due deliberation, or that it did not determine this question upon the fullest attainable information, and for the common good. We cannot say that the State has acted without reason nor ought we to proceed upon the theory that its action is a mere sham. Our duty, I submit, is to sustain the statute as not being in conflict with the Federal Constitution, for the reason — and such is an all sufficient reason — it is not shown to be plainly and palpably inconsistent with that instrument. Let the State alone in the management of its purely domestic affairs, so long as it does not appear beyond all question that it has violated the Federal Constitution. This view necessarily results from the principle that the health and safety of the people of a State are primarily for the State to guard and protect.

I take leave to say that the New York statute, in the particulars here involved, cannot be held to be in conflict with the Fourteenth Amendment, without enlarging the scope of the Amendment far beyond its original purpose and without bringing under the supervision of this court matters which have been supposed to belong exclusively to the legislative departments of the several States when exerting their conceded power to guard the health and safety of their citizens by such regulations as they in their wisdom deem best. . . .

. . . The judgment in my opinion should be affirmed.

Mr. Justice Holmes dissenting.

I regret sincerely that I am unable to agree with the judgment in this case, and that I think it my duty to express my dissent.

This case is decided upon an economic theory which a large part of the country does not entertain. If it were a question whether I agreed with that theory, I should desire to study it further and long before making up my mind. But I do not conceive that to be my duty, because I strongly believe that my agreement or disagreement has nothing to do with the right of a majority to embody their opinions in law. It is settled by various decisions of this court that state constitutions and state laws may regulate life in many ways which we as legislators might think as injudicious or if you like as tyrannical as this, and which equally with this interfere with the liberty to contract. Sunday laws and usury laws are ancient examples. A more modern one is the prohibition of lotteries. The liberty of the citizen to do as he likes so long as he does not interfere with the liberty of others to do the same, which has been a shibboleth for some well-known writers, is interfered with by school laws, by the Post Office, by every state or municipal institution which takes his money for purposes thought desirable, whether he likes it or not. The Fourteenth Amendment does not enact Mr. Herbert Spencer's Social Statics. . . . [A] constitution is not intended to embody a particular economic theory, whether of paternalism and the organic relation of the citizen to the State or of *laissez faire*. It is made for people of fundamentally differing views, and the accident of our finding certain opinions natural and familiar or novel and even shocking ought not to conclude our judgment upon the question whether statutes embodying them conflict with the Constitution of the United States.

General propositions do not decide concrete cases. The decision will depend on a judgment or intuition more subtle than any articulate major premise. But I think that the proposition just stated, if it is accepted, will carry us far toward the end. Every opinion tends to become a law. I think that the word liberty in the Fourteenth Amendment is perverted when it is held to prevent the natural outcome of a dominant opinion, unless it can be said that a rational and fair man necessarily would admit that the statute proposed would infringe fundamental principles as they have been understood by the traditions of our people and our law. It does not need research to show that no such sweeping condemnation can be passed upon the statute before us. A reasonable man might think it a proper measure on the score of health. Men whom I certainly could not pronounce unreasonable would uphold it as a first installment of a general regulation of the hours of work. Whether in the latter aspect it would be open to the charge of inequality I think it unnecessary to discuss.

## NOTES AND QUESTIONS

**1.** As the opinion in *Lochner* indicates, when faced with a due process challenge to a particular governmental regulation, a court must determine whether the law infringes a constitutionally recognized interest. But the question here wasn't one of procedural due process — the defendant in *Lochner* faced a criminal charge and, accordingly, was provided all the process the justice system could provide (at the time). The problem was that the law essentially criminalized the exercise of what the Court viewed as a protected interest. What, exactly, was the constitutional interest that the New York labor law undermined? How did the Court explain why, exactly, that interest should be considered to be protected under due process?

**2.** Having identified the interest implicated by the New York labor law, the Court proceeded to determine whether the state nonetheless could articulate some justification for its regulation. In the Court's view, how serious did the state's justification have to be? Recall that, in the First Amendment context, the Court talked about how laws that restrict speech on the basis of its content can be justified only under the most exacting scrutiny. Did the Court in *Lochner* apply the most exacting scrutiny to New York's labor law? Is that the correct show of deference in respect to a law that is, in essence, a simple police power regulation — that is, a law aimed at protecting the health, safety, and welfare of the citizenry?

**3.** Based upon your answers to these questions, can you see why *Lochner* is today regarded as a notorious decision? If not, consider this: on what basis did the Court conclude that the interest it deemed imperiled by the regulation was one that should receive the heightened protection afforded by substantive due process? As well, consider who is in the better position to determine whether such a law should be deemed necessary to the health and safety of the citizenry — the members of the U.S. Supreme Court, or the elected representatives of the people of New York?

**4.** Justice Holmes, in his dissent, suggested the doctrinal path that the Court eventually would follow in the area of substantive due process. As an initial matter, what kind of interests did Holmes believe warrant substantive due process protection? Where might a court locate these interests? Is it potentially a problem that they are not actually named in the text of the Constitution? If so, should they be recognized nonetheless, and how would a court go about doing that? These are the questions with which modern substantive due process cases have been concerned. Before we reach these questions and cases, though, let's see what became of the *Lochner* line of decisions, as illustrated by the next case.

## West Coast Hotel Co. v. Parrish
### 300 U.S. 379 (1937)

Mr. Chief Justice Hughes delivered the opinion of the Court.

This case presents the question of the constitutional validity of the minimum wage law of the State of Washington.

The Act, entitled "Minimum Wages for Women," authorizes the fixing of minimum wages for women and minors. . . . Further provisions required the [Industrial Welfare] Commission to ascertain the wages and conditions of labor of women and minors within the State. Public hearings were to be held. If after investigation the Commission found that in any occupation, trade or industry the wages paid to women were "inadequate to supply them necessary cost of living and to maintain the workers in health," the Commission was empowered to call a conference of representatives of employers and employees together with disinterested persons representing the public. The conference was to recommend to the Commission, on its request, an estimate of a minimum wage adequate for the purpose above stated, and on the approval of such a recommendation it became the duty of the Commission to issue an obligatory order fixing minimum wages. Any such order might be reopened and the question reconsidered with the aid of the former conference or a new one. Special licenses were authorized for the employment of women who were "physically defective or crippled by age or otherwise," and also for apprentices, at less than the prescribed minimum wage.

By a later Act the Industrial Welfare Commission was abolished and its duties were assigned to the Industrial Welfare Committee consisting of the Director of Labor and Industries, the Supervisor of Industrial Insurance, the Supervisor of Industrial Relations, the Industrial Statistician and the Supervisor of Women in Industry.

The appellant conducts a hotel. The appellee Elsie Parrish was employed as a chambermaid and (with her husband) brought this suit to recover the difference between the wages paid her and the minimum wage fixed pursuant to the state law. . . . The appellant challenged the act as repugnant to the due process clause of the Fourteenth Amendment of the Constitution of the United States. The Supreme Court of the State, reversing the trial court, sustained the statute and directed judgment for the plaintiffs. The case is here on appeal.

The appellant relies upon the decision of this Court in *Adkins v. Children's Hospital* (1923), which held invalid the District of Columbia Minimum Wage Act, which was attacked under the due process clause of the Fifth Amendment. . . .

The Supreme Court of Washington has upheld the minimum wage statute of that State. It has decided that the statute is a reasonable exercise of the police power of the State. In reaching that conclusion the state court has invoked principles long established by this Court in the application of the Fourteenth Amendment. The state court has refused to regard the decision in the *Adkins* case as determinative. . . . We are of the opinion that this ruling of the state court demands on our part a reexamination of the *Adkins* case. The importance of the question, in which many States having similar laws are concerned, the close division by which the decision in the *Adkins* case was reached, and the economic conditions which have supervened, and in the light of which the reasonableness of the exercise of the protective power of the State must be considered, make it not only appropriate, but we think imperative, that in deciding the present case the subject should receive fresh consideration.

. . . The constitutional provision invoked is the due process clause of the Fourteenth Amendment governing the States, as the due process clause invoked in the *Adkins* case governed Congress. In each case the violation alleged by those attacking minimum wage regulation for women is deprivation of freedom of contract. What is this freedom? The Constitution does not speak of freedom of contract. It speaks of liberty and prohibits the deprivation of liberty without due process of law. In prohibiting that deprivation the Constitution does not recognize an absolute and uncontrollable liberty. Liberty in each of its phases has its history and connotation. But the liberty safeguarded is liberty in a social organization which requires the protection of law against the evils which menace the health, safety, morals and welfare of the people. Liberty under the Constitution is thus necessarily subject to the restraints of due process, and regulation which is reasonable in relation to its subject and is adopted in the interests of the community is due process.

This essential limitation of liberty in general governs freedom of contract in particular. . . . This power under the Constitution to restrict freedom of contract has had many illustrations. That it may be exercised in the public interest with respect to contracts between employer and employee is undeniable. . . . In dealing with the relation of employer and employed, the legislature has necessarily a wide field of discretion in order that there may be suitable protection of health and safety, and that peace and good order may be promoted through regulations designed to insure wholesome conditions of work and freedom from oppression.

The point that has been strongly stressed that adult employees should be deemed competent to make their own contracts was decisively met nearly forty years ago in *Holden v. Hardy*, where we pointed out the inequality in the footing of the parties. We said:

The legislature has also recognized the fact, which the experience of legislators in many States has corroborated, that the proprietors of these establishments and their operatives do not stand upon an equality, and that their interests are, to a certain extent, conflicting. The former naturally desire to obtain as much labor as possible from their employes [sic], while the latter are often induced by the fear of discharge to conform to regulations which their judgment, fairly exercised, would pronounce to be detrimental to their health or strength. In other words, the proprietors lay down the rules and the laborers are practically constrained to obey them. In such cases self-interest is often an unsafe guide, and the legislature may properly interpose its authority.

And we added that the fact "that both parties are of full age and competent to contract does not necessarily deprive the State of the power to interfere where the parties do not stand upon an equality, or where the public health demands that one party to the contract shall be protected against himself." . . .

The minimum wage to be paid under the Washington statute is fixed after full consideration by representatives of employers, employees and the public. It may be assumed that the minimum wage is fixed in consideration of the service that [is] performed in the particular occupations under normal conditions. . . . The statement of Mr. Justice Holmes in the *Adkins* case is pertinent: "This statute does not compel anybody to pay anything. It simply forbids employment at rates below those fixed as the minimum requirement of health and right living. It is safe to assume that women will not be employed at even the lowest wages allowed unless they earn them, or unless the employer's business can sustain the burden. In short the law in its character and operation is like hundreds of so-called police laws that have been upheld." . . .

We think . . . that the decision in the *Adkins* case was a departure from the true application of the principles governing the regulation by the State of the relation of employer and employed. . . . What can be closer to the public interest than the health of women and their protection from unscrupulous and overreaching employers? And if the protection of women is a legitimate end of the exercise of state power, how can it be said that the requirement of the payment of a minimum wage fairly fixed in order to meet the very necessities of existence is not an admissible means to that end? The legislature of the State was clearly entitled to consider the situation of women in employment, the fact that they are in the class receiving the least pay, that their bargaining power is relatively weak, and that they are the ready victims of those who would take advantage of their necessitous circumstances. The legislature was entitled to adopt measures to reduce the evils of the "sweating system," the exploiting of workers at wages so low as to be insufficient to meet the bare cost of living, thus making their very helplessness the occasion of a most injurious competition. The legislature had the right to consider that its minimum wage requirements would be an important aid in carrying out its policy of protection. The adoption of similar requirements by many States evidences a deep-seated conviction both as to the presence of the evil and as to the means adapted to check it. Legislative response to that conviction cannot be regarded as arbitrary or capricious, and that is all we have to decide. Even if the wisdom of the policy be regarded as debatable and its effects uncertain, still the legislature is entitled to its judgment.

There is an additional and compelling consideration which recent economic experience has brought into a strong light. The exploitation of a class of workers who are in an unequal position with respect to bargaining power and are thus relatively defenceless against the denial of a living wage is not only detrimental to their health and well-being but casts a direct burden for their support upon the community. What these workers lose in wages the taxpayers are called upon to pay. The bare cost of living must be met. We may take judicial notice of the unparalleled demands for relief which arose during the recent period of depression and still continue to an alarming extent despite the degree of economic recovery which has been achieved. It is unnecessary to cite official statistics to establish what is of common knowledge through the length and breadth of the land. While in the instant case no factual brief has been presented, there is no reason to doubt that the State of Washington has encountered the same social problem that is present elsewhere. The community is not bound to provide what is in effect a subsidy for unconscionable employers. The community may direct its law-making power to correct the abuse which springs from their selfish disregard of the public interest. The argument that the legislation in question constitutes an arbitrary discrimination, because it does not extend to men, is unavailing. This Court has frequently held that the legislative authority, acting within its proper field, is not bound to extend its regulation to all cases which it might possibly reach. The legislature "is free to recognize degrees of harm and it may confine its restrictions to those classes of cases where the need is deemed to be dearest." . . . This familiar principle has repeatedly been applied to legislation which singles out women, and particular classes of women, in the exercise of the State's protective power. Their relative need in the presence of the evil, no less than the existence of the evil itself, is a matter for the legislative judgment.

Our conclusion is that the case of *Adkins v. Children's Hospital* should be, and it is, overruled. The judgment of the Supreme Court of the State of Washington is

*Affirmed.*

Mr. Justice Sutherland, dissenting:

. . . Neither the statute involved in the *Adkins* case nor the Washington statute, so far as it is involved here, has the slightest relation to the capacity or earning power of the employee, to the number of hours which constitute the day's work, the character of the place where the work is to be done, or the circumstances or surroundings of the employment. The sole basis upon which the question of validity rests is the assumption that the employee is entitled to receive a sum of money sufficient to provide a living for her, keep her in health and preserve her morals. And, as we pointed out at some length in that case, the question thus presented for the determination of the board cannot be solved by any general formula prescribed by a statutory bureau, since it is not a composite but an individual question to be answered for each individual, considered by herself.

### NOTES AND QUESTIONS

1. You don't need to know much about the *Adkins* case beyond what the majority indicates: there, the Supreme Court struck down a wage regulation by applying reasoning similar to what we saw in *Lochner*. Under the *Lochner-Adkins* approach to substantive due process, the Court sought to enforce a substantive constitutional protection of an individual's interest in entering into employment-type contracts. The Constitution, of course, doesn't protect that interest explicitly, but it does protect "liberty." *West Coast Hotel* employs a different understanding of the liberty protected by the due process clauses — something called "ordered liberty." What, exactly, is "ordered liberty," and how does it differ from the liberty that the Court sought to enforce in cases like *Lochner* and *Adkins*?

2. In a real sense, this case turns — as so many separation-of-powers cases do — on the Court's understanding of its role in policing the outcomes of the political process. The more that a court finds within the constitutional protection of liberty, the more work there will be for the courts, as there will be fewer cases in which the judiciary will defer to the political branches in the face of challenges to their regulatory authority under the police powers. *West Coast Hotel* is emblematic of the modern, post-*Lochner* determination that the Court's primary role is not to second-guess political decisionmaking — particularly when that political decisionmaking appears in the form of state regulations, which make up the largest body of restrictions on Americans as individuals. But, if the courts will not do so, then who will keep the political branches in check? Recall Justice Marshall's answer to this question in *Gibbons v. Ogden*, in which the Court addressed the scope of Congress's regulatory authority under the Commerce Clause.

3. *West Coast Hotel* put an end to *Lochner*-style substantive due process — but not to the framework of substantive due process itself. As we work through the materials in this chapter, you should be able to distinguish *Lochner* from the modern substantive due process cases — in other words, you should be able to distinguish between the now-rejected constitutional protection the Court afforded the interest of individuals working as many hours as they liked in a bakery and the protection the Court has afforded the interests at stake in the cases that follow.

### B. Incorporation and Unenumerated Rights

Before we turn to the modern substantive due process cases, it's important to understand a little something about the phenomenon known as "incorporation." You may recall that the first eight amendments to the U.S. Constitution refer to constitutional commitments to the protection of specific civil rights and liberties. Recall, too, that the guarantees contained in the Bill of Rights apply only to the actions of the federal government — the Supreme Court, in *Barron ex rel. Tiernan v. Mayor of Baltimore*, 32 U.S. 243 (1833), concluded that these amendments limit only the federal government and not the states.

Following the Civil War, the people ratified the Fourteenth Amendment, which provides that states may not abridge "the privileges or immunities of citizens of the United States" or deprive "any person of life, liberty, or property, without due process of law." By the end of the nineteenth century, the question arose whether "the privileges or immunities of citizens of the United States" included the rights contained in the first eight amendments. In the *Slaughter-House Cases*, 83 U.S. 36 (1873), the Court concluded that they did not.

The Privileges or Immunities Clause of the Fourteenth Amendment having proved a dead end, individual rights advocates turned to the Due Process Clause and found a receptive Supreme Court. In *Twining v. New Jersey*, 211 U.S. 78 (1908), the Court observed that "some of the right safeguarded by the first eight Amendments against National action [might] also be safeguarded against state action," but this was not "because those rights are enumerated in the first eight Amendments." Due process, the Court continued, contained within in it "immutable principles of justice which inhere in the very idea of free government which no member of the Union may disregard." *Id.* (internal quotation omitted). Later, in *Snyder v. Massachusetts*, 291 U.S. 97 (1934), the Court referred to rights that are "so rooted in the traditions and conscience of our people as to be ranked as fundamental, and, in *Palko v. Connecticut*, 302 U.S. 319 (1937), the Court included within due process rights that are "the very essence of a scheme of ordered liberty" and essential to "a fair and enlightened system of justice." Under these and like formulations, the Court held, for example, that the Fourteenth Amendment's Due Process Clause *incorporated* the First Amendment's protection of free speech. See *Gitlow v. New York*, 268 U.S. 652 (1925).

Eventually, through a jurisprudential approach called "selective incorporation," the Court would go on to hold, on a case-by-case basis, that due process protects against action by the states nearly all of the particular interests protected against action by the federal government under the first eight amendments. At this writing, the only rights that remain unincorporated are: the Third Amendment's protection against the quartering of soldiers; the Fifth Amendment's requirements of a grand jury indictment in criminal cases; and the Seventh Amendment's right to a jury trial in civil cases. See *McDonald v. City of Chicago*, 561 U.S. 742 n.13 (2010). Before 2010, this list included the Second Amendment's right to bear arms, an issue the Court addressed in *McDonald*; the Court added the right to be free from excessive fines in 2019 in *Timbs v. Indiana*, 586 U.S. ___.

Why is the phenomenon of incorporation important? Because it raises the question whether, in the Court's view, a particular right expressly contained in the Bill of Rights is so fundamental to our scheme of ordered liberty that it must be included among the interests protected by the Fourteenth Amendment's Due Process Clause against abridgment by state and local governments. That is in essence the same inquiry we will see the Court undertake in the substantive due process context — except that in the substantive due process cases, the question isn't whether a right *expressly named* in the Bill of Rights should be incorporated, but whether an *implicit* substantive liberty interest should be recognized and enforced through the Fourteenth Amendment's Due Process Clause (and, by logical extension, the Fifth Amendment's Due Process Clause).

## C. Modern Substantive Due Process: Personal Interests

### 1. Introduction to Unenumerated Rights

We begin our tour of the modern substantive due process cases with a post-*Lochner* decision that pre-dates *West Coast Hotel* and is still good law.

**Pierce v. Society of Sisters**
**268 U.S. 510 (1925)**

Mr. Justice McReynolds delivered the opinion of the Court.

These appeals are from decrees, based upon undenied allegations, which granted preliminary orders restraining appellants from threatening or attempting to enforce the Compulsory Education Act adopted November 7, 1922. . . . They present the same points of law; there are no controverted questions of fact. Rights said to be guaranteed by the federal Constitution were specially set up, and appropriate prayers asked for their protection.

The challenged Act, effective September 1, 1926, requires every parent, guardian or other person having control or charge or custody of a child between eight and sixteen years to send him "to a public school for the period of time a public school shall be held during the current year" in the district where the child resides; and failure so to do is declared a misdemeanor. . . . The manifest purpose is to compel general attendance at public schools by normal children, between eight and sixteen, who have not completed the eighth grade. And without doubt enforcement of the statute would seriously impair, perhaps destroy, the profitable features of appellees' business and greatly diminish the value of their property.

Appellee, the Society of Sisters, is an Oregon corporation, organized in 1880, with power to care for orphans, educate and instruct the youth, establish and maintain academies or schools, and acquire necessary real and personal property. It has long devoted its property and effort to the secular and religious education and care of children, and has acquired the valuable good will of many parents and guardians. It conducts interdependent primary and high schools and junior colleges, and maintains orphanages for the custody and control of children between eight and sixteen. In its primary schools many children between those ages are taught the subjects usually pursued in Oregon public schools during the first eight years. Systematic religious instruction and moral training according to the tenets of the Roman Catholic Church are also regularly provided. All courses of study, both temporal and religious, contemplate continuity of training under appellee's charge; the primary schools are essential to the system and the most profitable. It owns valuable buildings, especially constructed and equipped for school purposes. The business is remunerative — the annual income from primary schools exceeds thirty thousand dollars — and the successful conduct of this requires long time contracts with teachers and parents. The Compulsory Education Act of 1922 has already caused the withdrawal from its schools of children who would otherwise continue, and their income has steadily declined. The appellants, public officers, have proclaimed their purpose strictly to enforce the statute.

After setting out the above facts the Society's bill alleges that the enactment conflicts with the right of parents to choose schools where their children will receive appropriate mental and religious training, the right of the child to influence the parents' choice of a school, the right of schools and teachers therein to engage in a useful business or profession, and is accordingly repugnant to the Constitution and void. And, further, that unless enforcement of the measure is enjoined the corporation's business and property will suffer irreparable injury.

. . .

No question is raised concerning the power of the State reasonably to regulate all schools, to inspect, supervise and examine them, their teachers and pupils; to require that all children of proper age attend some school, that teachers shall be of good moral character and patriotic disposition, that certain studies plainly essential to good citizenship must be taught, and that nothing be taught which is manifestly inimical to the public welfare.

The inevitable practical result of enforcing the Act under consideration would be destruction of appellees' primary schools, and perhaps all other private primary schools for normal children within the State of Oregon. These parties are engaged in a kind of undertaking not inherently harmful, but long regarded as useful and meritorious. Certainly there is nothing in the present records to indicate that they have failed to discharge their obligations to patrons, students or the State. And there are no peculiar circumstances or present emergencies which demand extraordinary measures relative to primary education.

Under the doctrine of *Meyer v. Nebraska* (1923), we think it entirely plain that the Act of 1922 unreasonably interferes with the liberty of parents and guardians to direct the upbringing and education of children under their control. As often heretofore pointed out, rights guaranteed by the Constitution may not be abridged by legislation which has no reasonable relation to some purpose within the competency of the State. The fundamental theory of liberty upon which all governments in this Union repose excludes any general power of the State to standardize its children by forcing them to accept instruction from public teachers only. The child is not the mere creature of the State; those who nurture him and direct his destiny have the right, coupled with the high duty, to recognize and prepare him for additional obligations.

[Generally,] no person in any business has such an interest in possible customers as to enable him to restrain exercise of proper power of the State upon the ground that he will be deprived of patronage. But the injunctions here sought are not against the exercise of any *proper* power. Plaintiffs asked protection against arbitrary, unreasonable and unlawful interference with their patrons and the consequent destruction of their business and property. . . .

The decrees below are

*Affirmed.*

## NOTES & QUESTIONS

**1.** *Pierce* notes another case that post-dates *Lochner* and pre-dates *West Coast Hotel*: *Meyer v. Nebraska*, 262 U.S. 390 (1923), in which the Court held that due process protects the right of parents to raise children as they see fit. That case is also still good law. Indeed, you will see that both *Pierce* and *Meyer* remain touchstones in discussions about substantive due process, particularly in cases involving the regulation of parental and family interests.

**2.** How does the *Pierce* Court come to the conclusion that the right of parents to educate their children as they see fit should be deemed fundamental? It certainly seems like an interest that should be protected. But the Court did not engage in the modern analysis — that is, it did not ask whether the interest of parents in educating their children as they see fit should be deemed implicit in the concept of ordered liberty. That is because the "ordered liberty" understanding of due process, and the rejection of *Lochner*, would await the Court's decision in *West Coast Hotel*.

**3.** Though the *Pierce* Court does not apply the modern test, you should be able to distinguish *Pierce* and *Meyer* from *Lochner*. How do the interests asserted in each case substantively differ from each other? And in what respects do they differ?

### 2. Intimate Conduct

#### Griswold v. Connecticut
381 U.S. 479 (1965)

Mr. Justice Douglas delivered the opinion of the Court.

Appellant Griswold is Executive Director of the Planned Parenthood League of Connecticut. Appellant Buxton is a licensed physician and a professor at the Yale Medical School who served as Medical Director for the League at its Center in New Haven — a center open and operating from November 1 to November 10, 1961, when appellants were arrested.

meeting; it includes the right to express one's attitudes or philosophies by membership in a group or by affiliation with it or by other lawful means. Association in that context is a form of expression of opinion; and while it is not expressly included in the First Amendment its existence is necessary in making the express guarantees fully meaningful.

The foregoing cases suggest that specific guarantees in the Bill of Rights have penumbras, formed by emanations from those guarantees that help give them life and substance. Various guarantees create zones of privacy. The right of association contained in the penumbra of the First Amendment is one, as we have seen. The Third Amendment in its prohibition against the quartering of soldiers "in any house" in time of peace without the consent of the owner is another facet of that privacy. The Fourth Amendment explicitly affirms the "right of the people to be secure in their persons, houses, papers, and effects, against unreasonable searches and seizures." The Fifth Amendment in its Self-Incrimination Clause enables the citizen to create a zone of privacy which government may not force him to surrender to his detriment. The Ninth Amendment provides: "The enumeration in the Constitution, of certain rights, shall not be construed to deny or disparage others retained by the people."

The Fourth and Fifth Amendments were described in *Boyd v. United States* (1886), as protection against all governmental invasions "of the sanctity of a man's home and the privacies of life." We recently referred in *Mapp v. Ohio* (1961) to the Fourth Amendment as creating a "right to privacy, no less important than any other right carefully and particularly reserved to the people."

We have had many controversies over these penumbral rights of "privacy and repose." These cases bear witness that the right of privacy which presses for recognition here is a legitimate one.

The present case, then, concerns a relationship lying within the zone of privacy created by several fundamental constitutional guarantees. And it concerns a law which, in forbidding the *use* of contraceptives rather than regulating their manufacture or sale, seeks to achieve its goals by means having a maximum destructive impact upon that relationship. Such a law cannot stand in light of the familiar principle, so often applied by this Court, that a "governmental purpose to control or prevent activities constitutionally subject to state regulation may not be achieved by means which sweep unnecessarily broadly and thereby invade the area of protected freedoms." *NAACP*. Would we allow the police to search the sacred precincts of marital bedrooms for telltale signs of the use of contraceptives? The very idea is repulsive to the notions of privacy surrounding the marriage relationship.

We deal with a right of privacy older than the Bill of Rights — older than our political parties, older than our school system. Marriage is a coming together for better or for worse, hopefully enduring, and intimate to the degree of being sacred. It is an association that promotes a way of life, not causes; a harmony in living, not political faiths; a bilateral loyalty, not commercial or social projects. Yet it is an association for as noble a purpose as any involved in our prior decisions.

*Reversed.*

Mr. Justice Goldberg, whom The Chief Justice and Mr. Justice Brennan join, concurring.

I agree with the Court that Connecticut's birth-control law unconstitutionally intrudes upon the right of marital privacy, and I join in its opinion and judgment. . . . My conclusion that the concept of liberty . . . embraces the right of marital privacy though that right is not mentioned explicitly in the Constitution is supported both by numerous decisions of this Court, referred to in the Court's opinion, and by the language and history of the Ninth Amendment. In reaching the conclusion that the right of marital privacy is protected, as being within the protected penumbra of specific guarantees of the Bill of Rights, the Court refers to the Ninth Amendment. I add these words to emphasize the relevance of that Amendment to the Court's holding.

. . .

While this Court has had little occasion to interpret the Ninth Amendment, "[i]t cannot be presumed that any clause in the constitution is intended to be without effect." *Marbury v. Madison* (1803). In interpreting the Constitution, "real effect should be given to all the words it uses." *Myers v. United States* (1926). The Ninth Amendment to the Constitution may be regarded by some as a recent discovery and may be forgotten by others, but since 1791 it has been a basic part of the Constitution which we are sworn to uphold. To hold that a right so basic and fundamental and so deep-rooted in our society as the right of privacy in marriage may be infringed because that right is not guaranteed in so many words by the first eight amendments to the Constitution is to ignore the Ninth Amendment and to give it no effect whatsoever. Moreover, a judicial construction that this fundamental right is not protected by the Constitution because it is not mentioned in explicit terms by one of the first eight amendments or elsewhere in the Constitution would violate the Ninth Amendment, which specifically states that "[t]he enumeration in the Constitution, of certain rights, shall not be *construed* to deny or disparage others retained by the people." (Emphasis added.) . . . [T]he Ninth Amendment expressly recognizes [that] there are fundamental personal rights such as this one, which are protected from abridgment by the Government though not specifically mentioned in the Constitution.

[Justice Harlan dissented in an earlier case, *Poe v. Ullman*, 367 U.S. 497 (1961), concerning the constitutionality of the same law, and he concurred briefly in *Griswold*; his *Ullman* dissent, which explicated his view of due process, follows the excerpt of his *Griswold* concurrence:]

. . . In my view, the proper constitutional inquiry in this case is whether this Connecticut statute infringes the Due Process Clause of the Fourteenth Amendment because the enactment violates basic values "implicit in the concept of ordered liberty," *Palko v. Connecticut* (1937). For reasons stated at length in my dissenting opinion in *Poe v. Ullman* (1961), I believe that it does. While the relevant inquiry may be aided by resort to one or more of the provisions of the Bill of Rights, it is not dependent on them or any of their radiations. The Due Process Clause of the Fourteenth Amendment stands, in my opinion, on its own bottom.

[Harlan dissent, *Poe v. Ullman*: Due process has not been reduced to any formula; its content cannot be determined by reference to any code. The best that can be said is that through the course of this Court's decisions it has represented the balance which our Nation, built upon postulates of respect for the liberty of the individual, has struck between that liberty and the demands of organized society. If the supplying of content to this Constitutional concept has of necessity been a rational process, it certainly has not been one where judges have felt free to roam where unguided speculation might take them. The balance of which I speak is the balance struck by this country, having regard to what history teaches are the traditions from which it developed as well as the traditions from which it broke. That tradition is a living thing. A decision of this Court which radically departs from it could not long survive, while a decision which builds on what has survived is likely to be sound. No formula could serve as a substitute, in this area, for judgment and restraint.

It is this outlook which has led the Court continuingly to perceive distinctions in the imperative character of Constitutional provisions, since that character must be discerned from a particular provision's larger context. And inasmuch as this context is one not of words, but of history and purposes, the full scope of the liberty guaranteed by the Due Process Clause cannot be found in or limited by the precise terms of the specific guarantees elsewhere provided in the Constitution. This "liberty" is not a series of isolated points pricked out in terms of the taking of property; the freedom of speech, press, and religion; the right to keep and bear arms; the freedom from unreasonable searches and seizures; and so on. It is a rational continuum which, broadly speaking, includes a freedom from all substantial arbitrary impositions and purposeless restraints, and which also recognizes, what a reasonable and sensitive judgment must, that certain interests require particularly careful scrutiny of the state needs asserted to justify their abridgment.

[Appellants argue] that the judgment, implicit in this statute — that the use of contraceptives by married couples is immoral — is an irrational one, that in effect it subjects them in a very important matter to the arbitrary whim of the legislature, and that it does so for no good purpose. Where, as here, we are dealing with what must be considered "a basic liberty," . . . the mere assertion that the action of the State finds justification in the controversial realm of morals cannot justify alone any and every restriction it imposes.

. . .

It is in this area of sexual morality, which contains many proscriptions of consensual behavior having little or no direct impact on others, that the State of Connecticut has expressed its moral judgment that all use of contraceptives is improper. Appellants cite an impressive list of authorities who, from a great variety of points of view, commend the considered use of contraceptives by married couples. What they do not emphasize is that not too long ago the current of opinion was very probably quite the opposite, and that even today the issue is not free of controversy. Certainly, Connecticut's judgment is no more demonstrably correct or incorrect than are the varieties of judgment, expressed in law, on marriage and divorce, on adult consensual homosexuality, abortion, and sterilization, or euthanasia and suicide. If we had a case before us which required us to decide simply, and in abstraction, whether the moral judgment implicit in the application of the present statute to married couples was a sound one, the very controversial nature of these questions would, I think, require us to hesitate long before concluding that the Constitution precluded Connecticut from choosing as it has among these various views.

But, as might be expected, we are not presented simply with this moral judgment to be passed on as an abstract proposition. The secular state is not an examiner of consciences: it must operate in the realm of behavior, of overt actions, and where it does so operate, not only the underlying, moral purpose of its operations, but also the *choice of means* becomes relevant to any Constitutional judgment on what is done. . . .

Precisely what is involved here is this: the State is asserting the right to enforce its moral judgment by intruding upon the most intimate details of the marital relation with the full power of the criminal law. Potentially, this could allow the deployment of all the incidental machinery of the criminal law, arrests, searches and seizures; inevitably, it must mean at the very least the lodging of criminal charges, a public trial, and testimony as to the *corpus delicti*. Nor could any imaginable elaboration of presumptions, testimonial privileges, or other safeguards, alleviate the necessity for testimony as to the mode and manner of the married couples' sexual relations, or at least the opportunity for the accused to make denial of the charges. In sum, the statute allows the State to enquire into, prove and punish married people for the private use of their marital intimacy.

This, then, is the precise character of the enactment whose Constitutional measure we must take. The statute must pass a more rigorous Constitutional test than that going merely to the plausibility of its underlying rationale. This enactment involves what, by common understanding throughout the English-speaking world, must be granted to be a most fundamental aspect of "liberty," the privacy of the home in its most basic sense, and it is this which requires that the statute be subjected to strict scrutiny.

[Of course,] "[t]he family . . . is not beyond regulation," *Prince v. Massachusetts* (1944), and it would be an absurdity to suggest either that offenses may not be committed in the bosom of the family or that the home can be made a sanctuary for crime. The right of privacy most manifestly is not an absolute. Thus, I would not suggest that adultery, homosexuality, fornication and incest are immune from criminal enquiry, however privately practiced. So much has been explicitly recognized in acknowledging the State's rightful concern for its people's moral welfare. But not to discriminate between what is involved in this case and either the traditional offenses against good morals or crimes which, though they may be committed anywhere, happen to have been committed or concealed in the home, would entirely misconceive the argument that is being made.

Adultery, homosexuality and the like are sexual intimacies which the State forbids altogether, but the intimacy of husband and wife is necessarily an essential and accepted feature of the institution of marriage, an institution which the State not only must allow, but which always and in every age it has fostered and protected. It is one thing when the State exerts its power either to forbid extra-marital sexuality altogether, or to say who may marry, but it is quite another when, having acknowledged a marriage and the intimacies inherent in it, it undertakes to regulate by means of the criminal law the details of that intimacy.

In sum, even though the State has determined that the use of contraceptives is as iniquitous as any act of extra-marital sexual immorality, the intrusion of the whole machinery of the criminal law into the very heart of marital privacy, requiring husband and wife to render account before a criminal tribunal of their uses of that intimacy, is surely a very different thing indeed from punishing those who establish intimacies which the law has always forbidden and which can have no claim to social protection.

In my view the appellants have presented a very pressing claim for Constitutional protection. Such difficulty as the claim presents lies only in evaluating it against the State's countervailing contention that it be allowed to enforce, by whatever means it deems appropriate, its judgment of the immorality of the practice this law condemns. In resolving this conflict a number of factors compel me to conclude that the decision here must most emphatically be for the appellants. Since, as it appears to me, the statute marks an abridgment of important fundamental liberties protected by the Fourteenth Amendment, it will not do to urge in justification of that abridgment simply that the statute is rationally related to the effectuation of a proper state purpose. A closer scrutiny and stronger justification than that are required.

Though the State has argued the Constitutional permissibility of the moral judgment underlying this statute, neither its brief, nor its argument, nor anything in any of the opinions of its highest court in these or other cases even remotely suggests a justification for the obnoxiously intrusive means it has chosen to effectuate that policy. To me the very circumstance that Connecticut has not chosen to press the enforcement of this statute against individual users, while it nevertheless persists in asserting its right to do so at any time — in effect a right to hold this statute as an imminent threat to the privacy of the households of the State — conduces to the inference either that it does not consider the policy of the statute a very important one, or that it does not regard the means it has chosen for its effectuation as appropriate or necessary.]

Mr. Justice White, concurring in the judgment.

[T]his is not the first time this Court has had occasion to articulate that the liberty entitled to protection under the Fourteenth Amendment includes the right "to marry, establish a home and bring up children," *Meyer v. Nebraska* (1923), and "the liberty . . . to direct the upbringing and education of children," *Pierce v. Society of Sisters* (1925), and that these are among "the basic civil rights of man." *Skinner v. Oklahoma* (1942). These decisions affirm that there is a "realm of family life which the state cannot enter" without substantial justification. *Prince v. Massachusetts* (1944). Surely the right invoked in this case, to be free of regulation of the intimacies of the marriage relationship, "come[s] to this Court with a momentum for respect lacking when appeal is made to liberties which derive merely from shifting economic arrangements." *Kovacs v. Cooper* (1949) (opinion of Frankfurter, J.).

[T]he State claims but one justification for its anti-use statute. There is no serious contention that Connecticut thinks the use of artificial or external methods of contraception immoral or unwise in itself, or that the anti-use statute is founded upon any policy of promoting population expansion. Rather, the statute is said to serve the State's policy against all forms of promiscuous or illicit sexual relationships, be they premarital or extramarital, concededly a permissible and legitimate legislative goal.

Without taking issue with the premise that the fear of conception operates as a deterrent to such relationships in addition to the criminal proscriptions Connecticut has against such conduct, I wholly fail to see how the ban on the use of contraceptives by married couples in any way reinforces the State's ban on illicit sexual relationships. Connecticut does not bar the importation or possession of contraceptive devices; they are not considered contraband material under state law, and their availability in that State is not seriously disputed. The only way Connecticut seeks to limit or control the availability of such devices is through its general aiding and abetting statute whose operation in this context has been quite obviously ineffective and whose most serious use has been against birth-control clinics rendering advice to married, rather than unmarried, persons. Indeed, after over 80 years of the State's proscription of use, the legality of the sale of such devices to prevent disease has never been expressly passed upon, although it appears that sales have long occurred and have only infrequently been challenged. . . . Moreover, it would appear that the sale of contraceptives to prevent disease is plainly legal under Connecticut law.

In these circumstances one is rather hard pressed to explain how the ban on use by married persons in any way prevents use of such devices by persons engaging in illicit sexual relations and thereby contributes to the State's policy against such relationships. Neither the state courts nor the State before the bar of this Court has tendered such an explanation. It is purely fanciful to believe that the broad proscription on use facilitates discovery of use by persons engaging in a prohibited relationship or for some other reason makes such use more unlikely and thus can be supported by any sort of administrative consideration. Perhaps the theory is that the flat ban on use prevents married people from possessing contraceptives and without the ready availability of such devices for use in the marital relationship, there will be no or less temptation to use them in extramarital ones. This reasoning rests on the premise that married people will comply with the ban in regard to their marital relationship, notwithstanding total nonenforcement in this context and apparent nonenforcibility, but will not comply with criminal statutes prohibiting extramarital affairs and the anti-use statute in respect to illicit sexual relationships, a premise whose validity has not been demonstrated and whose intrinsic validity is not very evident. At most the broad ban is of marginal utility to the declared objective. A statute limiting its prohibition on use to persons engaging in the prohibited relationship would serve the end posited by Connecticut in the same way, and with the same effectiveness, or ineffectiveness, as the broad anti-use statute under attack in this case. I find nothing in this record justifying the sweeping scope of this statute, with its telling effect on the freedoms of married persons, and therefore conclude that it deprives such persons of liberty without due process of law.

Mr. Justice Black, with whom Mr. Justice Stewart joins, dissenting.

. . . [T]here is no provision of the Constitution which either expressly or impliedly vests power in this Court to sit as a supervisory agency over acts of duly constituted legislative bodies and set aside their laws because of the Court's belief that the legislative policies adopted are unreasonable, unwise, arbitrary, capricious or irrational. The adoption of such a loose, flexible, uncontrolled standard for holding laws unconstitutional, if ever it is finally achieved, will amount to a great unconstitutional shift of power to the courts which I believe and am constrained to say will be bad for the courts and worse for the country. Subjecting federal and state laws to such an unrestrained and unrestrainable judicial control as to the wisdom of legislative enactments would, I fear, jeopardize the separation of governmental powers that the Framers set up and at the same time threaten to take away much of the power of States to govern themselves which the Constitution plainly intended them to have.

. . . So far as I am concerned, Connecticut's law as applied here is not forbidden by any provision of the Federal Constitution as that Constitution was written, and I would therefore affirm.

Mr. Justice Stewart, whom Mr. Justice Black joins, dissenting.

Since 1879 Connecticut has had on its books a law which forbids the use of contraceptives by anyone. I think this is an uncommonly silly law. As a practical matter, the law is obviously unenforceable, except in the oblique context of the present case. As a philosophical matter, I believe the use of contraceptives in the relationship of marriage should be left to personal and private choice, based upon each individual's moral, ethical, and religious beliefs. As a matter of social policy, I think professional counsel about methods of birth control should be available to all, so that each individual's choice can be meaningfully made. But we are not asked in this case to say whether we think this law is unwise, or even asinine. We are asked to hold that it violates the United States Constitution. And that I cannot do.

. . . With all deference, I can find no . . . general right of privacy in the Bill of Rights, in any other part of the Constitution, or in any case ever before decided by this Court.

At the oral argument in this case we were told that the Connecticut law does not "conform to current community standards." But it is not the function of this Court to decide cases on the basis of community standards. We are here to decide cases "agreeably to the Constitution and laws of the United States." It is the essence of judicial duty to subordinate our own personal views, our own ideas of what legislation is wise and what is not. If, as I should surely hope, the law before us does not reflect the standards of the people of Connecticut, the people of Connecticut can freely exercise their true Ninth and Tenth Amendment rights to persuade their elected representatives to repeal it. That is the constitutional way to take this law off the books.

## NOTES AND QUESTIONS

**1.** To say that *Griswold* is an important case in constitutional law is perhaps an understatement. It is a case that has earned respect as precedent but remains controversial. One reason is the lack of unanimity among the justices as to why an individual interest in intimate conduct within marriage should be deemed fundamental (though a majority of them agreed that it is). On this point, who has the better of the argument — Justice Douglas, and his penumbral approach to privacy; Justice Goldberg, and his Ninth Amendment approach; or Justice Harlan, and his approach grounded in due process? Recall the *McDonald* case and you will know which approach ultimately won the day. That said, it's important to be able to distinguish between and among these approaches — and to understand why, ultimately, neither the approach espoused by Douglas nor the one favored by Goldberg won the day.

**2.** For all of the justices in the majority, the primary concern was to determine whether the asserted interest in intimate conduct within marriage should be deemed fundamental for purposes of due process — for once an interest is deemed to be fundamental, the state will have to carry a heavy burden to justify restricting that interest (as in, say, the context of restrictions on the content of speech under the First Amendment). One question (of the many) that *Griswold* does not answer is whether interests should be deemed fundamental for all purposes — or whether even interests that are not fundamental, but that are arguably related to the interest the Court found protected in *Griswold*, may be immune from regulation in certain instances, as the following case demonstrates.

### Lawrence v. Texas
### 539 U.S. 558 (2003)

Justice Kennedy delivered the opinion of the Court.

Liberty protects the person from unwarranted government intrusions into a dwelling or other private places. In our tradition the

State is not omnipresent in the home. And there are other spheres of our lives and existence, outside the home, where the State should not be a dominant presence. Freedom extends beyond spatial bounds. Liberty presumes an autonomy of self that includes freedom of thought, belief, expression, and certain intimate conduct. The instant case involves liberty of the person both in its spatial and in its more transcendent dimensions.

## I

The question before the Court is the validity of a Texas statute making it a crime for two persons of the same sex to engage in certain intimate sexual conduct.

In Houston, Texas, officers of the Harris County Police Department were dispatched to a private residence in response to a reported weapons disturbance. They entered an apartment where one of the petitioners, John Geddes Lawrence, resided. The right of the police to enter does not seem to have been questioned. The officers observed Lawrence and another man, Tyron Garner, engaging in a sexual act. The two petitioners were arrested, held in custody overnight, and charged and convicted before a Justice of the Peace.

The complaints described their crime as "deviate sexual intercourse, namely anal sex, with a member of the same sex (man)." The applicable state law is Tex. Penal Code Ann. § 21.06(a) (2003). It provides: "A person commits an offense if he engages in deviate sexual intercourse with another individual of the same sex." . . .

The petitioners exercised their right to a trial *de novo* in Harris County Criminal Court. They challenged the statute as a violation of the Equal Protection Clause of the Fourteenth Amendment and of a like provision of the Texas Constitution. Those contentions were rejected. The petitioners, having entered a plea of *nolo contendere*, were each fined $200 and assessed court costs of $141.25.

The Court of Appeals for the Texas Fourteenth District considered the petitioners' federal constitutional arguments under both the Equal Protection and Due Process Clauses of the Fourteenth Amendment. After hearing the case en banc the court, in a divided opinion, rejected the constitutional arguments and affirmed the convictions. The majority opinion indicates that the Court of Appeals considered our decision in *Bowers v. Hardwick* (1986), to be controlling on the federal due process aspect of the case. *Bowers* then being authoritative, this was proper.

We granted certiorari, to consider . . . [w]hether petitioners' criminal convictions for adult consensual sexual intimacy in the home violate their vital interests in liberty and privacy protected by the Due Process Clause of the Fourteenth Amendment[, and whether] *Bowers* should be overruled[.]

The petitioners were adults at the time of the alleged offense. Their conduct was in private and consensual.

## II

We conclude the case should be resolved by determining whether the petitioners were free as adults to engage in the private conduct in

*Using Harlan from Griswold?*

the exercise of their liberty under the Due Process Clause of the Fourteenth Amendment to the Constitution. For this inquiry we deem it necessary to reconsider the Court's holding in *Bowers*.

There are broad statements of the substantive reach of liberty under the Due Process Clause in earlier cases, including *Pierce v. Society of Sisters* (1925) and *Meyer v. Nebraska* (1923), but the most pertinent beginning point is our decision in *Griswold v. Connecticut* (1965).

In *Griswold* the Court invalidated a state law prohibiting the use of drugs or devices of contraception and counseling or aiding and abetting the use of contraceptives. The Court described the protected interest as a right to privacy and placed emphasis on the marriage relation and the protected space of the marital bedroom.

After *Griswold* it was established that the right to make certain decisions regarding sexual conduct extends beyond the marital relationship. In *Eisenstadt v. Baird* (1972), the Court invalidated a law prohibiting the distribution of contraceptives to unmarried persons. The case was decided under the Equal Protection Clause, but with respect to unmarried persons, the Court went on to state the fundamental proposition that the law impaired the exercise of their personal rights. ...

The facts in *Bowers* had some similarities to the instant case. A police officer, whose right to enter seems not to have been in question, observed Hardwick, in his own bedroom, engaging in intimate sexual conduct with another adult male. The conduct was in violation of a Georgia statute making it a criminal offense to engage in sodomy. One difference between the two cases is that the Georgia statute prohibited the conduct whether or not the participants were of the same sex, while the Texas statute, as we have seen, applies only to participants of the same sex. Hardwick was not prosecuted, but he brought an action in federal court to declare the state statute invalid. He alleged he was a practicing homosexual and that the criminal prohibition violated rights guaranteed to him by the Constitution. The Court, in an opinion by Justice White, sustained the Georgia law. Chief Justice Burger and Justice Powell joined the opinion of the Court and filed separate, concurring opinions. Four Justices dissented.

The Court began its substantive discussion in *Bowers* as follows: "The issue presented is whether the Federal Constitution confers a fundamental right upon homosexuals to engage in sodomy and hence invalidates the laws of the many States that still make such conduct illegal and have done so for a very long time." That statement, we now conclude, discloses the Court's own failure to appreciate the extent of the liberty at stake. To say that the issue in *Bowers* was simply the right to engage in certain sexual conduct demeans the claim the individual put forward, just as it would demean a married couple were it to be said marriage is simply about the right to have sexual intercourse. The laws involved in *Bowers* and here are, to be sure, statutes that purport to do no more than prohibit a particular sexual act. Their penalties and purposes, though, have more far-reaching consequences, touching upon the most private human conduct, sexual behavior, and in the most private of places, the home.

The statutes do seek to control a personal relationship that, whether or not entitled to formal recognition in the law, is within the liberty of persons to choose without being punished as criminals.

This, as a general rule, should counsel against attempts by the State, or a court, to define the meaning of the relationship or to set its boundaries absent injury to a person or abuse of an institution the law protects. It suffices for us to acknowledge that adults may choose to enter upon this relationship in the confines of their homes and their own private lives and still retain their dignity as free persons. When sexuality finds overt expression in intimate conduct with another person, the conduct can be but one element in a personal bond that is more enduring. The liberty protected by the Constitution allows homosexual persons the right to make this choice.

Having misapprehended the claim of liberty there presented to it, and thus stating the claim to be whether there is a fundamental right to engage in consensual sodomy, the *Bowers* Court said: "Proscriptions against that conduct have ancient roots." In academic writings, and in many of the scholarly *amicus* briefs filed to assist the Court in this case, there are fundamental criticisms of the historical premises relied upon by the majority and concurring opinions in *Bowers*. We need not enter this debate in the attempt to reach a definitive historical judgment, but the following considerations counsel against adopting the definitive conclusions upon which *Bowers* placed such reliance.

At the outset it should be noted that there is no longstanding history in this country of laws directed at homosexual conduct as a distinct matter. . . . [E]arly American sodomy laws were not directed at homosexuals as such but instead sought to prohibit nonprocreative sexual activity more generally. This does not suggest approval of homosexual conduct. It does tend to show that this particular form of conduct was not thought of as a separate category from like conduct between heterosexual persons.

Laws prohibiting sodomy do not seem to have been enforced against consenting adults acting in private. A substantial number of sodomy prosecutions and convictions for which there are surviving records were for predatory acts against those who could not or did not consent, as in the case of a minor or the victim of an assault. . . .

The policy of punishing consenting adults for private acts was not much discussed in the early legal literature. We can infer that one reason for this was the very private nature of the conduct. Despite the absence of prosecutions, there may have been periods in which there was public criticism of homosexuals as such and an insistence that the criminal laws be enforced to discourage their practices. But far from possessing "ancient roots," American laws targeting same-sex couples did not develop until the last third of the 20th century. The reported decisions concerning the prosecution of consensual, homosexual sodomy between adults for the years 1880-1995 are not always clear in the details, but a significant number involved conduct in a public place.

It was not until the 1970's that any State singled out same-sex relations for criminal prosecution, and only nine States have done so. Post-*Bowers* even some of these States did not adhere to the policy of suppressing homosexual conduct. Over the course of the last decades, States with same-sex prohibitions have moved toward abolishing them.

In summary, the historical grounds relied upon in *Bowers* are more complex than the majority opinion and the concurring opinion by Chief Justice Burger indicate. Their historical premises are not without doubt and, at the very least, are overstated.

It must be acknowledged, of course, that the Court in *Bowers* was making the broader point that for centuries there have been powerful voices to condemn homosexual conduct as immoral. The condemnation has been shaped by religious beliefs, conceptions of right and acceptable behavior, and respect for the traditional family. For many persons these are not trivial concerns but profound and deep convictions accepted as ethical and moral principles to which they aspire and which thus determine the course of their lives. These considerations do not answer the question before us, however. The issue is whether the majority may use the power of the State to enforce these views on the whole society through operation of the criminal law. . . .

The sweeping references by [in *Bowers*] to the history of Western civilization and to Judeo-Christian moral and ethical standards did not take account of other authorities pointing in an opposite direction. A committee advising the British Parliament recommended in 1957 repeal of laws punishing homosexual conduct. Parliament enacted the substance of those recommendations 10 years later.

Of even more importance, almost five years before *Bowers* was decided the European Court of Human Rights considered a case with parallels to *Bowers* and to today's case. An adult male resident in Northern Ireland alleged he was a practicing homosexual who desired to engage in consensual homosexual conduct. The laws of Northern Ireland forbade him that right. He alleged that he had been questioned, his home had been searched, and he feared criminal prosecution. The court held that the laws proscribing the conduct were invalid under the European Convention on Human Rights. In all countries that are members of the Council of Europe (21 nations then, 45 nations now), the decision is at odds with the premise in *Bowers* that the claim put forward was insubstantial in our Western civilization.

In our own constitutional system the deficiencies in *Bowers* became even more apparent in the years following its announcement. The 25 States with laws prohibiting the relevant conduct referenced in the *Bowers* decision are reduced now to 13, of which 4 enforce their laws only against homosexual conduct. In those States where sodomy is still proscribed, whether for same-sex or heterosexual conduct, there is a pattern of non-enforcement with respect to consenting adults acting in private. The State of Texas admitted in 1994 that as of that date it had not prosecuted anyone under those circumstances.

Two principal cases decided after *Bowers* cast its holding into even more doubt. In *Planned Parenthood, supra,* the Court reaffirmed the substantive force of the liberty protected by the Due Process Clause. The *Casey* decision again confirmed that our laws and tradition afford constitutional protection to personal decisions relating to marriage, procreation, contraception, family relationships, child rearing, and education. In explaining the respect the Constitution demands for the autonomy of the person in making these choices, we stated as follows:

> These matters, involving the most intimate and personal choices a person may make in a lifetime, choices central to personal dignity and autonomy, are central to the liberty protected by the Fourteenth Amendment. At the heart of liberty is the right to define one's own concept of existence, of meaning, of the universe, and of the mystery of human life. Beliefs about these matters could not define the attributes of personhood were they formed under compulsion of the State.

Persons in a homosexual relationship may seek autonomy for these purposes, just as heterosexual persons do. The decision in *Bowers* would deny them this right.

The second post-*Bowers* case of principal relevance is *Romer v. Evans* (1996). There the Court struck down class-based legislation directed at homosexuals as a violation of the Equal Protection Clause. *Romer* invalidated an amendment to Colorado's Constitution which named as a solitary class persons who were homosexuals, lesbians, or bisexual either by "orientation, conduct, practices or relationships" (internal quotation marks omitted), and deprived them of protection under state antidiscrimination laws. We concluded that the provision was "born of animosity toward the class of persons affected" and further that it had no rational relation to a legitimate governmental purpose.

As an alternative argument in this case, counsel for the petitioners and some *amici* contend that *Romer* provides the basis for declaring the Texas statute invalid under the Equal Protection Clause. That is a tenable argument, but we conclude the instant case requires us to address whether *Bowers* itself has continuing validity. Were we to hold the statute invalid under the Equal Protection Clause some might question whether a prohibition would be valid if drawn differently, say, to prohibit the conduct both between same-sex and different-sex participants.

Equality of treatment and the due process right to demand respect for conduct protected by the substantive guarantee of liberty are linked in important respects, and a decision on the latter point advances both interests. If protected conduct is made criminal and the law which does so remains unexamined for its substantive validity, its stigma might remain even if it were not enforceable as drawn for equal protection reasons. When homosexual conduct is made criminal by the law of the State, that declaration in and of itself is an invitation to subject homosexual persons to discrimination both in the public and in the private spheres. The central holding of *Bowers* has been brought in question by this case, and it should be addressed. Its continuance as precedent demeans the lives of homosexual persons.

The stigma this criminal statute imposes, moreover, is not trivial. The offense, to be sure, is but a class C misdemeanor, a minor offense in the Texas legal system. Still, it remains a criminal offense with all that imports for the dignity of the persons charged. The petitioners will bear on their record the history of their criminal convictions. Just this Term we rejected various challenges to state laws requiring the registration of sex offenders. We are advised that if Texas convicted an adult for private, consensual homosexual conduct under the statute here in question the convicted person would come within the registration laws of at least four States were he or she to be subject to their jurisdiction. This underscores the consequential nature of the punishment and the state-sponsored condemnation attendant to the criminal prohibition. Furthermore, the Texas criminal conviction carries with it the other collateral consequences always following a conviction, such as notations on job application forms, to mention but one example.

The foundations of *Bowers* have sustained serious erosion from our recent decisions in *Casey* and *Romer*. When our precedent has been thus weakened, criticism from other sources is of greater significance. In the United States criticism of *Bowers* has been substantial and continuing, disapproving of its reasoning in all respects, not just as to its historical assumptions. The courts of five different States have declined to follow it in interpreting provisions in their own state constitutions parallel to the Due Process Clause of the Fourteenth Amendment.

To the extent *Bowers* relied on values we share with a wider civilization, it should be noted that the reasoning and holding in *Bowers* have been rejected elsewhere. The European Court of Human Rights has followed not *Bowers* but its own decision in *Dudgeon v. United Kingdom* (ECHR 1981). Other nations, too, have taken action consistent with an affirmation of the protected right of homosexual adults to engage in intimate, consensual conduct. The right the petitioners seek in this case has been accepted as an integral part of human freedom in many other countries. There has been no showing that in this country the governmental interest in circumscribing personal choice is somehow more legitimate or urgent.

The doctrine of *stare decisis* is essential to the respect accorded to the judgments of the Court and to the stability of the law. It is not, however, an inexorable command. . . . The holding in *Bowers* . . . has not induced detrimental reliance comparable to some instances where recognized individual rights are involved. Indeed, there has been no individual or societal reliance on *Bowers* of the sort that could counsel against overturning its holding once there are compelling reasons to do so. *Bowers* itself causes uncertainty, for the precedents before and after its issuance contradict its central holding.

The rationale of *Bowers* does not withstand careful analysis. In his dissenting opinion in *Bowers* Justice Stevens came to these conclusions:

Our prior cases make two propositions abundantly clear. First, the fact that the governing majority in a State has traditionally viewed a particular practice as immoral is not a sufficient reason for upholding a law prohibiting the practice; neither history nor tradition could save a law prohibiting miscegenation from constitutional attack. Second, individual decisions by married persons, concerning the intimacies of their physical relationship, even when not intended to produce offspring, are a form of "liberty" protected by the Due Process Clause of the Fourteenth Amendment. Moreover, this protection extends to intimate choices by unmarried as well as married persons.

(footnotes and citations omitted).

Justice Stevens' analysis, in our view, should have been controlling in *Bowers* and should control here.

*Bowers* was not correct when it was decided, and it is not correct today. It ought not to remain binding precedent. *Bowers v. Hardwick* should be and now is overruled.

The present case does not involve minors. It does not involve persons who might be injured or coerced or who are situated in relationships where consent might not easily be refused. It does not involve public conduct or prostitution. It does not involve whether the government must give formal recognition to any relationship that homosexual persons seek to enter. The case does involve two adults who, with full and mutual consent from each other, engaged in sexual practices common to a homosexual lifestyle. The petitioners are entitled to respect for their private lives. The State cannot demean their existence or control their destiny by making their private sexual conduct a crime. Their right to liberty under the Due Process Clause gives them the full right to engage in their conduct without intervention of the government. "It is a promise of the Constitution that there is a realm of personal liberty which the government may not enter." *Casey*. The Texas statute furthers no legitimate state interest which can justify its intrusion into the personal and private life of the individual.

. . .

The judgment of the Court of Appeals for the Texas Fourteenth District is reversed, and the case is remanded for further proceedings not inconsistent with this opinion.

*It is so ordered.*

Justice O'Connor, concurring in the judgment.

The Court today overrules *Bowers v. Hardwick* (1986). I joined *Bowers,* and do not join the Court in overruling it. Nevertheless, I agree with the Court that Texas' statute banning same-sex sodomy is unconstitutional. Rather than relying on the substantive component of the Fourteenth Amendment's Due Process Clause, as the Court does, I base my conclusion on the Fourteenth Amendment's Equal Protection Clause.

The Equal Protection Clause of the Fourteenth Amendment "is essentially a direction that all persons similarly situated should be treated alike." *Cleburne v. Cleburne Living Center, Inc.* (1985). . . . The statute at issue here makes sodomy a crime only if a person "engages in deviate sexual intercourse with another individual of the same sex." Sodomy between opposite-sex partners, however, is not a crime in Texas. That is, Texas treats the same conduct differently based solely on the participants. Those harmed by this law are people who have a same-sex sexual orientation and thus are more likely to engage in behavior prohibited by § 21.06.

The Texas statute makes homosexuals unequal in the eyes of the law by making particular conduct — and only that conduct — subject to criminal sanction. It appears that prosecutions under Texas' sodomy law are rare. This case shows, however, that prosecutions under § 21.06 *do* occur. And while the penalty imposed on petitioners in this case was relatively minor, the consequences of conviction are not. It appears that petitioners' convictions, if upheld, would disqualify them from or restrict their ability to engage in a variety of professions, including medicine, athletic training, and interior design. Indeed, were petitioners to move to one of four States, their convictions would require them to register as sex offenders to local law enforcement.

And the effect of Texas' sodomy law is not just limited to the threat of prosecution or consequence of conviction. Texas' sodomy law brands all homosexuals as criminals, thereby making it more difficult for homosexuals to be treated in the same manner as everyone else. Indeed, Texas itself has previously acknowledged the collateral effects of the law, stipulating in a prior challenge to this action that the law "legally sanctions discrimination against [homosexuals] in a variety of ways unrelated to the criminal law," including in the areas of "employment, family issues, and housing." *State v. Morales* (Tex. App. 1992).

. . . I am confident, however, that so long as the Equal Protection Clause requires a sodomy law to apply equally to the private consensual conduct of homosexuals and heterosexuals alike, such a law would not long stand in our democratic society. . . .

A law branding one class of persons as criminal based solely on the State's moral disapproval of that class and the conduct associated with that class runs contrary to the values of the Constitution and the Equal Protection Clause, under any standard of review. I therefore concur in the Court's judgment that Texas' sodomy law banning "deviate sexual intercourse" between consenting adults of the same sex, but not between consenting adults of different sexes, is unconstitutional.

Justice Scalia, with whom The Chief Justice and Justice Thomas join, dissenting.

[The] Court embraces . . . Justice Stevens' declaration in his *Bowers* dissent, that "the fact that the governing majority in a State has traditionally viewed a particular practice as immoral is not a sufficient reason for upholding a law prohibiting the practice." This effectively decrees the end of all morals legislation. If, as the Court asserts, the promotion of majoritarian sexual morality is not even a *legitimate* state interest, none of the above-mentioned laws can survive rational-basis review.

Today's opinion is the product of a Court, which is the product of a law-profession culture, that has largely signed on to the so-called homosexual agenda, by which I mean the agenda promoted by some homosexual activists directed at eliminating the moral opprobrium that has traditionally attached to homosexual conduct. I noted in an earlier opinion the fact that the American Association of Law Schools (to which any reputable law school *must* seek to belong) excludes from membership any school that refuses to ban from its job-interview facilities a law firm (no matter how small) that does not wish to hire as a prospective partner a person who openly engages in homosexual conduct.

One of the most revealing statements in today's opinion is the Court's grim warning that the criminalization of homosexual conduct is "an invitation to subject homosexual persons to discrimination both in the public and in the private spheres." It is clear from this that the Court has taken sides in the culture war, departing from its role of assuring, as neutral observer, that the democratic rules of engagement are observed. Many Americans do not want persons who openly engage in homosexual conduct as partners in their business, as scoutmasters for their children, as teachers in their children's schools, or as boarders in their home. They view this as protecting themselves and their families from a lifestyle that they believe to be immoral and destructive. The Court views it as "discrimination" which it is the function of our judgments to deter. So imbued is the Court with the law profession's anti-anti-homosexual culture, that it is seemingly unaware that the attitudes of that culture are not obviously "mainstream"; that in most States what the Court calls "discrimination" against those who engage in homosexual acts is perfectly legal; that proposals to ban such "discrimination" under Title VII have repeatedly been rejected by Congress; that in some cases such "discrimination" is *mandated* by federal statute; and that in some cases such "discrimination" is a constitutional right.

Let me be clear that I have nothing against homosexuals, or any other group, promoting their agenda through normal democratic means. Social perceptions of sexual and other morality change over time, and every group has the right to persuade its fellow citizens that its view of such matters is the best. That homosexuals have achieved some success in that enterprise is attested to by the fact that Texas is one of the few remaining States that criminalize private, consensual homosexual acts. But persuading one's fellow citizens is one thing, and imposing one's views in absence of democratic majority will is something else. I would no more *require* a State to criminalize homosexual acts — or, for that matter, display *any* moral disapprobation of them — than I would *forbid* it to do so. What Texas has chosen to do is well within the range of traditional democratic action, and its hand should not be stayed through the invention of a brand-new "constitutional right" by a Court that is impatient of democratic change. It is indeed true that "later generations can see that laws once thought necessary and proper in fact serve only to oppress"; and when that happens, later generations can repeal those laws. But it is the premise of our system that those judgments are to be made by the people, and not imposed by a governing caste that knows best.

One of the benefits of leaving regulation of this matter to the people rather than to the courts is that the people, unlike judges, need not carry things to their logical conclusion. The people may feel that their disapprobation of homosexual conduct is strong enough to disallow homosexual marriage, but not strong enough to criminalize private homosexual acts — and may legislate accordingly. . . . At the end of its opinion — after having laid waste the foundations of our rational-basis jurisprudence — the Court says that the present case "does not involve whether the government must give formal recognition to any relationship that homosexual persons seek to enter." Do not believe it. More illuminating than this bald, unreasoned disclaimer is the progression of thought displayed by an earlier passage in the Court's opinion, which notes the constitutional protections afforded to "personal decisions relating to *marriage, procreation, contraception, family relationships, child rearing, and education,*" and then declares that "[p]ersons in a homosexual relationship may seek autonomy for these purposes, just as heterosexual persons do." (emphasis added). Today's opinion dismantles the structure of constitutional law that has permitted a distinction to be made between heterosexual and homosexual unions, insofar as formal recognition in marriage is concerned. If moral disapprobation of homosexual conduct is "no legitimate state interest" for purposes of proscribing that conduct; and if, as the Court coos (casting aside all pretense of neutrality), "[w]hen sexuality finds overt expression in intimate conduct with another person, the conduct can be but one element in a personal bond that is more enduring," what justification could there possibly be for denying the benefits of marriage to homosexual couples exercising "[t]he liberty protected by the Constitution"? Surely not the encouragement of procreation, since the sterile and the elderly are allowed to marry. This case "does not involve" the issue of homosexual marriage only if one entertains the belief that principle and logic have nothing to do with the decisions of this Court. Many will hope that, as the Court comfortingly assures us, this is so.

[Dissenting opinion of Justice Thomas omitted.]

## NOTES AND QUESTIONS

**1.** The primary concern of the majority in *Lawrence* was to make clear that *Bowers v. Hardwick*, 478 U.S. 186 (1986), should be overruled. The two cases seem to address the same issue, but the response from each court could not be more different.

**2.** One striking feature of *Lawrence* is the approach the majority adopts. Does the majority at any point explicitly mark the interest asserted — that is, the interest of consenting adults in engaging in intimate conduct — as fundamental for due process purposes? It points to cases in which similar interests have been held fundamental — *Griswold*, for example, and *Eisenstadt* — but never actually states that the interest in this case should be so viewed.

**3.** There is an approach to constitutional interpretation that values minimalism in judicial decisionmaking — an approach that requires a court to do no more than answer the question posed in the case before it, and to leave other, unanswered, and often larger, questions for another day. *See* Cass R. Sunstein, One Case at a Time: Judicial Minimalism on the Supreme Court (1999). *Lawrence* would seem to exemplify this approach, for its result arguably does not depend upon the Court holding the interest in certain intimate conduct asserted by the defendant to be fundamental.

**4.** If the interest asserted in *Lawrence* is not deemed fundamental, the question arises as to what level of scrutiny the regulation should receive. As noted above, the *Griswold* Court eschewed extended discussion of the framework of review fundamental rights receive, but you should recall, from the first chapter of this book, the cases discussing the First Amendment's freedom of speech, and you will see, throughout the rest of this chapter and the next, that deprivations of fundamental interests typically receive strict scrutiny from the courts. This means the government must demonstrate that the regulation is supported by a compelling interest and is narrowly tailored to achieve that interest. What interest did Texas argue supported its prohibition here? Had Texas argued other police power interests, such as health or safety, would the result have been the same?

**5.** Justice Scalia, in his dissent, prophecies that the courts will, after *Lawrence*, be emboldened to strike down all manner of police power regulations enacted by states — he names "criminal laws against fornication, bigamy, adultery, adult incest, bestiality, and obscenity." Can you distinguish between laws prohibiting these kinds of conduct, on the one hand, and the law Texas sought to defend in *Lawrence*, on the other? Does there exist a legitimate basis, other than morality, for prohibiting such conduct?

### 3. Family

### Moore v. City of East Cleveland
### 431 U.S. 494 (1977)

Mr. Justice Powell announced the judgment of the Court, and delivered an opinion in which Mr. Justice Brennan, Mr. Justice Marshall, and Mr. Justice Blackmun joined.

East Cleveland's housing ordinance, like many throughout the country, limits occupancy of a dwelling unit to members of a single family. But the ordinance contains an unusual and complicated definitional section that recognizes as a "family" only a few categories of related individuals. Because her family, living together in her home, fits none of those categories, appellant stands convicted of a criminal offense. The question in this case is whether the ordinance violates the Due Process Clause of the Fourteenth Amendment.

## I

Appellant, Mrs. Inez Moore, lives in her East Cleveland home together with her son, Dale Moore, Sr., and her two grandsons, Dale, Jr., and John Moore, Jr. The two boys are first cousins rather than brothers; we are told that John came to live with his grandmother and with the elder and younger Dale Moores after his mother's death.

In early 1973, Mrs. Moore received a notice of violation from the city, stating that John was an "illegal occupant" and directing her to comply with the ordinance. When she failed to remove him from her home, the city filed a criminal charge. Mrs. Moore moved to dismiss, claiming that the ordinance was constitutionally invalid on its face. Her motion was overruled, and upon conviction she was sentenced to five days in jail and a $25 fine. The Ohio Court of Appeals affirmed after giving full consideration to her constitutional claims, and the Ohio Supreme Court denied review. We noted probable jurisdiction of her appeal.

## II

The city argues that our decision in *Village of Belle Terre v. Boraas* (1974), requires us to sustain the ordinance attacked here. Belle Terre, like East Cleveland, imposed limits on the types of groups that could occupy a single dwelling unit. Applying the constitutional standard announced in this Court's leading land-use case, *Euclid v. Ambler Realty Co.* (1926), we sustained the Belle Terre ordinance on the ground that it bore a rational relationship to permissible state objectives.

But one overriding factor sets this case apart from *Belle Terre*. The ordinance there affected only *unrelated* individuals. It expressly allowed all who were related by "blood, adoption, or marriage" to live together, and in sustaining the ordinance we were careful to note that it promoted "family needs" and "family values." East Cleveland, in contrast, has chosen to regulate the occupancy of its housing by slicing deeply into the family itself. This is no mere incidental result of the ordinance. On its face it selects certain categories of relatives who may live together and declares that others may not. In particular, it makes a crime of a grandmother's choice to live with her grandson in circumstances like those presented here.

When a city undertakes such intrusive regulation of the family, neither *Belle Terre* nor *Euclid* governs; the usual judicial deference to the legislature is inappropriate. "This Court has long recognized that freedom of personal choice in matters of marriage and family life is one of the liberties protected by the Due Process Clause of the Fourteenth Amendment." *Cleveland Board of Education v. LaFleur* (1974). A host of cases, tracing their lineage to *Meyer v. Nebraska* (1923) and *Pierce v. Society of Sisters* (1925), have consistently acknowledged a "private realm of family life which the state cannot enter." *Prince v. Massachusetts* (1944). Of course, the family is not beyond regulation. But when the government intrudes on choices concerning family living arrangements, this Court must examine carefully the importance of the governmental interests advanced and the extent to which they are served by the challenged regulation.

When thus examined, this ordinance cannot survive. The city seeks to justify it as a means of preventing overcrowding, minimizing traffic and parking congestion, and avoiding an undue financial burden on East Cleveland's school system. Although these are legitimate goals, the ordinance before us serves them marginally, at best. For example, the ordinance permits any family consisting only of husband, wife, and unmarried children to live together, even if the family contains a half dozen licensed drivers, each with his or her own car. At the same time it forbids an adult brother and sister to share a household, even if both faithfully use public transportation. The ordinance would permit a grandmother to live with a single dependent son and children, even if his school-age children number a dozen, yet it forces Mrs. Moore to find another dwelling for her grandson John, simply because of the presence of his uncle and cousin in the same household. We need not labor the point. [The ordinance] has but a tenuous relation to alleviation of the conditions mentioned by the city.

### III

The city would distinguish the cases based on *Meyer* and *Pierce*. It points out that none of them "gives grandmothers any fundamental rights with respect to grandsons," and suggests that any constitutional right to live together as a family extends only to the nuclear family — essentially a couple and their dependent children.

To be sure, these cases did not expressly consider the family relationship presented here. They were immediately concerned with freedom of choice with respect to childbearing, or with the rights of parents to the custody and companionship of their own children, or with traditional parental authority in matters of child rearing and education. But unless we close our eyes to the basic reasons why certain rights associated with the family have been accorded shelter under the Fourteenth Amendment's Due Process Clause, we cannot avoid applying the force and rationale of these precedents to the family choice involved in this case.

Understanding those reasons requires careful attention to this Court's function under the Due Process Clause. . . .

Substantive due process has at times been a treacherous field for this Court. There *are* risks when the judicial branch gives enhanced protection to certain substantive liberties without the guidance of the more specific provisions of the Bill of Rights. As the history of the *Lochner* era demonstrates, there is reason for concern lest the only limits to such judicial intervention become the predilections of those who happen at the time to be Members of this Court. That history counsels caution and restraint. But it does not counsel abandonment, nor does it require what the city urges here: cutting off any protection of family rights at the first convenient, if arbitrary boundary — the boundary of the nuclear family.

Appropriate limits on substantive due process come not from drawing arbitrary lines but rather from careful "respect for the teachings of history [and] solid recognition of the basic values that underlie our society." *Griswold v. Connecticut* (1967) (Harlan, J., concurring). Our decisions establish that the Constitution protects the sanctity of the family precisely because the institution of the family is deeply rooted in this Nation's history and tradition. It is through the family that we inculcate and pass down many of our most cherished values, moral and cultural.

Ours is by no means a tradition limited to respect for the bonds uniting the members of the nuclear family. The tradition of uncles, aunts, cousins, and especially grandparents sharing a household along with parents and children has roots equally venerable and equally deserving of constitutional recognition. Over the years millions of our citizens have grown up in just such an environment, and most, surely, have profited from it. Even if conditions of modern society have brought about a decline in extended family households, they have not erased the accumulated wisdom of civilization, gained over the centuries and honored throughout our history, that supports a larger conception of the family. Out of choice, necessity, or a sense of family responsibility, it has been common for close relatives to draw together and participate in the duties and the satisfactions of a common home. Decisions concerning child rearing, which [many] cases have recognized as entitled to constitutional protection, long have been shared with grandparents or other relatives who occupy the same household — indeed who may take on major responsibility for the rearing of the children. Especially in times of adversity, such as the death of a spouse or economic need, the broader family has tended to come together for mutual sustenance and to maintain or rebuild a secure home life. This is apparently what happened here.

Whether or not such a household is established because of personal tragedy, the choice of relatives in this degree of kinship to live together may not lightly be denied by the State. *Pierce* struck down an Oregon law requiring all children to attend the State's public schools, holding that the Constitution "excludes any general power of the State to standardize its children by forcing them to accept instruction from public teachers only." By the same token the Constitution prevents East Cleveland from standardizing its children — and its adults — by forcing all to live in certain narrowly defined family patterns.

*Reversed.*

Mr. Justice Brennan, with whom Mr. Justice Marshall joins, concurring.

[T]he zoning power is not a license for local communities to enact senseless and arbitrary restrictions which cut deeply into private areas of protected family life. East Cleveland may not constitutionally define "family" as essentially confined to parents and the parents' own children. The plurality's opinion conclusively demonstrates that classifying family patterns in this eccentric way is not a rational means of achieving the ends East Cleveland claims for its ordinance, and further that the ordinance unconstitutionally abridges the "freedom of personal choice in matters of . . . family life [that] is one of the liberties protected by the Due Process Clause of the Fourteenth Amendment." *Cleveland Board of Education v. LaFleur* (1974). I write only to underscore the cultural myopia of the arbitrary boundary drawn by the East Cleveland ordinance in the light of the tradition of the American home that has been a feature of our society since our beginning as a Nation — the "tradition" in the plurality's words, "of uncles, aunts, cousins, and especially grandparents sharing a household along with parents and children. . . ." The line drawn by this ordinance displays a depressing insensitivity toward the economic and emotional needs of a very large part of our society. . . .

[Concurring opinion of Justice STEVENS omitted.]

[Dissenting opinion of Chief Justice BURGER omitted.]

Mr. Justice Stewart, with whom Mr. Justice Rehnquist joins, dissenting.

. . . Several decisions of the Court have identified specific aspects of what might broadly be termed "private family life" that are constitutionally protected against state interference. *See, e.g., Roe v. Wade* (1972) (woman's right to decide whether to terminate pregnancy); *Griswold v. Connecticut* (1967); *Eisenstadt v. Baird* (1972) (right to use contraceptives); *Pierce v. Society of Sisters* (parents' right to send children to private schools); *Meyer v. Nebraska* (parents' right to have children instructed in foreign language).

Although the appellant's desire to share a single-dwelling unit also involves "private family life" in a sense, that desire can hardly be equated with any of the interests protected in the cases just cited. The ordinance about which the appellant complains did not impede her choice to have or not to have children, and it did not dictate to her how her own children were to be nurtured and reared. The ordinance clearly does not prevent parents from living together or living with their unemancipated offspring.

But even though the Court's previous cases are not directly in point, the appellant contends that the importance of the "extended family" in American society requires us to hold that her decision to share her residence with her grandsons may not be interfered with by the State. This decision, like the decisions involved in bearing and raising children, is said to be an aspect of "family life" also entitled to substantive protection under the Constitution. Without pausing to inquire how far under this argument an "extended family" might extend, I cannot agree. When the Court has found that the Fourteenth Amendment placed a substantive limitation on a State's power to regulate, it has been in those rare cases in which the personal interests at issue have been deemed "implicit in the concept of ordered liberty." The interest that the appellant may have in permanently sharing a single kitchen and a suite of contiguous rooms with some of her relatives simply does not rise to that level. To equate this interest with the fundamental decisions to marry and to bear and raise children is to extend the limited substantive contours of the Due Process Clause beyond recognition. . . .

Mr. Justice White, dissenting.

. . . . What the deeply rooted traditions of the country are is arguable; which of them deserve the protection of the Due Process Clause is even more debatable. The suggested view would broaden enormously the horizons of the Clause; and, if the interest involved here is any measure of what the States would be forbidden to regulate, the courts would be substantively weighing and very likely invalidating a wide range of measures that Congress and state legislatures think appropriate to respond to a changing economic and social order. . . .

## NOTES AND QUESTIONS

**1.** What is the individual interest the *Moore* plurality deems protected under the doctrine of substantive due process? How does the plurality justify the inclusion of this interest among the others that are protected under substantive due process?

**2.** What level of scrutiny does the plurality apply to the municipal regulation at issue here? What kinds of interests did the municipality argue justify the regulation? Did the plurality credit those interests as valid — and, if it did, why did it nonetheless determine the regulation was unconstitutional?

**3.** At this point, you might want to start a running list of the interests protected under substantive due process. Each, for reasons that should become more clear as we move through these cases, should be articulated narrowly rather than broadly.

### Troxel v. Granville
### 530 U.S. 57 (2000)

Justice O'Connor announced the judgment of the Court and delivered an opinion, in which The Chief Justice, Justice Ginsburg, and Justice Breyer join.

Section 26.10.160(3) of the Revised Code of Washington permits "[a]ny person" to petition a superior court for visitation rights "at any time," and authorizes that court to grant such visitation rights whenever "visitation may serve the best interest of the child." Petitioners Jenifer and Gary Troxel petitioned a Washington Superior Court for the right to visit their grandchildren, Isabelle and Natalie Troxel. Respondent Tommie Granville, the mother of Isabelle and Natalie, opposed the petition. The case ultimately reached the Washington Supreme Court, which held that § 26.10.160(3) unconstitutionally interferes with the fundamental right of parents to rear their children.

I

Tommie Granville and Brad Troxel shared a relationship that ended in June 1991. The two never married, but they had two daughters, Isabelle and Natalie. Jenifer and Gary Troxel are Brad's parents, and thus the paternal grandparents of Isabelle and Natalie. After Tommie and Brad separated in 1991, Brad lived with his parents and regularly brought his daughters to his parents' home for weekend visitation. Brad committed suicide in May 1993. Although the Troxels at first continued to see Isabelle and Natalie on a regular basis after their son's death, Tommie Granville informed the Troxels in October 1993 that she wished to limit their visitation with her daughters to one short visit per month.

In December 1993, the Troxels commenced the present action by filing, in the Washington Superior Court for Skagit County, a petition to obtain visitation rights with Isabelle and Natalie. . . . Section 26.10.160(3) provides: "Any person may petition the court for visitation rights at any time including, but not limited to, custody proceedings. The court may order visitation rights for any person when visitation may serve the best interest of the child whether or not there has been any change of circumstances." At trial, the Troxels requested two weekends of overnight visitation per month and two weeks of visitation each summer. Granville did not oppose visitation altogether, but instead asked the court to order one day of visitation per month with no overnight stay. In 1995, the Superior Court issued an oral ruling and entered a visitation decree ordering visitation one weekend per month, one week during the summer, and four hours on both of the petitioning grandparents' birthdays.

Granville appealed, during which time she married Kelly Wynn. Before addressing the merits of Granville's appeal, the Washington Court of Appeals remanded the case to the Superior Court for entry of written findings of fact and conclusions of law. On remand, the Superior Court found that visitation was in Isabelle's and Natalie's best interests. . . . Approximately nine months after the Superior Court entered its order on remand, Granville's husband formally adopted Isabelle and Natalie.

[T]he Washington Supreme Court [held] the Troxels could not obtain visitation of Isabelle and Natalie pursuant to § 26.10.160(3). The court rested its decision on the Federal Constitution, holding that § 26.10.160(3) unconstitutionally infringes on the fundamental right of parents to rear their children. . . . The Washington Supreme Court held that "[p]arents have a right to limit visitation of their children with third persons," and that between parents and judges, "the parents should be the ones to choose whether to expose their children to certain people or ideas." . . .

We granted certiorari, and now affirm the judgment.

## II

The demographic changes of the past century make it difficult to speak of an average American family. The composition of families varies greatly from household to household. While many children may have two married parents and grandparents who visit regularly, many other children are raised in single-parent households. In 1996, children living with only one parent accounted for 28 percent of all children under age 18 in the United States. Understandably, in these single-parent households, persons outside the nuclear family are called upon with increasing frequency to assist in the everyday tasks of child rearing. In many cases, grandparents play an important role. For example, in 1998, approximately 4 million children — or 5.6

percent of all children under age 18 — lived in the household of their grandparents.

The nationwide enactment of nonparental visitation statutes is assuredly due, in some part, to the States' recognition of these changing realities of the American family. Because grandparents and other relatives undertake duties of a parental nature in many households, States have sought to ensure the welfare of the children therein by protecting the relationships those children form with such third parties. The States' nonparental visitation statutes are further supported by a recognition, which varies from State to State, that children should have the opportunity to benefit from relationships with statutorily specified persons — for example, their grandparents. The extension of statutory rights in this area to persons other than a child's parents, however, comes with an obvious cost. For example, the State's recognition of an independent third-party interest in a child can place a substantial burden on the traditional parent-child relationship. Contrary to Justice Stevens' accusation, our description of state nonparental visitation statutes in these terms, of course, is not meant to suggest that "children are so much chattel." Rather, our terminology is intended to highlight the fact that these statutes can present questions of constitutional import. In this case, we are presented with just such a question. Specifically, we are asked to decide whether § 26.10.160(3), as applied to Tommie Granville and her family, violates the Federal Constitution.

The Fourteenth Amendment provides that no State shall "deprive any person of life, liberty, or property, without due process of law." We have long recognized that the Amendment's Due Process Clause, like its Fifth Amendment counterpart, "guarantees more than fair process." *Washington v. Glucksberg* (1997). The Clause also includes a substantive component that "provides heightened protection against government interference with certain fundamental rights and liberty interests." *Id.*

The liberty interest at issue in this case — the interest of parents in the care, custody, and control of their children — is perhaps the oldest of the fundamental liberty interests recognized by this Court. More than 75 years ago, in *Meyer v. Nebraska* (1923), we held that the "liberty" protected by the Due Process Clause includes the right of parents to "establish a home and bring up children" and "to control the education of their own." Two years later, in *Pierce v. Society of Sisters* (1925), we again held that the "liberty of parents and guardians" includes the right "to direct the upbringing and education of children under their control." We explained in *Pierce* that "[t]he child is not the mere creature of the State; those who nurture him and direct his destiny have the right, coupled with the high duty, to recognize and prepare him for additional obligations." We returned to the subject in *Prince v. Massachusetts* (1944), and again confirmed that there is a constitutional dimension to the right of parents to direct the upbringing of their children. "It is cardinal with us that the custody, care and nurture of the child reside first in the parents, whose primary function and freedom include preparation for obligations the state can neither supply nor hinder."

In subsequent cases also, we have recognized the fundamental right of parents to make decisions concerning the care, custody, and control of their children. In light of this extensive precedent, it cannot now be doubted that the Due Process Clause of the Fourteenth Amendment protects the fundamental right of parents to make decisions concerning the care, custody, and control of their children.

Section 26.10.160(3), as applied to Granville and her family in this case, unconstitutionally infringes on that fundamental parental right. The Washington nonparental visitation statute is breathtakingly broad. According to the statute's text, "[a]*ny person* may petition the court for visitation rights *at any time*," and the court may grant such visitation rights whenever "visitation may serve *the best interest of the child.*" § 26.10.160(3) (emphases added). That language effectively permits any third party seeking visitation to subject any decision by a parent concerning visitation of the parent's children to state-court review. Once the visitation petition has been filed in court and the matter is placed before a judge, a parent's decision that visitation would not be in the child's best interest is accorded no deference. Section 26.10.160(3) contains no requirement that a court accord the parent's decision any presumption of validity or any weight whatsoever. Instead, the Washington statute places the best-interest determination solely in the hands of the judge. Should the judge disagree with the parent's estimation of the child's best interests, the judge's view necessarily prevails. Thus, in practical effect, in the State of Washington a court can disregard and overturn *any* decision by a fit custodial parent concerning visitation whenever a third party affected by the decision files a visitation petition, based solely on the judge's determination of the child's best interests. . . .

Turning to the facts of this case, the record reveals that the Superior Court's order was based on precisely the type of mere disagreement we have just described and nothing more. The Superior Court's order was not founded on any special factors that might justify the State's interference with Granville's fundamental right to make decisions concerning the rearing of her two daughters. To be sure, this case involves a visitation petition filed by grandparents soon after the death of their son — the father of Isabelle and Natalie — but the combination of several factors here compels our conclusion that § 26.10.160(3), as applied, exceeded the bounds of the Due Process Clause.

First, the Troxels did not allege, and no court has found, that Granville was an unfit parent. That aspect of the case is important, for there is a presumption that fit parents act in the best interests of their children. . . . Accordingly, so long as a parent adequately cares for his or her children (*i.e.*, is fit), there will normally be no reason for the State to inject itself into the private realm of the family to further question the ability of that parent to make the best decisions concerning the rearing of that parent's children.

The problem here is not that the Washington Superior Court intervened, but that when it did so, it gave no special weight at all to Granville's determination of her daughters' best interests. More importantly, it appears that the Superior Court applied exactly the opposite presumption. . . . The judge's comments suggest that he presumed the grandparents' request should be granted unless the children would be "impact[ed] adversely." In effect, the judge placed on Granville, the fit custodial parent, the burden of *disproving* that visitation would be in the best interest of her daughters. The judge reiterated moments later: "I think [visitation with the Troxels] would be in the best interest of the children and I haven't been shown it is not in [the] best interest of the children."

The decisional framework employed by the Superior Court directly contravened the traditional presumption that a fit parent will act in the best interest of his or her child. In that respect, the court's presumption failed to provide any protection for Granville's fundamental constitutional right to make decisions concerning the rearing of her own daughters. In an ideal world, parents might always seek to cultivate the bonds between grandparents and their grandchildren. Needless to say, however, our world is far from perfect, and in it the decision whether such an intergenerational relationship would be beneficial in any specific case is for the parent to make in the first instance. And, if a fit parent's decision of the kind at issue here becomes subject to judicial review, the court must accord at least some special weight to the parent's own determination.

Finally, we note that there is no allegation that Granville ever sought to cut off visitation entirely. Rather, the present dispute originated when Granville informed the Troxels that she would prefer to restrict their visitation with Isabelle and Natalie to one short visit per month and special holidays. In the Superior Court proceedings Granville did not oppose visitation but instead asked that the duration of any visitation order be shorter than that requested by the Troxels. While the Troxels requested two weekends per month and two full weeks in the summer, Granville asked the Superior Court to order only one day of visitation per month (with no overnight stay) and participation in the Granville family's holiday celebrations. The Superior Court gave no weight to Granville's having assented to visitation even before the filing of any visitation petition or subsequent court intervention. The court instead rejected Granville's proposal and settled on a middle ground, ordering one weekend of visitation per month, one week in the summer, and time on both of the petitioning grandparents' birthdays. Significantly, many other States expressly provide by statute that courts may not award visitation unless a parent has denied (or unreasonably denied) visitation to the concerned third party.

Considered together with the Superior Court's reasons for awarding visitation to the Troxels, the combination of these factors demonstrates that the visitation order in this case was an unconstitutional infringement on Granville's fundamental right to make decisions concerning the care, custody, and control of her two daughters. The Washington Superior Court failed to accord the determination of Granville, a fit custodial parent, any material weight. [Its] slender findings, in combination with the court's announced presumption in favor of grandparent visitation and its failure to accord significant weight to Granville's already having offered meaningful visitation to the Troxels, show that this case involves nothing more than a simple disagreement between the Washington Superior Court and Granville concerning her children's best interests.... As we have explained, the Due Process Clause does not permit a State to infringe on the fundamental right of parents to make child rearing decisions simply because a state judge believes a "better" decision could be made. Neither the Washington nonparental visitation statute generally — which places no limits on either the persons who may petition for visitation or the circumstances in which such a petition may be granted — nor the Superior Court in this specific case required anything more. Accordingly, we hold that § 26.10.160(3), as applied in this case, is unconstitutional.

Because we rest our decision on the sweeping breadth of § 26.10.160(3) and the application of that broad, unlimited power in this case, we do not consider the primary constitutional question passed on by the Washington Supreme Court — whether the Due Process Clause requires all nonparental visitation statutes to include a showing of harm or potential harm to the child as a condition precedent to granting visitation. We do not, and need not, define today the precise scope of the parental due process right in the visitation context. In this respect, we agree with Justice Kennedy that the constitutionality of any standard for awarding visitation turns on the specific manner in which that standard is applied and that the constitutional protections in this area are best "elaborated with care." Because much state-court adjudication in this context occurs on a case-by-case basis, we would be hesitant to hold that specific nonparental visitation statutes violate the Due Process Clause as a *per se* matter.

... We therefore hold that the application of § 26.10.160(3) to Granville and her family violated her due process right to make decisions concerning the care, custody, and control of her daughters.

Accordingly, the judgment of the Washington Supreme Court is affirmed.

*It is so ordered.*

[Concurring opinion of Justice Souter omitted.]

Justice Thomas, concurring in the judgment.

... I agree with the plurality that this Court's recognition of a fundamental right of parents to direct the upbringing of their children resolves this case. Our decision in *Pierce v. Society of Sisters* (1925), holds that parents have a fundamental constitutional right to rear their children, including the right to determine who shall educate and socialize them. . . . Here, the State of Washington lacks even a legitimate governmental interest — to say nothing of a compelling one — in second-guessing a fit parent's decision regarding visitation with third parties. On this basis, I would affirm the judgment below.

Justice Stevens, dissenting.

A parent's rights with respect to her child have . . . never been regarded as absolute, but rather are limited by the existence of an actual, developed relationship with a child, and are tied to the presence or absence of some embodiment of family. These limitations have arisen, not simply out of the definition of parenthood itself, but because of this Court's assumption that a parent's interests in a child must be balanced against the State's long-recognized interests as *parens patriae*, and, critically, the child's own complementary interest in preserving relationships that serve her welfare and protection.

While this Court has not yet had occasion to elucidate the nature of a child's liberty interests in preserving established familial or family-like bonds, it seems to me extremely likely that, to the extent parents and families have fundamental liberty interests in preserving such intimate relationships, so, too, do children have these interests, and so, too, must their interests be balanced in the equation. At a minimum, our prior cases recognizing that children are, generally speaking, constitutionally protected actors require that this Court reject any suggestion that when it comes to parental rights, children are so much chattel. The constitutional protection against arbitrary state interference with parental rights should not be extended to prevent the States from protecting children against the arbitrary exercise of parental authority that is not in fact motivated by an interest in the welfare of the child. . . .

Justice Scalia, dissenting.

Judicial vindication of "parental rights" under a Constitution that does not even mention them requires (as Justice Kennedy's opinion rightly points out) not only a judicially crafted definition of parents, but also — unless, as no one believes, the parental rights are to be absolute — judicially approved assessments of "harm to the child" and judicially defined gradations of other persons (grandparents, extended family, adoptive family in an adoption later found to be invalid, long-term guardians, etc.) who may have some claim against the wishes of the parents. If we embrace this unenumerated right, I think it obvious — whether we affirm or reverse the judgment here, or remand as Justice Stevens or Justice Kennedy would do — that we will be ushering in a new regime of judicially prescribed, and federally prescribed, family law. I have no reason to believe that federal judges will be better at this than state legislatures; and state legislatures have the great advantages of doing harm in a more circumscribed area, of being able to correct their mistakes in a flash, and of being removable by the people.

For these reasons, I would reverse the judgment below.

Justice Kennedy, dissenting.

. . . As our case law has developed, the custodial parent has a constitutional right to determine, without undue interference by the State, how best to raise, nurture, and educate the child. The parental right stems from the liberty protected by the Due Process Clause of the Fourteenth Amendment. *Pierce* and *Meyer*, had they been decided in recent times, may well have been grounded upon First Amendment principles protecting freedom of speech, belief, and religion. Their formulation and subsequent interpretation have been quite different, of course; and they long have been interpreted to have found in

Fourteenth Amendment concepts of liberty an independent right of the parent in the "custody, care and nurture of the child," free from state intervention. The principle exists, then, in broad formulation; yet courts must use considerable restraint, including careful adherence to the incremental instruction given by the precise facts of particular cases, as they seek to give further and more precise definition to the right.

The State Supreme Court sought to give content to the parent's right by announcing a categorical rule that third parties who seek visitation must always prove the denial of visitation would harm the child. After reviewing some of the relevant precedents, the Supreme Court of Washington concluded "[t]he requirement of harm is the sole protection that parents have against pervasive state interference in the parenting process." For that reason, "[s]hort of preventing harm to the child," the court considered the best interests of the child to be "insufficient to serve as a compelling state interest overruling a parent's fundamental rights."

While it might be argued as an abstract matter that in some sense the child is always harmed if his or her best interests are not considered, the law of domestic relations, as it has evolved to this point, treats as distinct the two standards, one harm to the child and the other the best interests of the child. The judgment of the Supreme Court of Washington rests on that assumption, and I, too, shall assume that there are real and consequential differences between the two standards.

On the question whether one standard must always take precedence over the other in order to protect the right of the parent or parents, "[o]ur Nation's history, legal traditions, and practices" do not give us clear or definitive answers. *Washington v. Glucksberg* (1997). The consensus among courts and commentators is that at least through the 19th century there was no legal right of visitation; court-ordered visitation appears to be a 20th-century phenomenon. . . .

To say that third parties have had no historical right to petition for visitation does not necessarily imply, as the Supreme Court of Washington concluded, that a parent has a constitutional right to prevent visitation in all cases not involving harm. True, this Court has acknowledged that States have the authority to intervene to prevent harm to children, but that is not the same as saying that a heightened harm to the child standard must be satisfied in every case in which a third party seeks a visitation order. . . . The State Supreme Court's conclusion that the Constitution forbids the application of the best interests of the child standard in any visitation proceeding, however, appears to rest upon assumptions the Constitution does not require.

My principal concern is that the holding seems to proceed from the assumption that the parent or parents who resist visitation have always been the child's primary caregivers and that the third parties who seek visitation have no legitimate and established relationship with the child. That idea, in turn, appears influenced by the concept that the conventional nuclear family ought to establish the visitation standard for every domestic relations case. As we all know, this is simply not the structure or prevailing condition in many households. For many boys and girls a traditional family with two or even one permanent and caring parent is simply not the reality of their childhood. This may be so whether their childhood has been marked by tragedy or filled with considerable happiness and fulfillment.

Cases are sure to arise — perhaps a substantial number of cases — in which a third party, by acting in a caregiving role over a significant period of time, has developed a relationship with a child which is not necessarily subject to absolute parental veto. Some pre-existing relationships, then, serve to identify persons who have a strong attachment to the child with the concomitant motivation to act in a responsible way to ensure the child's welfare. As the State Supreme Court was correct to acknowledge, those relationships can be so enduring that "in certain circumstances where a child has enjoyed a substantial relationship with a third person, arbitrarily depriving the child of the relationship could cause severe psychological harm to the child"; and harm to the adult may also ensue. In the design and elaboration of their visitation laws, States may be entitled to consider that certain relationships are such that to avoid the risk of harm, a best interests standard can be employed by their domestic relations courts in some circumstances.

Indeed, contemporary practice should give us some pause before rejecting the best interests of the child standard in all third-party visitation cases, as the Washington court has done. The standard has been recognized for many years as a basic tool of domestic relations law in visitation proceedings. Since 1965 all 50 States have enacted a third-party visitation statute of some sort. Each of these statutes, save one, permits a court order to issue in certain cases if visitation is found to be in the best interests of the child. While it is unnecessary for us to consider the constitutionality of any particular provision in the case now before us, it can be noted that the statutes also include a variety of methods for limiting parents' exposure to third-party visitation petitions and for ensuring parental decisions are given respect. Many States limit the identity of permissible petitioners by restricting visitation petitions to grandparents, or by requiring petitioners to show a substantial relationship with a child, or both. The statutes vary in other respects — for instance, some permit visitation petitions when there has been a change in circumstances such as divorce or death of a parent. . . .

In light of the inconclusive historical record and case law, as well as the almost universal adoption of the best interests standard for visitation disputes, I would be hard pressed to conclude the right to be free of such review in all cases is itself "implicit in the concept of ordered liberty." Glucksberg (quoting *Palko v. Connecticut* (1937)). In my view, it would be more appropriate to conclude that the constitutionality of the application of the best interests standard depends on more specific factors. In short, a fit parent's right vis-à-vis a complete stranger is one thing; her right vis-à-vis another parent or a *de facto* parent may be another. The protection the Constitution requires, then, must be elaborated with care, using the discipline and instruction of the case law system. We must keep in mind that family courts in the 50 States confront these factual variations each day, and are best situated to consider the unpredictable, yet inevitable, issues that arise. . . .

## NOTES AND QUESTIONS

**1.** Once again: another fundamental interest, another plurality opinion. But this decision appears to be less controversial: in many ways, the fundamental interest the plurality recognizes in *Troxel* seems a logical extension of interests the Court has recognized as fundamental for some time, going back to cases like *Meyer* and *Pierce*. And yet, Justice Scalia will have none of it. What is his basis for dissenting to the recognition of such an interest — a basis that lies at the heart of all his dissents in these cases?

**2.** In light of Justice Scalia's dissent, you can see that, as suggested earlier, substantive due process cases, too, may be seen as a species of separation of powers. And, in this regard, it is important to remember that, in most cases, the courts will categorize most asserted interests as ordinary liberty interests — along the lines of the interest in contracting for hours of employment — and not fundamental interests — like the interest of parents in the care, custody, and control of their children. Only when an interest is deemed by a court to be fundamental will heightened scrutiny apply, at which point the odds are strong the regulation at issue will be struck down. For all other interests, though, rational basis scrutiny applies, and those citizens who object to the law's reach must voice their concerns through the political process.

### 4. Marriage

**Loving v. Virginia**
**388 U.S. 1 (1967)**

Mr. Chief Justice Warren delivered the opinion of the Court.

This case presents a constitutional question never addressed by this Court: whether a statutory scheme adopted by the State of Virginia to prevent marriages between persons solely on the basis of racial classifications violates the Equal Protection and Due Process Clauses of the Fourteenth Amendment. For reasons which seem to us to reflect the central meaning of those constitutional commands, we conclude that these statutes cannot stand consistently with the Fourteenth Amendment.

In June 1958, two residents of Virginia, Mildred Jeter, a Negro woman, and Richard Loving, a white man, were married in the District of Columbia pursuant to its laws. Shortly after their marriage, the Lovings returned to Virginia and established their marital abode in Caroline County. At the October Term, 1958, of the Circuit Court of Caroline County, a grand jury issued an indictment charging the Lovings with violating Virginia's ban on interracial marriages. On January 6, 1959, the Lovings pleaded guilty to the charge and were sentenced to one year in jail; however, the trial judge suspended the sentence for a period of 25 years on the condition that the Lovings leave the State and not return to Virginia together for 25 years. He stated in an opinion that: "Almighty God created the races white, black, yellow, malay and red, and he placed them on separate continents. And but for the interference with his arrangement there would be no cause for such marriages. The fact that he separated the races shows that he did not intend for the races to mix."

After their convictions, the Lovings took up residence in the District of Columbia. On November 6, 1963, they filed a motion in the state trial court to vacate the judgment and set aside the sentence on the ground that the statutes which they had violated were repugnant to the Fourteenth Amendment. The motion not having been decided by October 28, 1964, the Lovings instituted a class action in the United States District Court for the Eastern District of Virginia requesting that a three-judge court be convened to declare the Virginia anti-miscegenation statutes unconstitutional and to enjoin state officials from enforcing their convictions. On January 22, 1965, the state trial judge denied the motion to vacate the sentences, and the Lovings perfected an appeal to the Supreme Court of Appeals of Virginia. On February 11, 1965, the three-judge District Court continued the case to allow the Lovings to present their constitutional claims to the highest state court.

The Supreme Court of Appeals upheld the constitutionality of the anti-miscegenation statutes and, after modifying the sentence, affirmed the convictions. The Lovings appealed this decision, and we noted probable jurisdiction on December 12, 1966, 385 U.S. 986.

The two statutes under which appellants were convicted and sentenced are part of a comprehensive statutory scheme aimed at prohibiting and punishing interracial marriages. The Lovings were convicted of violating § 20-58 of the Virginia Code:

> *Leaving State to evade law.* — If any white person and colored person shall go out of this State, for the purpose of being married, and with the intention of returning, and be married out of it, and afterwards return to and reside in it, cohabiting as man and wife, they shall be punished as provided in § 20-59, and the marriage shall be governed by the same law as if it had been solemnized in this State. The fact of their cohabitation here as man and wife shall be evidence of their marriage.

Section 20-59, which defines the penalty for miscegenation, provides:

> *Punishment for marriage.* — If any white person intermarry with a colored person, or any colored person intermarry with a white person, he shall be guilty of a felony and shall be punished by confinement in the penitentiary for not less than one nor more than five years.

Other central provisions in the Virginia statutory scheme are § 20-57, which automatically voids all marriages between "a white person and a colored person" without any judicial proceeding, and §§ 20-54 and 1-14 which, respectively, define "white persons" and "colored persons and Indians" for purposes of the statutory prohibitions. The Lovings have never disputed in the course of this litigation that Mrs. Loving is a "colored person" or that Mr. Loving is a "white person" within the meanings given those terms by the Virginia statutes.

Virginia is now one of 16 States which prohibit and punish marriages on the basis of racial classifications. Penalties for miscegenation arose as an incident to slavery and have been common in Virginia since the colonial period. The present statutory scheme dates from the adoption of the Racial Integrity Act of 1924, passed during the period of extreme nativism which followed the end of the First World War. The central features of this Act, and current Virginia law, are the absolute prohibition of a "white person" marrying other than another "white person," a prohibition against issuing marriage licenses until the issuing official is satisfied that the applicants' statements as to their race are correct, certificates of "racial composition" to be kept by both local and state registrars, and the carrying forward of earlier prohibitions against racial intermarriage.

## I.

In upholding the constitutionality of these provisions in the decision below, the Supreme Court of Appeals of Virginia referred to its 1955 decision in *Naim v. Naim* (Va. 1955), as stating the reasons supporting the validity of these laws. In *Naim*, the state court concluded that the State's legitimate purposes were "to preserve the racial integrity of its citizens," and to prevent "the corruption of blood," "a mongrel breed of citizens," and "the obliteration of racial pride," obviously an endorsement of the doctrine of White Supremacy. The court also reasoned that marriage has traditionally been subject to state regulation without federal intervention, and, consequently, the regulation of marriage should be left to exclusive state control by the Tenth Amendment.

While the state court is no doubt correct in asserting that marriage is a social relation subject to the State's police power, the State does not contend in its argument before this Court that its powers to regulate marriage are unlimited notwithstanding the commands of the Fourteenth Amendment. Nor could it do so in light of *Meyer v. Nebraska* (1923). . . .

## II.

These statutes also deprive the Lovings of liberty without due process of law in violation of the Due Process Clause of the Fourteenth Amendment. The freedom to marry has long been recognized as one of the vital personal rights essential to the orderly pursuit of happiness by free men.

Marriage is one of the "basic civil rights of man," fundamental to our very existence and survival. To deny this fundamental freedom on so unsupportable a basis as the racial classifications embodied in these statutes, classifications so directly subversive of the principle of equality at the heart of the Fourteenth Amendment, is surely to deprive all the State's citizens of liberty without due process of law. The Fourteenth Amendment requires that the freedom of choice to marry not be restricted by invidious racial discriminations. Under our

Constitution, the freedom to marry, or not marry, a person of another race resides with the individual and cannot be infringed by the State.

These convictions must be reversed.

*It is so ordered.*

[Concurring opinion of Justice Stewart omitted.]

### NOTES AND QUESTIONS

**1.** The Court holds here, without further explanation, that marriage is a basic civil right. Setting this statement aside, can you construct an argument that marriage is, in fact, distinguishable in some way from all the other interests the Court has deemed fundamental? Indeed, in a sense it may share more with a woman's right to choose than the other interests explored in these cases.

**2.** Accepting that marriage is different, the Court has often endeavored to analyze restrictions on the right to marry in the context of equal protection doctrine, to which we turn in the next chapter.

**3.** *Loving* is the seminal case on marriage, and yet the substantive due process analysis is sparse. Is there enough in the opinion, considering the factual context and historical background, from which to conclude other kinds of absolute marriage bans should also be declared unconstitutional?

### Obergefell v. Hodges
### 576 U.S. __ (2015)

Justice Kennedy delivered the opinion of the Court.

The Constitution promises liberty to all within its reach, a liberty that includes certain specific rights that allow persons, within a lawful realm, to define and express their identity. The petitioners in these cases seek to find that liberty by marrying someone of the same sex and having their marriages deemed lawful on the same terms and conditions as marriages between persons of the opposite sex.

#### I

These cases come from Michigan, Kentucky, Ohio, and Tennessee, States that define marriage as a union between one man and one woman. The petitioners are 14 same-sex couples and two men whose same-sex partners are deceased. The respondents are state officials responsible for enforcing the laws in question. The petitioners claim the respondents violate the Fourteenth Amendment by denying them the right to marry or to have their marriages, lawfully performed in another State, given full recognition.

Petitioners filed these suits in United States District Courts in their home States. Each District Court ruled in their favor. . . . The respondents appealed the decisions against them to the United States Court of Appeals for the Sixth Circuit. It consolidated the cases and reversed the judgments of the District Courts. The Court of Appeals held that a State has no constitutional obligation to license same-sex marriages or to recognize same-sex marriages performed out of State.

The petitioners sought certiorari. This Court granted review, limited to two questions. The first, presented by the cases from

Michigan and Kentucky, is whether the Fourteenth Amendment requires a State to license a marriage between two people of the same sex. The second, presented by the cases from Ohio, Tennessee, and, again, Kentucky, is whether the Fourteenth Amendment requires a State to recognize a same-sex marriage licensed and performed in a State which does grant that right.

## II

[M]arriage was once viewed as an arrangement by the couple's parents based on political, religious, and financial concerns; but by the time of the Nation's founding it was understood to be a voluntary contract between a man and a woman. As the role and status of women changed, the institution further evolved. Under the centuries-old doctrine of coverture, a married man and woman were treated by the State as a single, male-dominated legal entity. As women gained legal, political, and property rights, and as society began to understand that women have their own equal dignity, the law of coverture was abandoned. These and other developments in the institution of marriage over the past centuries were not mere superficial changes. Rather, they worked deep transformations in its structure, affecting aspects of marriage long viewed by many as essential.

These new insights have strengthened, not weakened, the institution of marriage. Indeed, changed understandings of marriage are characteristic of a Nation where new dimensions of freedom become apparent to new generations, often through perspectives that begin in pleas or protests and then are considered in the political sphere and the judicial process.

[In *Bowers v. Hardwick* (1986), the Court] upheld the constitutionality of a Georgia law deemed to criminalize certain homosexual acts. Ten years later, in *Romer v. Evans* (1996), the Court invalidated an amendment to Colorado's Constitution that sought to foreclose any branch or political subdivision of the State from protecting persons against discrimination based on sexual orientation. Then, in 2003, the Court overruled *Bowers,* holding that laws making same-sex intimacy a crime "demea[n] the lives of homosexual persons." *Lawrence v. Texas.*

Against this background, the legal question of same-sex marriage arose. . . .

Numerous cases about same-sex marriage have reached the United States Courts of Appeals in recent years. In accordance with the judicial duty to base their decisions on principled reasons and neutral discussions, without scornful or disparaging commentary, courts have written a substantial body of law considering all sides of these issues. That case law helps to explain and formulate the underlying principles this Court now must consider. With the exception of the opinion here under review and one other, the Courts of Appeals have held that excluding same-sex couples from marriage violates the Constitution. There also have been many thoughtful District Court decisions addressing same-sex marriage — and most of them, too, have concluded same-sex couples must be allowed to marry. In addition the highest courts of many States have contributed to this ongoing dialogue in decisions interpreting their own State Constitutions. . . .

### III

. . . The fundamental liberties protected by [the Due Process] Clause include most of the rights enumerated in the Bill of Rights. In addition these liberties extend to certain personal choices central to individual dignity and autonomy, including intimate choices that define personal identity and beliefs.

The identification and protection of fundamental rights is an enduring part of the judicial duty to interpret the Constitution. That responsibility, however, "has not been reduced to any formula." *Poe v. Ullman* (1961) (Harlan, J., dissenting). Rather, it requires courts to exercise reasoned judgment in identifying interests of the person so fundamental that the State must accord them its respect. That process is guided by many of the same considerations relevant to analysis of other constitutional provisions that set forth broad principles rather than specific requirements. History and tradition guide and discipline this inquiry but do not set its outer boundaries. That method respects our history and learns from it without allowing the past alone to rule the present.

The nature of injustice is that we may not always see it in our own times. The generations that wrote and ratified the Bill of Rights and the Fourteenth Amendment did not presume to know the extent of freedom in all of its dimensions, and so they entrusted to future generations a charter protecting the right of all persons to enjoy liberty as we learn its meaning. When new insight reveals discord between the Constitution's central protections and a received legal stricture, a claim to liberty must be addressed.

Applying these established tenets, the Court has long held the right to marry is protected by the Constitution. In *Loving v. Virginia* (1967), which invalidated bans on interracial unions, a unanimous Court held marriage is "one of the vital personal rights essential to the orderly pursuit of happiness by free men." . . . Over time and in other contexts, the Court has reiterated that the right to marry is fundamental under the Due Process Clause.

It cannot be denied that this Court's cases describing the right to marry presumed a relationship involving opposite-sex partners. The Court, like many institutions, has made assumptions defined by the world and time of which it is a part. This was evident in *Baker v. Nelson*, a one-line summary decision issued in 1972, holding the exclusion of same-sex couples from marriage did not present a substantial federal question.

Still, there are other, more instructive precedents. This Court's cases have expressed constitutional principles of broader reach. In defining the right to marry these cases have identified essential attributes of that right based in history, tradition, and other constitutional liberties inherent in this intimate bond. And in assessing whether the force and rationale of its cases apply to same-sex couples, the Court must respect the basic reasons why the right to marry has been long protected.

This analysis compels the conclusion that same-sex couples may exercise the right to marry. The four principles and traditions to be discussed demonstrate that the reasons marriage is fundamental under the Constitution apply with equal force to same-sex couples.

A first premise of the Court's relevant precedents is that the right to personal choice regarding marriage is inherent in the concept of individual autonomy. This abiding connection between marriage and liberty is why *Loving* invalidated interracial marriage bans under the Due Process Clause. Like choices concerning contraception, family relationships, procreation, and childrearing, all of which are protected by the Constitution, decisions concerning marriage are among the most intimate that an individual can make. . . .

The nature of marriage is that, through its enduring bond, two persons together can find other freedoms, such as expression, intimacy, and spirituality. This is true for all persons, whatever their sexual orientation. There is dignity in the bond between two men or two women who seek to marry and in their autonomy to make such profound choices.

A second principle in this Court's jurisprudence is that the right to marry is fundamental because it supports a two-person union unlike any other in its importance to the committed individuals. This point was central to *Griswold v. Connecticut* (1965), which held the Constitution protects the right of married couples to use contraception. Suggesting that marriage is a right "older than the Bill of Rights," *Griswold* described marriage this way:

> Marriage is a coming together for better or for worse, hopefully enduring, and intimate to the degree of being sacred. It is an association that promotes a way of life, not causes; a harmony in living, not political faiths; a bilateral loyalty, not commercial or social projects. Yet it is an association for as noble a purpose as any involved in our prior decisions.

. . .

A third basis for protecting the right to marry is that it safeguards children and families and thus draws meaning from related rights of childrearing, procreation, and education. The Court has recognized these connections by describing the varied rights as a unified whole. . . . Under the laws of the several States, some of marriage's protections for children and families are material. But marriage also confers more profound benefits. By giving recognition and legal structure to their parents' relationship, marriage allows children "to understand the integrity and closeness of their own family and its concord with other families in their community and in their daily lives." *United States v. Windsor* (2013). Marriage also affords the permanency and stability important to children's best interests.

As all parties agree, many same-sex couples provide loving and nurturing homes to their children, whether biological or adopted. And hundreds of thousands of children are presently being raised by such couples. Most States have allowed gays and lesbians to adopt, either as individuals or as couples, and many adopted and foster children have same-sex parents. This provides powerful confirmation from the law itself that gays and lesbians can create loving, supportive families.

Excluding same-sex couples from marriage thus conflicts with a central premise of the right to marry. Without the recognition, stability, and predictability marriage offers, their children suffer the stigma of knowing their families are somehow lesser. They also suffer the significant material costs of being raised by unmarried parents, relegated through no fault of their own to a more difficult and uncertain family life. The marriage laws at issue here thus harm and humiliate the children of same-sex couples.

That is not to say the right to marry is less meaningful for those who do not or cannot have children. An ability, desire, or promise to procreate is not and has not been a prerequisite for a valid marriage in any State. In light of precedent protecting the right of a married couple not to procreate, it cannot be said the Court or the States have conditioned the right to marry on the capacity or commitment to procreate. The constitutional marriage right has many aspects, of which childbearing is only one.

Fourth and finally, this Court's cases and the Nation's traditions make clear that marriage is a keystone of our social order. . . . This idea has been reiterated even as the institution has evolved in substantial ways over time, superseding rules related to parental consent, gender, and race once thought by many to be essential. Marriage remains a building block of our national community.

For that reason, just as a couple vows to support each other, so does society pledge to support the couple, offering symbolic recognition and material benefits to protect and nourish the union. Indeed, while the States are in general free to vary the benefits they confer on all married couples, they have throughout our history made marriage the basis for an expanding list of governmental rights, benefits, and responsibilities. These aspects of marital status include: taxation; inheritance and property rights; rules of intestate succession; spousal privilege in the law of evidence; hospital access; medical decisionmaking authority; adoption rights; the rights and benefits of survivors; birth and death certificates; professional ethics rules; campaign finance restrictions; workers' compensation benefits; health insurance; and child custody, support, and visitation rules. Valid marriage under state law is also a significant status for over a thousand provisions of federal law. The States have contributed to the fundamental character of the marriage right by placing that institution at the center of so many facets of the legal and social order.

There is no difference between same- and opposite-sex couples with respect to this principle. Yet by virtue of their exclusion from that institution, same-sex couples are denied the constellation of benefits that the States have linked to marriage. This harm results in more than just material burdens. Same-sex couples are consigned to an instability many opposite-sex couples would deem intolerable in their own lives. As the State itself makes marriage all the more precious by the significance it attaches to it, exclusion from that status has the effect of teaching that gays and lesbians are unequal in important respects. It demeans gays and lesbians for the State to lock them out of a central institution of the Nation's society. Same-sex couples, too, may aspire to the transcendent purposes of marriage and seek fulfillment in its highest meaning.

The limitation of marriage to opposite-sex couples may long have seemed natural and just, but its inconsistency with the central meaning of the fundamental right to marry is now manifest. With that knowledge must come the recognition that laws excluding same-sex couples from the marriage right impose stigma and injury of the kind prohibited by our basic charter.

[T]he right to marry is a fundamental right inherent in the liberty of the person, and under the Due Process and Equal Protection Clauses of the Fourteenth Amendment couples of the same-sex may not be deprived of that right and that liberty. The Court now holds that same-sex couples may exercise the fundamental right to marry. No longer may this liberty be denied to them. *Baker v. Nelson* must be and now is overruled, and the State laws challenged by Petitioners in these cases are now held invalid to the extent they exclude same-sex couples from civil marriage on the same terms and conditions as opposite-sex couples.

## IV

There may be an initial inclination in these cases to proceed with caution — to await further legislation, litigation, and debate. The respondents warn there has been insufficient democratic discourse before deciding an issue so basic as the definition of marriage. In its ruling on the cases now before this Court, the majority opinion for the Court of Appeals made a cogent argument that it would be appropriate for the respondents' States to await further public discussion and political measures before licensing same-sex marriages.

Yet there has been far more deliberation than this argument acknowledges. There have been referenda, legislative debates, and grassroots campaigns, as well as countless studies, papers, books, and other popular and scholarly writings. There has been extensive litigation in state and federal courts. Judicial opinions addressing the issue have been informed by the contentions of parties and counsel, which, in turn, reflect the more general, societal discussion of same-sex marriage and its meaning that has occurred over the past decades. As more than 100 *amici* make clear in their filings, many of the central institutions in American life — state and local governments, the military, large and small businesses, labor unions, religious organizations, law enforcement, civic groups, professional organizations, and universities — have devoted substantial attention to the question. This has led to an enhanced understanding of the issue — an understanding reflected in the arguments now presented for resolution as a matter of constitutional law.

Of course, the Constitution contemplates that democracy is the appropriate process for change, so long as that process does not abridge fundamental rights. . . . Indeed, it is most often through democracy that liberty is preserved and protected in our lives. But . . . when the rights of persons are violated, "the Constitution requires redress by the courts," notwithstanding the more general value of democratic decisionmaking. *Schuette v. BAMN* (2014). This holds true even when protecting individual rights affects issues of the utmost importance and sensitivity.

The dynamic of our constitutional system is that individuals need not await legislative action before asserting a fundamental right. The Nation's courts are open to injured individuals who come to them to vindicate their own direct, personal stake in our basic charter. An individual can invoke a right to constitutional protection when he or she is harmed, even if the broader public disagrees and even if the legislature refuses to act. . . . It is of no moment whether advocates of same-sex marriage now enjoy or lack momentum in the democratic process. The issue before the Court here is the legal question whether the Constitution protects the right of same-sex couples to marry.

. . . Were the Court to uphold the challenged laws as constitutional, it would teach the Nation that these laws are in accord with our society's most basic compact. Were the Court to stay its hand to allow slower, case-by-case determination of the required availability of specific public benefits to same-sex couples, it still would deny gays and lesbians many rights and responsibilities intertwined with marriage.

The respondents also argue allowing same-sex couples to wed will harm marriage as an institution by leading to fewer opposite-sex marriages. This may occur, the respondents contend, because licensing same-sex marriage severs the connection between natural procreation and marriage. . . . The respondents have not shown a foundation for the conclusion that allowing same-sex marriage will cause the harmful outcomes they describe. Indeed, with respect to this asserted basis for excluding same-sex couples from the right to marry, it is appropriate to observe these cases involve only the rights of two consenting adults whose marriages would pose no risk of harm to themselves or third parties.

Finally, it must be emphasized that religions, and those who adhere to religious doctrines, may continue to advocate with utmost, sincere conviction that, by divine precepts, same-sex marriage should not be condoned. The First Amendment ensures that religious organizations and persons are given proper protection as they seek to teach the principles that are so fulfilling and so central to their lives and faiths, and to their own deep aspirations to continue the family structure they have long revered. The same is true of those who oppose same-sex marriage for other reasons. In turn, those who believe allowing same-sex marriage is proper or indeed essential, whether as a matter of religious conviction or secular belief, may engage those who disagree with their view in an open and searching debate. The Constitution, however, does not permit the State to bar same-sex couples from marriage on the same terms as accorded to couples of the opposite sex.

## V

These cases also present the question whether the Constitution requires States to recognize same-sex marriages validly performed out of State. [The] recognition bans inflict substantial and continuing harm on same-sex couples.

Being married in one State but having that valid marriage denied in another is one of "the most perplexing and distressing complication[s]" in the law of domestic relations. *Williams v. North Carolina* (1942) (internal quotation marks omitted). Leaving the current state of affairs in place would maintain and promote instability and uncertainty. For some couples, even an ordinary drive into a neighboring State to visit family or friends risks causing severe hardship in the event of a spouse's hospitalization while across state lines. In light of the fact that many States already allow same-sex marriage — and hundreds of thousands of these marriages already have occurred — the disruption caused by the recognition bans is significant and ever-growing.

As counsel for the respondents acknowledged at argument, if States are required by the Constitution to issue marriage licenses to same-sex couples, the justifications for refusing to recognize those marriages performed elsewhere are undermined. The Court, in this decision, holds same-sex couples may exercise the fundamental right to marry in all States. It follows that the Court also must hold — and it now does hold — that there is no lawful basis for a State to refuse to recognize a lawful same-sex marriage performed in another State on the ground of its same-sex character.

\* \* \*

The judgment of the Court of Appeals for the Sixth Circuit is reversed.

*It is so ordered.*

Chief Justice Roberts, with whom Justice Scalia and Justice Thomas join, dissenting.

[T]he majority's approach has no basis in principle or tradition, except for the unprincipled tradition of judicial policymaking that characterized discredited decisions such as *Lochner v. New York* (1905). Stripped of its shiny rhetorical gloss, the majority's argument is that the Due Process Clause gives same-sex couples a fundamental right to marry because it will be good for them and for society. If I were a legislator, I would certainly consider that view as a matter of social policy. But as a judge, I find the majority's position indefensible as a matter of constitutional law.

Petitioners' "fundamental right" claim falls into the most sensitive category of constitutional adjudication. Petitioners do not contend that their States' marriage laws violate an *enumerated* constitutional right, such as the freedom of speech protected by the First Amendment. . . . Allowing unelected federal judges to select which unenumerated rights rank as "fundamental" — and to strike down state laws on the basis of that determination — raises obvious concerns about the judicial role. . . .

[The majority] relies primarily on precedents discussing the fundamental "right to marry." These cases do not hold, of course, that anyone who wants to get married has a constitutional right to do so.

They instead require a State to justify barriers to marriage as that institution has always been understood. . . .

None of the laws at issue in those cases purported to change the core definition of marriage as the union of a man and a woman. . . . Removing racial barriers to marriage [in *Loving*] did not change what a marriage was any more than integrating schools changed what a school was. As the majority admits, the institution of "marriage" discussed in every one of these cases "presumed a relationship involving opposite-sex partners."

In short, the "right to marry" cases stand for the important but limited proposition that particular restrictions on access to marriage *as traditionally defined* violate due process. These precedents say nothing at all about a right to make a State change its definition of marriage, which is the right petitioners actually seek here. Neither petitioners nor the majority cites a single case or other legal source providing any basis for such a constitutional right. None exists, and that is enough to foreclose their claim.

. . . The truth is that today's decision rests on nothing more than the majority's own conviction that same-sex couples should be allowed to marry because they want to, and that "it would disparage their choices and diminish their personhood to deny them this right." Whatever force that belief may have as a matter of moral philosophy, it has no more basis in the Constitution than did the naked policy preferences adopted in *Lochner*.

I respectfully dissent.

Justice Scalia, with whom Justice Thomas joins, dissenting.

I join The Chief Justice's opinion in full. I write separately to call attention to this Court's threat to American democracy.

The substance of today's decree is not of immense personal importance to me. The law can recognize as marriage whatever sexual attachments and living arrangements it wishes, and can accord them favorable civil consequences, from tax treatment to rights of inheritance. Those civil consequences — and the public approval that conferring the name of marriage evidences — can perhaps have adverse social effects, but no more adverse than the effects of many other controversial laws. So it is not of special importance to me what the law says about marriage. It is of overwhelming importance, however, who it is that rules me. Today's decree says that my Ruler, and the Ruler of 320 million Americans coast-to-coast, is a majority of the nine lawyers on the Supreme Court. The opinion in these cases is the furthest extension in fact — and the furthest extension one can even imagine — of the Court's claimed power to create "liberties" that the Constitution and its Amendments neglect to mention. This practice of constitutional revision by an unelected committee of nine, always accompanied (as it is today) by extravagant praise of liberty, robs the People of the most important liberty they asserted in the Declaration of Independence and won in the Revolution of 1776: the freedom to govern themselves.

[The majority] opinion is couched in a style that is as pretentious as its content is egotistic. It is one thing for separate concurring or dissenting opinions to contain extravagances, even silly extravagances, of thought and expression; it is something else for the official opinion of the Court to do so. Of course the opinion's showy profundities are often profoundly incoherent. "The nature of marriage is that, through its enduring bond, two persons together can find other freedoms, such as expression, intimacy, and spirituality." (Really? Who ever thought that intimacy and spirituality [whatever that means] were freedoms? And if intimacy is, one would think Freedom of Intimacy is abridged rather than expanded by marriage. Ask the nearest hippie. Expression, sure enough, *is* a freedom, but anyone in a long-lasting marriage will attest that that happy state constricts, rather than expands, what one can prudently say.) Rights, we are told, can "rise . . . from a better informed understanding of how constitutional imperatives define a liberty that remains urgent in our own era." (Huh? How can a better informed understanding of how constitutional imperatives [whatever that means] define [whatever that means] an urgent liberty [never mind], give birth to a right?) . . . I could go on. The world does not expect logic and precision in poetry or inspirational pop-philosophy; it demands them in the law. The stuff contained in today's opinion has to diminish this Court's reputation for clear thinking and sober analysis.

* * *

. . . With each decision of ours that takes from the People a question properly left to them — with each decision that is unabashedly based not on law, but on the "reasoned judgment" of a bare majority of this Court — we move one step closer to being reminded of our impotence.

[Dissenting opinion of Justice Thomas omitted.]

[Dissenting opinion of Justice Alito omitted.]

## NOTES AND QUESTIONS

**1.** Is *Obergefell* simply *Loving* redux? If so, why didn't Justice Kennedy, writing for the majority, just say that? In what way does he see the interest in marriage connecting to the other interests deemed fundamental under substantive due process? In other words, what links them all — and may at least partially explain what it means for a right to be implicit in the concept of ordered liberty?

**2.** Chief Justice Roberts, in his dissent, sees the majority's decision here as identical to the incorrect decision of the *Lochner* majority. Why? In what ways are the decisions alike? Does accepting the premise of the Chief Justice's argument mean it is necessary to reject the existence of any unenumerated right under the rubric of substantive due process?

**3.** To say that Justice Scalia is unhappy with the reasoning in the *Obergefell* majority opinion is perhaps an understatement. What is his basis for disagreement — and what is his primary anxiety?

**4.** To return to Justice Kennedy's majority opinion: what limits does it suggest on the scope of the individual interest in marriage? Does this decision open the door to plural marriage? Does it suggest that other marriage restrictions that have been deemed reasonable —

restrictions based, for example, upon age, or relation of the parties —
may now be subject to challenge?

### 5. The Right to Die
### Cruzan v. Director, Missouri Department of Health
### 497 U.S. 261 (1990)

Chief Justice Rehnquist delivered the opinion of the Court.

Petitioner Nancy Beth Cruzan was rendered incompetent as a result of severe injuries sustained during an automobile accident. Copetitioners Lester and Joyce Cruzan, Nancy's parents and coguardians, sought a court order directing the withdrawal of their daughter's artificial feeding and hydration equipment after it became apparent that she had virtually no chance of recovering her cognitive faculties. The Supreme Court of Missouri held that because there was no clear and convincing evidence of Nancy's desire to have life-sustaining treatment withdrawn under such circumstances, her parents lacked authority to effectuate such a request. We granted certiorari and now affirm.

. . .

After it had become apparent that Nancy Cruzan had virtually no chance of regaining her mental faculties, her parents asked hospital employees to terminate the artificial nutrition and hydration procedures. All agree that such a removal would cause her death. The employees refused to honor the request without court approval. The parents then sought and received authorization from the state trial court for termination. The court found that a person in Nancy's condition had a fundamental right under the State and Federal Constitutions to refuse or direct the withdrawal of "death prolonging procedures." The court also found that Nancy's "expressed thoughts at age twenty-five in somewhat serious conversation with a housemate friend that if sick or injured she would not wish to continue her life unless she could live at least halfway normally suggests that given her present condition she would not wish to continue on with her nutrition and hydration."

The Supreme Court of Missouri reversed by a divided vote. . . . The court found that Cruzan's statements to her roommate regarding her desire to live or die under certain conditions were "unreliable for the purpose of determining her intent," "and thus insufficient to support the co-guardians['] claim to exercise substituted judgment on Nancy's behalf." It rejected the argument that Cruzan's parents were entitled to order the termination of her medical treatment, concluding that "no person can assume that choice for an incompetent in the absence of the formalities required under Missouri's Living Will statutes or the clear and convincing, inherently reliable evidence absent here." . . .

We granted certiorari to consider the question whether Cruzan has a right under the United States Constitution which would require the hospital to withdraw life-sustaining treatment from her under these circumstances.

At common law, even the touching of one person by another without consent and without legal justification was a battery. Before the turn of the century, this Court observed that "[n]o right is held more sacred, or is more carefully guarded, by the common law, than the right of every individual to the possession and control of his own person, free from all restraint or interference of others, unless by clear and unquestionable authority of law." *Union Pacific R. Co. v. Botsford* (1891). This notion of bodily integrity has been embodied in the requirement that informed consent is generally required for medical treatment. Justice Cardozo, while on the Court of Appeals of New York, aptly described this doctrine: "Every human being of adult years and sound mind has a right to determine what shall be done with his own body; and a surgeon who performs an operation without his patient's consent commits an assault, for which he is liable in damages." *Schloendorff v. Society of New York Hospital* (N.Y. 1914). The informed consent doctrine has become firmly entrenched in American tort law.

[T]he common-law doctrine of informed consent is viewed as generally encompassing the right of a competent individual to refuse medical treatment. . . . In this Court, the question is simply and starkly whether the United States Constitution prohibits Missouri from choosing the rule of decision which it did. This is the first case in which we have been squarely presented with the issue whether the United States Constitution grants what is in common parlance referred to as a "right to die." . . .

The Fourteenth Amendment provides that no State shall "deprive any person of life, liberty, or property, without due process of law." The principle that a competent person has a constitutionally protected liberty interest in refusing unwanted medical treatment may be inferred from our prior decisions. . . .

But determining that a person has a "liberty interest" under the Due Process Clause does not end the inquiry; "whether respondent's constitutional rights have been violated must be determined by balancing his liberty interests against the relevant state interests." *Youngberg v. Romeo* (1982).

Petitioners insist that under the general holdings of our cases, the forced administration of life-sustaining medical treatment, and even of artificially delivered food and water essential to life, would implicate a competent person's liberty interest. Although we think the logic of the cases discussed above would embrace such a liberty interest, the dramatic consequences involved in refusal of such treatment would inform the inquiry as to whether the deprivation of that interest is constitutionally permissible. But for purposes of this case, we assume that the United States Constitution would grant a competent person a constitutionally protected right to refuse lifesaving hydration and nutrition.

Petitioners go on to assert that an incompetent person should possess the same right in this respect as is possessed by a competent person. . . . The difficulty with petitioners' claim is that in a sense it begs the question: An incompetent person is not able to make an informed and voluntary choice to exercise a hypothetical right to refuse treatment or any other right. Such a "right" must be exercised for her, if at all, by some sort of surrogate. Here, Missouri has in effect recognized that under certain circumstances a surrogate may act for the patient in electing to have hydration and nutrition withdrawn in such a way as to cause death, but it has established a procedural safeguard to assure that the action of the surrogate conforms as best it may to the wishes expressed by the patient while competent. Missouri requires that evidence of the incompetent's wishes as to the withdrawal of treatment be proved by clear and convincing evidence. The question, then, is whether the United States Constitution forbids the establishment of this procedural requirement by the State. We hold that it does not.

Whether or not Missouri's clear and convincing evidence requirement comports with the United States Constitution depends in part on what interests the State may properly seek to protect in this situation. Missouri relies on its interest in the protection and preservation of human life, and there can be no gainsaying this interest. As a general matter, the States — indeed, all civilized nations — demonstrate their commitment to life by treating homicide as a serious crime. . . . We do not think a State is required to remain neutral in the face of an informed and voluntary decision by a physically able adult to starve to death.

But in the context presented here, a State has more particular interests at stake. The choice between life and death is a deeply personal decision of obvious and overwhelming finality. We believe Missouri may legitimately seek to safeguard the personal element of this choice through the imposition of heightened evidentiary requirements. It cannot be disputed that the Due Process Clause protects an interest in life as well as an interest in refusing life-sustaining medical treatment. Not all incompetent patients will have loved ones available to serve as surrogate decisionmakers. And even where family members are present, "[t]here will, of course, be some unfortunate situations in which family members will not act to protect a patient." *In re Jobes* (N.J. 1987). A State is entitled to guard against potential abuses in such situations. Similarly, a State is entitled to consider that a judicial proceeding to make a determination regarding an incompetent's wishes may very well not be an adversarial one, with the added guarantee of accurate fact-finding that the adversary process brings with it. Finally, we think a State may properly decline to make judgments about the "quality" of life that a particular individual may enjoy, and simply assert an unqualified interest in the preservation of human life to be weighed against the constitutionally protected interests of the individual.

In our view, Missouri has permissibly sought to advance these interests through the adoption of a "clear and convincing" standard of proof to govern such proceedings. "The function of a standard of proof, as that concept is embodied in the Due Process Clause and in the realm of factfinding, is to 'instruct the factfinder concerning the degree of confidence our society thinks he should have in the correctness of factual conclusions for a particular type of adjudication.' " *Addington v. Texas* (1979) (quoting *In re Winship* (1970) (Harlan, J., concurring)). "This Court has mandated an intermediate standard of proof — 'clear and convincing evidence' — when the individual interests at stake in a state proceeding are both 'particularly important' and 'more substantial than mere loss of money.' " *Santosky v. Kramer* (1982) (quoting *Addington*). Thus, such a standard has been required in deportation proceedings, in denaturalization proceedings, in civil commitment proceedings, and in proceedings for the termination of parental rights. . . .

We think it self-evident that the interests at stake in the instant proceedings are more substantial, both on an individual and societal level, than those involved in a run-of-the-mine civil dispute. But not only does the standard of proof reflect the importance of a particular adjudication, it also serves as "a societal judgment about how the risk of error should be distributed between the litigants." *Santosky*. The more stringent the burden of proof a party must bear, the more that party bears the risk of an erroneous decision. We believe that Missouri may permissibly place an increased risk of an erroneous decision on those seeking to terminate an incompetent individual's life-sustaining treatment. An erroneous decision not to terminate results in a maintenance of the status quo; the possibility of subsequent developments such as advancements in medical science, the discovery of new evidence regarding the patient's intent, changes in the law, or simply the unexpected death of the patient despite the administration of life-sustaining treatment at least create the potential that a wrong decision will eventually be corrected or its impact mitigated. An erroneous decision to withdraw life-sustaining treatment, however, is not susceptible of correction. In *Santosky*, one of the factors which led the Court to require proof by clear and convincing evidence in a proceeding to terminate parental rights was that a decision in such a case was final and irrevocable. The same must surely be said of the decision to discontinue hydration and nutrition of a patient such as Nancy Cruzan, which all agree will result in her death.

It is also worth noting that most, if not all, States simply forbid oral testimony entirely in determining the wishes of parties in transactions which, while important, simply do not have the consequences that a decision to terminate a person's life does. . . . There is no doubt that statutes requiring wills to be in writing, and statutes of frauds which require that a contract to make a will be in writing, on occasion frustrate the effectuation of the intent of a particular decedent, just as Missouri's requirement of proof in this case may have frustrated the effectuation of the not-fully-expressed desires of Nancy Cruzan. But the Constitution does not require general rules to work faultlessly; no general rule can.

In sum, we conclude that a State may apply a clear and convincing evidence standard in proceedings where a guardian seeks to discontinue nutrition and hydration of a person diagnosed to be in a persistent vegetative state. We note that many courts which have adopted some sort of substituted judgment procedure in situations like this, whether they limit consideration of evidence to the prior expressed wishes of the incompetent individual, or whether they allow more general proof of what the individual's decision would have been, require a clear and convincing standard of proof for such evidence.

The Supreme Court of Missouri held that in this case the testimony adduced at trial did not amount to clear and convincing proof of the patient's desire to have hydration and nutrition withdrawn. In so doing, it reversed a decision of the Missouri trial court which had found that the evidence "suggest[ed]" Nancy Cruzan would not have desired to continue such measures, but which had not adopted the standard of "clear and convincing evidence" enunciated by the Supreme Court. The testimony adduced at trial consisted primarily of Nancy Cruzan's statements made to a housemate about a year before her accident that she would not want to live should she face life as a "vegetable," and other observations to the same effect. The observations did not deal in terms with withdrawal of medical treatment or of hydration and nutrition. We cannot say that the Supreme Court of Missouri committed constitutional error in reaching the conclusion that it did.

[There is no doubt] that Nancy Cruzan's mother and father are loving and caring parents. If the State were required by the United States Constitution to repose a right of "substituted judgment" with anyone, the Cruzans would surely qualify. But we do not think the Due Process Clause requires the State to repose judgment on these matters with anyone but the patient herself. Close family members may have a strong feeling — a feeling not at all ignoble or unworthy, but not entirely disinterested, either — that they do not wish to witness the continuation of the life of a loved one which they regard as hopeless, meaningless, and even degrading. But there is no automatic assurance that the view of close family members will necessarily be the same as the patient's would have been had she been confronted with the prospect of her situation while competent. All of the reasons previously discussed for allowing Missouri to require clear and convincing evidence of the patient's wishes lead us to conclude that the State may choose to defer only to those wishes, rather than confide the decision to close family members.

The judgment of the Supreme Court of Missouri is

*Affirmed.*

Justice O'Connor, concurring.

I agree that a protected liberty interest in refusing unwanted medical treatment may be inferred from our prior decisions, and that the refusal of artificially delivered food and water is encompassed within that liberty interest. I write separately to clarify why I believe this to be so.

As the Court notes, the liberty interest in refusing medical treatment flows from decisions involving the State's invasions into the body. Because our notions of liberty are inextricably entwined with our idea of physical freedom and self-determination, the Court has often deemed state incursions into the body repugnant to the interests protected by the Due Process Clause. The State's imposition of medical treatment on an unwilling competent adult necessarily involves some form of restraint and intrusion. A seriously ill or dying patient whose wishes are not honored may feel a captive of the machinery required for life-sustaining measures or other medical interventions. Such forced treatment may burden that individual's liberty interests as much as any state coercion.

The State's artificial provision of nutrition and hydration implicates identical concerns. Artificial feeding cannot readily be distinguished from other forms of medical treatment. Whether or not the techniques used to pass food and water into the patient's alimentary tract are termed "medical treatment," it is clear they all involve some degree of intrusion and restraint. . . . Accordingly, the liberty guaranteed by the Due Process Clause must protect, if it protects anything, an individual's deeply personal decision to reject medical treatment, including the artificial delivery of food and water.

. . .

Today's decision, holding only that the Constitution permits a State to require clear and convincing evidence of Nancy Cruzan's desire to have artificial hydration and nutrition withdrawn, does not preclude a future determination that the Constitution requires the States to implement the decisions of a patient's duly appointed surrogate. Nor does it prevent States from developing other approaches for protecting an incompetent individual's liberty interest in refusing medical treatment. [N]o national consensus has yet emerged on the best solution for this difficult and sensitive problem. Today we decide only that one State's practice does not violate the Constitution; the more challenging task of crafting appropriate procedures for safeguarding incompetents' liberty interests is entrusted to the "laboratory" of the States, *New State Ice Co. v. Liebmann* (1932) (Brandeis, J., dissenting), in the first instance.

Justice Scalia, concurring.

[I do not] suggest that I would think it desirable, if we were sure that Nancy Cruzan wanted to die, to keep her alive by the means at issue here. I assert only that the Constitution has nothing to say about the subject. To raise up a constitutional right here we would have to create out of nothing (for it exists neither in text nor tradition) some constitutional principle whereby, although the State may insist that an individual come in out of the cold and eat food, it may not insist that he take medicine; and although it may pump his stomach empty of poison he has ingested, it may not fill his stomach with food he has failed to ingest. Are there, then, no reasonable and humane limits that ought not to be exceeded in requiring an individual to preserve his own life? There obviously are, but they are not set forth in the Due Process Clause. What assures us that those limits will not be exceeded is the same constitutional guarantee that is the source of most of our protection — what protects us, for example, from being assessed a tax of 100% of our income above the subsistence level, from being forbidden to drive cars, or from being required to send our children to school for 10 hours a day, none of which horribles are categorically prohibited by the Constitution. Our salvation is the Equal Protection Clause, which requires the democratic majority to accept for themselves and their loved ones what they impose on you and me. This Court need not, and has no authority to, inject itself into every field of human activity where irrationality and oppression may theoretically occur, and if it tries to do so it will destroy itself.

Justice Brennan, with whom Justice Marshall and Justice Blackmun join, dissenting.

The only state interest asserted here is a general interest in the preservation of life. But the State has no legitimate general interest in someone's life, completely abstracted from the interest of the person living that life, that could outweigh the person's choice to avoid medical treatment. . . . [T]he State's general interest in life must accede to Nancy Cruzan's particularized and intense interest in self-determination in her choice of medical treatment. There is simply nothing legitimately within the State's purview to be gained by superseding her decision.

. . . I cannot agree with the majority that where it is not possible to determine what choice an incompetent patient would make, a State's role as *parens patriae* permits the State automatically to make that choice itself. Under fair rules of evidence, it is improbable that a court could not determine what the patient's choice would be. Under the rule of decision adopted by Missouri and upheld today by this Court, such occasions might be numerous. But in neither case does it follow that it is constitutionally acceptable for the State invariably to assume the role of deciding for the patient. A State's legitimate interest in safeguarding a patient's choice cannot be furthered by simply appropriating it.

The majority justifies its position by arguing that, while close family members may have a strong feeling about the question, "there is no automatic assurance that the view of close family members will necessarily be the same as the patient's would have been had she been confronted with the prospect of her situation while competent." I cannot quarrel with this observation. But it leads only to another question: Is there any reason to suppose that a State is *more* likely to make the choice that the patient would have made than someone who knew the patient intimately? To ask this is to answer it. . . .

A State's inability to discern an incompetent patient's choice still need not mean that a State is rendered powerless to protect that choice. But I would find that the Due Process Clause prohibits a State from doing more than that. A State may ensure that the person who makes the decision on the patient's behalf is the one whom the patient himself would have selected to make that choice for him. And a State may exclude from consideration anyone having improper motives. But a State generally must either repose the choice with the person whom the patient himself would most likely have chosen as proxy or leave the decision to the patient's family.

[Dissenting opinion of Justice Stevens omitted.]

## NOTES AND QUESTIONS

1. In this case, Chief Justice Rehnquist, writing for the majority, does much to clarify the modern Court's thinking when it seeks to determine whether an unenumerated right should be deemed fundamental under substantive due process. Consider where he begins his analysis — with rights established under common law regarding unwanted touching. He next suggests that the existence of these common-law rights lead to the conclusion that competent individuals enjoy a similar, constitutional right as against the state when it comes to unwanted life-sustained medical treatment. But that does not answer the question posed in *Cruzan* — namely, whether incompetent individuals enjoy a similar interest — and that issue is the one upon which the Court must evaluate Missouri's regulation here.

2. Missouri elected to require that anyone wishing to decide for patients who can no longer speak for themselves to end their lives must establish, by clear and convincing evidence, that such was a patient's wish. It is that evidentiary standard that the Court scrutinizes, once again looking at ends and means. Why does the Court in the end determine that the state's evidentiary standard is appropriate? Does that mean that a lesser standard — say, preponderance of the evidence — would be unconstitutional? What about a higher standard — say, proof beyond a reasonable doubt?

## Washington v. Glucksberg
### 521 U.S. 702 (1997)

Chief Justice Rehnquist delivered the opinion of the Court.

The question presented in this case is whether Washington's prohibition against "caus[ing]" or "aid[ing]" a suicide offends the Fourteenth Amendment to the United States Constitution. We hold that it does not.

It has always been a crime to assist a suicide in the State of Washington. In 1854, Washington's first Territorial Legislature outlawed "assisting another in the commission of self-murder." Today, Washington law provides: "A person is guilty of promoting a suicide attempt when he knowingly causes or aids another person to attempt suicide." Wash. Rev. Code § 9A.36.060(1) (1994). "Promoting a suicide attempt" is a felony, punishable by up to five years' imprisonment and up to a $10,000 fine. §§ 9A.36.060(2) and 9A.20.021(1)(c). At the same time, Washington's Natural Death Act, enacted in 1979, states that the "withholding or withdrawal of life-sustaining treatment" at a patient's direction "shall not, for any purpose, constitute a suicide." Wash. Rev. Code § 70.122.070(1).

Petitioners in this case are the State of Washington and its Attorney General. Respondents Harold Glucksberg, M.D., Abigail Halperin, M.D., Thomas A. Preston, M.D., and Peter Shalit, M.D., are physicians who practice in Washington. These doctors occasionally treat terminally ill, suffering patients, and declare that they would assist these patients in ending their lives if not for Washington's assisted-suicide ban. In January 1994, respondents, along with three gravely ill, pseudonymous plaintiffs who have since died and Compassion in Dying, a nonprofit organization that counsels people considering physician-assisted suicide, sued in the United States District Court, seeking a declaration that Wash. Rev. Code § 9A. 36.060(1) (1994) is, on its face, unconstitutional.

The plaintiffs asserted "the existence of a liberty interest protected by the Fourteenth Amendment which extends to a personal choice by a mentally competent, terminally ill adult to commit physician-assisted suicide." Relying primarily on *Planned Parenthood of Southeastern Pa. v. Casey* (1992) and *Cruzan v. Director, Mo. Dept. of Health* (1990), the District Court agreed, and concluded that Washington's assisted-suicide ban is unconstitutional because it "places an undue burden on the exercise of [that] constitutionally protected liberty interest." . . .

A panel of the Court of Appeals for the Ninth Circuit reversed, emphasizing that "[i]n the two hundred and five years of our existence no constitutional right to aid in killing oneself has ever been asserted and upheld by a court of final jurisdiction." The Ninth Circuit reheard the case en banc, reversed the panel's decision, and affirmed the District Court. Like the District Court, the en banc Court of Appeals emphasized our *Casey* and *Cruzan* decisions. The court also discussed what it described as "historical" and "current societal attitudes" toward suicide and assisted suicide, and concluded that "the Constitution encompasses a due process liberty interest in controlling the time and manner of one's death — that there is, in short, a constitutionally-recognized 'right to die.' " After "[w]eighing and then balancing" this interest against Washington's various interests, the court held that the State's assisted-suicide ban was unconstitutional "as applied to terminally ill competent adults who wish to hasten their deaths with medication prescribed by their physicians." . . . We granted certiorari and now reverse.

## I

We begin, as we do in all due process cases, by examining our Nation's history, legal traditions, and practices. In almost every State — indeed, in almost every western democracy — it is a crime to assist a suicide. The States' assisted-suicide bans are not innovations. Rather, they are longstanding expressions of the States' commitment to the protection and preservation of all human life. Indeed, opposition to and condemnation of suicide — and, therefore, of assisting suicide — are consistent and enduring themes of our philosophical, legal, and cultural heritages.

More specifically, for over 700 years, the Anglo-American common-law tradition has punished or otherwise disapproved of both suicide and assisting suicide. . . . Sir William Blackstone, whose Commentaries on the Laws of England not only provided a definitive summary of the common law but was also a primary legal authority for 18th- and 19th-century American lawyers, referred to suicide as "self-murder" and "the pretended heroism, but real cowardice, of the Stoic philosophers, who destroyed themselves to avoid those ills which they had not the fortitude to endure. . . ." 4 W. Blackstone, Commentaries *189. Blackstone emphasized that "the law has . . .

ranked [suicide] among the highest crimes," although, anticipating later developments, he conceded that the harsh and shameful punishments imposed for suicide "borde[r] a little upon severity."

For the most part, the early American Colonies adopted the common-law approach. For example, the legislators of the Providence Plantations, which would later become Rhode Island, declared, in 1647, that "[s]elf-murder is by all agreed to be the most unnatural, and it is by this present Assembly declared, to be that, wherein he that doth it, kills himself out of a premeditated hatred against his own life or other humor: . . . his goods and chattels are the king's custom, but not his debts nor lands; but in case he be an infant, a lunatic, mad or distracted man, he forfeits nothing." The Earliest Acts and Laws of the Colony of Rhode Island and Providence Plantations 1647-1719 (J. Cushing ed. 1977). . . .

Over time, however, the American Colonies abolished these harsh common-law penalties. William Penn abandoned the criminal-forfeiture sanction in Pennsylvania in 1701, and the other Colonies (and later, the other States) eventually followed this example. . . . [T]he movement away from the common law's harsh sanctions did not represent an acceptance of suicide; rather, as Chief Justice Swift observed, this change reflected the growing consensus that it was unfair to punish the suicide's family for his wrongdoing. Nonetheless, although States moved away from Blackstone's treatment of suicide, courts continued to condemn it as a grave public wrong.

That suicide remained a grievous, though non-felonious, wrong is confirmed by the fact that colonial and early state legislatures and courts did not retreat from prohibiting assisting suicide. . . . The earliest American statute explicitly to outlaw assisting suicide was enacted in New York in 1828, and many of the new States and Territories followed New York's example. . . . By the time the Fourteenth Amendment was ratified, it was a crime in most States to assist a suicide.

Though deeply rooted, the States' assisted-suicide bans have in recent years been reexamined and, generally, reaffirmed. Because of advances in medicine and technology, Americans today are increasingly likely to die in institutions, from chronic illnesses. Public concern and democratic action are therefore sharply focused on how best to protect dignity and independence at the end of life, with the result that there have been many significant changes in state laws and in the attitudes these laws reflect. Many States, for example, now permit "living wills," surrogate health-care decisionmaking, and the withdrawal or refusal of life-sustaining medical treatment. At the same time, however, voters and legislators continue for the most part to reaffirm their States' prohibitions on assisting suicide.

The Washington statute at issue in this case was enacted in 1975 as part of a revision of that State's criminal code. Four years later, Washington passed its Natural Death Act, which specifically stated that the "withholding or withdrawal of life-sustaining treatment . . . shall not, for any purpose, constitute a suicide" and that "[n]othing in this chapter shall be construed to condone, authorize, or approve mercy killing. . . ." In 1991, Washington voters rejected a ballot initiative which, had it passed, would have permitted a form of physician-assisted suicide. Washington then added a provision to the Natural Death Act expressly excluding physician-assisted suicide.

California voters rejected an assisted-suicide initiative similar to Washington's in 1993. On the other hand, in 1994, voters in Oregon enacted, also through ballot initiative, that State's "Death With Dignity Act," which legalized physician-assisted suicide for competent, terminally ill adults. Since the Oregon vote, many proposals to legalize assisted-suicide have been and continue to be introduced in the States' legislatures. . . .

Attitudes toward suicide itself have changed . . . , but our laws have consistently condemned, and continue to prohibit, assisting suicide. Despite changes in medical technology and notwithstanding an increased emphasis on the importance of end-of-life decisionmaking, we have not retreated from this prohibition. Against this backdrop of history, tradition, and practice, we now turn to respondents' constitutional claim.

## II

The Due Process Clause guarantees more than fair process, and the "liberty" it protects includes more than the absence of physical restraint. The Clause also provides heightened protection against government interference with certain fundamental rights and liberty interests. In a long line of cases, we have held that, in addition to the specific freedoms protected by the Bill of Rights, the "liberty" specially protected by the Due Process Clause includes the rights to marry, to have children, to direct the education and upbringing of one's children, to marital privacy, to use contraception, to bodily integrity, and to abortion. We have also assumed, and strongly suggested, that the Due Process Clause protects the traditional right to refuse unwanted life-saving medical treatment.

But we "ha[ve] always been reluctant to expand the concept of substantive due process because guide posts for responsible decisionmaking in this uncharted area are scarce and open-ended." *Collins v. City of Harker Heights, Texas* (1992). By extending constitutional protection to an asserted right or liberty interest, we, to a great extent, place the matter outside the arena of public debate and legislative action. We must therefore "exercise the utmost care whenever we are asked to break new ground in this field," *id.*, lest the liberty protected by the Due Process Clause be subtly transformed into the policy preferences of the Members of this Court, *Moore v. City of East Cleveland* (1977) (plurality opinion).

Our established method of substantive-due-process analysis has two primary features: First, we have regularly observed that the Due Process Clause specially protects those fundamental rights and liberties which are, objectively, "deeply rooted in this Nation's history and tradition," *id.* (plurality opinion); and "implicit in the concept of ordered liberty," such that "neither liberty nor justice would exist if they were sacrificed," *Palko v. Connecticut* (1937). Second, we have required in substantive-due-process cases a "careful description" of the asserted fundamental liberty interest. Our Nation's history, legal traditions, and practices thus provide the crucial "guide posts for responsible decisionmaking," *Collins*, that direct and restrain our exposition of the Due Process Clause. As we stated recently in *Reno v. Flores* (1993), the Fourteenth Amendment "forbids the government to infringe . . . 'fundamental' liberty interests *at all*, no matter what process is provided, unless the infringement is narrowly tailored to serve a compelling state interest."

. . . In our view . . . the development of this Court's substantive-due-process jurisprudence has been a process whereby the outlines of the "liberty" specially protected by the Fourteenth Amendment — never fully clarified, to be sure, and perhaps not capable of being fully clarified — have at least been carefully refined by concrete examples involving fundamental rights found to be deeply rooted in our legal tradition. This approach tends to rein in the subjective elements that are necessarily present in due process judicial review. In addition, by establishing a threshold requirement — that a challenged state action implicate a fundamental right — before requiring more than a reasonable relation to a legitimate state interest to justify the action, it avoids the need for complex balancing of competing interests in every case.

Turning to the claim at issue here, the Court of Appeals stated that "[p]roperly analyzed, the first issue to be resolved is whether there is a liberty interest in determining the time and manner of one's death," or, in other words, "[i]s there a right to die?" Similarly, respondents assert a "liberty to choose how to die" and a right to "control of one's final days," and describe the asserted liberty as "the right to choose a humane, dignified death," and "the liberty to shape death." As noted above, we have a tradition of carefully formulating the interest at stake in substantive dueprocess cases. For example, although *Cruzan* is often described as a "right to die" case, we were, in fact, more precise: We assumed that the Constitution granted competent persons a "constitutionally protected right to refuse lifesaving hydration and nutrition." The Washington statute at issue in this case prohibits "aid[ing] another person to attempt suicide," and, thus, the question before us is whether the "liberty" specially protected by the Due Process Clause includes a right to commit suicide which itself includes a right to assistance in doing so.

We now inquire whether this asserted right has any place in our Nation's traditions. Here, as discussed *supra*, we are confronted with a consistent and almost universal tradition that has long rejected the asserted right, and continues explicitly to reject it today, even for terminally ill, mentally competent adults. To hold for respondents, we would have to reverse centuries of legal doctrine and practice, and strike down the considered policy choice of almost every State.

Respondents contend, however, that the liberty interest they assert *is* consistent with this Court's substantive-due process line of cases, if not with this Nation's history and practice. Pointing to *Casey* and *Cruzan*, respondents read our jurisprudence in this area as reflecting a general tradition of "self-sovereignty," and as teaching that the "liberty" protected by the Due Process Clause includes "basic and intimate exercises of personal autonomy." According to respondents, our liberty jurisprudence, and the broad, individualistic principles it reflects, protects the "liberty of competent, terminally ill adults to make end-of-life decisions free of undue government interference." The question presented in this case, however, is whether the protections of the Due Process Clause include a right to commit suicide with another's assistance. With this "careful description" of respondents' claim in mind, we turn to *Casey* and *Cruzan*.

. . .

Respondents contend that in *Cruzan* we "acknowledged that competent, dying persons have the right to direct the removal of life-sustaining medical treatment and thus hasten death," and that "the constitutional principle behind recognizing the patient's liberty to direct the withdrawal of artificial life support applies at least as strongly to the choice to hasten impending death by consuming lethal medication." Similarly, the Court of Appeals concluded that "*Cruzan*, by recognizing a liberty interest that includes the refusal of artificial provision of life-sustaining food and water, necessarily recognize[d] a liberty interest in hastening one's own death."

The right assumed in *Cruzan*, however, was not simply deduced from abstract concepts of personal autonomy. Given the common-law rule that forced medication was a battery, and the long legal tradition protecting the decision to refuse unwanted medical treatment, our assumption was entirely consistent with this Nation's history and constitutional traditions. The decision to commit suicide with the assistance of another may be just as personal and profound as the decision to refuse unwanted medical treatment, but it has never enjoyed similar legal protection. Indeed, the two acts are widely and reasonably regarded as quite distinct. In *Cruzan* itself, we recognized that most States outlawed assisted suicide — and even more do today — and we certainly gave no intimation that the right to refuse unwanted medical treatment could be somehow transmuted into a right to assistance in committing suicide.

[T]he Court's opinion in *Casey* described, in a general way and in light of our prior cases, those personal activities and decisions that this Court has identified as so deeply rooted in our history and traditions, or so fundamental to our concept of constitutionally ordered liberty, that they are protected by the Fourteenth Amendment. The opinion moved from the recognition that liberty necessarily includes freedom of conscience and belief about ultimate considerations to the observation that "though the abortion decision may originate within the zone of conscience and belief, it is *more than a philosophic exercise*." *Casey* (emphasis added). That many of the rights and liberties protected by the Due Process Clause sound in personal autonomy does not warrant the sweeping conclusion that any and all important, intimate, and personal decisions are so protected, and *Casey* did not suggest otherwise.

The history of the law's treatment of assisted suicide in this country has been and continues to be one of the rejection of nearly all efforts to permit it. That being the case, our decisions lead us to conclude that the asserted "right" to assistance in committing suicide is not a fundamental liberty interest protected by the Due Process Clause. The Constitution also requires, however, that Washington's assisted-suicide ban be rationally related to legitimate government interests. This requirement is unquestionably met here. As the court below recognized, Washington's assisted-suicide ban implicates a number of state interests.

First, Washington has an "unqualified interest in the preservation of human life." *Cruzan*. The State's prohibition on assisted suicide, like all homicide laws, both reflects and advances its commitment to this interest. . . .

Relatedly, all admit that suicide is a serious public-health problem, especially among persons in otherwise vulnerable groups. The State has an interest in preventing suicide, and in studying, identifying, and treating its causes.

Those who attempt suicide — terminally ill or not — often suffer from depression or other mental disorders. Research indicates, however, that many people who request physician-assisted suicide withdraw that request if their depression and pain are treated.

[There is also] an interest in protecting the integrity and ethics of the medical profession. In contrast to the Court of Appeals' conclusion that "the integrity of the medical profession would [not] be threatened in any way by [physician-assisted suicide]," the American Medical Association, like many other medical and physicians' groups, has concluded that "[p]hysician-assisted suicide is fundamentally incompatible with the physician's role as healer." American Medical Association, Code of Ethics § 2.211 (1994). And physician-assisted suicide could, it is argued, undermine the trust that is essential to the doctor-patient relationship by blurring the time-honored line between healing and harming.

Next, the State has an interest in protecting vulnerable groups — including the poor, the elderly, and disabled persons — from abuse, neglect, and mistakes. [There exists] the real risk of subtle coercion and undue influence in end-of-life situations. . . . If physician-assisted suicide were permitted, many might resort to it to spare their families the substantial financial burden of end-of-life health-care costs.

The State's interest here goes beyond protecting the vulnerable from coercion; it extends to protecting disabled and terminally ill people from prejudice, negative and inaccurate stereotypes, and "societal indifference." The State's assisted-suicide ban reflects and reinforces its policy that the lives of terminally ill, disabled, and elderly people must be no less valued than the lives of the young and healthy, and that a seriously disabled person's suicidal impulses should be interpreted and treated the same way as anyone else's.

Finally, the State may fear that permitting assisted suicide will start it down the path to voluntary and perhaps even involuntary euthanasia. The Court of Appeals struck down Washington's assisted-suicide ban only "as applied to competent, terminally ill adults who wish to hasten their deaths by obtaining medication prescribed by their doctors." Washington insists, however, that the impact of the court's decision will not and cannot be so limited. If suicide is protected as a matter of constitutional right, it is argued, "every man and woman in the United States must enjoy it." The Court of Appeals' decision, and its expansive reasoning, provide ample support for the State's concerns. The court noted, for example, that the "decision of a duly appointed surrogate decision maker is for all legal purposes the decision of the patient himself," that "in some instances, the patient may be unable to self-administer the drugs and . . . administration by the physician . . . may be the only way the patient may be able to receive them," and that not only physicians, but also family members and loved ones, will inevitably participate in assisting suicide. Thus, it turns out that what is couched as a limited right to "physician-assisted suicide" is likely, in effect, a much broader license, which could prove extremely difficult to police and contain. Washington's ban on assisting suicide prevents such erosion.

[The Court] need not weigh exactly the relative strengths of these various interests. They are unquestionably important and legitimate, and Washington's ban on assisted suicide is at least reasonably related to their promotion and protection. We therefore hold that Wash. Rev. Code § 9A.36.060(1) (1994) does not violate the Fourteenth Amendment, either on its face or "as applied to competent, terminally ill adults who wish to hasten their deaths by obtaining medication prescribed by their doctors."

\* \* \*

Throughout the Nation, Americans are engaged in an earnest and profound debate about the morality, legality, and practicality of physician-assisted suicide. Our holding permits this debate to continue, as it should in a democratic society. The decision of the en banc Court of Appeals is reversed, and the case is remanded for further proceedings consistent with this opinion.

*It is so ordered.*

[Concurring opinion of Justice O'Connor omitted.]

[Concurring opinion of Justice Stevens omitted.]

[Concurring opinion of Justice Souter omitted.]

[Concurring opinion of Justice Ginsburg omitted.]

[Concurring opinion of Justice Breyer omitted.]

## NOTES AND QUESTIONS

**1.** In this case, Chief Justice Rehnquist makes clear both the Court's approach to determining whether a particular interest should be deemed fundamental, and the appropriate level of scrutiny that follows depending upon that initial determination. That initial inquiry is twofold: first, is there a history and tradition of legal protection of the interest in question and, second, can it be said that this interest, though unenumerated, is implicit in the concept of ordered liberty? If the answer to either of these inquiries is in the negative, the interest cannot be deemed fundamental, and the court will apply rational basis scrutiny to regulation of that interest. If the answer to these questions is "yes," the second step is to provide a careful description of the right in question. Why might that be important for a court to articulate?

**2.** *Glucksberg* nonetheless leaves many questions about the proper analysis unanswered. What constitutes an interest that is implicit in the concept of ordered liberty remains ill-defined; the legal history in this case was relatively easy to discern and unequivocal. In cases in which the history is unavailable, lawyers have recourse to precedent, but it remains to be seen whether the Court will seriously entertain an approach to determining whether an interest is fundamental by examining its proximal relation to interests already so determined, notwithstanding that such reasoning is the common law system's stock-in-trade.

### 6. Choice

In 1973, the Court decided *Roe v. Wade*, 410 U.S. 113, in which it held that a woman's right to choose whether to have an abortion was protected under substantive due process. Writing for the majority, Justice Harry Blackmun reasoned that, while the Constitution "does not explicitly mention any right of privacy ... the Court has recognized that a right of personal privacy, or a guarantee of certain areas or zones of privacy, does exist under the Constitution." He continued:

> In varying contexts, the Court or individual Justices have, indeed, found at least the roots of that right in the First Amendment; in the Fourth and Fifth Amendments; in the penumbras of the Bill of Rights; in the Ninth Amendment; or in the concept of liberty guaranteed by the first section of the Fourteenth Amendment. These decisions make it clear that only personal rights that can be deemed "fundamental" or "implicit in the concept of ordered liberty," *Palko v. Connecticut* (1937), are included in this guarantee of personal privacy. They also make it clear that the right has some extension to activities relating to marriage, procreation, contraception, family relationships, and child rearing and education.
>
> This right of privacy, whether it be founded in the Fourteenth Amendment's concept of personal liberty and restrictions upon state action, as we feel it is ... is broad enough to encompass a woman's decision whether or not to terminate her pregnancy. The detriment that the State would impose upon the pregnant woman by denying this choice altogether is apparent. Specific and direct harm medically diagnosable even in early pregnancy may be involved. Maternity, or additional offspring, may force upon the woman a distressful life and future. Psychological harm may be imminent. Mental and physical health may be taxed by child care. There is also the distress, for all concerned, associated with the unwanted child, and there is the problem of bringing a child into a family already unable, psychologically and otherwise, to care for it. In other cases, as in this one, the

additional difficulties and continuing stigma of unwed motherhood may be involved. All these are factors the woman and her responsible physician necessarily will consider in consultation.

While the Court concluded that a woman's right to choose was fundamental, it recognized that "[t]he situation ... is inherently different from marital intimacy, or bedroom possession of obscene material, or marriage, or procreation, or education," and that "it is reasonable and appropriate for a State to decide that at some point in time another interest, that of health of the mother or that of potential human life, becomes significantly involved." It subsequently and famously adopted a trimester framework for assessing the constitutionality of regulations affecting a woman's right to choose:

> (a) For the stage prior to approximately the end of the first trimester, the abortion decision and its effectuation must be left to the medical judgment of the pregnant woman's attending physician.
>
> (b) For the stage subsequent to approximately the end of the first trimester, the State, in promoting its interest in the health of the mother, may, if it chooses, regulate the abortion procedure in ways that are reasonably related to maternal health.
>
> (c) For the stage subsequent to viability, the State in promoting its interest in the potentiality of human life may, if it chooses, regulate, and even proscribe, abortion except where it is necessary, in appropriate medical judgment, for the preservation of the life or health of the mother.

Almost immediately following *Roe*, states challenged the decision's premises with a variety of regulations designed to restrict women from exercising the right to choose, or at least to deter them from doing so. And many of those challenges included invitations to the Court to overturn *Roe* wholesale. That did not happen, but nearly 20 years after *Roe* was decided, a plurality of the Court in *Planned Parenthood v. Casey*, 505 U.S. 833 (1992), articulated a new approach to the issues raised by the constitutional protection of a woman's right to choose. Together, Justices Sandra Day O'Connor, Anthony Kennedy, and David Souter signed an opinion embracing the core of *Roe*, affirming that the Constitution protects a woman's right to choose as fundamental. "Neither the Bill of Rights nor the specific practices of States at the time of the adoption of the Fourteenth Amendment," the plurality held, "marks the outer limits of the substantive sphere of liberty which the Fourteenth Amendment protects." "The Constitution," the plurality continued, "places limits on a State's right to interfere with a person's most basic decisions about family and parenthood, as well as bodily integrity." Where choice is concerned, the plurality concluded that "[t]he destiny of [a] woman must be shaped to a large extent on her own conception of her spiritual imperatives and her place in society."

Nonetheless, the Casey plurality jettisoned *Roe*'s trimester framework. In its place, it drew a line at fetal viability: a "woman's right to terminate her pregnancy before viability is the most central principle of *Roe v. Wade*. It is a rule of law and a component of liberty we cannot renounce." The plurality continued:

> Though the woman has a right to choose to terminate or continue her pregnancy before viability, it does not at all follow that the State is prohibited from taking steps to ensure that this choice is thoughtful and informed. Even in the earliest stages of pregnancy, the State may enact rules and regulations designed to encourage her to know that there are philosophic and social arguments of great weight that can be brought to bear in favor of continuing the pregnancy to full term and that there are procedures and institutions to allow adoption of unwanted children as well as a certain degree of state assistance if the mother chooses to raise the child herself. . . . It follows that States are free to enact laws to provide a reasonable framework for a woman to make a decision that has such profound and lasting meaning. ...
>
> [The State's] substantial interest in potential life leads to the conclusion that not all regulations must be deemed unwarranted. Not all burdens on the right to decide whether to terminate a pregnancy will be undue. In our view, the undue burden standard is the appropriate means of reconciling the State's interest with the woman's constitutionally protected liberty.
>
> [A] statute which, while furthering the interest in potential life or some other valid state interest, has the effect of placing a substantial obstacle in the path of a woman's choice cannot be considered a permissible means of serving its legitimate ends. . . .

Applying the "undue burden" test, the plurality upheld the restrictions on choice at issue, save a provision requiring spousal notification requirement, which the plurality concluded would likely impose a substantial obstacle to choice: "For the great many women who are victims of abuse inflicted by their husbands, or whose children are the victims of such abuse, a spousal notice requirement enables the husband to wield an effective veto over his wife's decision." The joint opinion by Justices O'Connor, Souter, and Kennedy effectively displaced *Roe* as the most important case securing constitutional protection for a woman's right to choose.

In 2021, the Court heard arguments in *Dobbs v. Jackson Women's Health Organization*, reviewing a Court of Appeals decision striking down Mississippi's prohibition on choice after the fifteenth week of pregnancy; in 2022, the Court overturned *Roe* and *Casey*.

### Dobbs v. Jackson Women's Health Organization
### 597 U.S. ___ (2022)

Justice ALITO delivered the opinion of the Court.

In defending [its] law, [Mississippi's] primary argument is that we should reconsider and overrule *Roe* and *Casey* and once again allow each State to regulate abortion as its citizens wish. On the other side, respondents and the Solicitor General ask us to reaffirm *Roe* and *Casey*, and they contend that the Mississippi law cannot stand if we do so. ...

We hold that *Roe* and *Casey* must be overruled. The Constitution makes no reference to abortion, and no such right is implicitly protected by any constitutional provision, including the one on which the defenders of *Roe* and *Casey* now chiefly rely—the Due Process Clause of the Fourteenth Amendment. That provision has been held to guarantee some rights that are not mentioned in the Constitution, but any such right must be "deeply rooted in this Nation's history and tradition" and "implicit in the concept of ordered liberty." *Washington v. Glucksberg* (1997) (internal quotation marks omitted).

The right to abortion does not fall within this category. Until the latter part of the 20th century, such a right was entirely unknown in American law. Indeed, when the Fourteenth Amendment was adopted, three quarters of the States made abortion a crime at all stages of pregnancy. The abortion right is also critically different from any other right that this Court has held to fall within the Fourteenth Amendment's protection of "liberty." *Roe*'s defenders characterize the abortion right as similar to the rights recognized in past decisions involving matters such as intimate sexual relations, contraception, and marriage, but abortion is fundamentally different, as both *Roe* and *Casey* acknowledged, because it destroys what those decisions called "fetal life" and what the law now before us describes as an "unborn human being."

*Stare decisis*, the doctrine on which *Casey*'s controlling opinion was based, does not compel unending adherence to *Roe*'s abuse of judicial authority. *Roe* was egregiously wrong from the start. Its reasoning was exceptionally weak, and the decision has had damaging consequences. And far from bringing about a national settlement of the abortion issue, *Roe* and *Casey* have enflamed debate and deepened division.

It is time to heed the Constitution and return the issue of abortion to the people's elected representatives. ...

I

The law at issue in this case, Mississippi's Gestational Age Act, contains this central provision: "Except in a medical emergency or in the case of a severe fetal abnormality, a person shall not intentionally or knowingly perform ... or induce an abortion of an unborn human being if the probable gestational age of the unborn human being has been determined to be greater than fifteen (15) weeks."

[R]espondents are ... Jackson Women's Health Organization, and one of its doctors. On the day the Gestational Age Act was enacted, respondents filed suit in Federal District Court against various Mississippi officials, alleging that the Act violated this Court's precedents establishing a constitutional right to abortion. The District Court granted summary judgment in favor of respondents and permanently enjoined enforcement of the Act[.] The Fifth Circuit affirmed. ...

We granted certiorari to resolve the question whether "all pre-viability prohibitions on elective abortions are unconstitutional." ...

**II**

[We address the question whether the Constitution protects a woman's right to choose in three steps:] First, we explain the standard that our cases have used in determining whether the Fourteenth Amendment's reference to "liberty" protects a particular right. Second, we examine whether the right at issue in this case is rooted in our Nation's history and tradition and whether it is an essential component of what we have described as "ordered liberty." Finally, we consider whether a right to obtain an abortion is part of a broader entrenched right that is supported by other precedents.

**A**

*Roe* ... held that the abortion right, which is not mentioned in the Constitution, is part of a right to privacy, which is also not mentioned. And that privacy right, *Roe* observed, had been found to spring from no fewer than five different constitutional provisions—the First, Fourth, Fifth, Ninth, and Fourteenth Amendments.

... The *Casey* Court did not defend this unfocused analysis and instead grounded its decision solely on the theory that the right to obtain an abortion is part of the "liberty" protected by the Fourteenth Amendment's Due Process Clause.

We discuss this theory in depth below, but before doing so, we briefly address one additional constitutional provision that some of respondents' *amici* have now offered as yet another potential home for the abortion right: the Fourteenth Amendment's Equal Protection Clause. Neither *Roe* nor *Casey* saw fit to invoke this theory, and it is squarely foreclosed by our precedents, which establish that a State's regulation of abortion is not a sex-based classification and is thus not subject to the "heightened scrutiny" that applies to such classifications. The regulation of a medical procedure that only one sex can undergo does not trigger heightened constitutional scrutiny unless the regulation is a "mere pretex[t] designed to effect an invidious discrimination against members of one sex or the other." *Geduldig v. Aiello* (1974). And as the Court has stated, the "goal of preventing abortion" does not constitute "invidiously discriminatory animus" against women. *Bray v. Alexandria Women's Health Clinic* (1993) (internal quotation marks omitted). Accordingly, laws regulating or prohibiting abortion are not subject to heightened scrutiny. Rather, they are governed by the same standard of review as other health and safety measures.

With this new theory addressed, we turn to *Casey*'s bold assertion that the abortion right is an aspect of the "liberty" protected by the Due Process Clause of the Fourteenth Amendment.

The underlying theory on which this argument rests—that the Fourteenth Amendment's Due Process Clause provides substantive, as well as procedural, protection for "liberty"—has long been controversial. But our decisions have held that the Due Process Clause protects two categories of substantive rights.

The first consists of rights guaranteed by the first eight Amendments. Those Amendments originally applied only to the Federal Government, but this Court has held that the Due Process Clause of the Fourteenth Amendment "incorporates" the great majority of those rights and thus makes them equally applicable to the States. The second category—which is the one in question here—comprises a select list of fundamental rights that are not mentioned anywhere in the Constitution.

In deciding whether a right falls into either of these categories, the Court has long asked whether the right is "deeply rooted in [our] history and tradition" and whether it is essential to our Nation's "scheme of ordered liberty." *Timbs v. Indiana* (2019) (internal quotation marks omitted). And in conducting this inquiry, we have engaged in a careful analysis of the history of the right at issue.

[Historical inquiries] are essential whenever we are asked to recognize a new component of the "liberty" protected by the Due Process Clause because the term "liberty" alone provides little guidance. "Liberty" is a capacious term. As Lincoln once said: "We all declare for Liberty; but in using the same word we do not all mean the same thing." ...

In interpreting what is meant by the Fourteenth Amendment's reference to "liberty," we must guard against the natural human tendency to confuse what that Amendment protects with our own ardent views about the liberty that Americans should enjoy. That is why the Court has long been "reluctant" to recognize rights that are not mentioned in the Constitution. ...

On occasion, when the Court has ignored the "[a]ppropriate limits" imposed by "respect for the teachings of history," *Moore v. City of East Cleveland* (1977) ( (plurality opinion), it has fallen into the freewheeling judicial policymaking that characterized discredited decisions such as *Lochner v. New York* (1905). The Court must not fall prey to such an unprincipled approach. Instead, guided by the history and tradition that map the essential components of our Nation's concept of ordered liberty, we must ask what the *Fourteenth Amendment* means by the term "liberty." When we engage in that inquiry in the present case, the clear answer is that the Fourteenth Amendment does not protect the right to an abortion.

**B**

Until the latter part of the 20th century, there was no support in American law for a constitutional right to obtain an abortion. No state constitutional provision had recognized such a right. Until a few years before *Roe* was handed down, no federal or state court had recognized such a right. Nor had any scholarly treatise of which we are aware. And although law review articles are not reticent about advocating new rights, the earliest article proposing a constitutional right to abortion that has come to our attention was published only a few years before *Roe*.

Not only was there no support for such a constitutional right until shortly before *Roe*, but abortion had long been a *crime* in every single State. At common law, abortion was criminal in at least some stages of pregnancy and was regarded as unlawful and could have very serious consequences at all stages. American law followed the common law until a wave of statutory restrictions in the 1800s expanded criminal liability for abortions. By the time of the adoption of the Fourteenth Amendment, three-quarters of the States had made abortion a crime at any stage of pregnancy, and the remaining States would soon follow.

[By the time *Roe* was decided and] by the *Roe* Court's own count, a substantial majority [of States]—30 []—still prohibited abortion at all stages except to save the life of the mother. ... In short, the "Court's opinion in *Roe* itself convincingly refutes the notion that the abortion liberty is deeply rooted in the history or tradition of our people." *Thornburgh v. American College of Obstetricians and Gynecologists* (1986) (White, J., dissenting).

The inescapable conclusion is that a right to abortion is not deeply rooted in the Nation's history and traditions. On the contrary, an unbroken tradition of prohibiting abortion on pain of criminal punishment persisted from the earliest days of the common law until 1973. The Court in *Roe* could have said of abortion exactly what *Glucksberg* said of assisted suicide: "Attitudes toward [abortion] have changed since Bracton, but our laws have consistently condemned, and continue to prohibit, [that practice]."

[S]upporters of *Roe* and *Casey* contend that the abortion right is an integral part of a broader entrenched right. *Roe* termed this a right to privacy, and *Casey* described it as the freedom to make "intimate and personal choices" that are "central to personal dignity and autonomy." *Casey* elaborated: "At the heart of liberty is the right to define one's own concept of existence, of meaning, of the universe, and of the mystery of human life."

The Court did not claim that this broadly framed right is absolute, and no such claim would be plausible. While individuals are certainly free *to think* and *to say* what they wish about "existence," "meaning," the "universe," and "the mystery of human life," they are not always free *to act* in accordance with those thoughts. License to act on the basis of such beliefs may correspond to one of the many understandings of "liberty," but it is certainly not "ordered liberty."

Ordered liberty sets limits and defines the boundary between competing interests. *Roe* and *Casey* each struck a particular balance between the interests of a woman who wants an abortion and the interests of what they termed "potential life." But the people of the various States may evaluate those interests differently.... Our Nation's historical understanding of ordered liberty does not prevent the people's elected representatives from deciding how abortion should be regulated.

Nor does the right to obtain an abortion have a sound basis in precedent. *Casey* relied on cases involving the right to marry a person of a different race, *Loving v. Virginia* (1967); the right to marry while in prison, *Turner v. Safley* (1987); the right to obtain contraceptives, *Griswold v. Connecticut* (1965), *Eisenstadt v. Baird* (1972), *Carey v. Population Services, Int'l* (1977); the right to reside with relatives,

They gave information, instruction, and medical advice to *married persons* as to the means of preventing conception. . . .

The appellants were found guilty as accessories and fined $100 each, against the claim that the accessory statute as so applied violated the Fourteenth Amendment. . . .

We think that appellants have standing to raise the constitutional rights of the married people with whom they had a professional relationship. . . .

Coming to the merits, we are met with a wide range of questions that implicate the Due Process Clause of the Fourteenth Amendment. Overtones of some arguments suggest that *Lochner v. New York* (1905) should be our guide. But we decline that invitation. . . . We do not sit as a super-legislature to determine the wisdom, need, and propriety of laws that touch economic problems, business affairs, or social conditions. This law, however, operates directly on an intimate relation of husband and wife and their physician's role in one aspect of that relation.

The association of people is not mentioned in the Constitution nor in the Bill of Rights. The right to educate a child in a school of the parents' choice — whether public or private or parochial — is also not mentioned. Nor is the right to study any particular subject or any foreign language. Yet the First Amendment has been construed to include certain of those rights.

By *Pierce v. Society of Sisters* (1925), the right to educate one's children as one chooses is made applicable to the States by the force of the First and Fourteenth Amendments. By *Meyer v. Nebraska* (1923), the same dignity is given the right to study the German language in a private school. In other words, the State may not, consistently with the spirit of the First Amendment, contract the spectrum of available knowledge. The right of freedom of speech and press includes not only the right to utter or to print, but the right to distribute, the right to receive, the right to read and freedom of inquiry, freedom of thought, and freedom to teach — indeed the freedom of the entire university community. Without those peripheral rights the specific rights would be less secure. And so we reaffirm the principle of the *Pierce* and the *Meyer* cases.

In *NAACP v. Alabama* (1958), we protected the "freedom to associate and privacy in one's associations," noting that freedom of association was a peripheral First Amendment right. Disclosure of membership lists of a constitutionally valid association, we held, was invalid "as entailing the likelihood of a substantial restraint upon the exercise by petitioner's members of their right to freedom of association." In other words, the First Amendment has a penumbra where privacy is protected from governmental intrusion. In like context, we have protected forms of "association" that are not political in the customary sense but pertain to the social, legal, and economic benefit of the members. . . .

Those cases involved more than the "right of assembly" — a right that extends to all irrespective of their race or ideology. The right of "association," like the right of belief, is more than the right to attend a

*Moore v. East Cleveland* (1977); the right to make decisions about the education of one's children, *Pierce v. Society of Sisters* (1925), *Meyer v. Nebraska* (1923); the right not to be sterilized without consent, *Skinner v. Oklahoma ex rel. Williamson* (1942); and the right in certain circumstances not to undergo involuntary surgery, forced administration of drugs, or other substantially similar procedures, *Winston v. Lee* (1985), *Washington v. Harper* (1990), *Rochin v. California* (1952). Respondents and the Solicitor General also rely on post-*Casey* decisions like *Lawrence v. Texas* (2003) (right to engage in private, consensual sexual acts), and *Obergefell v. Hodges* (2015) (right to marry a person of the same sex).

These attempts to justify abortion through appeals to a broader right to autonomy and to define one's "concept of existence" prove too much. *Casey*. Those criteria, at a high level of generality, could license fundamental rights to illicit drug use, prostitution, and the like. None of these rights has any claim to being deeply rooted in history.

[margin note: except they do if you look past Puritan bans]

What sharply distinguishes the abortion right from the rights recognized in the cases on which *Roe* and *Casey* rely is something that both those decisions acknowledged: Abortion destroys what those decisions call "potential life" and what the law at issue in this case regards as the life of an "unborn human being." None of the other decisions cited by *Roe* and *Casey* involved the critical moral question posed by abortion. They are therefore inapposite. They do not support the right to obtain an abortion, and by the same token, our conclusion that the Constitution does not confer such a right does not undermine them in any way.

[margin note: They do Please shut up Several of these are "critical moral questions"]

## III

We next consider whether the doctrine of *stare decisis* counsels continued acceptance of *Roe* and *Casey*. *Stare decisis* plays an important role in our case law, and we have explained that it serves many valuable ends. It protects the interests of those who have taken action in reliance on a past decision. It "reduces incentives for challenging settled precedents, saving parties and courts the expense of endless relitigation." *Kimble v. Marvel Entertainment* (2015). It fosters "evenhanded" decisionmaking by requiring that like cases be decided in a like manner. *Payne v. Tennessee* (1991). It "contributes to the actual and perceived integrity of the judicial process." *Id*. And it restrains judicial hubris and reminds us to respect the judgment of those who have grappled with important questions in the past. ...

We have long recognized, however, that *stare decisis* is "not an inexorable command," *Pearson v. Callahan* (2009) (internal quotation marks omitted), and it "is at its weakest when we interpret the Constitution," *Agostini v. Felton* (1997). It has been said that it is sometimes more important that an issue "be settled than that it be settled right." *Kimble* (quoting *Burnet v. Coronado Oil & Gas Co*. (1932) (Brandeis, J., dissenting)). But when it comes to the interpretation of the Constitution—the "great charter of our liberties," which was meant "to endure through a long lapse of ages," *Martin v. Hunter's Lessee* (1816) (opinion for the Court by Story, J.)—we place a high value on having the matter "settled right." In addition, when one of our constitutional decisions goes astray, the country is usually stuck with the bad decision unless we correct our own mistake. An erroneous constitutional decision can be fixed by amending the Constitution, but our Constitution is notoriously hard to amend. ...

No Justice of this Court has ever argued that the Court should *never* overrule a constitutional decision, but overruling a precedent is a serious matter. It is not a step that should be taken lightly. ...

In this case, five factors weigh strongly in favor of overruling *Roe* and *Casey*: the nature of their error, the quality of their reasoning, the "workability" of the rules they imposed on the country, their disruptive effect on other areas of the law, and the absence of concrete reliance.

*The nature of the Court's error.* An erroneous interpretation of the Constitution is always important, but some are more damaging than others.

The infamous decision in *Plessy v. Ferguson*, was one such decision. It betrayed our commitment to "equality before the law." *Id.* (Harlan, J., dissenting). It was "egregiously wrong" on the day it was decided, see *Ramos v. Louisiana* (2020) (opinion of KAVANAUGH, J.), and as the Solicitor General agreed at oral argument, it should have been overruled at the earliest opportunity.

*Roe* was also egregiously wrong and deeply damaging. For reasons already explained, *Roe*'s constitutional analysis was far outside the bounds of any reasonable interpretation of the various constitutional provisions to which it vaguely pointed.

*Roe* was on a collision course with the Constitution from the day it was decided, *Casey* perpetuated its errors, and those errors do not concern some arcane corner of the law of little importance to the American people. Rather, wielding nothing but "raw judicial power," *Roe* (White, J., dissenting), the Court usurped the power to address a question of profound moral and social importance that the Constitution unequivocally leaves for the people. *Casey* described itself as calling both sides of the national controversy to resolve their debate, but in doing so, *Casey* necessarily declared a winning side. Those on the losing side—those who sought to advance the State's interest in fetal life—could no longer seek to persuade their elected representatives to adopt policies consistent with their views. The Court short-circuited the democratic process by closing it to the large number of Americans who dissented in any respect from *Roe*. ...

*The quality of the reasoning.* Under our precedents, the quality of the reasoning in a prior case has an important bearing on whether it should be reconsidered. [We have] explained why *Roe* was incorrectly decided, but that decision was more than just wrong. It stood on exceptionally weak grounds.

*Roe* found that the Constitution implicitly conferred a right to obtain an abortion, but it failed to ground its decision in text, history, or precedent. ...

The weaknesses in *Roe*'s reasoning are well-known. Without any grounding in the constitutional text, history, or precedent, it imposed on the entire country a detailed set of rules much like those that one might expect to find in a statute or regulation. ... This elaborate scheme was the Court's own brainchild. Neither party advocated the trimester framework; nor did either party or any *amicus* argue that "viability" should mark the point at which the scope of the abortion right and a State's regulatory authority should be substantially transformed.

Not only did this scheme resemble the work of a legislature, but the Court made little effort to explain how these rules could be deduced from any of the sources on which constitutional decisions are usually based. ...

*Roe* featured a lengthy survey of history, but much of its discussion was irrelevant, and the Court made no effort to explain why it was included. For example, multiple paragraphs were devoted to an account of the views and practices of ancient civilizations where infanticide was widely accepted. When it came to the most important historical fact—how the States regulated abortion when the Fourteenth Amendment was adopted—the Court said almost nothing. It allowed that States had tightened their abortion laws "in the middle and late 19th century," but it implied that these laws might have been enacted not to protect fetal life but to further "a Victorian social concern" about "illicit sexual conduct."

*Roe*'s failure even to note the overwhelming consensus of state laws in effect in 1868 is striking, and what it said about the common law was simply wrong. ...

After surveying history, the opinion spent many paragraphs conducting the sort of fact-finding that might be undertaken by a legislative committee. ...

Finally, after all this, the Court turned to precedent. Citing a broad array of cases, the Court found support for a constitutional "right of personal privacy," but it conflated two very different meanings of the term: the right to shield information from disclosure and the right to make and implement important personal decisions without governmental interference. Only the cases involving this second sense of the term could have any possible relevance to the abortion issue, and some of the cases in that category involved personal decisions that were obviously very, very far afield. See *Pierce* (right to send children to religious school); *Meyer* (right to have children receive German language instruction).

What remained was a handful of cases having something to do with marriage. But none of these decisions involved what is distinctive about abortion: its effect on what *Roe* termed "potential life."

When the Court summarized the basis for the scheme it imposed on the country, it asserted that its rules were "consistent with" the following: (1) "the relative weights of the respective interests involved," (2) "the lessons and examples of medical and legal history," (3) "the lenity of the common law," and (4) "the demands of the profound problems of the present day." Put aside the second and third factors, which were based on the Court's flawed account of history, and what remains are precisely the sort of considerations that legislative bodies often take into account when they draw lines that accommodate competing interests. The scheme *Roe* produced *looked* like legislation, and the Court provided the sort of explanation that might be expected from a legislative body.

What *Roe* did not provide was any cogent justification for the lines it drew. ... An even more glaring deficiency was *Roe*'s failure to justify the critical distinction it drew between pre- and post-viability abortions. [The arbitrary line the Court drew] has not found much support among philosophers and ethicists who have attempted to justify a right to abortion. Some have argued that a fetus should not be entitled to legal protection until it acquires the characteristics that they regard as defining what it means to be a "person." Among the characteristics that have been offered as essential attributes of "personhood" are sentience, self-awareness, the ability to reason, or some combination thereof. By this logic, it would be an open question whether even born individuals, including young children or those afflicted with certain developmental or medical conditions, merit protection as "persons." But even if one takes the view that "personhood" begins when a certain attribute or combination of attributes is acquired, it is very hard to see why viability should mark the point where "personhood" begins.

The most obvious problem with any such argument is that viability is heavily dependent on factors that have nothing to do with the characteristics of a fetus. One is the state of neonatal care at a particular point in time. Due to the development of new equipment and improved practices, the viability line has changed over the years. In the 19th century, a fetus may not have been viable until the 32d or 33d week of pregnancy or even later. When *Roe* was decided, viability was gauged at roughly 28 weeks. Today, respondents draw the line at 23 or 24 weeks. So, according to *Roe*'s logic, States now have a compelling interest in protecting a fetus with a gestational age of, say, 26 weeks, but in 1973 States did not have an interest in protecting an identical fetus. How can that be?

Viability also depends on the "quality of the available medical facilities." *Colautti v. Franklin* (1979). Thus, a 24-week-old fetus may be viable if a woman gives birth in a city with hospitals that provide advanced care for very premature babies, but if the woman travels to a remote area far from any such hospital, the fetus may no longer be viable. On what ground could the constitutional status of a fetus depend on the pregnant woman's location? And if viability is meant to mark a line having universal moral significance, can it be that a fetus that is viable in a big city in the United States has a privileged moral status not enjoyed by an identical fetus in a remote area of a poor country?

In addition, as the Court once explained, viability is not really a hard-and-fast line. A physician determining a particular fetus's odds of surviving outside the womb must consider "a number of variables," including "gestational age," "fetal weight," a woman's "general health and nutrition," the "quality of the available medical facilities," and other factors. *Id.* It is thus "only with difficulty" that a physician can estimate the "probability" of a particular fetus's survival. *Id.* And even if each fetus's probability of survival could be ascertained with certainty, settling on a "probabilit[y] of survival" that should count as "viability" is another matter. *Id.* Is a fetus viable with a 10 percent chance of survival? 25 percent? 50 percent? Can such a judgment be made by a State? And can a State specify a gestational age limit that applies in all cases? Or must these difficult questions be left entirely to the individual "attending physician on the particular facts of the case before him"? *Id.*

The viability line, which *Casey* termed *Roe*'s central rule, makes no sense, and it is telling that other countries almost uniformly eschew such a line. The Court thus asserted raw judicial power to impose, as a matter of constitutional law, a uniform viability rule that allowed the States less freedom to regulate abortion than the majority of western democracies enjoy.

When *Casey* revisited *Roe* almost 20 years later, very little of *Roe*'s reasoning was defended or preserved. The Court abandoned any reliance on a privacy right and instead grounded the abortion right entirely on the Fourteenth Amendment's Due Process Clause. The Court did not reaffirm *Roe*'s erroneous account of abortion history. In fact, none of the Justices in the majority said anything about the history of the abortion right. And as for precedent, the Court relied on essentially the same body of cases that *Roe* had cited. Thus, with respect to the standard grounds for constitutional decision making—text, history, and precedent—*Casey* did not attempt to bolster *Roe*'s reasoning.

The Court also made no real effort to remedy one of the greatest weaknesses in *Roe*'s analysis: its much-criticized discussion of viability. The Court retained what it called *Roe*'s "central holding"—that a State may not regulate pre-viability abortions for the purpose of protecting fetal life—but it provided no principled defense of the viability line. Instead, it merely rephrased what *Roe* had said, stating that viability marked the point at which "the independent existence of a second life can in reason and fairness be the object of state protection that now overrides the rights of the woman." Why "reason and fairness" demanded that the line be drawn at viability the Court did not explain. And the Justices who authored the controlling opinion conspicuously failed to say that they agreed with the viability rule; instead, they candidly acknowledged "the reservations [some] of us may have in reaffirming [that] holding of *Roe.*"

The controlling opinion criticized and rejected *Roe*'s trimester scheme, and substituted a new "undue burden" test, but the basis for this test was obscure. ... *Casey*, in short, either refused to reaffirm or rejected important aspects of *Roe*'s analysis, failed to remedy glaring deficiencies in *Roe*'s reasoning, endorsed what it termed *Roe*'s central holding while suggesting that a majority might not have thought it was correct, provided no new support for the abortion right other than *Roe*'s status as precedent, and imposed a new and problematic test with no firm grounding in constitutional text, history, or precedent.

*Workability.* Our precedents counsel that another important consideration in deciding whether a precedent should be overruled is whether the rule it imposes is workable—that is, whether it can be understood and applied in a consistent and predictable manner. *Casey*'s "undue burden" test has scored poorly on the workability scale.

Problems begin with the very concept of an "undue burden." ... The *Casey* plurality tried to put meaning into the "undue burden" test by setting out three subsidiary rules, but these rules created their own problems. The first rule is that "a provision of law is invalid, if its purpose or effect is to place a *substantial obstacle* in the path of a woman seeking an abortion before the fetus attains viability." (emphasis added). But whether a particular obstacle qualifies as "substantial" is often open to reasonable debate. ...

This ambiguity is a problem, and the second rule, which applies at all stages of a pregnancy, muddies things further. It states that measures designed "to ensure that the woman's choice is informed" are constitutional so long as they do not impose "an undue burden on the right." To the extent that this rule applies to pre-viability abortions, it overlaps with the first rule and appears to impose a different standard. Consider a law that imposes an insubstantial obstacle but serves little purpose. As applied to a pre-viability abortion, would such a regulation be constitutional on the ground that it does not impose a "*substantial* obstacle"? Or would it be unconstitutional on the ground that it creates an "*undue* burden" because the burden it imposes, though slight, outweighs its negligible benefits? *Casey* does not say, and this ambiguity would lead to confusion down the line.

The third rule complicates the picture even more. Under that rule, "*[u]nnecessary health* regulations that have the purpose or effect of presenting a *substantial obstacle* to a woman seeking an abortion impose an *undue burden* on the right." (emphasis added). This rule contains no fewer than three vague terms. It includes the two already discussed—"undue burden" and "substantial obstacle"—even though they are inconsistent. And it adds a third ambiguous term when it refers to "*unnecessary* health regulations." ... *Casey* did not explain the sense in which the term is used in this rule.

In addition to these problems, one more applies to all three rules. They all call on courts to examine a law's effect on women, but a regulation may have a very different impact on different women for a variety of reasons, including their places of residence, financial resources, family situations, work and personal obligations, knowledge about fetal development and abortion, psychological and emotional disposition and condition, and the firmness of their desire to obtain abortions. In order to determine whether a regulation presents a substantial obstacle to women, a court needs to know which set of women it should have in mind and how many of the women in this set must find that an obstacle is "substantial."

*Casey* provided no clear answer to these questions. It said that a regulation is unconstitutional if it imposes a substantial obstacle "in a large fraction of cases in which [it] is relevant," but there is obviously no clear line between a fraction that is "large" and one that is not. Nor is it clear what the Court meant by "cases in which" a regulation is "relevant."

*Effect on other areas of law.* *Roe* and *Casey* have led to the distortion of many important but unrelated legal doctrines, and that effect provides further support for overruling those decisions. ...

The Court's abortion cases have diluted the strict standard for facial constitutional challenges. They have ignored the Court's third-party standing doctrine. They have disregarded standard *res judicata* principles. They have flouted the ordinary rules on the severability of unconstitutional provisions, as well as the rule that statutes should be read where possible to avoid unconstitutionality. And they have distorted First Amendment doctrines.

*Reliance interests.* We last consider whether overruling *Roe* and *Casey* will upend substantial reliance interests.

Traditional reliance interests arise "where advance planning of great precision is most obviously a necessity." *Casey* (joint opinion). In *Casey*, the controlling opinion conceded that those traditional reliance interests were not implicated because getting an abortion is generally "unplanned activity," and "reproductive planning could take virtually immediate account of any sudden restoration of state authority to ban abortions." For these reasons, we agree with the *Casey* plurality that conventional, concrete reliance interests are not present here.

Unable to find reliance in the conventional sense, the controlling opinion in *Casey* perceived a more intangible form of reliance. It wrote that "people [had] organized intimate relationships and made choices that define their views of themselves and their places in society ... in reliance on the availability of abortion in the event that contraception should fail" and that "[t]he ability of women to participate equally in the economic and social life of the Nation has been facilitated by their ability to control their reproductive lives." But this Court is ill-equipped to assess "generalized assertions about the national psyche." *Id.* (opinion of Rehnquist, C. J.). *Casey*'s notion of reliance thus finds little support in our cases, which instead emphasize very concrete reliance interests, like those that develop in "cases involving property and contract rights." *Payne*.

When a concrete reliance interest is asserted, courts are equipped to evaluate the claim, but assessing the novel and intangible form of reliance endorsed by the *Casey* plurality is another matter. That form of reliance depends on an empirical question that is hard for anyone—and in particular, for a court—to assess, namely, the effect of the abortion right on society and in particular on the lives of women. ...

Our decision returns the issue of abortion to ... legislative bodies, and it allows women on both sides of the abortion issue to seek to affect the legislative process by influencing public opinion, lobbying legislators, voting, and running for office. Women are not without electoral or political power. It is noteworthy that the percentage of women who register to vote and cast ballots is consistently higher than the percentage of men who do so. In the last election in November 2020, women, who make up around 51.5 percent of the population of Mississippi, constituted 55.5 percent of the voters who cast ballots.

Unable to show concrete reliance on *Roe* and *Casey* themselves, the Solicitor General suggests that overruling those decisions would "threaten the Court's precedents holding that the Due Process Clause protects other rights." That is not correct for reasons we have already discussed. As even the *Casey* plurality recognized, "[a]bortion is a unique act" because it terminates "life or potential life." And to ensure that our decision is not misunderstood or mischaracterized, we emphasize that our decision concerns the constitutional right to abortion and no others right. Nothing in this opinion should be understood to cast doubt on precedents that do not concern abortion.

## IV

Having shown that traditional *stare decisis* factors do not weigh in favor of retaining *Roe* or *Casey*, we must address one final argument that featured prominently in the *Casey* plurality opinion.

The argument was cast in different terms, but stated simply, it was essentially as follows. The American people's belief in the rule of law would be shaken if they lost respect for this Court as an institution that decides important cases based on principle, not "social and political pressures." There is a special danger that the public will perceive a decision as having been made for unprincipled reasons when the Court overrules a controversial "watershed" decision, such as *Roe*. A decision overruling *Roe* would be perceived as having been made "under fire" and as a "surrender to political pressure," therefore the preservation of public approval of the Court weighs heavily in favor of retaining *Roe*.

This analysis starts out on the right foot but ultimately veers off course. The *Casey* plurality was certainly right that it is important for the public to perceive that our decisions are based on principle, and we should make every effort to achieve that objective by issuing opinions that carefully show how a proper understanding of the law leads to the results we reach. But we cannot exceed the scope of our authority under the Constitution, and we cannot allow our decisions to be affected by any extraneous influences such as concern about the public's reaction to our work. That is true both when we initially decide a constitutional issue *and* when we consider whether to overrule a prior decision. ...

The *Casey* plurality "call[ed] the contending sides of a national controversy to end their national division," and claimed the authority to impose a permanent settlement of the issue of a constitutional abortion right simply by saying that the matter was closed. That unprecedented claim exceeded the power vested in us by the Constitution. ... Our sole authority is to exercise "judgment"—which is to say, the authority to judge what the law means and how it should apply to the case at hand. The Court has no authority to decree that an erroneous precedent is *permanently* exempt from evaluation under traditional *stare decisis* principles. A precedent of this Court is subject to the usual principles of *stare decisis* under which adherence to precedent is the norm but not an inexorable command. If the rule were otherwise, erroneous decisions like *Plessy* and *Lochner* would still be the law. That is not how *stare decisis* operates.

The *Casey* plurality also misjudged the practical limits of this Court's influence. *Roe* certainly did not succeed in ending division on the issue of abortion. On the contrary, *Roe* "inflamed" a national issue that has remained bitterly divisive for the past half century. *Casey* (opinion of Scalia, J.)....

We do not pretend to know how our political system or society will respond to today's decision overruling *Roe* and *Casey*. And even if we could foresee what will happen, we would have no authority to let that knowledge influence our decision. We can only do our job, which is to interpret the law, apply longstanding principles of *stare decisis*, and decide this case accordingly.

We therefore hold that the Constitution does not confer a right to abortion. *Roe* and *Casey* must be overruled, and the authority to regulate abortion must be returned to the people and their elected representatives.

**VI**

We must now decide what standard will govern if state abortion regulations undergo constitutional challenge and whether the law before us satisfies the appropriate standard.

Under our precedents, rational-basis review is the appropriate standard for such challenges. As we have explained, procuring an abortion is not a fundamental constitutional right because such a right has no basis in the Constitution's text or in our Nation's history.

It follows that the States may regulate abortion for legitimate reasons, and when such regulations are challenged under the Constitution, courts cannot "substitute their social and economic beliefs for the judgment of legislative bodies." *Ferguson*. ...

A law regulating abortion, like other health and welfare laws ... must be sustained if there is a rational basis on which the legislature could have thought that it would serve legitimate state interests. *Williamson v. Lee Optical of Okla., Inc.* (1955). These legitimate interests include respect for and preservation of prenatal life at all stages of development; the protection of maternal health and safety; the elimination of particularly gruesome or barbaric medical procedures; the preservation of the integrity of the medical profession; the mitigation of fetal pain; and the prevention of discrimination on the basis of race, sex, or disability.

These legitimate interests justify Mississippi's Gestational Age Act. Except "in a medical emergency or in the case of a severe fetal abnormality," the statute prohibits abortion "if the probable gestational age of the unborn human being has been determined to be greater than fifteen (15) weeks." [I]t follows that respondents' constitutional challenge must fail.

## VII

The judgment of the Fifth Circuit is reversed, and the case is remanded for further proceedings consistent with this opinion.

It is so ordered.

Justice THOMAS, concurring.

The Court today declines to disturb substantive due process jurisprudence generally or the doctrine's application in other, specific contexts. Cases like *Griswold v. Connecticut* (1965) (right of married persons to obtain contraceptives); *Lawrence v. Texas* (2003) (right to engage in private, consensual sexual acts); and *Obergefell v. Hodges* (2015) (right to same-sex marriage), are not at issue. The Court's abortion cases are unique, and no party has asked us to decide "whether our entire Fourteenth Amendment jurisprudence must be preserved or revised," *McDonald* (opinion of THOMAS, J.). Thus, I agree that "[n]othing in [the Court's] opinion should be understood to cast doubt on precedents that do not concern abortion."

For that reason, in future cases, we should reconsider all of this Court's substantive due process precedents, including *Griswold*, *Lawrence*, and *Obergefell*. Because any substantive due process decision is "demonstrably erroneous," *Ramos v. Louisiana* (2020) (THOMAS, J., concurring in judgment), we have a duty to "correct the error" established in those precedents, *Gamble v. United States* (2019). After overruling these demonstrably erroneous decisions, the question would remain whether other constitutional provisions guarantee the myriad rights that our substantive due process cases have generated. For example, we could consider whether any of the rights announced in this Court's substantive due process cases are "privileges or immunities of citizens of the United States" protected by the Fourteenth Amendment. Amdt. 14, § 1. To answer that question, we would need to decide important antecedent questions, including whether the Privileges or Immunities Clause protects *any* rights that are not enumerated in the Constitution and, if so, how to identify those rights. That said, even if the Clause does protect unenumerated rights, the Court conclusively demonstrates that abortion is not one of them under any plausible interpretive approach.

Justice KAVANAUGH, concurring.

The Constitution does not grant the nine unelected Members of this Court the unilateral authority to rewrite the Constitution to create new rights and liberties based on our own moral or policy views. ... This Court therefore does not possess the authority either to declare a constitutional right to abortion *or* to declare a constitutional prohibition of abortion.

[T]he Constitution is neutral on the issue of abortion and allows the people and their elected representatives to address the issue through the democratic process. In my respectful view, the Court in *Roe* therefore erred by taking sides on the issue of abortion.

After today's decision, the nine Members of this Court will no longer decide the basic legality of pre-viability abortion for all 330 million Americans. That issue will be resolved by the people and their representatives in the democratic process in the States or Congress. But the parties' arguments have raised other related questions, and I address some of them here.

*First* is the question of how this decision will affect other precedents involving issues such as contraception and marriage. I emphasize what the Court today states: Overruling *Roe* does *not* mean the overruling of those precedents, and does *not* threaten or cast doubt on those precedents.

*Second*, as I see it, some of the other abortion-related legal questions raised by today's decision are not especially difficult as a constitutional matter. For example, may a State bar a resident of that State from traveling to another State to obtain an abortion? In my view, the answer is no based on the constitutional right to interstate travel. May a State retroactively impose liability or punishment for an abortion that occurred before today's decision takes effect? In my view, the answer is no based on the Due Process Clause or the *Ex Post Facto* Clause.

Other abortion-related legal questions may emerge in the future. But this Court will no longer decide the fundamental question of whether abortion must be allowed throughout the United States through 6 weeks, or 12 weeks, or 15 weeks, or 24 weeks, or some other line. The Court will no longer decide how to evaluate the interests of the pregnant woman and the interests in protecting fetal life throughout pregnancy. Instead, those difficult moral and policy questions will be decided, as the Constitution dictates, by the people and their elected representatives through the constitutional processes of democratic self-government.

The Court's decision today properly returns the Court to a position of judicial neutrality on the issue of abortion, and properly restores the people's authority to resolve the issue of abortion through the processes of democratic self-government established by the Constitution.

In my judgment, on the issue of abortion, the Constitution is neither pro-life nor pro-choice. The Constitution is neutral, and this Court likewise must be scrupulously neutral. The Court today properly heeds the constitutional principle of judicial neutrality and returns the issue of abortion to the people and their elected representatives in the democratic process.

Chief Justice ROBERTS, concurring in the judgment.

We granted certiorari to decide one question: "Whether all pre-viability prohibitions on elective abortions are unconstitutional." That question is directly implicated here: Mississippi's Gestational Age Act (2018) generally prohibits abortion after the fifteenth week of pregnancy—several weeks before a fetus is regarded as "viable" outside the womb. In urging our review, Mississippi stated that its case was "an ideal vehicle" to "reconsider the bright-line viability rule," and that a judgment in its favor would "not require the Court to overturn" [*Roe* and *Casey*.]

Today, the Court nonetheless rules for Mississippi by doing just that. I would take a more measured course. I agree with the Court that the viability line established by *Roe* and *Casey* should be discarded under a straightforward *stare decisis* analysis. That line never made any sense. Our abortion precedents describe the right at issue as a woman's right to choose to terminate her pregnancy. That right should therefore extend far enough to ensure a reasonable opportunity to choose, but need not extend any further—certainly not all the way to viability. Mississippi's law allows a woman three months to obtain an abortion, well beyond the point at which it is considered "late" to discover a pregnancy. See A. Ayoola, Late Recognition of Unintended Pregnancies, 32 Pub. Health Nursing 462 (2015) (pregnancy is discoverable and ordinarily discovered by six weeks of gestation). I see no sound basis for questioning the adequacy of that opportunity.

But that is all I would say, out of adherence to a simple yet fundamental principle of judicial restraint: If it is not necessary to decide more to dispose of a case, then it is necessary *not* to decide more. Perhaps we are not always perfect in following that command, and certainly there are cases that warrant an exception. But this is not one of them. Surely we should adhere closely to principles of judicial restraint here, where the broader path the Court chooses entails repudiating a constitutional right we have not only previously recognized, but also expressly reaffirmed applying the doctrine of *stare decisis*. The Court's opinion is thoughtful and thorough, but those virtues cannot compensate for the fact that its dramatic and consequential ruling is unnecessary to decide the case before us.

[Overruling the viability rule] is sufficient to resolve this case in Mississippi's favor. The law at issue allows abortions up through fifteen weeks, providing an adequate opportunity to exercise the right *Roe* protects. By the time a pregnant woman has reached that point, her pregnancy is well into the second trimester. Pregnancy tests are now inexpensive and accurate, and a woman ordinarily discovers she is pregnant by six weeks of gestation. Almost all know by the end of the first trimester. Safe and effective abortifacients, moreover, are now readily available, particularly during those early stages. Given all this, it is no surprise that the vast majority of abortions happen in the first trimester. Presumably most of the remainder would also take place earlier if later abortions were not a legal option. Ample evidence thus suggests that a 15-week ban provides sufficient time, absent rare circumstances, for a woman "to decide for herself" whether to terminate her pregnancy. *Webster v. Reproductive Health Services* (1989) (plurality opinion).

Both the Court's opinion and the dissent display a relentless freedom from doubt on the legal issue that I cannot share. I am not sure, for example, that a ban on terminating a pregnancy from the moment of conception must be treated the same under the Constitution as a ban after fifteen weeks. ... I would decide the question we granted review to answer—whether the previously recognized abortion right bars all abortion restrictions prior to viability, such that a ban on abortions after fifteen weeks of pregnancy is necessarily unlawful. The answer to that question is no, and there is no need to go further to decide this case.

I therefore concur only in the judgment.

Justice BREYER, Justice SOTOMAYOR, and Justice KAGAN, dissenting.

For half a century, *Roe v. Wade* (1973) and *Planned Parenthood v Casey* (1992) have protected the liberty and equality of women. *Roe* held, and *Casey* reaffirmed, that the Constitution safeguards a woman's right to decide for herself whether to bear a child. *Roe* held, and *Casey* reaffirmed, that in the first stages of pregnancy, the government could not make that choice for women. ... Respecting a woman as an autonomous being, and granting her full equality, meant giving her substantial choice over this most personal and most consequential of all life decisions.

*Roe* and *Casey* well understood the difficulty and divisiveness of the abortion issue. The Court knew that Americans hold profoundly different views about the "moral[ity]" of "terminating a pregnancy, even in its earliest stage." *Casey*. And the Court recognized that "the State has legitimate interests from the outset of the pregnancy in protecting" the "life of the fetus that may become a child." *Id*. So the Court struck a balance, as it often does when values and goals compete. It held that the State could prohibit abortions after fetal viability, so long as the ban contained exceptions to safeguard a woman's life or health. It held that even before viability, the State could regulate the abortion procedure in multiple and meaningful ways. But until the viability line was crossed, the Court held, a State could not impose a "substantial obstacle" on a woman's "right to elect the procedure" as she (not the government) thought proper, in light of all the circumstances and complexities of her own life. *Id*.

Today, the Court discards that balance. It says that from the very moment of fertilization, a woman has no rights to speak of. A State can force her to bring a pregnancy to term, even at the steepest personal and familial costs. An abortion restriction, the majority holds, is permissible whenever rational, the lowest level of scrutiny known to the law. And because, as the Court has often stated, protecting fetal life is rational, States will feel free to enact all manner of restrictions. The Mississippi law at issue here bars abortions after the 15th week of pregnancy. Under the majority's ruling, though, another State's law could do so after ten weeks, or five or three or one—or, again, from the moment of fertilization. States have already passed such laws, in anticipation of today's ruling. More will follow. Some States have enacted laws extending to all forms of abortion procedure, including taking medication in one's own home. They have passed laws without any exceptions for when the woman is the victim of rape or incest. Under those laws, a woman will have to bear her rapist's child or a young girl her father's—no matter if doing so will destroy her life. So too, after today's ruling, some States may compel women to carry to term a fetus with severe physical anomalies—for example, one afflicted with Tay-Sachs disease, sure to die within a few years of birth. States may even argue that a prohibition on abortion need make no provision for protecting a woman from risk of death or physical harm. Across a vast array of circumstances, a

State will be able to impose its moral choice on a woman and coerce her to give birth to a child.

Enforcement of all these draconian restrictions will also be left largely to the States' devices. A State can of course impose criminal penalties on abortion providers, including lengthy prison sentences. But some States will not stop there. Perhaps, in the wake of today's decision, a state law will criminalize the woman's conduct too, incarcerating or fining her for daring to seek or obtain an abortion. And as Texas has recently shown, a State can turn neighbor against neighbor, enlisting fellow citizens in the effort to root out anyone who tries to get an abortion, or to assist another in doing so.

The majority tries to hide the geographically expansive effects of its holding. Today's decision, the majority says, permits "each State" to address abortion as it pleases. That is cold comfort, of course, for the poor woman who cannot get the money to fly to a distant State for a procedure. Above all others, women lacking financial resources will suffer from today's decision. In any event, interstate restrictions will also soon be in the offing. After this decision, some States may block women from traveling out of State to obtain abortions, or even from receiving abortion medications from out of State. Some may criminalize efforts, including the provision of information or funding, to help women gain access to other States' abortion services. Most threatening of all, no language in today's decision stops the Federal Government from prohibiting abortions nationwide, once again from the moment of conception and without exceptions for rape or incest. If that happens, "the views of [an individual State's] citizens" will not matter. The challenge for a woman will be to finance a trip not to "New York [or] California" but to Toronto. (KAVANAUGH, J., concurring).

Whatever the exact scope of the coming laws, one result of today's decision is certain: the curtailment of women's rights, and of their status as free and equal citizens. Yesterday, the Constitution guaranteed that a woman confronted with an unplanned pregnancy could (within reasonable limits) make her own decision about whether to bear a child, with all the life-transforming consequences that act involves. And in thus safeguarding each woman's reproductive freedom, the Constitution also protected "[t]he ability of women to participate equally in [this Nation's] economic and social life." *Casey*. But no longer. As of today, this Court holds, a State can always force a woman to give birth, prohibiting even the earliest abortions. A State can thus transform what, when freely undertaken, is a wonder into what, when forced, may be a nightmare. Some women, especially women of means, will find ways around the State's assertion of power. Others—those without money or childcare or the ability to take time off from work—will not be so fortunate. Maybe they will try an unsafe method of abortion, and come to physical harm, or even die. Maybe they will undergo pregnancy and have a child, but at significant personal or familial cost. At the least, they will incur the cost of losing control of their lives. The Constitution will, today's majority holds, provide no shield, despite its guarantees of liberty and equality for all.

And no one should be confident that this majority is done with its work. The right *Roe* and *Casey* recognized does not stand alone. To the contrary, the Court has linked it for decades to other settled freedoms involving bodily integrity, familial relationships, and procreation. Most obviously, the right to terminate a pregnancy arose straight out of the right to purchase and use contraception. See *Griswold v. Connecticut* (1965); *Eisenstadt v. Baird* (1972). In turn, those rights led, more recently, to rights of same-sex intimacy and marriage. See *Lawrence v. Texas* (2003); *Obergefell v. Hodges* (2015). They are all part of the same constitutional fabric, protecting autonomous decisionmaking over the most personal of life decisions. The majority (or to be more accurate, most of it) is eager to tell us today that nothing it does "cast[s] doubt on precedents that do not concern abortion." (THOMAS, J., concurring) (advocating the overruling of *Griswold*, *Lawrence*, and *Obergefell*). But how could that be? The lone rationale for what the majority does today is that the right to elect an abortion is not "deeply rooted in history": Not until *Roe*, the majority argues, did people think abortion fell within the Constitution's guarantee of liberty. The same could be said, though, of most of the rights the majority claims it is not tampering with. The majority could write just as long an opinion showing, for example, that until the mid-20th century, "there was no support in American law for a constitutional right to obtain [contraceptives]." So one of two things must be true. Either the majority does not really believe in its own reasoning. Or if it does, all rights that have no history stretching back to the mid-19th century are insecure. Either the mass of the majority's opinion is hypocrisy, or additional constitutional rights are under threat. It is one or the other.

One piece of evidence on that score seems especially salient: The majority's cavalier approach to overturning this Court's precedents. *Stare decisis* is the Latin phrase for a foundation stone of the rule of law: that things decided should stay decided unless there is a very good reason for change. It is a doctrine of judicial modesty and humility. Those qualities are not evident in today's opinion. The majority has no good reason for the upheaval in law and society it sets off. *Roe* and *Casey* have been the law of the land for decades, shaping women's expectations of their choices when an unplanned pregnancy occurs. Women have relied on the availability of abortion both in structuring their relationships and in planning their lives. The legal framework *Roe* and *Casey* developed to balance the competing interests in this sphere has proved workable in courts across the country. No recent developments, in either law or fact, have eroded or cast doubt on those precedents. Nothing, in short, has changed. Indeed, the Court in *Casey* already found all of that to be true. *Casey* is a precedent about precedent. It reviewed the same arguments made here in support of overruling *Roe*, and it found that doing so was not warranted. The Court reverses course today for one reason and one reason only: because the composition of this Court has changed. *Stare decisis*, this Court has often said, "contributes to the actual and perceived integrity of the judicial process" by ensuring that decisions are "founded in the law rather than in the proclivities of individuals." *Payne v. Tennessee* (1991). Today, the proclivities of individuals rule. The Court departs from its obligation to faithfully and impartially apply the law. …

Quoting Justice Stewart, *Casey* explained that to [overrule *Roe*]—to reverse prior law "upon a ground no firmer than a change in [the Court's] membership"—would invite the view that "this institution is little different from the two political branches of the Government." No view, *Casey* thought, could do "more lasting injury to this Court and to the system of law which it is our abiding mission to serve." For overruling *Roe*, *Casey* concluded, the Court would pay a "terrible price."

The Justices who wrote those words—O'Connor, Kennedy, and Souter—they were judges of wisdom. They would not have won any contests for the kind of ideological purity some court watchers want Justices to deliver. But if there were awards for Justices who left this Court better than they found it? And who for that reason left this country better? And the rule of law stronger? Sign those Justices up.

They knew that "the legitimacy of the Court [is] earned over time." They also would have recognized that it can be destroyed much more quickly. They worked hard to avert that outcome in *Casey*. The American public, they thought, should never conclude that its constitutional protections hung by a thread—that a new majority, adhering to a new "doctrinal school," could "by dint of numbers" alone expunge their rights. It is hard—no, it is impossible—to conclude that anything else has happened here. One of us once said that "[i]t is not often in the law that so few have so quickly changed so much." S. Breyer, Breaking the Promise of *Brown*: The Resegregation of America's Schools 30 (2022). For all of us, in our time on this Court, that has never been more true than today. In overruling *Roe* and *Casey*, this Court betrays its guiding principles.

With sorrow—for this Court, but more, for the many millions of American women who have today lost a fundamental constitutional protection—we dissent.

## NOTES AND QUESTIONS

1. It is not often the Court revisits and overturns a precedent. *Lawrence v. Texas*, 539 U.S. 558 (2003) revisited and overturned *Bowers v. Hardwick*, 478 U.S. 186 (1986). *Brown v. Board of Education*, 347 U.S. 483 (1954) revisited and overturned *Plessy v. Ferguson*, 163 U.S. 537 (both of which are discussed in the next chapter, covering the Equal Protection Clause). Can *Dobbs* be distinguished from these earlier examples?

2. Aside from eliminating a woman's right to choose as a fundamental interest under substantive due process, the majority maintains that the only legitimate fundamental interests are those that can be supported through the nation's legal history and traditions. The *Dobbs* majority's view of history has been the subject of criticism. *See, e.g.*, Joint Organization of American Historians and the American

Historical Association Statement on the *Dobbs v. Jackson* Decision (July 2022) (noting that the "opinion inadequately represents the history of the common law, the significance of quickening in state law and practice in the United States, and the nineteenth-century forces that turned early abortion into a crime").

3. Apart from questions about the ability of judges and lawyers to "do" history, what does the *Dobbs* decision mean for other fundamental interests, like the right of same-sex couples to marry, that the Court has concluded were implicit in the concept of ordered liberty, but without historical support?

4. On what basis did Chief Justice Roberts write separately? What does his solo concurrence indicate about the majority's willingness to revisit settled law?

5. The majority's desire to overturn *Roe* seemed to turn in part on the inability of the Court to resolve a hotly contested social issue. Isn't that true of almost any individual rights issue that makes its way into the courts? Is Justice Alito correct in his assertion that the issue of choice may be uniquely different?

6. How likely is it that, going forward, the Supreme Court will be able to avoid cases involving legal issues related to state regulation of a woman's right to choose?

### 7. Economic Substantive Due Process, Revisited

Notwithstanding the end to unmoored substantive due process that the Court signaled with *West Coast Hotel v. Parrish*, the spirit of *Lochner* survives. As you may have noticed, that spirit lives on, first, as a rhetorical tool most often deployed by justices dissenting to substantive due process decisions they suspect lack precisely the kind of constitutional grounding in text and history that doomed *Lochner*. And, second, that spirit lives on in substantive due process cases at both the state and federal levels.

At the state level, consider, for example, *Department of Insurance v. Dade County Consumer Advocate's Office*, 492 So. 2d 1031 (Fla. 1986), in which the Florida Supreme Court held unconstitutional a statute prohibiting insurance agents from accepting commissions than those set by the state. The court found "no identifiable relationship between" the regulation and "a legitimate state purpose in safeguarding the public health, safety or general welfare. Insurance agents' commissions do not affect the net insurance premium and are unrelated to the actuarial soundness of insurance policies." *Id.*

Remember that, when a state high court resolves an issue by relying upon its state constitution, it effectively insulates its decision from further review by the U.S. Supreme Court, for each state high court is final in its authority to determine the meaning of the state constitution. Further, just because the U.S. Supreme Court has decided an issue in a particular way doesn't mean a state court must follow suit. The state court is free to reject the federal reasoning, even when the issue involves the interpretation of a parallel constitutional provision — here, the Due Process Clause.

Why might a state high court be in a different position vis-à-vis economic substantive due process than the U.S. Supreme Court? Would the embrace of economic substantive due process be less problematic for a state court? Is this decision immune from the criticism that the majority has simply substituted its judgment for the legislature's? Or is the decision democracy-enhancing, to the extent the court is forcing the state legislature — in a way that the U.S. Supreme Court could not force the Congress — to regulate in the face of actual, as opposed to perceived, threats to public health, safety, or the general welfare?

What follows is an example in federal constitutional law in which the kind of doctrinal analysis embraced by *Lochner* continues to hold sway. The case involves the commercial speech doctrine and it returns us to the realm of the First Amendment's protection of free expression.

### Sorrell v. IMS Health, Inc.
### 564 U.S. __ (2011)

Justice Kennedy delivered the opinion of the Court.

Vermont law restricts the sale, disclosure, and use of pharmacy records that reveal the prescribing practices of individual doctors. . . . Vermont argues that its prohibitions safeguard medical privacy and diminish the likelihood that marketing will lead to prescription decisions not in the best interests of patients or the State. It can be assumed that these interests are significant. Speech in aid of pharmaceutical marketing, however, is a form of expression protected by the Free Speech Clause of the First Amendment. As a consequence, Vermont's statute must be subjected to heightened judicial scrutiny. The law cannot satisfy that standard.

#### I

Pharmaceutical manufacturers promote their drugs to doctors through a process called "detailing." This often involves a scheduled visit to a doctor's office to persuade the doctor to prescribe a particular pharmaceutical. Detailers bring drug samples as well as medical studies that explain the "details" and potential advantages of various prescription drugs. Interested physicians listen, ask questions, and receive followup data. Salespersons can be more effective when they know the background and purchasing preferences of their clientele, and pharmaceutical salespersons are no exception. Knowledge of a physician's prescription practices — called "prescriber-identifying information" — enables a detailer better to ascertain which doctors are likely to be interested in a particular drug and how best to present a particular sales message. Detailing is an expensive undertaking, so pharmaceutical companies most often use it to promote high-profit brand-name drugs protected by patent. Once a brand-name drug's patent expires, less expensive bioequivalent generic alternatives are manufactured and sold.

Pharmacies, as a matter of business routine and federal law, receive prescriber-identifying information when processing prescriptions. Many pharmacies sell this information to "data miners," firms that analyze prescriber-identifying information and produce reports on prescriber behavior. Data miners lease these reports to pharmaceutical manufacturers subject to nondisclosure agreements. Detailers, who represent the manufacturers, then use the reports to refine their marketing tactics and increase sales.

In 2007, Vermont enacted the Prescription Confidentiality Law. The measure is also referred to as Act 80. . . . The central provision of the present case is § 4631(d).

> A health insurer, a self-insured employer, an electronic transmission intermediary, a pharmacy, or other similar entity shall not sell, license, or exchange for value regulated records containing prescriber-identifiable information, nor permit the use of regulated records containing prescriber-identifiable information for marketing or promoting a prescription drug, unless the prescriber consents. . . . Pharmaceutical manufacturers and pharmaceutical marketers shall not use prescriber-identifiable information for marketing or promoting a prescription drug unless the prescriber consents. . . .

The quoted provision has three component parts. The provision begins by prohibiting pharmacies, health insurers, and similar entities from selling prescriber-identifying information, absent the prescriber's consent. The parties here dispute whether this clause applies to all sales or only to sales for marketing. The provision then goes on to prohibit pharmacies, health insurers, and similar entities from allowing prescriber-identifying information to be used for marketing, unless the prescriber consents. This prohibition in effect bars pharmacies from disclosing the information for marketing purposes. Finally, the provision's second sentence bars pharmaceutical manufacturers and pharmaceutical marketers from using prescriber-identifying information for marketing, again absent the prescriber's consent. The Vermont attorney general may pursue civil remedies against violators.

Separate statutory provisions elaborate the scope of the prohibitions set out in § 4631(d). "Marketing" is defined to include "advertising, promotion, or any activity" that is "used to influence sales or the market share of a prescription drug." Section 4631(c)(1) further provides that Vermont's Department of Health must allow "a prescriber to give consent for his or her identifying information to be used for the purposes" identified in § 4631(d). Finally, the Act's prohibitions on sale, disclosure, and use are subject to a list of exceptions. For example, prescriber-identifying information may be disseminated or used for "health care research"; to enforce "compliance" with health insurance formularies, or preferred drug lists; for "care management educational communications provided to" patients on such matters as "treatment options"; for law enforcement operations; and for purposes "otherwise provided by law."

. . . Contending that § 4631(d) violates their First Amendment rights as incorporated by the Fourteenth Amendment, the respondents [three Vermont data miners and an association of pharmaceutical manufacturers that produce brand-name drugs] sought declaratory and injunctive relief against the petitioners, the Attorney General and other officials of the State of Vermont.

After a bench trial, the United States District Court for the District of Vermont denied relief. . . . The United States Court of Appeals for the Second Circuit reversed and remanded. It held that § 4631(d) violates the First Amendment by burdening the speech of pharmaceutical marketers and data miners without an adequate justification. . . .

## II

On its face, Vermont's law enacts content-and speaker-based restrictions on the sale, disclosure, and use of prescriber-identifying information. The provision first forbids sale subject to exceptions based in large part on the content of a purchaser's speech. For example, those who wish to engage in certain "educational communications," may purchase the information. The measure then bars any disclosure when recipient speakers will use the information for marketing. Finally, the provision's second sentence prohibits pharmaceutical manufacturers from using the information for marketing. The statute thus disfavors marketing, that is, speech with a particular content. More than that, the statute disfavors specific speakers, namely pharmaceutical manufacturers. As a result of these content- and speaker-based rules, detailers cannot obtain prescriber-identifying information, even though the information may be purchased or acquired by other speakers with diverse purposes and viewpoints. Detailers are likewise barred from using the information for marketing, even though the information may be used by a wide range of other speakers. For example, it appears that Vermont could supply academic organizations with prescriber-identifying information to use in countering the messages of brand-name pharmaceutical manufacturers and in promoting the prescription of generic drugs. But § 4631(d) leaves detailers no means of purchasing, acquiring, or using prescriber-identifying information. The law on its face burdens disfavored speech by disfavored speakers.

Any doubt that § 4631(d) imposes an aimed, content-based burden on detailers is dispelled by the record and by formal legislative findings. As the District Court noted, "[p]harmaceutical manufacturers are essentially the only paying customers of the data vendor industry"; and the almost invariable rule is that detailing by pharmaceutical manufacturers is in support of brand-name drugs. Vermont's law thus has the effect of preventing detailers — and only detailers — from communicating with physicians in an effective and informative manner. Formal legislative findings accompanying § 4631(d) confirm that the law's express purpose and practical effect are to diminish the effectiveness of marketing by manufacturers of brand-name drugs. Just as the "inevitable effect of a statute on its face may render it unconstitutional," a statute's stated purposes may also be considered. *United States v. O'Brien* (1968). Here, the Vermont Legislature explained that detailers, in particular those who promote brand-name drugs, convey messages that "are often in conflict with the goals of the state." The legislature designed § 4631(d) to target those speakers and their messages for disfavored treatment. "In its practical operation," Vermont's law "goes even beyond mere content discrimination, to actual viewpoint discrimination." *R.A.V. v. St. Paul* (1992). Given the legislature's expressed statement of purpose, it is apparent that § 4631(d) imposes burdens that are based on the content of speech and that are aimed at a particular viewpoint.

Act 80 is designed to impose a specific, content-based burden on protected expression. It follows that heightened judicial scrutiny is warranted. . . . Lawmakers may no more silence unwanted speech by burdening its utterance than by censoring its content. . . . A government bent on frustrating an impending demonstration might pass a law demanding two years' notice before the issuance of parade permits. Even if the hypothetical measure on its face appeared neutral as to content and speaker, its purpose to suppress speech and its unjustified burdens on expression would render it unconstitutional. Commercial speech is no exception.

. . . § 4631(d) imposes more than an incidental burden on protected expression. Both on its face and in its practical operation, Vermont's law imposes a burden based on the content of speech and the identity of the speaker. While the burdened speech results from an economic motive, so too does a great deal of vital expression. Vermont's law does not simply have an effect on speech, but is directed at certain content and is aimed at particular speakers. The Constitution "does not enact Mr. Herbert Spencer's Social Statics." *Lochner v. New York* (1905) (Holmes, J., dissenting). It does enact the First Amendment.

[The State] contends that heightened judicial scrutiny is unwarranted in this case because sales, transfer, and use of prescriber-identifying information are conduct, not speech. Consistent with that submission, the United States Court of Appeals for the First Circuit has characterized prescriber-identifying information as a mere "commodity" with no greater entitlement to First Amendment protection than "beef jerky." In contrast the courts below concluded that a prohibition on the sale of prescriber-identifying information is a content-based rule akin to a ban on the sale of cookbooks, laboratory results, or train schedules.

This Court has held that the creation and dissemination of information are speech within the meaning of the First Amendment. Facts, after all, are the beginning point for much of the speech that is most essential to advance human knowledge and to conduct human affairs. There is thus a strong argument that prescriber-identifying information is speech for First Amendment purposes.

The State asks for an exception to the rule that information is speech, but there is no need to consider that request in this case. The State has imposed content- and speaker-based restrictions on the availability and use of prescriber-identifying information. So long as they do not engage in marketing, many speakers can obtain and use the information. But detailers cannot. Vermont's statute could be compared with a law prohibiting trade magazines from purchasing or using ink. Like that hypothetical law, § 4631(d) imposes a speaker- and content-based burden on protected expression, and that circumstance is sufficient to justify application of heightened scrutiny. As a consequence, this case can be resolved even assuming, as the State argues, that prescriber-identifying information is a mere commodity.

[I]t is the State's burden to justify its content-based law as consistent with the First Amendment. To sustain the targeted, content-based burden § 4631(d) imposes on protected expression, [the commercial speech doctrine requires that] the State must show at least that the statute directly advances a substantial governmental interest and that the measure is drawn to achieve that interest. . . .

The State's asserted justifications for § 4631(d) come under two general headings. First, the State contends that its law is necessary to protect medical privacy, including physician confidentiality, avoidance of harassment, and the integrity of the doctor-patient relationship. Second, the State argues that § 4631(d) is integral to the achievement of policy objectives — namely, improved public health and reduced healthcare costs. Neither justification withstands scrutiny.

**1**

Vermont argues that its physicians have a "reasonable expectation" that their prescriber-identifying information "will not be used for purposes other than . . . filling and processing" prescriptions. It may be assumed that, for many reasons, physicians have an interest in keeping their prescription decisions confidential. But § 4631(d) is not drawn to serve that interest. Under Vermont's law, pharmacies may share prescriber-identifying information with anyone for any reason save one: They must not allow the information to be used for marketing. Exceptions further allow pharmacies to sell prescriber-identifying information for certain purposes, including "health care research." And the measure permits insurers, researchers, journalists, the State itself, and others to use the information. All but conceding that § 4631(d) does not in itself advance confidentiality interests, the State suggests that other laws might impose separate bars on the disclosure of prescriber-identifying information. But the potential effectiveness of other measures cannot justify the distinctive set of prohibitions and sanctions imposed by § 4631(d).

[Here,] Vermont made prescriber-identifying information available to an almost limitless audience. The explicit structure of the statute allows the information to be studied and used by all but a narrow class of disfavored speakers. Given the information's widespread availability and many permissible uses, the State's asserted interest in physician confidentiality does not justify the burden that § 4631(d) places on protected expression.

The State points out that it allows doctors to forgo the advantages of § 4631(d) by consenting to the sale, disclosure, and use of their prescriber-identifying information. It is true that private decisionmaking can avoid governmental partiality and thus insulate privacy measures from First Amendment challenge. But that principle is inapposite here. Vermont has given its doctors a contrived choice: Either consent, which will allow your prescriber-identifying information to be disseminated and used without constraint; or, withhold consent, which will allow your information to be used by those speakers whose message the State supports. Section 4631(d) may offer a limited degree of privacy, but only on terms favorable to the speech the State prefers. This is not to say that all privacy measures must avoid content-based rules. Here, however, the State has conditioned privacy on acceptance of a content-based rule that is not drawn to serve the State's asserted interest. To obtain the limited privacy allowed by § 4631(d), Vermont physicians are forced to acquiesce in the State's goal of burdening disfavored speech by disfavored speakers.

Respondents suggest that a further defect of § 4631(d) lies in its presumption of applicability absent a physician's election to the contrary. Vermont's law might burden less speech if it came into operation only after an individual choice, but a revision to that effect would not necessarily save § 4631(d). Even reliance on a prior election would not suffice, for instance, if available categories of coverage by design favored speakers of one political persuasion over another. Rules that burden protected expression may not be sustained when the options provided by the State are too narrow to advance legitimate interests or too broad to protect speech. As already explained, § 4631(d) permits extensive use of prescriber-identifying information and so does not advance the State's asserted interest in physician confidentiality. The limited range of available privacy options instead reflects the State's impermissible purpose to burden disfavored speech. Vermont's argument accordingly fails, even if the availability and scope of private election might be relevant in other contexts, as when the statute's design is unrelated to any purpose to advance a preferred message.

The State also contends that § 4631(d) protects doctors from "harassing sales behaviors." "Some doctors in Vermont are experiencing an undesired increase in the aggressiveness of pharmaceutical sales representatives," the Vermont Legislature found, "and a few have reported that they felt coerced and harassed." It is doubtful that concern for "a few" physicians who may have "felt coerced and harassed" by pharmaceutical marketers can sustain a broad content-based rule like § 4631(d). [And] the State offers no explanation why remedies other than content-based rules would be inadequate. Physicians can, and often do, simply decline to meet with detailers, including detailers who use prescriber-identifying information. Doctors who wish to forgo detailing altogether are free to give "No Solicitation" or "No Detailing" instructions to their office managers or to receptionists at their places of work. . . .

Vermont argues that detailers' use of prescriber-identifying information undermines the doctor-patient relationship by allowing detailers to influence treatment decisions. According to the State, "unwanted pressure occurs" when doctors learn that their prescription decisions are being "monitored" by detailers. Some physicians accuse detailers of "spying" or of engaging in "underhanded" conduct in order to "subvert" prescription decisions. And Vermont claims that detailing makes people "anxious" about whether doctors have their patients' best interests at heart. But the State does not explain why detailers' use of prescriber-identifying information is more likely to prompt these objections than many other uses permitted by § 4631(d). In any event, this asserted interest is contrary to basic First Amendment principles. . . . The more benign and, many would say, beneficial speech of pharmaceutical marketing is also entitled to the protection of the First Amendment. If pharmaceutical marketing affects treatment decisions, it does so because doctors find it persuasive. Absent circumstances far from those presented here, the fear that speech might persuade provides no lawful basis for quieting it.

**2**

The State contends that § 4631(d) advances important public policy goals by lowering the costs of medical services and promoting public health. If prescriber-identifying information were available for use by detailers, the State contends, then detailing would be effective in promoting brand-name drugs that are more expensive and less safe than generic alternatives. This logic is set out at length in the legislative findings accompanying § 4631(d). Yet at oral argument here, the State declined to acknowledge that § 4631(d)'s objective purpose and practical effect were to inhibit detailing and alter doctors' prescription decisions. The State's reluctance to embrace its own legislature's rationale reflects the vulnerability of its position.

While Vermont's stated policy goals may be proper, § 4631(d) does not advance them in a permissible way. . . . The State seeks to achieve its policy objectives through the indirect means of restraining certain speech by certain speakers — that is, by diminishing detailers' ability to influence prescription decisions. Those who seek to censor or burden free expression often assert that disfavored speech has adverse effects. But the "fear that people would make bad decisions if given truthful information" cannot justify content-based burdens on speech. *Thompson v. Western States Medical Center* (2002). . . .

As Vermont's legislative findings acknowledge, the premise of § 4631(d) is that the force of speech can justify the government's attempts to stifle it. Indeed the State defends the law by insisting that "pharmaceutical marketing has a strong influence on doctors' prescribing practices." This reasoning is incompatible with the First Amendment. In an attempt to reverse a disfavored trend in public opinion, a State could not ban campaigning with slogans, picketing with signs, or marching during the daytime. Likewise the State may not seek to remove a popular but disfavored product from the marketplace by prohibiting truthful, nonmisleading advertisements that contain impressive endorsements or catchy jingles. That the State finds expression too persuasive does not permit it to quiet the speech or to burden its messengers.

. . . The State may not burden the speech of others in order to tilt public debate in a preferred direction. . . .

It is true that content-based restrictions on protected expression are sometimes permissible, and that principle applies to commercial speech. . . . The Court has noted, for example, that "a State may choose to regulate price advertising in one industry but not in others, because the risk of fraud . . . is in its view greater there." *R.A.V. v. St. Paul* (1992). Here, however, Vermont has not shown that its law has a neutral justification.

The State nowhere contends that detailing is false or misleading within the meaning of this Court's First Amendment precedents. Nor does the State argue that the provision challenged here will prevent false or misleading speech. The State's interest in burdening the speech of detailers instead turns on nothing more than a difference of opinion.

\* \* \*

. . . The State has burdened a form of protected expression that it found too persuasive. At the same time, the State has left unburdened those speakers whose messages are in accord with its own views. This the State cannot do.

The judgment of the Court of Appeals is affirmed.

*It is so ordered.*

Justice Breyer, with whom Justice Ginsburg and Justice Kagan join, dissenting.

The Vermont statute before us adversely affects expression in one, and only one, way. It deprives pharmaceutical and data-mining companies of data, collected pursuant to the government's regulatory mandate, that could help pharmaceutical companies create better sales messages. In my view, this effect on expression is inextricably related to a lawful governmental effort to regulate a commercial enterprise. The First Amendment does not require courts to apply a special "heightened" standard of review when reviewing such an effort. And, in any event, the statute meets the First Amendment standard this Court has previously applied when the government seeks to regulate commercial speech. For any or all of these reasons, the Court should uphold the statute as constitutional.

. . . Since ordinary regulatory programs can affect speech, particularly commercial speech, in myriad ways, to apply a "heightened" First Amendment standard of review whenever such a program burdens speech would transfer from legislatures to judges the primary power to weigh ends and to choose means, threatening to distort or undermine legitimate legislative objectives. To apply a "heightened" standard of review in such cases as a matter of course would risk what then-Justice Rehnquist, dissenting in *Central Hudson Gas & Electric Corp. v. Public Service Comm'n of New York* (1980), described as a "retur[n] to the bygone era of *Lochner v. New York* (1905), in which it was common practice for this Court to strike down economic regulations adopted by a State based on the Court's own notions of the most appropriate means for the State to implement its considered policies."

There are several reasons why the Court should review Vermont's law "under the standard appropriate for the review of economic regulation." . . . For one thing, Vermont's statute neither forbids nor requires anyone to say anything, to engage in any form of symbolic speech, or to endorse any particular point of view, whether ideological or related to the sale of a product.

For another thing, the same First Amendment standards that apply to Vermont here would apply to similar regulatory actions taken by other States or by the Federal Government acting, for example, through Food and Drug Administration (FDA) regulation. . . .

Further, the statute's requirements form part of a traditional, comprehensive regulatory regime. The pharmaceutical drug industry has been heavily regulated at least since 1906. Longstanding statutes and regulations require pharmaceutical companies to engage in complex drug testing to ensure that their drugs are both "safe" and "effective." Only then can the drugs be marketed, at which point drug companies are subject to the FDA's exhaustive regulation of the content of drug labels and the manner in which drugs can be advertised and sold.

Finally, Vermont's statute is directed toward information that exists only by virtue of government regulation. Under federal law, certain drugs can be dispensed only by a pharmacist operating under the orders of a medical practitioner. Vermont regulates the qualifications, the fitness, and the practices of pharmacists themselves, and requires pharmacies to maintain a "patient record system" that, among other things, tracks who prescribed which drugs. But for these regulations, pharmacies would have no way to know who had told customers to buy which drugs (as is the case when a doctor tells a patient to take a daily dose of aspirin).

Regulators will often find it necessary to create tailored restrictions on the use of information subject to their regulatory jurisdiction. A car dealership that obtains credit scores for customers who want car loans can be prohibited from using credit data to search for new customers. Medical specialists who obtain medical records for their existing patients cannot purchase those records in order to identify new patients. Or, speaking hypothetically, a public utilities commission that directs local gas distributors to gather usage information for individual customers might permit the distributors to share the data with researchers (trying to lower energy costs) but forbid sales of the data to appliance manufacturers seeking to sell gas stoves.

. . . [R]egulatory actions of the kind present here have not previously been thought to raise serious additional constitutional concerns under the First Amendment. The ease with which one can point to actual or hypothetical examples with potentially adverse speech-related effects at least roughly comparable to those at issue here indicates the danger of applying a "heightened" or "intermediate" standard of First Amendment review where typical regulatory actions affect commercial speech (say, by withholding information that a commercial speaker might use to shape the content of a message).

Thus, it is not surprising that, until today, this Court has *never* found that the *First Amendment* prohibits the government from restricting the use of information gathered pursuant to a regulatory mandate — whether the information rests in government files or has remained in the hands of the private firms that gathered it. . . .

[G]iven the sheer quantity of regulatory initiatives that touch upon commercial messages, the Court's vision of its reviewing task threatens to return us to a happily bygone era when judges scrutinized legislation for its interference with economic liberty. History shows that the power was much abused and resulted in the constitutionalization of economic theories preferred by individual jurists. By inviting courts to scrutinize whether a State's legitimate regulatory interests can be achieved in less restrictive ways whenever they touch (even indirectly) upon commercial speech, today's majority risks repeating the mistakes of the past in a manner not anticipated by our precedents.

[T]he statute before us satisfies the "intermediate" standards this Court has applied to restrictions on commercial speech. *A fortiori* it satisfies less demanding standards that are more appropriately applied in this kind of commercial regulatory case — a case where the government seeks typical regulatory ends (lower drug prices, more balanced sales messages) through the use of ordinary regulatory means (limiting the commercial use of data gathered pursuant to a regulatory mandate). The speech-related consequences here are indirect, incidental, and entirely commercial.

The Court reaches its conclusion through the use of important First Amendment categories — "content-based," "speaker-based," and "neutral" — but without taking full account of the regulatory context, the nature of the speech effects, the values these First Amendment categories seek to promote, and prior precedent. At best the Court opens a Pandora's Box of First Amendment challenges to many ordinary regulatory practices that may only incidentally affect a commercial message. At worst, it reawakens *Lochner*'s pre-New Deal threat of substituting judicial for democratic decisionmaking where ordinary economic regulation is at issue.

Regardless, whether we apply an ordinary commercial speech standard or a less demanding standard, I believe Vermont's law is consistent with the First Amendment. And with respect, I dissent.

## NOTES AND QUESTIONS

**1.** A central feature of Justice Kennedy's opinion for the majority is that the Vermont law regulates speech, not conduct, which, as you may recall from the first chapter of this book, triggers heightened scrutiny under the First Amendment. Is prescriber-identifying information speech? The First Circuit thought otherwise — that court concluded that such information is a commodity and, therefore, subject to regulation like any other commodity. And if it is true that facts are themselves speech, what other kinds of state police power regulations might be subject to heightened scrutiny?

**2.** Before *Sorrell*, the Court treated regulations of commercial speech — that is, speech that essentially proposes a commercial transaction — more deferentially than regulation of political speech, which lies at the core of the First Amendment. It may be that the Court is unwilling to determine whether particular speech should be classified as either "commercial" or "political." But that reluctance, as Justice Breyer warned in his dissent, will lead the Court to impose heightened scrutiny on all manner of economic regulations previously thought immune from such challenges — and involve the courts in policing such regulations in a way that forces judges to make determinations about whether a legislature's judgment regarding, say, the importance of individual patient privacy, should be upheld.

**3.** Does the difference between this decision and *Lochner* lie in the fact that here, the plaintiffs claimed a violation of the First Amendment as opposed to substantive due process? Was the problem with *Lochner* that the interest at stake was unenumerated, or that it was not truly fundamental? Or was it that the *Lochner* Court simply failed to recognize the legislature's legitimate regulatory interests and superior competence in such matters? Take comfort in knowing that there are no easy answers to these questions.

## 8. Recognizing New Fundamental Interests Under the U.S. Constitution

### District Attorney's Office v. Osborne
### 557 U.S. 52 (2009)

Chief Justice Roberts delivered the opinion of the Court.

DNA testing has an unparalleled ability both to exonerate the wrongly convicted and to identify the guilty. It has the potential to significantly improve both the criminal justice system and police investigative practices. The Federal Government and the States have recognized this, and have developed special approaches to ensure that this evidentiary tool can be effectively incorporated into established criminal procedure — usually but not always through legislation.

Against this prompt and considered response, the respondent, William Osborne, proposes a different approach: the recognition of a freestanding and far-reaching constitutional right of access to this new type of evidence. The nature of what he seeks is confirmed by his decision to file this lawsuit in federal court under 42 U.S.C. § 1983, not within the state criminal justice system. This approach would take the development of rules and procedures in this area out of the hands of legislatures and state courts shaping policy in a focused manner and turn it over to federal courts applying the broad parameters of the Due Process Clause. There is no reason to constitutionalize the issue in this way. Because the decision below would do just that, we reverse.

### I

This lawsuit arose out of a violent crime committed 16 years ago, which has resulted in a long string of litigation in the state and federal courts. . . . Osborne and Jackson were convicted by an Alaska jury of kidnaping, assault, and sexual assault. They were acquitted of an additional count of sexual assault and of attempted murder. Finding it "nearly miraculous" that [the victim] had survived, the trial judge sentenced Osborne to 26 years in prison, with 5 suspended. His conviction and sentence were affirmed on appeal.

Osborne then sought post-conviction relief in Alaska state court. He claimed that he had asked his attorney, Sidney Billingslea, to seek more discriminating restriction-fragment-length-polymorphism (RFLP) DNA testing during trial, and argued that she was constitutionally ineffective for not doing so. Billingslea testified that after investigation, she had concluded that further testing would do more harm than good. . . . The Alaska Court of Appeals concluded that Billingslea's decision had been strategic and rejected Osborne's claim.

In this proceeding, Osborne also sought the DNA testing that Billingslea had failed to perform, relying on an Alaska post-conviction statute, Alaska Stat. § 12.72 (2008), and the State and Federal Constitutions. In two decisions, the Alaska Court of Appeals concluded that Osborne had no right to the RFLP test. According to the court, § 12.72 "apparently" did not apply to DNA testing that had been available at trial. The court found no basis in our precedents for recognizing a federal constitutional right to DNA evidence. After a remand for further findings, the Alaska Court of Appeals concluded that Osborne could not claim a state constitutional right either, because the other evidence of his guilt was too strong and RFLP testing was not likely to be conclusive. . . .

The court relied heavily on the fact that Osborne had confessed to some of his crimes in a 2004 application for parole — in which it is a crime to lie. . . . He repeated this confession before the parole board. Despite this acceptance of responsibility, the board did not grant him discretionary parole. In 2007, he was released on mandatory parole, but he has since been rearrested for another offense, and the State has petitioned to revoke this parole.

Meanwhile, Osborne had also been active in federal court, suing state officials under 42 U.S.C. § 1983. He claimed that the Due Process Clause and other constitutional provisions gave him a constitutional right to access the DNA evidence for what is known as short-tandem-repeat (STR) testing (at his own expense). This form of testing is more discriminating than the DQ Alpha or RFLP methods available at the time of Osborne's trial. The District Court first dismissed the claim. . . . The United States Court of Appeals for the Ninth Circuit reversed, concluding that § 1983 was the proper vehicle for Osborne's claims, while "express[ing] no opinion as to whether Osborne ha[d] been deprived of a federally protected right."

On cross-motions for summary judgment after remand, the District Court concluded that "there *does* exist, *under the unique and specific facts presented*, a very limited constitutional right to the testing sought." The court relied on several factors: that the testing Osborne sought had been unavailable at trial, that the testing could be accomplished at almost no cost to the State, and that the results were likely to be material. It therefore granted summary judgment in favor of Osborne.

The Court of Appeals affirmed. . . . We granted certiorari to decide whether Osborne's claims could be pursued using § 1983, and whether he has a right under the Due Process Clause to obtain post-conviction access to the State's evidence for DNA testing. We now reverse on the latter ground.

## II

Modern DNA testing can provide powerful new evidence unlike anything known before. Since its first use in criminal investigations in the mid-1980s, there have been several major advances in DNA technology, culminating in STR technology. It is now often possible to determine whether a biological tissue matches a suspect with near certainty. While of course many criminal trials proceed without any forensic and scientific testing at all, there is no technology comparable to DNA testing for matching tissues when such evidence is at issue. DNA testing has exonerated wrongly convicted people, and has confirmed the convictions of many others.

At the same time, DNA testing alone does not always resolve a case. Where there is enough other incriminating evidence and an explanation for the DNA result, science alone cannot prove a prisoner innocent. The availability of technologies not available at trial cannot mean that every criminal conviction, or even every criminal conviction involving biological evidence, is suddenly in doubt. The dilemma is how to harness DNA's power to prove innocence without unnecessarily overthrowing the established system of criminal justice.

That task belongs primarily to the legislature. "[T]he States are currently engaged in serious, thoughtful examinations," *Washington v. Glucksberg* (1997), of how to ensure the fair and effective use of this testing within the existing criminal justice framework. Forty-six States have already enacted statutes dealing specifically with access to DNA evidence. The Federal Government has also passed the Innocence Protection Act of 2004, which allows federal prisoners to move for court-ordered DNA testing under certain specified conditions. That Act also grants money to States that enact comparable statutes, and as a consequence has served as a model for some state legislation. . . .

Alaska is one of a handful of States yet to enact legislation specifically addressing the issue of evidence requested for DNA testing. But that does not mean that such evidence is unavailable for those seeking to prove their innocence. Instead, Alaska courts are addressing how to apply existing laws for discovery and post-conviction relief to this novel technology. The same is true with respect to other States that do not have DNA-specific statutes.

First, access to evidence is available under Alaska law for those who seek to subject it to newly available DNA testing that will prove them to be actually innocent. Under the State's general post-conviction relief statute, a prisoner may challenge his conviction when "there exists evidence of material facts, not previously presented and heard by the court, that requires vacation of the conviction or sentence in the interest of justice." Such a claim is exempt from otherwise applicable time limits if "newly discovered evidence," pursued with due diligence, "establishes by clear and convincing evidence that the applicant is innocent."

Both parties agree that under these provisions, "a defendant is entitled to post-conviction relief if the defendant presents newly discovered evidence that establishes by clear and convincing evidence that the defendant is innocent." If such a claim is brought, state law permits general discovery. Alaska courts have explained that these procedures are available to request DNA evidence for newly available testing to establish actual innocence.

In addition to this statutory procedure, the Alaska Court of Appeals has invoked a widely accepted three-part test to govern additional rights to DNA access under the State Constitution. Drawing on the experience with DNA evidence of State Supreme Courts around the country, the Court of Appeals . . . was "prepared to hold, . . . that a defendant who seeks post-conviction DNA testing . . . must show (1) that the conviction rested primarily on eyewitness identification evidence, (2) that there was a demonstrable doubt concerning the defendant's identification as the perpetrator, and (3) that scientific testing would likely be conclusive on this issue." Thus, the Alaska courts have suggested that even those who do not get discovery under the State's criminal rules have available to them a safety valve under the State Constitution.

This is the background against which the Federal Court of Appeals ordered the State to turn over the DNA evidence in its possession, and it is our starting point in analyzing Osborne's constitutional claims.

## IV
### A

"No State shall . . . deprive any person of life, liberty, or property, without due process of law." U.S. Const., Amdt. 14, § 1; accord Amdt. 5. This Clause imposes procedural limitations on a State's power to take away protected entitlements. Osborne argues that access to the State's evidence is a "process" needed to vindicate his right to prove himself innocent and get out of jail. Process is not an end in itself, so a necessary premise of this argument is that he has an entitlement (what our precedents call a "liberty interest") to prove his innocence even after a fair trial has proved otherwise. We must first examine this asserted liberty interest to determine what process (if any) is due.

In identifying his potential liberty interest, Osborne first attempts to rely on the Governor's constitutional authority to "grant pardons, commutations, and reprieves." Alaska Const., Art. III, § 21. That claim can be readily disposed of. We have held that noncapital defendants do not have a liberty interest in traditional state executive clemency, to which no particular claimant is *entitled* as a matter of state law. Osborne therefore cannot challenge the constitutionality of any procedures available to vindicate an interest in state clemency.

Osborne does, however, have a liberty interest in demonstrating his innocence with new evidence under state law. As explained, Alaska law provides that those who use "newly discovered evidence" to "establis[h] by clear and convincing evidence that [they are] innocent" may obtain "vacation of [their] conviction or sentence in the interest of justice." . . . The Court of Appeals went too far, however, in concluding that the Due Process Clause requires that certain familiar pre-conviction trial rights be extended to protect Osborne's post-conviction liberty interest. . . . A criminal defendant proved guilty after a fair trial does not have the same liberty interests as a free man. At trial, the defendant is presumed innocent and may demand that the government prove its case beyond reasonable doubt. But "[o]nce a defendant has been afforded a fair trial and convicted of the offense for which he was charged, the presumption of innocence disappears." *Herrera v. Collins* (1993). . . .

The State accordingly has more flexibility in deciding what procedures are needed in the context of postconviction relief. "[W]hen a State chooses to offer help to those seeking relief from convictions," due process does not "dictat[e] the exact form such assistance must assume." *Pennsylvania v. Finley* (1987). Osborne's right to due process is not parallel to a trial right, but rather must be analyzed in light of the fact that he has already been found guilty at a fair trial, and has only a limited interest in post-conviction relief. . . .

[T]he question is whether consideration of Osborne's claim within the framework of the State's procedures for post-conviction relief "offends some principle of justice so rooted in the traditions and conscience of our people as to be ranked as fundamental," or "transgresses any recognized principle of fundamental fairness in operation." *Medina v. California* (1992) (internal quotation marks omitted). Federal courts may upset a State's post-conviction relief procedures only if they are fundamentally inadequate to vindicate the substantive rights provided.

We see nothing inadequate about the procedures Alaska has provided to vindicate its state right to post-conviction relief in general, and nothing inadequate about how those procedures apply to those who seek access to DNA evidence. Alaska provides a substantive right to be released on a sufficiently compelling showing of new evidence that establishes innocence. It exempts such claims from otherwise applicable time limits. The State provides for discovery in post-conviction proceedings, and has — through judicial decision — specified that this discovery procedure is available to those seeking access to DNA evidence. These procedures are not without limits. The evidence must indeed be newly available to qualify under Alaska's statute, must have been diligently pursued, and must also be sufficiently material. These procedures are similar to those provided for DNA evidence by federal law and the law of other States, and they are not inconsistent with the "traditions and conscience of our people" or with "any recognized principle of fundamental fairness." *Medina* (internal quotation marks omitted).

And there is more. While the Alaska courts have not had occasion to conclusively decide the question, the Alaska Court of Appeals has suggested that the State Constitution provides an additional right of access to DNA. In expressing its "reluctan[ce] to hold that Alaska law offers no remedy" to those who belatedly seek DNA testing, and in invoking the three-part test used by other state courts, the court indicated that in an appropriate case the State Constitution may provide a failsafe even for those who cannot satisfy the statutory requirements under general postconviction procedures.

To the degree there is some uncertainty in the details of Alaska's newly developing procedures for obtaining post-conviction access to DNA, we can hardly fault the State for that. Osborne has brought this § 1983 action without ever using these procedures in filing a state or federal habeas claim relying on actual innocence. In other words, he has not tried to use the process provided to him by the State or attempted to vindicate the liberty interest that is now the centerpiece of his claim. When Osborne *did* request DNA testing in state court, he sought RFLP testing that had been available at trial, not the STR testing he now seeks, and the state court relied on that fact in denying him testing under Alaska law.

His attempt to sidestep state process through a new federal lawsuit puts Osborne in a very awkward position. If he simply seeks the DNA through the State's discovery procedures, he might well get it. If he does not, it may be for a perfectly adequate reason, just as the federal statute and all state statutes impose conditions and limits on access to DNA evidence. It is difficult to criticize the State's procedures when Osborne has not invoked them. This is not to say that Osborne must exhaust state-law remedies. But it is Osborne's burden to demonstrate the inadequacy of the state-law procedures available to him in state post-conviction relief. These procedures are adequate on their face, and without trying them, Osborne can hardly complain that they do not work in practice.

. . .

## B

[Osborne also] seeks to defend the judgment on the basis of substantive due process as well. He asks that we recognize a freestanding right to DNA evidence untethered from the liberty interests he hopes to vindicate with it. We reject the invitation and conclude, in the circumstances of this case, that there is no such substantive due process right. "As a general matter, the Court has always been reluctant to expand the concept of substantive due process because guideposts for responsible decisionmaking in this unchartered area are scarce and open-ended." *Collins v. Harker Heights* (1992). Osborne seeks access to state evidence so that he can apply new DNA-testing technology that might prove him innocent. There is no long history of such a right, and "[t]he mere novelty of such a claim is reason enough to doubt that 'substantive due process' sustains it." *Reno v. Flores* (1993).

And there are further reasons to doubt. The elected governments of the States are actively confronting the challenges DNA technology poses to our criminal justice systems and our traditional notions of finality, as well as the opportunities it affords. To suddenly constitutionalize this area would short-circuit what looks to be a prompt and considered legislative response. The first DNA testing statutes were passed in 1994 and 1997. In the past decade, 44 States and the Federal Government have followed suit, reflecting the increased availability of DNA testing. As noted, Alaska itself is considering such legislation. "By extending constitutional protection to an asserted right or liberty interest, we, to a great extent, place the matter outside the arena of public debate and legislative action. We must therefore exercise the utmost care whenever we are asked to break new ground in this field." *Glucksberg* (internal quotation marks omitted). . . . If we extended substantive due process to this area, we would cast these statutes into constitutional doubt and be forced to take over the issue of DNA access ourselves. We are reluctant to enlist the Federal Judiciary in creating a new constitutional code of rules for handling DNA.

Establishing a freestanding right to access DNA evidence for testing would force us to act as policymakers, and our substantive-due-process rulemaking authority would not only have to cover the right of access but a myriad of other issues. We would soon have to decide if there is a constitutional obligation to preserve forensic evidence that might later be tested. If so, for how long? Would it be different for different types of evidence? Would the State also have some obligation to gather such evidence in the first place? How much, and when? No doubt there would be a miscellany of other minor directives.

In this case, the evidence has already been gathered and preserved, but if we extend substantive due process to this area, these questions would be before us in short order, and it is hard to imagine what tools federal courts would use to answer them. At the end of the day, there is no reason to suppose that their answers to these questions would be any better than those of state courts and legislatures, and good reason to suspect the opposite.

\* \* \*

DNA evidence will undoubtedly lead to changes in the criminal justice system. It has done so already. The question is whether further change will primarily be made by legislative revision and judicial interpretation of the existing system, or whether the Federal Judiciary must leap ahead — revising (or even discarding) the system by creating a new constitutional right and taking over responsibility for refining it.

Federal courts should not presume that state criminal procedures will be inadequate to deal with technological change. The criminal justice system has historically accommodated new types of evidence, and is a time-tested means of carrying out society's interest in convicting the guilty while respecting individual rights. That system, like any human endeavor, cannot be perfect. DNA evidence shows that it has not been. But there is no basis for Osborne's approach of assuming that because DNA has shown that these procedures are not flawless, DNA evidence must be treated as categorically outside the process, rather than within it. That is precisely what his § 1983 suit seeks to do, and that is the contention we reject.

The judgment of the Court of Appeals is reversed, and the case is remanded for further proceedings consistent with this opinion.

*It is so ordered.*

[Concurring opinion of Justice Alito omitted.]

Justice Stevens, with whom Justice Ginsburg and Justice Breyer join, dissenting.

[W]hile a prisoner's "rights may be diminished by the needs and exigencies of the institutional environment[,] . . . [t]here is no iron curtain drawn between the Constitution and the prisons of this country." *Wolff v. McDonnell* (1974). Our cases have recognized protected interests in a variety of post-conviction contexts, extending substantive constitutional protections to state prisoners on the premise that the Due Process Clause of the Fourteenth Amendment requires States to respect certain fundamental liberties in the post-conviction context. It is therefore far too late in the day to question the basic proposition that convicted persons such as Osborne retain a constitutionally protected measure of interest in liberty, including the fundamental liberty of freedom from physical restraint.

Recognition of this right draws strength from the fact that 46 States and the Federal Government have passed statutes providing access to evidence for DNA testing, and 3 additional states (including Alaska) provide similar access through court-made rules alone. These legislative developments are consistent with recent trends in legal ethics recognizing that prosecutors are obliged to disclose all forms of exculpatory evidence that come into their possession following conviction. The fact that nearly all the States have now recognized some post-conviction right to DNA evidence makes it more, not less, appropriate to recognize a limited federal right to such evidence in cases where litigants are unfairly barred from obtaining relief in state court.

[Further,] the State has failed to provide any concrete reason for denying Osborne the DNA testing he seeks, and none is apparent. Because Osborne has offered to pay for the tests, cost is not a factor. And as the State now concedes, there is no reason to doubt that such testing would provide conclusive confirmation of Osborne's guilt or revelation of his innocence. In the courts below, the State refused to provide an explanation for its refusal to permit testing of the evidence, and in this Court, its explanation has been, at best, unclear. Insofar as the State has articulated any reason at all, it appears to be a generalized interest in protecting the finality of the judgment of conviction from any possible future attacks.

While we have long recognized that States have an interest in securing the finality of their judgments, finality is not a stand-alone value that trumps a State's overriding interest in ensuring that justice is done in its courts and secured to its citizens. Indeed, when absolute proof of innocence is readily at hand, a State should not shrink from the possibility that error may have occurred. . . . DNA evidence has led to an extraordinary series of exonerations, not only in cases where the trial evidence was weak, but also in cases where the convicted parties confessed their guilt and where the trial evidence against them appeared overwhelming. The examples provided by *amici* of the power of DNA testing serve to convince me that the fact of conviction is not sufficient to justify a State's refusal to perform a test that will conclusively establish innocence or guilt.

This conclusion draws strength from the powerful state interests that offset the State's purported interest in finality *per se*. When a person is convicted for a crime he did not commit, the true culprit escapes punishment. DNA testing may lead to his identification. Crime victims, the law enforcement profession, and society at large share a strong interest in identifying and apprehending the actual perpetrators of vicious crimes, such as the rape and attempted murder that gave rise to this case.

The arbitrariness of the State's conduct is highlighted by comparison to the private interests it denies. It seems to me obvious that if a wrongly convicted person were to produce proof of his actual innocence, no state interest would be sufficient to justify his continued punitive detention. If such proof can be readily obtained without imposing a significant burden on the State, a refusal to provide access to such evidence is wholly unjustified.

. . . I am left to conclude that the State's failure to provide Osborne access to the evidence constitutes arbitrary action that offends basic principles of due process. On that basis, I would affirm the judgment of the Ninth Circuit.

[Dissenting opinion of Justice Souter omitted.]

### NOTES AND QUESTIONS

**1.** In this case we see the ways in which one can challenge the same statutory regime using both procedural and substantive due process arguments. As to procedural due process: by this point you should be sufficiently familiar with the approach set out in *Mathews* to appreciate the analysis the majority employed, and to anticipate the result the majority reached.

**2.** As to substantive due process: on the understanding that this decision pre-dates Dobbs, the majority opinion by Chief Justice Roberts nonetheless raises some interesting questions about jurisprudential methodology. The first part of the analysis of the interest at stake, from *Glucksberg*, looks to a history of legal protection of the interest. Here, nearly all the states recognize and protect the right at issue as a matter of statute, which raises a question: why isn't this evidence of a legal tradition sufficient for the majority, which demanded instead a longer history of such protection?

## Chapter 9
## The Religion Clauses

In addition to protecting the freedom of speech, the First Amendment provides that "Congress shall make no law respecting an establishment of religion, or prohibiting the free exercise thereof. . . ." Our discussion of what are known as the Establishment Clause and the Free Exercise Clause follows, rather than precedes, study of the constitutional protections of liberty and equality because the U.S. Supreme Court's approach to implementing the religion clauses does not track its doctrinal work in those other areas of individual rights protection. While in those contexts the doctrinal analyses employed by the courts — tiered scrutiny that depends upon the nature of the interest at risk — often are so similar as to seem, at certain points, interchangeable, the Supreme Court has yet to settle on a single approach to implementing the Establishment Clause. To be sure, the Court has provided more clarity in its free exercise jurisprudence, which in recent years shares connections with the modern approach to equal protection. Still, as two commentators recently observed, "[t]he Court's record on religious freedom [has been] vilified for its lack of consistent and coherent principles, its uncritical use of mechanical tests and misleading metaphors, and its massive pile of divided and discordant opinions." John Witte, Jr. & Joel A. Nichols, Religions and the American Constitutional Experiment 3 (4th ed. 2016).

In this chapter we'll look at some of those mechanical tests and misleading metaphors for which the Court has been vilified, and we'll try and make some sense of the divided and discordant opinions in the cases involving the religion clauses. After all, as lawyers you will need to be able to make something of these provisions, and the cases do provide some guideposts as to how they should be implemented in particular situations.

### A. The Establishment Clause

#### Town of Greece v. Galloway
#### 572 U.S. 565 (2014)

Justice Kennedy delivered the opinion of the Court, except as to Part II-B [Roberts, C.J., and Alito, J., joined the opinion in full, and Scalia and Thomas, JJ., joined except as to Part II-B].

The Court must decide whether the town of Greece, New York, imposes an impermissible establishment of religion by opening its monthly board meetings with a prayer. It must be concluded, consistent with the Court's opinion in *Marsh v. Chambers* (1983) that no violation of the Constitution has been shown.

I

Greece, a town with a population of 94,000, is in upstate New York. For some years, it began its monthly town board meetings with a moment of silence. In 1999, the newly elected town supervisor, John Auberger, decided to replicate the prayer practice he had found meaningful while serving in the county legislature. Following the roll call and recitation of the Pledge of Allegiance, Auberger would invite a local clergyman to the front of the room to deliver an invocation. After the prayer, Auberger would thank the minister for serving as the board's "chaplain for the month" and present him with a commemorative plaque. The prayer was intended to place town board members in a solemn and deliberative frame of mind, invoke divine guidance in town affairs, and follow a tradition practiced by Congress and dozens of state legislatures.

The town followed an informal method for selecting prayer givers, all of whom were unpaid volunteers. A town employee would call the congregations listed in a local directory until she found a minister available for that month's meeting. The town eventually compiled a list of willing "board chaplains" who had accepted invitations and agreed to return in the future. The town at no point excluded or denied an opportunity to a would-be prayer giver. Its leaders maintained that a minister or layperson of any persuasion, including an atheist, could give the invocation. But nearly all of the congregations in town were Christian; and from 1999 to 2007, all of the participating ministers were too.

Greece neither reviewed the prayers in advance of the meetings nor provided guidance as to their tone or content, in the belief that exercising any degree of control over the prayers would infringe both the free exercise and speech rights of the ministers. The town instead left the guest clergy free to compose their own devotions. The resulting prayers often sounded both civic and religious themes. Typical were invocations that asked the divinity to abide at the meeting and bestow blessings on the community. . . . Some of the ministers spoke in a distinctly Christian idiom; and a minority invoked religious holidays, scripture, or doctrine. . . .

Respondents Susan Galloway and Linda Stephens attended town board meetings to speak about issues of local concern, and they objected that the prayers violated their religious or philosophical views. . . . After respondents complained that Christian themes pervaded the prayers, to the exclusion of citizens who did not share those beliefs, the town invited a Jewish layman and the chairman of the local Baha'i temple to deliver prayers. A Wiccan priestess who had read press reports about the prayer controversy requested, and was granted, an opportunity to give the invocation.

Galloway and Stephens brought suit in the United States District Court for the Western District of New York. They alleged that the town violated the First Amendment's Establishment Clause by preferring Christians over other prayer givers and by sponsoring sectarian prayers, such as those given "in Jesus' name." They did not seek an end to the prayer practice, but rather requested an injunction that would limit the town to "inclusive and ecumenical" prayers that referred only to a "generic God" and would not associate the government with any one faith or belief.

The District Court on summary judgment upheld the prayer practice as consistent with the First Amendment. . . . The Court of Appeals for the Second Circuit reversed. It held that some aspects of the prayer program, viewed in their totality by a reasonable observer, conveyed the message that Greece was endorsing Christianity. . . .

Having granted certiorari to decide whether the town's prayer practice violates the Establishment Clause, the Court now reverses the judgment of the Court of Appeals.

## II

In *Marsh*, the Court found no First Amendment violation in the Nebraska Legislature's practice of opening its sessions with a prayer delivered by a chaplain paid from state funds. The decision concluded that legislative prayer, while religious in nature, has long been understood as compatible with the Establishment Clause. As practiced by Congress since the framing of the Constitution, legislative prayer lends gravity to public business, reminds lawmakers to transcend petty differences in pursuit of a higher purpose, and expresses a common aspiration to a just and peaceful society. The Court has considered this symbolic expression to be a "tolerable acknowledgement of beliefs widely held," rather than a first, treacherous step towards establishment of a state church.

. . . The Court in *Marsh* found . . . history supported the conclusion that legislative invocations are compatible with the Establishment Clause. The First Congress made it an early item of business to appoint and pay official chaplains, and both the House and Senate have maintained the office virtually uninterrupted since that time. When *Marsh* was decided, in 1983, legislative prayer had persisted in the Nebraska Legislature for more than a century, and the majority of the other States also had the same, consistent practice. Although no information has been cited by the parties to indicate how many local legislative bodies open their meetings with prayer, this practice too has historical precedent. . . .

Yet *Marsh* must not be understood as permitting a practice that would amount to a constitutional violation if not for its historical foundation. . . . That the First Congress provided for the appointment of chaplains only days after approving language for the First Amendment demonstrates that the Framers considered legislative prayer a benign acknowledgment of religion's role in society. In the 1850's, the judiciary committees in both the House and Senate reevaluated the practice of official chaplaincies after receiving petitions to abolish the office. The committees concluded that the office posed no threat of an establishment because lawmakers were not compelled to attend the daily prayer; no faith was excluded by law, nor any favored, and the cost of the chaplain's salary imposed a vanishingly small burden on taxpayers. *Marsh* stands for the proposition that it is not necessary to define the precise boundary of the Establishment Clause where history shows that the specific practice is permitted. Any test the Court adopts must acknowledge a practice that was accepted by the Framers and has withstood the critical scrutiny of time and political change. A test that would sweep away what has so long been settled would create new controversy and begin anew the very divisions along religious lines that the Establishment Clause seeks to prevent.

The Court's inquiry, then, must be to determine whether the prayer practice in the town of Greece fits within the tradition long followed in Congress and the state legislatures. Respondents assert that the town's prayer exercise falls outside that tradition and transgresses the Establishment Clause for two independent but mutually reinforcing reasons. First, they argue that *Marsh* did not approve prayers containing sectarian language or themes. . . . Second, they argue that the setting and conduct of the town board meetings create social pressures that force nonadherents to remain in the room or even feign participation in order to avoid offending the representatives who sponsor the prayer and will vote on matters citizens bring before the board. The sectarian content of the prayers compounds the subtle coercive pressures, they argue, because the nonbeliever who might tolerate ecumenical prayer is forced to do the same for prayer that might be inimical to his or her beliefs.

### A

Respondents maintain that prayer must be nonsectarian, or not identifiable with any one religion; and they fault the town for permitting guest chaplains to deliver prayers that "use overtly Christian terms" or "invoke specifics of Christian theology." . . . They argue that prayer which contemplates "the workings of the Holy Spirit, the events of Pentecost, and the belief that God 'has raised up the Lord Jesus' and 'will raise us, in our turn, and put us by His side' " would be impermissible, as would any prayer that reflects dogma particular to a single faith tradition.

An insistence on nonsectarian or ecumenical prayer as a single, fixed standard is not consistent with the tradition of legislative prayer outlined in the Court's cases. The Court found the prayers in *Marsh* consistent with the First Amendment not because they espoused only a generic theism but because our history and tradition have shown that prayer in this limited context could "coexis[t] with the principles of disestablishment and religious freedom." The Congress that drafted the First Amendment would have been accustomed to invocations containing explicitly religious themes of the sort respondents find objectionable. . . . Congress continues to permit its appointed and visiting chaplains to express themselves in a religious idiom. It acknowledges our growing diversity not by proscribing sectarian content but by welcoming ministers of many creeds.

. . . *Marsh* nowhere suggested that the constitutionality of legislative prayer turns on the neutrality of its content. . . . Nor did the Court imply the rule that prayer violates the Establishment Clause any time it is given in the name of a figure deified by only one faith or creed. To the contrary, the Court instructed that the "content of the prayer is not of concern to judges," provided "there is no indication that the prayer opportunity has been exploited to proselytize or advance any one, or to disparage any other, faith or belief."

To hold that invocations must be nonsectarian would force the legislatures that sponsor prayers and the courts that are asked to decide these cases to act as supervisors and censors of religious speech, a rule that would involve government in religious matters to a far greater degree than is the case under the town's current practice of neither editing or approving prayers in advance nor criticizing their content after the fact. Our Government is prohibited from prescribing prayers to be recited in our public institutions in order to promote a preferred system of belief or code of moral behavior. It would be but a few steps removed from that prohibition for legislatures to require chaplains to redact the religious content from their message in order to make it acceptable for the public sphere. Government may not mandate a civic religion that stifles any but the most generic reference to the sacred any more than it may prescribe a religious orthodoxy.

Respondents argue, in effect, that legislative prayer may be addressed only to a generic God. The law and the Court could not draw this line for each specific prayer or seek to require ministers to set aside their nuanced and deeply personal beliefs for vague and artificial ones. There is doubt, in any event, that consensus might be reached as to what qualifies as generic or nonsectarian. . . . Because it is unlikely that prayer will be inclusive beyond dispute, it would be unwise to adopt what respondents think is the next-best option: permitting those religious words, and only those words, that are acceptable to the majority, even if they will exclude some. The First Amendment is not a majority rule, and government may not seek to define permissible categories of religious speech. Once it invites prayer into the public sphere, government must permit a prayer giver to address his or her own God or gods as conscience dictates, unfettered by what an administrator or judge considers to be nonsectarian.

In rejecting the suggestion that legislative prayer must be nonsectarian, the Court does not imply that no constraints remain on its content. The relevant constraint derives from its place at the opening of legislative sessions, where it is meant to lend gravity to the occasion and reflect values long part of the Nation's heritage. Prayer that is solemn and respectful in tone, that invites lawmakers to reflect upon shared ideals and common ends before they embark on the fractious business of governing, serves that legitimate function. If the course and practice over time shows that the invocations denigrate nonbelievers or religious minorities, threaten damnation, or preach conversion, many present may consider the prayer to fall short of the desire to elevate the purpose of the occasion and to unite lawmakers in their common effort. That circumstance would present a different case than the one presently before the Court.

. . . Our tradition assumes that adult citizens, firm in their own beliefs, can tolerate and perhaps appreciate a ceremonial prayer delivered by a person of a different faith.

The prayers delivered in the town of Greece do not fall outside the tradition this Court has recognized. A number of the prayers did invoke the name of Jesus, the Heavenly Father, or the Holy Spirit, but they also invoked universal themes, as by celebrating the changing of the seasons or calling for a "spirit of cooperation" among town leaders. . . .

## B

Respondents further seek to distinguish the town's prayer practice from the tradition upheld in *Marsh* on the ground that it coerces participation by nonadherents. They and some *amici* contend that prayer conducted in the intimate setting of a town board meeting differs in fundamental ways from the invocations delivered in Congress and state legislatures, where the public remains segregated from legislative activity and may not address the body except by occasional invitation. Citizens attend town meetings, on the other hand, to accept awards; speak on matters of local importance; and petition the board for action that may affect their economic interests, such as the granting of permits, business licenses, and zoning variances. Respondents argue that the public may feel subtle pressure to participate in prayers that violate their beliefs in order to please the board members from whom they are about to seek a favorable ruling. In their view the fact that board members in small towns know many of their constituents by name only increases the pressure to conform.

. . . On the record in this case the Court is not persuaded that the town of Greece, through the act of offering a brief, solemn, and respectful prayer to open its monthly meetings, compelled its citizens to engage in a religious observance. . . . The prayer opportunity in this case must be evaluated against the backdrop of historical practice. As a practice that has long endured, legislative prayer has become part of our heritage and tradition, part of our expressive idiom, similar to the Pledge of Allegiance, inaugural prayer, or the recitation of "God save the United States and this honorable Court" at the opening of this Court's sessions. It is presumed that the reasonable observer is acquainted with this tradition and understands that its purposes are to lend gravity to public proceedings and to acknowledge the place religion holds in the lives of many private citizens, not to afford government an opportunity to proselytize or force truant constituents into the pews. That many appreciate these acknowledgments of the divine in our public institutions does not suggest that those who disagree are compelled to join the expression or approve its content.

The principal audience for these invocations is not, indeed, the public but lawmakers themselves, who may find that a moment of prayer or quiet reflection sets the mind to a higher purpose and thereby eases the task of governing. . . . To be sure, many members of the public find these prayers meaningful and wish to join them. But their purpose is largely to accommodate the spiritual needs of lawmakers and connect them to a tradition dating to the time of the Framers. For members of town boards and commissions, who often serve part-time and as volunteers, ceremonial prayer may also reflect the values they hold as private citizens. The prayer is an opportunity for them to show who and what they are without denying the right to dissent by those who disagree.

The analysis would be different if town board members directed the public to participate in the prayers, singled out dissidents for opprobrium, or indicated that their decisions might be influenced by a person's acquiescence in the prayer opportunity. No such thing occurred in the town of Greece. . . . Nothing in the record indicates that town leaders allocated benefits and burdens based on participation in the prayer, or that citizens were received differently depending on whether they joined the invocation or quietly declined. In no instance did town leaders signal disfavor toward nonparticipants or suggest that their stature in the community was in any way diminished. A practice that classified citizens based on their religious views would violate the Constitution, but that is not the case before this Court.

In their declarations in the trial court, respondents stated that the prayers gave them offense and made them feel excluded and disrespected. Offense, however, does not equate to coercion. Adults often encounter speech they find disagreeable; and an Establishment Clause violation is not made out any time a person experiences a sense of affront from the expression of contrary religious views in a legislative forum, especially where, as here, any member of the public is welcome in turn to offer an invocation reflecting his or her own convictions. [I]n the general course legislative bodies do not engage in impermissible coercion merely by exposing constituents to prayer they would rather not hear and in which they need not participate.

[Here], the prayer is delivered during the ceremonial portion of the town's meeting. Board members are not engaged in policymaking at this time, but in more general functions, such as swearing in new police officers, inducting high school athletes into the town hall of fame, and presenting proclamations to volunteers, civic groups, and senior citizens. It is a moment for town leaders to recognize the achievements of their constituents and the aspects of community life that are worth celebrating. By inviting ministers to serve as chaplain for the month, and welcoming them to the front of the room alongside civic leaders, the town is acknowledging the central place that religion, and religious institutions, hold in the lives of those present. Indeed, some congregations are not simply spiritual homes for town residents but also the provider of social services for citizens regardless of their beliefs. The inclusion of a brief, ceremonial prayer as part of a larger exercise in civic recognition suggests that its purpose and effect are to acknowledge religious leaders and the institutions they represent rather than to exclude or coerce nonbelievers.

Ceremonial prayer is but a recognition that, since this Nation was founded and until the present day, many Americans deem that their own existence must be understood by precepts far beyond the authority of government to alter or define and that willing participation in civic affairs can be consistent with a brief acknowledgment of their belief in a higher power, always with due respect for those who adhere to other beliefs. The prayer in this case has a permissible ceremonial purpose. It is not an unconstitutional establishment of religion.

\* \* \*

The town of Greece does not violate the First Amendment by opening its meetings with prayer that comports with our tradition and does not coerce participation by nonadherents. The judgment of the U.S. Court of Appeals for the Second Circuit is reversed.

*It is so ordered.*

[Concurring opinion of Justice Alito omitted.]

[Concurring opinion of Justice Thomas omitted.]

[Dissenting opinion of Justice Breyer omitted.]

Justice Kagan, with whom Justice Ginsburg, Justice Breyer, and Justice Sotomayor join, dissenting.

. . . I think the Town of Greece's prayer practices violate [the] norm of religious equality — the breathtakingly generous constitutional idea that our public institutions belong no less to the Buddhist or Hindu than to the Methodist or Episcopalian. I do not contend that principle translates here into a bright separationist line. To the contrary, I agree with the Court's decision in *Marsh*, upholding the Nebraska Legislature's tradition of beginning each session with a chaplain's prayer. And I believe that pluralism and inclusion in a town hall can satisfy the constitutional requirement of neutrality; such a forum need not become a religion-free zone. But still, the Town of Greece should lose this case. The practice at issue here differs from the one sustained in *Marsh* because Greece's town meetings involve participation by ordinary citizens, and the invocations given — directly to those citizens — were predominantly sectarian in content. Still more, Greece's Board did nothing to recognize religious diversity: In arranging for clergy members to open each meeting, the Town never sought (except briefly when this suit was filed) to involve, accommodate, or in any way reach out to adherents of non-Christian religions. So month in and month out for over a decade, prayers steeped in only one faith, addressed toward members of the public, commenced meetings to discuss local affairs and distribute government benefits. In my view, that practice does not square with the First Amendment's promise that every citizen, irrespective of her religion, owns an equal share in her government.

. . . I agree with the majority that the issue here is "whether the prayer practice in the Town of Greece fits within the tradition long followed in Congress and the state legislatures."

[Here, the town hall] is a kind of hybrid. Greece's Board indeed has legislative functions, as Congress and state assemblies do — and that means some opening prayers are allowed there. But . . . the Board's meetings are also occasions for ordinary citizens to engage with and petition their government, often on highly individualized matters. That feature calls for Board members to exercise special care to ensure that the prayers offered are inclusive — that they respect each and every member of the community as an equal citizen. But the Board, and the clergy members it selected, made no such effort. Instead, the prayers given in Greece, addressed directly to the Town's citizenry, were *more* sectarian, and *less* inclusive, than anything this Court sustained in *Marsh*. For those reasons, the prayer in Greece departs from the legislative tradition that the majority takes as its benchmark.

. . . *Marsh* upheld prayer addressed to legislators alone, in a proceeding in which citizens had no role — and even then, only when it did not "proselytize or advance" any single religion. It was that legislative prayer practice (not every prayer in a body exercising any legislative function) that the Court found constitutional given its "unambiguous and unbroken history." But that approved practice, as I have shown, is not Greece's. None of the history *Marsh* cited — and none the majority details today — supports calling on citizens to pray, in a manner consonant with only a single religion's beliefs, at a participatory public proceeding, having both legislative and adjudicative components. Or to use the majority's phrase, no "history shows that th[is] specific practice is permitted." And so, contra the majority, Greece's prayers cannot simply ride on the constitutional coattails of the legislative tradition *Marsh* described. The Board's practice must, in its own particulars, meet constitutional requirements.

And the guideposts for addressing that inquiry include the principles of religious neutrality. . . . The government (whether federal, state, or local) may not favor, or align itself with, any particular creed. And that is nowhere more true than when officials and citizens come face to face in their shared institutions of governance. In performing civic functions and seeking civic benefits, each person of this nation must experience a government that belongs to one and all, irrespective of belief. And for its part, each government must ensure that its participatory processes will not classify those citizens by faith, or make relevant their religious differences.

To decide how Greece fares on that score, think . . . about how its prayer practice works, meeting after meeting. . . . Let's say that a Muslim citizen of Greece goes before the Board to share her views on policy or request some permit. Maybe she wants the Board to put up a traffic light at a dangerous intersection; or maybe she needs a zoning variance to build an addition on her home. But just before she gets to say her piece, a minister deputized by the Town asks her to pray "in the name of God's only son Jesus Christ." She must think — it is hardly paranoia, but only the truth — that Christian worship has become entwined with local governance. And now she faces a choice — to pray alongside the majority as one of that group or somehow to register her deeply felt difference. She is a strong person, but that is no easy call — especially given that the room is small and her every action (or inaction) will be noticed. She does not wish to be rude to her neighbors, nor does she wish to aggravate the Board members whom she will soon be trying to persuade. And yet she does not want to acknowledge Christ's divinity, any more than many of her neighbors would want to deny that tenet. So assume she declines to participate with the others in the first act of the meeting — or even, as the majority proposes, that she stands up and leaves the room altogether. At the least, she becomes a different kind of citizen, one who will not join in the religious practice that the Town Board has chosen as reflecting its own and the community's most cherished beliefs. And she thus stands at a remove, based solely on religion, from her fellow citizens and her elected representatives.

Everything about that situation, I think, infringes the First Amendment. . . . That the Town Board selects, month after month and year after year, prayer-givers who will reliably speak in the voice of Christianity, and so places itself behind a single creed. That in offering those sectarian prayers, the Board's chosen clergy members repeatedly call on individuals, prior to participating in local governance, to join in a form of worship that may be at odds with their own beliefs. That the clergy thus put some residents to the unenviable choice of either pretending to pray like the majority or declining to join its communal activity, at the very moment of petitioning their elected leaders. That the practice thus divides the citizenry, creating one class that shares the Board's own evident religious beliefs and another (far smaller) class that does not. And that the practice also alters a dissenting citizen's relationship with her government, making her religious difference salient when she seeks only to engage her elected representatives as would any other citizen.

None of this means that Greece's town hall must be religion- or prayer-free. . . . When citizens of all faiths come to speak to each other and their elected representatives in a legislative session, the government must take especial care to ensure that the prayers they hear will seek to include, rather than serve to divide. No more is required — but that much is crucial — to treat every citizen, of whatever religion, as an equal participant in her government.

And contrary to the majority's . . . view, that is not difficult to do. If the Town Board had let its chaplains know that they should speak in nonsectarian terms, common to diverse religious groups, then no one would have valid grounds for complaint. Priests and ministers, rabbis and imams give such invocations all the time; there is no great mystery to the project. . . . Or if the Board preferred, it might have invited clergy of many faiths to serve as chaplains, as the majority notes that Congress does. When one month a clergy member refers to Jesus, and the next to Allah or Jehovah — as the majority hopefully though counterfactually suggests happened here — the government does not identify itself with one religion or align itself with that faith's citizens, and the effect of even sectarian prayer is transformed. So Greece had multiple ways of incorporating prayer into its town meetings — reflecting all the ways that prayer (as most of us know from daily life) can forge common bonds, rather than divide.

But Greece could not do what it did: infuse a participatory government body with one (and only one) faith, so that month in and month out, the citizens appearing before it become partly defined by their creed — as those who share, and those who do not, the community's majority religious belief. In this country, when citizens go before the government, they go not as Christians or Muslims or Jews (or what have you), but just as Americans (or here, as Grecians). That is what it means to be an equal citizen, irrespective of religion.

And that is what the Town of Greece precluded by so identifying itself with a single faith.

[T]he not-so-implicit message of the majority's opinion — "What's the big deal, anyway?" — is mistaken. The content of Greece's prayers *is* a big deal, to Christians and non-Christians alike. A person's response to the doctrine, language, and imagery contained in those invocations reveals a core aspect of identity — who that person is and how she faces the world. And the responses of different individuals, in Greece and across this country, of course vary. Contrary to the majority's apparent view, such sectarian prayers are not "part of our expressive idiom" or "part of our heritage and tradition," assuming the word "our" refers to all Americans. They express beliefs that are fundamental to some, foreign to others — and because that is so they carry the ever-present potential to both exclude and divide. The majority, I think, assesses too lightly the significance of these religious differences, and so fears too little the "religiously based divisiveness that the Establishment Clause seeks to avoid." *Van Orden v. Perry* (2005) (Breyer, J., concurring in judgment). I would treat more seriously the multiplicity of Americans' religious commitments, along with the challenge they can pose to the project — the distinctively American project — of creating one from the many, and governing all as united.

## NOTES AND QUESTIONS

**1.** Both the majority and the dissent in *Town of Greece* begin from the proposition that certain kinds of public religious events have attained a level of constitutional validity as a result of their historical pedigree. The question, then, is whether the prayers that open meetings of Greece's town board qualify for inclusion within this class of constitutionally acceptable public events. How do Justices Kennedy and Kagan each approach this question?

**2.** Justice Kennedy, in his opinion, asks whether any members of the audience who witnessed the prayer preceding the meetings would have felt coerced to observe an essentially religious ritual, in violation of the Establishment Clause. He is here applying what has become known as the "coercion test." In effect, the coercion test prohibits those publicly supported religious activities that effectively mandate participation: as Kennedy once put it, "the Constitution guarantees that government may not coerce anyone to support or participate in religion or its exercise." *Lee v. Weisman*, 505 U.S. 577 (1992). In applying the test here, note that Kennedy writes only for a plurality of the Court.

**3.** What we see in this case is differing applications of the kind of historical-practice analysis the Court has begun to embrace in respect to other individual rights provisions, like the Second Amendment. Can you identify the elements of that analysis in the Establishment Clause context? What facts would you need to know to argue that a particular public prayer event falls on one side or other of the constitutional line? Consider, for example, that all of the justices appear to agree that certain kinds of religious invocations at public ceremonies are constitutional — why?

**4.** The differences in outcome that the majority and dissent reach here seem to depend upon two considerations. First, how open-ended should the court's understanding of historical practice analysis be? Couldn't it be said of the historical-practice analysis that it might be easily manipulated by legislatures interested in subjugating religious minorities? Second, whose perspective should a court take in determining whether a particular practice strays too far from those which history has validated — the perspective of the prayer-proponents, or the prayer-opponents? If the latter, does the analysis threaten to stray into the question whether the state is promoting religious activity or coercing participation in religious activity?

**5.** In *American Legion v. Amerian Humanist Ass'n*, 588 U.S. ___ (2019), the Court addressed a challenge on Establishment Clause grounds to the display of a cross erected as a tribute to 49 soldiers who lost their lives in World War I. Justice Alito, writing for the plurality, ruled that the Court would, in evaluating such challenges, apply "a presumption of constitutionality for longstanding monuments, symbols, and practices." He explained the four considerations guiding the Court: First, "these cases often concern monuments, symbols, or practices that were first established long ago, and in such cases, identifying their original purpose or purposes may be especially difficult." Second, "as time goes by, the purposes associated with an established monument, symbol, or practice often multiply." Third, "just as the purpose for maintaining a monument, symbol, or practice may evolve, "[t]he 'message' conveyed ... may change over time." (quoting *Pleasant Grove City v. Summum* (2009)). Finally, "when time's passage imbues a religiously expressive monument, symbol, or practice with this kind of familiarity and historical significance, removing it may no longer appear neutral, especially to the local community for which it has taken on particular meaning." He concluded that the cross in question did not violate the Establishment Clause:

> The cross is undoubtedly a Christian symbol, but that fact should not blind us to everything else that the Bladensburg Cross has come to represent. For some, that monument is a symbolic resting place for ancestors who never returned home. For others, it is a place for the community to gather and honor all veterans and their sacrifices for our Nation. For others still, it is a historical landmark. For many of these people, destroying or defacing the Cross that has stood undisturbed for nearly a century would not be neutral and would not further the ideals of respect and tolerance embodied in the First Amendment. For all these reasons, the Cross does not offend the Constitution.

**6.** What, if any, are the benefits of these considerations to judicial evaluation of Establishment Clause claims? What are the potential detriments?

**7.** In the 2019 term, the Court addressed another aspect of the Establishment Clause's reach in *Lady of Guadalupe v. Morrissey-Berru*. There, the Court held that the Establishment Clause precludes judicial intervention in employment disputes "involving teachers at religious schools who are entrusted with the responsibility of instructing their students in the faith." The 7-2 decision expands the extent to which religious institutions are essentially immune from suit on the grounds of discrimination in employment.

## B. The Free Exercise Clause

### Employment Division v. Smith
### 494 U.S. 872 (1990)

Justice Scalia delivered the opinion of the Court.

This case requires us to decide whether the Free Exercise Clause of the First Amendment permits the State of Oregon to include religiously inspired peyote use within the reach of its general criminal prohibition on use of that drug, and thus permits the State to deny unemployment benefits to persons dismissed from their jobs because of such religiously inspired use.

### I

Oregon law prohibits the knowing or intentional possession of a "controlled substance" unless the substance has been prescribed by a medical practitioner. The law defines "controlled substance" as a drug classified in Schedules I through V of the Federal Controlled Substances Act, as modified by the State Board of Pharmacy. Persons who violate this provision by possessing a controlled substance listed on Schedule I are "guilty of a Class B felony." As compiled by the State Board of Pharmacy under its statutory authority, Schedule I contains the drug peyote, a hallucinogen. . . .

Respondents Alfred Smith and Galen Black (hereinafter respondents) were fired from their jobs with a private drug rehabilitation organization because they ingested peyote for sacramental purposes at a ceremony of the Native American Church, of which both are members. When respondents applied to petitioner Employment Division (hereinafter petitioner) for unemployment compensation, they were determined to be ineligible for benefits because they had been discharged for work-related "misconduct." The Oregon Court of Appeals reversed that determination, holding that the denial of benefits violated respondents' free exercise rights under the First Amendment.

On appeal to the Oregon Supreme Court, petitioner argued that the denial of benefits was permissible because respondents' consumption of peyote was a crime under Oregon law. [T]he court concluded that respondents were entitled to payment of unemployment benefits. We granted certiorari.

Before this Court in 1987, petitioner continued to maintain that the illegality of respondents' peyote consumption was relevant to their constitutional claim. We agreed, concluding that "if a State has prohibited through its criminal laws certain kinds of religiously motivated conduct without violating the First Amendment, it certainly follows that it may impose the lesser burden of denying unemployment compensation benefits to persons who engage in that conduct." *Employment Div., Dept. of Human Resources of Oregon v. Smith* (1988) (*Smith I*). We noted, however, that the Oregon Supreme Court had not decided whether respondents' sacramental use of peyote was in fact proscribed by Oregon's controlled substance law, and that this issue was a matter of dispute between the parties. . . . Accordingly, we vacated the judgment of the Oregon Supreme Court and remanded for further proceedings.

On remand, the Oregon Supreme Court held that respondents' religiously inspired use of peyote fell within the prohibition of the Oregon statute, which "makes no exception for the sacramental use" of the drug. It then considered whether that prohibition was valid under the Free Exercise Clause, and concluded that it was not. The court therefore reaffirmed its previous ruling that the State could not deny unemployment benefits to respondents for having engaged in that practice.

We again granted certiorari.

## II

[T]he Oregon Supreme Court has confirmed that Oregon does prohibit the religious use of peyote[;] we proceed to consider whether that prohibition is permissible under the Free Exercise Clause.

### A

The Free Exercise Clause of the First Amendment, which has been made applicable to the States by incorporation into the Fourteenth Amendment, provides that "Congress shall make no law respecting an establishment of religion, or *prohibiting the free exercise thereof.* . . ." U.S. Const., Amdt. 1 (emphasis added). The free exercise of religion means, first and foremost, the right to believe and profess whatever religious doctrine one desires. Thus, the First Amendment obviously excludes all "governmental regulation of religious *beliefs* as such." *Sherbert v. Verner* (1963). The government may not compel affirmation of religious belief, punish the expression of religious doctrines it believes to be false, impose special disabilities on the basis of religious views or religious status, or lend its power to one or the other side in controversies over religious authority or dogma.

But the "exercise of religion" often involves not only belief and profession but the performance of (or abstention from) physical acts: assembling with others for a worship service, participating in sacramental use of bread and wine, proselytizing, abstaining from certain foods or certain modes of transportation. It would be true, we think (though no case of ours has involved the point), that a State would be "prohibiting the free exercise [of religion]" if it sought to ban such acts or abstentions only when they are engaged in for religious reasons, or only because of the religious belief that they display. . . .

Respondents in the present case, however, seek to carry the meaning of "prohibiting the free exercise [of religion]" one large step further. . . . They assert . . . that "prohibiting the free exercise [of religion]" includes requiring any individual to observe a generally applicable law that requires (or forbids) the performance of an act that his religious belief forbids (or requires). As a textual matter, we do not think the words must be given that meaning. It is no more necessary to regard the collection of a general tax, for example, as "prohibiting the free exercise [of religion]" by those citizens who believe support of organized government to be sinful, than it is to regard the same tax as "abridging the freedom . . . of the press" of those publishing companies that must pay the tax as a condition of staying in business. It is a permissible reading of the text, in the one case as in the other, to say that if prohibiting the exercise of religion (or burdening the activity of printing) is not the object of the tax but merely the incidental effect of a generally applicable and otherwise valid provision, the First Amendment has not been offended.

Our decisions reveal that the latter reading is the correct one. We have never held that an individual's religious beliefs excuse him from compliance with an otherwise valid law prohibiting conduct that the State is free to regulate. On the contrary, the record of more than a century of our free exercise jurisprudence contradicts that proposition. . . . [In] *Reynolds v. United States* (1879), [for example,] we rejected the claim that criminal laws against polygamy could not be constitutionally applied to those whose religion commanded the practice. . . .

[T]he right of free exercise does not relieve an individual of the obligation to comply with a "valid and neutral law of general applicability on the ground that the law proscribes (or prescribes) conduct that his religion prescribes (or proscribes)." *United States v. Lee* (1982) (Stevens, J., concurring in judgment). . . . Our most recent decision involving a neutral, generally applicable regulatory law that compelled activity forbidden by an individual's religion was *United States v. Lee*. There, an Amish employer, on behalf of himself and his employees, sought exemption from collection and payment of Social Security taxes on the ground that the Amish faith prohibited participation in governmental support programs. We rejected the claim that an exemption was constitutionally required. There would be no way, we observed, to distinguish the Amish believer's objection to Social Security taxes from the religious objections that others might have to the collection or use of other taxes. . . .

Respondents urge us to hold, quite simply, that when otherwise prohibitable conduct is accompanied by religious convictions, not only the convictions but the conduct itself must be free from governmental regulation. We have never held that, and decline to do so now. There being no contention that Oregon's drug law represents an attempt to regulate religious beliefs, the communication of religious beliefs, or the raising of one's children in those beliefs, the rule to which we have adhered ever since *Reynolds* plainly controls. . . .

**B**

Respondents argue that even though exemption from generally applicable criminal laws need not automatically be extended to religiously motivated actors, at least the claim for a religious exemption must be evaluated under the balancing test set forth in

*Sherbert v. Verner.* Under the *Sherbert* test, governmental actions that substantially burden a religious practice must be justified by a compelling governmental interest. Applying that test we have, on three occasions, invalidated state unemployment compensation rules that conditioned the availability of benefits upon an applicant's willingness to work under conditions forbidden by his religion. . . .

Even if we were inclined to breathe into *Sherbert* some life beyond the unemployment compensation field, we would not apply it to require exemptions from a generally applicable criminal law. The *Sherbert* test, it must be recalled, was developed in a context that lent itself to individualized governmental assessment of the reasons for the relevant conduct. [A] distinctive feature of unemployment compensation programs is that their eligibility criteria invite consideration of the particular circumstances behind an applicant's unemployment. . . . [O]ur decisions in the unemployment cases stand for the proposition that where the State has in place a system of individual exemptions, it may not refuse to extend that system to cases of "religious hardship" without compelling reason.

Whether or not the decisions are that limited, they at least have nothing to do with an across-the-board criminal prohibition on a particular form of conduct. Although, as noted earlier, we have sometimes used the *Sherbert* test to analyze free exercise challenges to such laws, we have never applied the test to invalidate one. We conclude today that the sounder approach, and the approach in accord with the vast majority of our precedents, is to hold the test inapplicable to such challenges. The government's ability to enforce generally applicable prohibitions of socially harmful conduct, like its ability to carry out other aspects of public policy, "cannot depend on measuring the effects of a governmental action on a religious objector's spiritual development." *Lyng v. Northwest Indian Cemetery Protective Assn* (1988). To make an individual's obligation to obey such a law contingent upon the law's coincidence with his religious beliefs, except where the State's interest is "compelling" — permitting him, by virtue of his beliefs, "to become a law unto himself," *Reynolds* — contradicts both constitutional tradition and common sense.

The "compelling government interest" requirement seems benign, because it is familiar from other fields. But using it as the standard that must be met before the government may accord different treatment on the basis of race, or before the government may regulate the content of speech, is not remotely comparable to using it for the purpose asserted here. What it produces in those other fields — equality of treatment and an unrestricted flow of contending speech — are constitutional norms; what it would produce here — a private right to ignore generally applicable laws — is a constitutional anomaly.

Nor is it possible to limit the impact of respondents' proposal by requiring a "compelling state interest" only when the conduct prohibited is "central" to the individual's religion. It is no more appropriate for judges to determine the "centrality" of religious beliefs before applying a "compelling interest" test in the free exercise field, than it would be for them to determine the "importance" of ideas before applying the "compelling interest" test in the free speech field. What principle of law or logic can be brought to bear to contradict a believer's assertion that a particular act is "central" to his personal faith? . . . Repeatedly and in many different contexts, we have warned that courts must not presume to determine the place of a particular belief in a religion or the plausibility of a religious claim.

If the "compelling interest" test is to be applied at all, then, it must be applied across the board, to all actions thought to be religiously commanded. Moreover, if "compelling interest" really means what it says (and watering it down here would subvert its rigor in the other fields where it is applied), many laws will not meet the test. Any society adopting such a system would be courting anarchy, but that danger increases in direct proportion to the society's diversity of religious beliefs, and its determination to coerce or suppress none of them. Precisely because . . . we value and protect . . . religious divergence, we cannot afford the luxury of deeming *presumptively invalid*, as applied to the religious objector, every regulation of conduct that does not protect an interest of the highest order. The rule respondents favor would open the prospect of constitutionally required religious exemptions from civic obligations of almost every conceivable kind — ranging from compulsory military service, to the payment of taxes, to health and safety regulation such as manslaughter and child neglect laws, compulsory vaccination laws, drug laws, and traffic laws, to social welfare legislation such as minimum wage laws, child labor laws, animal cruelty laws, and laws providing for equality of opportunity for the races. The First Amendment's protection of religious liberty does not require this.

Values that are protected against government interference through enshrinement in the Bill of Rights are not thereby banished from the political process. Just as a society that believes in the negative protection accorded to the press by the First Amendment is likely to enact laws that affirmatively foster the dissemination of the printed word, so also a society that believes in the negative protection accorded to religious belief can be expected to be solicitous of that value in its legislation as well. It is therefore not surprising that a number of States have made an exception to their drug laws for sacramental peyote use. But to say that a nondiscriminatory religious-practice exemption is permitted, or even that it is desirable, is not to say that it is constitutionally required, and that the appropriate occasions for its creation can be discerned by the courts. It may fairly be said that leaving accommodation to the political process will place at a relative disadvantage those religious practices that are not widely engaged in; but that unavoidable consequence of democratic government must be preferred to a system in which each conscience is a law unto itself or in which judges weigh the social importance of all laws against the centrality of all religious beliefs.

\* \* \*

Because respondents' ingestion of peyote was prohibited under Oregon law, and because that prohibition is constitutional, Oregon may, consistent with the Free Exercise Clause, deny respondents unemployment compensation when their dismissal results from use of the drug. The decision of the Oregon Supreme Court is accordingly reversed.

*It is so ordered.*

[Concurring opinion of Justice O'Connor omitted.]

[Dissenting opinion of Justice Blackmun omitted.]

## NOTES AND QUESTIONS

**1.** The majority opinion does not apply strict scrutiny — or any kind of heightened scrutiny — to the Oregon law prohibiting peyote use. Following *Smith*, in what situations might a court apply heightened scrutiny to a claimed violation of the right to free exercise of one's religion? Does *Smith* essentially obviate the possibility of a federal judicial remedy when free exercise rights are undermined? To whom would the majority urge the aggrieved to appeal?

**2.** Generally applicable laws, of course, typically reflect generally applicable norms. What is the likelihood such a law would affect the exercise of religious conduct associated with any mainstream Christian religion? In light of your answer to that question, can you draw a connection between *Smith*, and its reorientation of free exercise jurisprudence, and *Washington v. Davis* (1986), which we read in the last chapter, and which served to fundamentally reorient the Supreme Court's equal protection jurisprudence?

**3.** Though *Smith* served to significantly re-orient free exercise jurisprudence, the Court soon began to retreat from its broadest implications.

### Church of the Lukumi Babalu Aye v. City of Hialeah
### 508 U.S. 520 (1993)

Justice Kennedy delivered the opinion of the Court.

The principle that government may not enact laws that suppress religious belief or practice is so well understood that few violations are recorded in our opinions. Concerned that this fundamental nonpersecution principle of the First Amendment was implicated here, however, we granted certiorari.

Our review confirms that the laws in question were enacted by officials who did not understand, failed to perceive, or chose to ignore the fact that their official actions violated the Nation's essential commitment to religious freedom. The challenged laws had an impermissible object; and in all events the principle of general applicability was violated because the secular ends asserted in defense of the laws were pursued only with respect to conduct motivated by religious beliefs. We invalidate the challenged enactments and reverse the judgment of the Court of Appeals.

## I

Petitioner Church of the Lukumi Babalu Aye, Inc. (Church), is a not-for-profit corporation organized under Florida law in 1973. The Church and its congregants practice the Santeria religion. The president of the Church is petitioner Ernesto Pichardo, who is also the Church's priest and holds the religious title of *Italero*, the second highest in the Santeria faith. In April 1987, the Church leased land in the city of Hialeah, Florida, and announced plans to establish a house of worship as well as a school, cultural center, and museum. Pichardo indicated that the Church's goal was to bring the practice of the Santeria faith, including its ritual of animal sacrifice, into the open. The Church began the process of obtaining utility service and receiving the necessary licensing, inspection, and zoning approvals. Although the Church's efforts at obtaining the necessary licenses and permits were far from smooth, it appears that it received all needed approvals by early August 1987.

The prospect of a Santeria church in their midst was distressing to many members of the Hialeah community, and the announcement of the plans to open a Santeria church in Hialeah prompted the city council to hold an emergency public session on June 9, 1987. . . .

A summary suffices here, beginning with the enactments passed at the June 9 meeting. First, the city council adopted Resolution 87-66, which noted the "concern" expressed by residents of the city "that certain religions may propose to engage in practices which are inconsistent with public morals, peace or safety," and declared that "[t]he City reiterates its commitment to a prohibition against any and all acts of any and all religious groups which are inconsistent with public morals, peace or safety." Next, the council approved an emergency ordinance, which incorporated in full, except as to penalty, Florida's animal cruelty laws. Among other things, the incorporated state law subjected to criminal punishment "[w]hoever . . . unnecessarily or cruelly . . . kills any animal."

The city council desired to undertake further legislative action, but Florida law prohibited a municipality from enacting legislation relating to animal cruelty that conflicted with state law. To obtain clarification, Hialeah's city attorney requested an opinion from the attorney general of Florida as to whether § 828.12 prohibited "a religious group from sacrificing an animal in a religious ritual or practice" and whether the city could enact ordinances "making religious animal sacrifice unlawful." The attorney general . . . advised that religious animal sacrifice was against state law, so that a city ordinance prohibiting it would not be in conflict.

The city council responded at first with a hortatory enactment, Resolution 87-90, that noted its residents' "great concern regarding the possibility of public ritualistic animal sacrifices" and the state-law prohibition. The resolution declared the city policy "to oppose the ritual sacrifices of animals" within Hialeah and announced that any person or organization practicing animal sacrifice "will be prosecuted."

In September 1987, the city council adopted three substantive ordinances addressing the issue of religious animal sacrifice. Ordinance 87-52 defined "sacrifice" as "to unnecessarily kill, torment, torture, or mutilate an animal in a public or private ritual or ceremony not for the primary purpose of food consumption," and prohibited owning or possessing an animal "intending to use such animal for food purposes." It restricted application of this prohibition, however, to any individual or group that "kills, slaughters or sacrifices animals for any type of ritual, regardless of whether or not the flesh or blood of the animal is to be consumed." The ordinance contained an exemption for slaughtering by "licensed establishment[s]" of animals "specifically raised for food purposes." Declaring, moreover, that the city council "has determined that the sacrificing of animals within the city limits is contrary to the public health, safety, welfare and morals of the community," the city council adopted Ordinance 87-71. That ordinance defined "sacrifice" as had Ordinance 87-52, and then provided that "[i]t shall be unlawful for any person, persons, corporations or associations to sacrifice any animal within the corporate limits of the City of Hialeah, Florida." The final Ordinance, 87-72, defined "slaughter" as "the killing of animals for food" and prohibited slaughter outside of areas zoned for slaughterhouse use. The ordinance provided an exemption, however, for the slaughter or processing for sale of "small numbers of hogs and/or cattle per week in accordance with an exemption provided by state law." All ordinances and resolutions passed the city council by unanimous vote. Violations of each of the four ordinances were punishable by fines not exceeding $500 or imprisonment not exceeding 60 days, or both.

Following enactment of these ordinances, the Church and Pichardo filed this action . . . in the United States District Court for the Southern District of Florida. . . . [T]he District Court [upheld the prohibition on ritual sacrifice and the] Court of Appeals for the Eleventh Circuit affirmed in a one-paragraph *per curiam* opinion. [T]he Court of Appeals stated simply that it concluded the ordinances were consistent with the Constitution. . . .

## II

The Free Exercise Clause of the First Amendment, which has been applied to the States through the Fourteenth Amendment, provides that "Congress shall make no law respecting an establishment of religion, or *prohibiting the free exercise thereof.* . . ." (Emphasis added.) The city does not argue that Santeria is not a "religion" within the meaning of the First Amendment. Nor could it. Although the practice of animal sacrifice may seem abhorrent to some, "religious beliefs need not be acceptable, logical, consistent, or comprehensible to others in order to merit First Amendment protection." *Thomas v. Review Bd. of Indiana Employment Security Div.* (1981). . . . Neither the city nor the courts below, moreover, have [sic] questioned the sincerity of petitioners' professed desire to conduct animal sacrifices for religious reasons. . . .

In addressing the constitutional protection for free exercise of religion, our cases establish the general proposition that a law that is neutral and of general applicability need not be justified by a compelling governmental interest even if the law has the incidental effect of burdening a particular religious practice. Neutrality and general applicability are interrelated, and, as becomes apparent in this case, failure to satisfy one requirement is a likely indication that the other has not been satisfied. A law failing to satisfy these requirements must be justified by a compelling governmental interest and must be narrowly tailored to advance that interest. These ordinances fail to satisfy the *Smith* requirements. We begin by discussing neutrality.

### A

[I]f the object of a law is to infringe upon or restrict practices because of their religious motivation, the law is not neutral, and it is invalid unless it is justified by a compelling interest and is narrowly tailored to advance that interest. There are, of course, many ways of demonstrating that the object or purpose of a law is the suppression of religion or religious conduct. . . .

We reject the contention advanced by the city that our inquiry must end with the text of the laws at issue. Facial neutrality is not determinative. The Free Exercise Clause ... "forbids subtle departures from neutrality," *Gilette v. United States* (1971), and "covert suppression of particular religious beliefs," *Bowen v. Roy* (1986) (opinion of Burger, C.J.). Official action that targets religious conduct for distinctive treatment cannot be shielded by mere compliance with the requirement of facial neutrality. . . .

The record in this case compels the conclusion that suppression of the central element of the Santeria worship service was the object of the ordinances. First, though use of the words "sacrifice" and "ritual" does not compel a finding of improper targeting of the Santeria religion, the choice of these words is support for our conclusion. There are further respects in which the text of the city council's enactments discloses the improper attempt to target Santeria. Resolution 87-66, adopted June 9, 1987, recited that "residents and citizens of the City of Hialeah have expressed their concern that certain religions may propose to engage in practices which are inconsistent with public morals, peace or safety," and "reiterate[d]" the city's commitment to prohibit "any and all [such] acts of any and all religious groups." No one suggests, and on this record it cannot be maintained, that city officials had in mind a religion other than Santeria.

It becomes evident that these ordinances target Santeria sacrifice when the ordinances' operation is considered. Apart from the text, the effect of a law in its real operation is strong evidence of its object. . . . [Here,] the ordinances when considered together disclose an object remote from these legitimate concerns. The design of these laws accomplishes . . . an impermissible attempt to target petitioners and their religious practices.

It is a necessary conclusion that almost the only conduct subject to Ordinances 87-40, 87-52, and 87-71 is the religious exercise of Santeria church members. The texts show that they were drafted in tandem to achieve this result. We begin with Ordinance 87-71. It prohibits the sacrifice of animals, but defines sacrifice as "to unnecessarily kill . . . an animal in a public or private ritual or ceremony not for the primary purpose of food consumption." The definition excludes almost all killings of animals except for religious sacrifice, and the primary purpose requirement narrows the proscribed category even further, in particular by exempting kosher slaughter. . . . The net result . . . is that few if any killings of animals are prohibited other than Santeria sacrifice, which is proscribed because it occurs during a ritual or ceremony and its primary purpose is . . . not food consumption. Indeed, careful drafting ensured that, although Santeria sacrifice is prohibited, killings that are no more necessary or humane in almost all other circumstances are unpunished.

Operating in similar fashion is Ordinance 87-52, which prohibits the "possess[ion], sacrifice, or slaughter" of an animal with the "inten[t] to use such animal for food purposes." This prohibition, extending to the keeping of an animal as well as the killing itself, applies if the animal is killed in "any type of ritual" and there is an intent to use the animal for food, whether or not it is in fact consumed for food. The ordinance exempts, however, "any licensed [food] establishment" with regard to "any animals which are specifically raised for food purposes," if the activity is permitted by zoning and other laws. This exception, too, seems intended to cover kosher slaughter. Again, the burden of the ordinance, in practical terms, falls on Santeria adherents but almost no others: If the killing is — unlike most Santeria sacrifices — unaccompanied by the intent to use the animal for food, then it is not prohibited by Ordinance 87-52; if the killing is specifically for food but does not occur during the course of "any type of ritual," it again falls outside the prohibition; and if the killing is for food and occurs during the course of a ritual, it is still exempted if it occurs in a properly zoned and licensed establishment and involves animals "specifically raised for food purposes." . . .

Ordinance 87-40 incorporates the Florida animal cruelty statute, Fla. Stat. § 828.12 (1987). Its prohibition is broad on its face, punishing "[w]hoever . . . unnecessarily . . . kills any animal." The city claims that this ordinance is the epitome of a neutral prohibition. The problem, however, is the interpretation given to the ordinance by respondent and the Florida attorney general. Killings for religious reasons are deemed unnecessary, whereas most other killings fall outside the prohibition. The city, on what seems to be a *per se* basis, deems hunting, slaughter of animals for food, eradication of insects and pests, and euthanasia as necessary. There is no indication in the record that respondent has concluded that hunting or fishing for sport is unnecessary. . . . As we noted in *Employment Div., Dept. of Human Resources of Ore. v. Smith* (1990), in circumstances in which individualized exemptions from a general requirement are available, the government "may not refuse to extend that system to cases of 'religious hardship' without compelling reason." Respondent's application of the ordinance's test of necessity devalues religious reasons for killing by judging them to be of lesser import than nonreligious reasons. Thus, religious practice is being singled out for discriminatory treatment.

We also find significant evidence of the ordinances' improper targeting of Santeria sacrifice in the fact that they proscribe more religious conduct than is necessary to achieve their stated ends. . . . The legitimate governmental interests in protecting the public health and preventing cruelty to animals could be addressed by restrictions stopping far short of a flat prohibition of all Santeria sacrificial practice. If improper disposal, not the sacrifice itself, is the harm to be prevented, the city could have imposed a general regulation on the disposal of organic garbage. It did not do so. Indeed, counsel for the city conceded at oral argument that, under the ordinances, Santeria sacrifices would be illegal even if they occurred in licensed, inspected, and zoned slaughterhouses. Thus, these broad ordinances prohibit Santeria sacrifice even when it does not threaten the city's interest in the public health. . . .

Under similar analysis, narrower regulation would achieve the city's interest in preventing cruelty to animals. With regard to the city's interest in ensuring the adequate care of animals, regulation of conditions and treatment, regardless of why an animal is kept, is the logical response to the city's concern, not a prohibition on possession for the purpose of sacrifice. The same is true for the city's interest in prohibiting cruel methods of killing. Under federal and Florida law and Ordinance 87-40, which incorporates Florida law in this regard, killing an animal by the "simultaneous and instantaneous severance of the carotid arteries with a sharp instrument" — the method used in kosher slaughter — is approved as humane. . . . If the city has a real concern that other methods are less humane, however, the subject of the regulation should be the method of slaughter itself, not a religious classification that is said to bear some general relation to it.

Ordinance 87-72 — unlike the three other ordinances — does appear to apply to substantial nonreligious conduct and not to be overbroad. For our purposes here, however, the four substantive ordinances may be treated as a group for neutrality purposes. Ordinance 87-72 was passed the same day as Ordinance 87-71 and was enacted, as were the three others, in direct response to the opening of the Church. It would be implausible to suggest that the three other ordinances, but not Ordinance 87-72, had as their object the suppression of religion. We need not decide whether Ordinance 87-72 could survive constitutional scrutiny if it existed separately; it must be invalidated because it functions, with the rest of the enactments in question, to suppress Santeria religious worship.

[Here], the neutrality inquiry leads to one conclusion: The ordinances had as their object the suppression of religion. The pattern we have recited discloses animosity to Santeria adherents and their religious practices; the ordinances by their own terms target this religious exercise; the texts of the ordinances were gerrymandered with care to proscribe religious killings of animals but to exclude almost all secular killings; and the ordinances suppress much more religious conduct than is necessary in order to achieve the legitimate ends asserted in their defense. These ordinances are not neutral, and the court below committed clear error in failing to reach this conclusion.

**B**

We turn next to a second requirement of the Free Exercise Clause, the rule that laws burdening religious practice must be of general applicability. . . . The principle that government, in pursuit of legitimate interests, cannot in a selective manner impose burdens only on conduct motivated by religious belief is essential to the protection of the rights guaranteed by the Free Exercise Clause. . . . In this case we need not define with precision the standard used to evaluate whether a prohibition is of general application, for these ordinances fall well below the minimum standard necessary to protect First Amendment rights.

Respondent claims that Ordinances 87-40, 87-52, and 87-71 advance two interests: protecting the public health and preventing cruelty to animals. The ordinances are underinclusive for those ends. They fail to prohibit nonreligious conduct that endangers these interests in a similar or greater degree than Santeria sacrifice does. The underinclusion is substantial, not inconsequential. Despite the city's proffered interest in preventing cruelty to animals, the ordinances are drafted with care to forbid few killings but those occasioned by religious sacrifice. Many types of animal deaths or kills for nonreligious reasons are either not prohibited or approved by express provision. For example, fishing — which occurs in Hialeah — is legal. Extermination of mice and rats within a home is also permitted. Florida law incorporated by Ordinance 87-40 sanctions euthanasia of "stray, neglected, abandoned, or unwanted animals"; destruction of animals judicially removed from their owners "for humanitarian reasons" or when the animal "is of no commercial value"; the infliction of pain or suffering "in the interest of medical science"; the placing of poison in one's yard or enclosure; and the use of a live animal "to pursue or take wildlife or to participate in any hunting," and "to hunt wild hogs."

The city . . . asserts, however, that animal sacrifice is "different" from the animal killings that are permitted by law. According to the city, it is "self-evident" that killing animals for food is "important"; the eradication of insects and pests is "obviously justified"; and the euthanasia of excess animals "makes sense." These *ipse dixits* do not explain why religion alone must bear the burden of the ordinances, when many of these secular killings fall within the city's interest in preventing the cruel treatment of animals.

The ordinances are also underinclusive with regard to the city's interest in public health, which is threatened by the disposal of animal carcasses in open public places and the consumption of uninspected meat. Neither interest is pursued by respondent with regard to conduct that is not motivated by religious conviction. The health risks posed by the improper disposal of animal carcasses are the same whether

Santeria sacrifice or some nonreligious killing preceded it. The city does not, however, prohibit hunters from bringing their kill to their houses, nor does it regulate disposal after their activity. Despite substantial testimony at trial that the same public health hazards result from improper disposal of garbage by restaurants, restaurants are outside the scope of the ordinances. Improper disposal is a general problem that causes substantial health risks, but which respondent addresses only when it results from religious exercise.

The ordinances are underinclusive as well with regard to the health risk posed by consumption of uninspected meat. Under the city's ordinances, hunters may eat their kill and fishermen may eat their catch without undergoing governmental inspection. Likewise, state law requires inspection of meat that is sold but exempts meat from animals raised for the use of the owner and "members of his household and nonpaying guests and employees." The asserted interest in inspected meat is not pursued in contexts similar to that of religious animal sacrifice.

Ordinance 87-72, which prohibits the slaughter of animals outside of areas zoned for slaughterhouses, is underinclusive on its face. The ordinance includes an exemption for "any person, group, or organization" that "slaughters or processes for sale, small numbers of hogs and/or cattle per week in accordance with an exemption provided by state law." Respondent has not explained why commercial operations that slaughter "small numbers" of hogs and cattle do not implicate its professed desire to prevent cruelty to animals and preserve the public health. Although the city has classified Santeria sacrifice as slaughter, subjecting it to this ordinance, it does not regulate other killings for food in like manner.

We conclude, in sum, that each of Hialeah's ordinances pursues the city's governmental interests only against conduct motivated by religious belief. . . .

### III

A law burdening religious practice that is not neutral or not of general application must undergo the most rigorous of scrutiny. [*Wisconsin v. Yoder* (1972).] . . . A law that targets religious conduct for distinctive treatment or advances legitimate governmental interests only against conduct with a religious motivation will survive strict scrutiny only in rare cases. It follows from what we have already said that these ordinances cannot withstand this scrutiny.

First, even were the governmental interests compelling, the ordinances are not drawn in narrow terms to accomplish those interests. As we have discussed, all four ordinances are overbroad or underinclusive in substantial respects. The proffered objectives are not pursued with respect to analogous nonreligious conduct, and those interests could be achieved by narrower ordinances that burdened religion to a far lesser degree. The absence of narrow tailoring suffices to establish the invalidity of the ordinances.

Respondent has not demonstrated, moreover, that, in the context of these ordinances, its governmental interests are compelling. Where government restricts only conduct protected by the First Amendment and fails to enact feasible measures to restrict other conduct producing substantial harm or alleged harm of the same sort, the interest given in justification of the restriction is not compelling. . . .

*Reversed.*

[Concurring opinion of Justice Scalia omitted.]

[Concurring opinion of Justice Souter omitted.]

[Concurring opinion of Justice Blackmun omitted.]

## NOTES AND QUESTIONS

**1.** *Church of the Lukumi Babalu Aye* clears up some of the confusion created by *Employment Division v. Smith* (1989), at least as to when a court will apply heightened scrutiny to an alleged free exercise violation. Again, note that the initial requirement that must be satisfied in such a challenge is whether a genuinely religious belief or practice has been placed at risk by the law in question. In no case have we seen the government challenge the legitimacy of a religious practice or belief; neither has the Supreme Court second-guessed such legitimacy. Why might that be so? Does that mean that *any* asserted religious practice or belief will (or should) qualify for free exercise protection?

**2.** As Justice Kennedy explains in the majority opinion, free exercise claims essentially may receive two kinds of judicial scrutiny: highly deferential review should the challenged law prove to be neutral and generally applicable, and strict scrutiny when the law proves not to be. In this case, why were the city's laws, considered together, neither neutral nor generally applicable? Following that determination, was there much left for the Court to analyze in respect to the law's constitutionality?

**3.** If the criminal law in *Smith* prohibiting the use of certain drugs generally had nonetheless contained individualized exceptions legalizing their use for, say, scientific experiments about the long-term effects of using certain drugs, or for treatment of certain kinds of psychological conditions, would the absence of an exception for religious use necessarily have meant the law was not neutral? What does it mean for an exception to be "individualized"?

### Roman Catholic Diocese of Brooklyn v. Cuomo
### 592 U.S. ___ (2020)

PER CURIAM.

The application for injunctive relief presented to JUSTICE BREYER and by him referred to the Court is granted. Respondent is enjoined from enforcing Executive Order 202.68's 10- and 25-person occupancy limits on applicant pending disposition of the appeal in the United States Court of Appeals for the Second Circuit and disposition of the petition for a writ of certiorari, if such writ is timely sought. Should the petition for a writ of certiorari be denied, this order shall terminate automatically. In the event the petition for a writ of certiorari is granted, the order shall terminate upon the sending down of the judgment of this Court.

* * * * * *

This emergency application and another, Agudath Israel of America, et al. v. Cuomo, present the same issue, and this opinion addresses both cases.

Both applications seek relief from an Executive Order issued by the Governor of New York that imposes very severe restrictions on attendance at religious services in areas classified as "red" or "orange" zones. In red zones, no more than 10 persons may attend each religious service, and in orange zones, attendance is capped at 25. The two applications, one filed by the Roman Catholic Diocese of Brooklyn and the other by Agudath Israel of America and affiliated entities, contend that these restrictions violate the Free Exercise Clause of the First Amendment, and they ask us to enjoin enforcement of the restrictions while they pursue appellate review. Citing a variety of remarks made by the Governor, Agudath Israel argues that the Governor specifically targeted the Orthodox Jewish community and gerrymandered the boundaries of red and orange zones to ensure that heavily Orthodox areas were included. Both the Diocese and Agudath Israel maintain that the regulations treat houses of worship much more harshly than comparable secular facilities. And they tell us without contradiction that they have complied with all public health guidance, have implemented additional precautionary measures, and have operated at 25% or 33% capacity for months without a single outbreak.

The applicants have clearly established their entitlement to relief pending appellate review. They have shown that their First Amendment claims are likely to prevail, that denying them relief would lead to irreparable injury, and that granting relief would not harm the public interest. Because of the need to issue an order promptly, we provide only a brief summary of the reasons why immediate relief is essential.

*Likelihood of success on the merits.* The applicants have made a strong showing that the challenged restrictions violate "the minimum requirement of neutrality" to religion. *Church of Lukumi Babalu Aye, Inc. v. Hialeah* (1993). As noted by the dissent in the court below, statements made in connection with the challenged rules can be viewed as targeting the "ultra-Orthodox [Jewish] community." (Park, J., dissenting). But even if we put those comments aside, the regulations cannot be viewed as neutral because they single out houses of worship for especially harsh treatment.

In a red zone, while a synagogue or church may not admit more than 10 persons, businesses categorized as "essential" may admit as many people as they wish. And the list of "essential" businesses includes things such as acupuncture facilities, camp grounds, garages, as well as many whose services are not limited to those that can be regarded as essential, such as all plants manufacturing chemicals and microelectronics and all transportation facilities. The disparate treatment is even more striking in an orange zone. While attendance at houses of worship is limited to 25 persons, even non-essential businesses may decide for themselves how many persons to admit.

These categorizations lead to troubling results. At the hearing in the District Court, a health department official testified about a large store in Brooklyn that could "literally have hundreds of people shopping there on any given day." Yet a nearby church or synagogue would be prohibited from allowing more than 10 or 25 people inside for a worship service. And the Governor has stated that factories and schools have contributed to the spread of COVID-19, but they are treated less harshly than the Diocese's churches and Agudath Israel's synagogues, which have admirable safety records.

Because the challenged restrictions are not "neutral" and of "general applicability," they must satisfy "strict scrutiny," and this means that they must be "narrowly tailored" to serve a "compelling" state interest. *Church of Lukumi*. Stemming the spread of COVID-19 is unquestionably a compelling interest, but it is hard to see how the challenged regulations can be regarded as "narrowly tailored." They are far more restrictive than any COVID-related regulations that have previously come before the Court, much tighter than those adopted by many other jurisdictions hard-hit by the pandemic, and far more severe than has been shown to be required to prevent the spread of the virus at the applicants' services. The District Court noted that "there ha[d] not been any COVID-19 outbreak in any of the Diocese's churches since they reopened," and it praised the Diocese's record in combatting the spread of the disease. It found that the Diocese had been constantly "ahead of the curve, enforcing stricter safety protocols than the State required." Similarly, Agudath Israel notes that "[t]he Governor does not dispute that [it] ha[s] rigorously implemented and adhered to all health protocols and that there has been no outbreak of COVID-19 in [its] congregations."

Not only is there no evidence that the applicants have contributed to the spread of COVID-19 but there are many other less restrictive rules that could be adopted to minimize the risk to those attending religious services. Among other things, the maximum attendance at a religious service could be tied to the size of the church or synagogue. Almost all of the 26 Diocese churches immediately affected by the Executive Order can seat at least 500 people, about 14 can accommodate at least 700, and 2 can seat over 1,000. Similarly, Agudath Israel of Kew Garden Hills can seat up to 400. It is hard to believe that admitting more than 10 people to a 1,000-seat church or 400-seat synagogue would create a more serious health risk than the many other activities that the State allows. [Valid point]

*Irreparable harm.* There can be no question that the challenged restrictions, if enforced, will cause irreparable harm. "The loss of First Amendment freedoms, for even minimal periods of time, unquestionably constitutes irreparable injury." *Elrod v. Burns* (1976) (plurality). If only 10 people are admitted to each service, the great majority of those who wish to attend Mass on Sunday or services in a synagogue on Shabbat will be barred. And while those who are shut out may in some instances be able to watch services on television, such remote viewing is not the same as personal attendance. Catholics who watch a Mass at home cannot receive communion, and there are important religious traditions in the Orthodox Jewish faith that require personal attendance.

*Public interest.* Finally, it has not been shown that granting the applications will harm the public. As noted, the State has not claimed that attendance at the applicants' services has resulted in the spread of the disease. And the State has not shown that public health would be imperiled if less restrictive measures were imposed.

Members of this Court are not public health experts, and we should respect the judgment of those with special expertise and responsibility in this area. But even in a pandemic, the Constitution cannot be put away and forgotten. The restrictions at issue here, by effectively barring many from attending religious services, strike at the very heart of the First Amendment's guarantee of religious liberty. Before allowing this to occur, we have a duty to conduct a serious examination of the need for such a drastic measure.

The dissenting opinions argue that we should withhold relief because the relevant circumstances have now changed. After the applicants asked this Court for relief, the Governor reclassified the areas in question from orange to yellow, and this change means that the applicants may hold services at 50% of their maximum occupancy. The dissents would deny relief at this time but allow the Diocese and Agudath Israel to renew their requests if this recent reclassification is reversed.

There is no justification for that proposed course of action. It is clear that this matter is not moot. And injunctive relief is still called for because the applicants remain under a constant threat that the area in question will be reclassified as red or orange. The Governor regularly changes the classification of particular areas without prior notice. If that occurs again, the reclassification will almost certainly bar individuals in the affected area from attending services before judicial relief can be obtained. At most Catholic churches, Mass is celebrated daily, and "Orthodox Jews pray in [Agudath Israel's] synagogues every day." Moreover, if reclassification occurs late in a week, as has happened in the past, there may not be time for applicants to seek and obtain relief from this Court before another Sabbath passes. Thirteen days have gone by since the Diocese filed its application, and Agudath Israel's application was filed over a week ago. While we could presumably act more swiftly in the future, there is no guarantee that we could provide relief before another weekend passes. The applicants have made the showing needed to obtain relief, and there is no reason why they should bear the risk of suffering further irreparable harm in the event of another reclassification.

For these reasons, we hold that enforcement of the Governor's severe restrictions on the applicants' religious services must be enjoined.

*It is so ordered.*

Justice GORSUCH, concurring.

Government is not free to disregard the First Amendment in times of crisis. At a minimum, that Amendment prohibits government officials from treating religious exercises worse than comparable secular activities, unless they are pursuing a compelling interest and using the least restrictive means available. Yet recently, during the COVID pandemic, certain States seem to have ignored these long-settled principles.

Today's case supplies just the latest example. New York's Governor has asserted the power to assign different color codes to different parts of the State and govern each by executive decree. In "red zones," houses of worship are all but closed—limited to a maximum of 10 people. In the Orthodox Jewish community that limit might operate to exclude all women, considering 10 men are necessary to establish a *minyan,* or a quorum. In "orange zones," it's not much different. Churches and synagogues are limited to a maximum of 25 people. These restrictions apply even to the largest cathedrals and synagogues, which ordinarily hold hundreds. And the restrictions apply no matter the precautions taken, including social distancing, wearing masks, leaving doors and windows open, forgoing singing, and disinfecting spaces between services.

At the same time, the Governor has chosen to impose *no* capacity restrictions on certain businesses he considers "essential." And it turns out the businesses the Governor considers essential include hardware stores, acupuncturists, and liquor stores. Bicycle repair shops, certain signage companies, accountants, lawyers, and insurance agents are all essential too. So, at least according to the Governor, it may be unsafe to go to church, but it is always fine to pick up another bottle of wine, shop for a new bike, or spend the afternoon exploring your distal points and meridians. Who knew public health would so perfectly align with secular convenience?

As almost everyone on the Court today recognizes, squaring the Governor's edicts with our traditional First Amendment rules is no easy task. People may gather inside for extended periods in bus stations and airports, in laundromats and banks, in hardware stores and liquor shops. No apparent reason exists why people may not gather, subject to identical restrictions, in churches or synagogues, especially when religious institutions have made plain that they stand ready, able, and willing to follow all the safety precautions required of "essential" businesses and perhaps more besides. The only explanation for treating religious places differently seems to be a judgment that what happens there just isn't as "essential" as what happens in secular spaces. Indeed, the Governor is remarkably frank about this: In his judgment laundry and liquor, travel and tools, are all "essential" while traditional religious exercises are not. *That* is exactly the kind of discrimination the First Amendment forbids.

It is time—past time—to make plain that, while the pandemic poses many grave challenges, there is no world in which the Constitution tolerates color-coded executive edicts that reopen liquor stores and bike shops but shutter churches, synagogues, and mosques.

Justice KAVANAUGH, concurring.

The State's discrimination against religion raises a serious First Amendment issue and triggers heightened scrutiny, requiring the State to provide a sufficient justification for the discrimination. But New

York has not sufficiently justified treating houses of worship more severely than secular businesses.

The State argues that it has not impermissibly discriminated against religion because some secular businesses such as movie theaters must remain closed and are thus treated less favorably than houses of worship. But under this Court's precedents, it does not suffice for a State to point out that, as compared to houses of worship, *some* secular businesses are subject to similarly severe or even more severe restrictions. Rather, once a State creates a favored class of businesses, as New York has done in this case, the State must justify why houses of worship are excluded from that favored class. Here, therefore, the State must justify imposing a 10-person or 25-person limit on houses of worship but not on favored secular businesses. The State has not done so.

To be clear, the COVID-19 pandemic remains extraordinarily serious and deadly. And at least until vaccines are readily available, the situation may get worse in many parts of the United States. Federal courts ... must afford substantial deference to state and local authorities about how best to balance competing policy considerations during the pandemic. But judicial deference in an emergency or a crisis does not mean wholesale judicial abdication, especially when important questions of religious discrimination, racial discrimination, free speech, or the like are raised.

In light of the devastating pandemic, I do not doubt the State's authority to impose tailored restrictions—even very strict restrictions—on attendance at religious services and secular gatherings alike. But the New York restrictions on houses of worship are not tailored to the circumstances given the First Amendment interests at stake. ...

Chief Justice ROBERTS, dissenting.

I would not grant injunctive relief under the present circumstances. There is simply no need to do so. After the Diocese and Agudath Israel filed their applications, the Governor revised the designations of the affected areas. None of the houses of worship identified in the applications is now subject to any fixed numerical restrictions. At these locations, the applicants can hold services with up to 50% of capacity, which is at least as favorable as the relief they currently seek.

Justice BREYER, with whom Justice SOTOMAYOR and Justice KAGAN join, dissenting.

New York regulations designed to fight the rapidly spreading—and, in many cases, fatal—COVID-19 virus permit the Governor to identify hot spots where infection rates have spiked and to designate those hot spots as red zones, the immediately surrounding areas as orange zones, and the outlying areas as yellow zones. The regulations impose restrictions within these zones (with the strictest restrictions in the red zones and the least strict restrictions in the yellow zones) to curb transmission of the virus and prevent spread into nearby areas. In October, the Governor designated red, orange, and yellow zones in parts of Brooklyn and Queens. Among other things, the restrictions in these zones limit the number of persons who can be present at one extraordinary remedy of injunction." (internal quotation marks omitted).

COVID-19 has infected more than 12 million Americans and caused more than 250,000 deaths nationwide. At least 26,000 of those deaths have occurred in the State of New York, with 16,000 in New York City alone. And the number of COVID-19 cases is many times the number of deaths. The Nation is now experiencing a second surge of infections. In New York, for example, the 7-day average of new confirmed cases per day has risen from around 700 at the end of the summer to over 4,800 last week. Nationwide, the number of new confirmed cases per day is now higher than it has ever been.

At the same time, members of the scientific and medical communities tell us that the virus is transmitted from person to person through respiratory droplets produced when a person or group of people talk, sing, cough, or breathe near each other. Thus, according to experts, the risk of transmission is higher when people are in close contact with one another for prolonged periods of time, particularly indoors or in other enclosed spaces. The nature of the epidemic, the spikes, the uncertainties, and the need for quick action, taken together, mean that the State has countervailing arguments based upon health, safety, and administrative considerations that must be balanced against the applicants' First Amendment challenges. That fact, along with others that JUSTICE SOTOMAYOR describes, means that the applicants' claim of a constitutional violation (on which they base their request for injunctive relief) is far from clear. (All of these matters could be considered and discussed in the ordinary course of proceedings at a later date.) At the same time, the public's serious health and safety needs, which call for swift government action in ever changing circumstances, also mean that it is far from clear that "the balance of equities tips in [the applicants'] favor," or "that an injunction is in the public interest." *Winter v. Natural Resources Defense Council, Inc.* (2008).

Justice SOTOMAYOR, with whom Justice KAGAN joins, dissenting.

Amidst a pandemic that has already claimed over a quarter million American lives, the Court today enjoins one of New York's public health measures aimed at containing the spread of COVID-19 in areas facing the most severe outbreaks. Earlier this year, this Court twice stayed its hand when asked to issue similar extraordinary relief. I see no justification for the Court's change of heart, and I fear that granting applications such as the one filed by the Roman Catholic Diocese of Brooklyn (Diocese) will only exacerbate the Nation's suffering.

*South Bay Pentecostal Church v. Newsom*, 592 U.S. ___ (2021), and *Calvary Chapel Dayton Valley v. Sisolak*, ___ U.S. ___ (2020), provided a clear and workable rule to state officials seeking to control the spread of COVID-19: They may restrict attendance at houses of worship so long as comparable secular institutions face restrictions that are at least equally as strict. See *South Bay* (ROBERTS, C. J., concurring). New York's safety measures fall comfortably within those bounds. Like the States in *South Bay* and *Calvary Chapel*, New

York applies "[s]imilar or more severe restrictions . . . to comparable secular gatherings, including lectures, concerts, movie showings, spectator sports, and theatrical performances, where large groups of people gather in close proximity for extended periods of time." Likewise, New York "treats more leniently only dissimilar activities, such as operating grocery stores, banks, and laundromats, in which people neither congregate in large groups nor remain in close proximity for extended periods." *Id.* That should be enough to decide this case.

The Diocese attempts to get around *South Bay* and *Calvary Chapel* by disputing New York's conclusion that attending religious services poses greater risks than, for instance, shopping at big box stores. But the District Court rejected that argument as unsupported by the factual record. Undeterred, JUSTICE GORSUCH offers up his own examples of secular activities he thinks might pose similar risks as religious gatherings, but which are treated more leniently under New York's rules (*e.g.*, going to the liquor store or getting a bike repaired). But JUSTICE GORSUCH does not even try to square his examples with the conditions medical experts tell us facilitate the spread of COVID-19: large groups of people gathering, speaking, and singing in close proximity indoors for extended periods of time. Unlike religious services, which "have every one of th[ose] risk factors," bike repair shops and liquor stores generally do not feature customers gathering inside to sing and speak together for an hour or more at a time. *Id.* ("Epidemiologists and physicians generally agree that religious services are among the riskiest activities"). Justices of this Court play a deadly game in second guessing the expert judgment of health officials about the environments in which a contagious virus, now infecting a million Americans each week, spreads most easily.

In truth, this case is easier than *South Bay* and *Calvary Chapel*. While the state regulations in those cases generally applied the same rules to houses of worship and secular institutions where people congregate in large groups, New York treats houses of worship far more favorably than their secular comparators. And whereas the restrictions in *South Bay* and *Calvary Chapel* applied statewide, New York's fixed-capacity restrictions apply only in specially designated areas experiencing a surge in COVID-19 cases.

\* \* \*

. . . The Constitution does not forbid States from responding to public health crises through regulations that treat religious institutions equally or more favorably than comparable secular institutions, particularly when those regulations save lives. Because New York's COVID-19 restrictions do just that, I respectfully dissent.

### NOTES AND QUESTIONS

**1.** The critical case for understanding the Per Curiam opinion is *Church of the Lukumi Babalu Aye v. City of Hialeah*, which is applicable when it seems like government is targeting religion or religious institutions for particular treatment. Why does the Per Curiam majority conclude this is such a case?

**2.** Chief Justice Roberts argues that the time is not right for judicial intervention by the Court. Why not? In what way does his concurring opinion epitomize his minimalist approach to constitutional decision-making?

**3.** As so often seems to be the case, the dissenters and the Per Curiam justices (and especially Justice Gorsuch) seem to be talking past each other. On what basic point do the dissenters disagree with the Per Curiam justices when it comes to the classifications at issue here? Why do the dissenters appear to be urging deference to the government, at least at this stage in the proceedings?

**4.** As should be clear, the Court has emphasized in recent cases that, where generally applicable laws contain exceptions, religious exercise may not be treated differently. For example, the Court has held that "a State violates the Free Exercise Clause when it excludes religious observers from otherwise available public benefits." *Carson v. Makin*, 596 U.S. ___ (2022). In *Carson*, the Court concluded that the state of Maine could not justify "carv[ing] out private religious schools from those eligible to receive such funds." The *Carson* majority saw no Establishment Clause impediment to what amounted to state funding of religious education. The next case further explores the tension and relationship between the religion clauses.

## Kennedy v. Bremerton School District
### 597 U.S. ___ (2022)

Justice GORSUCH delivered the opinion of the Court.

Joseph Kennedy ... made it a practice to give "thanks through prayer on the playing field" at the conclusion of each game. In his prayers, Mr. Kennedy sought to express gratitude for "what the players had accomplished and for the opportunity to be part of their lives through the game of football." Mr. Kennedy offered his prayers after the players and coaches had shaken hands, by taking a knee at the 50-yard line and praying "quiet[ly]" for "approximately 30 seconds."

Initially, Mr. Kennedy prayed on his own. But over time, some players asked whether they could pray alongside him. Mr. Kennedy responded by saying, "This is a free country. You can do what you want." The number of players who joined Mr. Kennedy eventually grew to include most of the team, at least after some games. Sometimes team members invited opposing players to join. Other times Mr. Kennedy still prayed alone. Eventually, Mr. Kennedy began incorporating short motivational speeches with his prayer when others were present. Separately, the team at times engaged in pregame or postgame prayers in the locker room. It seems this practice was a "school tradition" that predated Mr. Kennedy's tenure. Mr. Kennedy explained that he "never told any student that it was important they participate in any religious activity." In particular, he "never pressured or encouraged any student to join" his postgame midfield prayers.

[T]he District's superintendent first learned of them only in September 2015, after an employee from another school commented positively on the school's practices to Bremerton's principal. At that point, the District reacted quickly. On September 17, the superintendent sent Mr. Kennedy a letter. In it, the superintendent identified "two problematic practices" in which Mr. Kennedy had engaged. First, Mr. Kennedy had provided "inspirational talk[s]" that included "overtly religious references" likely constituting "prayer" with the students "at midfield following the completion of ... game[s]." Second, he had led "students and coaching staff in a prayer" in the locker-room tradition that "predated [his] involvement with the program."

The District explained that it sought to establish "clear parameters" "going forward." It instructed Mr. Kennedy to avoid any motivational "talks with students" that "include[d] religious expression, including prayer," and to avoid "suggest[ing], encourag[ing] (or discourag[ing]), or supervis[ing]" any prayers of students, which students remained free to "engage in." The District also explained that any religious activity on Mr. Kennedy's part must be "nondemonstrative (*i.e.*, not outwardly discernible as religious activity)" if "students are also engaged in religious conduct" in order to "avoid the perception of endorsement." In offering these directives, the District appealed to what it called a "direct tension between" the "Establishment Clause" and "a school employee's [right to] free[ly] exercise" his religion. To resolve that "tension," the District explained, an employee's free exercise rights "must yield so far as necessary to avoid school endorsement of religious activities."

After receiving the District's September 17 letter, Mr. Kennedy ended the tradition, predating him, of offering locker-room prayers. He also ended his practice of incorporating religious references or prayer into his postgame motivational talks to his team on the field. Mr. Kennedy further felt pressured to abandon his practice of saying his own quiet, on-field postgame prayer. Driving home after a game, however, Mr. Kennedy felt upset that he had "broken [his] commitment to God" by not offering his own prayer, so he turned his car around and returned to the field. By that point, everyone had left the stadium, and he walked to the 50-yard line and knelt to say a brief prayer of thanks.

On October 14, through counsel, Mr. Kennedy sent a letter to school officials informing them that, because of his "sincerely-held religious beliefs," he felt "compelled" to offer a "post-game personal prayer" of thanks at midfield. He asked the District to allow him to continue that "private religious expression" alone. Consistent with the District's policy, Mr. Kennedy explained that he "neither requests, encourages, nor discourages students from participating in" these prayers. Mr. Kennedy emphasized that he sought only the opportunity to "wai[t] until the game is over and the players have left the field and then wal[k] to mid-field to say a short, private, personal prayer." He "told everybody" that it would be acceptable to him to pray "when the kids went away from [him]." He later clarified that this meant he was even willing to say his "prayer while the players were walking to the locker room" or "bus," and then catch up with his team. However, Mr. Kennedy objected to the logical implication of the District's September 17 letter, which he understood as banning him "from bowing his head" in the vicinity of students, and as requiring him to "flee the scene if students voluntarily [came] to the same area" where he was praying. After all, District policy prohibited him from "discourag[ing]" independent student decisions to pray.

On October 16, shortly before the game that day, the District responded with another letter. The District acknowledged that Mr. Kennedy "ha[d] complied" with the "directives" in its September 17 letter. Yet instead of accommodating Mr. Kennedy's request to offer a brief prayer on the field while students were busy with other activities —whether heading to the locker room, boarding the bus, or perhaps singing the school fight song—the District issued an ultimatum. It forbade Mr. Kennedy from engaging in "any overt actions" that could "appea[r] to a reasonable observer to endorse ... prayer ... while he is on duty as a District-paid coach." ...

After receiving this letter, Mr. Kennedy offered a brief prayer following the October 16 game. When he bowed his head at midfield after the game, "most [Bremerton] players were ... engaged in the traditional singing of the school fight song to the audience." Though Mr. Kennedy was alone when he began to pray, players from the other team and members of the community joined him before he finished his prayer.

[T]he District wrote Mr. Kennedy again [on October 23, shortly before that evening's game]. It ... explained that a "reasonable observer" could think government endorsement of religion had occurred when a "District employee, on the field only by virtue of his employment with the District, still on duty" engaged in "overtly religious conduct." The District thus made clear that the only option it would offer Mr. Kennedy was to allow him to pray after a game in a "private location" behind closed doors and "not observable to students or the public."

After the October 23 game ended, Mr. Kennedy knelt at the 50-yard line, where "no one joined him," and bowed his head for a "brief, quiet prayer." The superintendent informed the District's board that this prayer "moved closer to what we want," but nevertheless remained "unconstitutional." After the final relevant football game on October 26, Mr. Kennedy again knelt alone to offer a brief prayer as the players engaged in postgame traditions. While he was praying, other adults gathered around him on the field. Later, Mr. Kennedy rejoined his players for a postgame talk, after they had finished singing the school fight song.

Shortly after the October 26 game, the District placed Mr. Kennedy on paid administrative leave and prohibited him from "participat[ing], in any capacity, in ... football program activities." ...

[M]r. Kennedy received "uniformly positive evaluations" every other year of his coaching career, [yet] after the 2015 season ended in November, the District gave him a poor performance evaluation. The evaluation advised against rehiring Mr. Kennedy on the grounds that he "failed to follow district policy" regarding religious expression and "failed to supervise student-athletes after games." Mr. Kennedy did not return for the next season.

... Mr. Kennedy sued in federal court, alleging that the District's actions violated the First Amendment's Free Speech and Free Exercise Clauses. ... Rejecting Mr. Kennedy's free speech claim, the [district court] concluded that because Mr. Kennedy "was hired precisely to occupy" an "influential role for student athletes," any speech he uttered was offered in his capacity as a government employee and unprotected by the First Amendment. ...

The Ninth Circuit [agreed and later] denied a petition to rehear the case en banc. ... We granted certiorari.

**III**

[T]he Free Exercise and Free Speech Clauses of the First Amendment ... work in tandem. Where the Free Exercise Clause protects religious exercises, whether communicative or not, the Free Speech Clause provides overlapping protection for expressive religious activities. ...

[A] plaintiff bears certain burdens to demonstrate an infringement of his rights under the Free Exercise and Free Speech Clauses. If the plaintiff carries these burdens, the focus then shifts to the defendant to show that its actions were nonetheless justified and tailored consistent with the demands of our case law. We begin by examining whether Mr. Kennedy has discharged his burdens, first under the Free Exercise Clause, then under the Free Speech Clause.

**A**

The Free Exercise Clause ... protects not only the right to harbor religious beliefs inwardly and secretly. It does perhaps its most important work by protecting the ability of those who hold religious beliefs of all kinds to live out their faiths in daily life through "the performance of (or abstention from) physical acts." *Employment Div., Dept. of Human Resources of Ore. v. Smith* (1990).

[A] plaintiff may carry the burden of proving a free exercise violation in various ways, including by showing that a government entity has burdened his sincere religious practice pursuant to a policy that is not "neutral" or "generally applicable." *Id*. Should a plaintiff make a showing like that, this Court will find a First Amendment violation unless the government can satisfy "strict scrutiny" by demonstrating its course was justified by a compelling state interest and was narrowly tailored in pursuit of that interest. *Church of the Lukumi Bablau Aye, Inc. v. Hialeah* (1993).

That Mr. Kennedy has discharged his burdens is effectively undisputed. No one questions that he seeks to engage in a sincerely motivated religious exercise. The exercise in question involves, as Mr. Kennedy has put it, giving "thanks through prayer" briefly and by himself "on the playing field" at the conclusion of each game he coaches. ...

Nor does anyone question that, in forbidding Mr. Kennedy's brief prayer, the District failed to act pursuant to a neutral and generally applicable rule. A government policy will not qualify as neutral if it is "specifically directed at ... religious practice." *Smith*. A policy can fail this test if it "discriminate[s] on its face," or if a religious exercise is otherwise its "object." *Lukumi*. A government policy will fail the general applicability requirement if it "prohibits religious conduct while permitting secular conduct that undermines the government's asserted interests in a similar way," or if it provides "a mechanism for individualized exemptions." *Fulton v. Philadelphia* (2021). Failing either the neutrality or general applicability test is sufficient to trigger strict scrutiny.

In this case, the District's challenged policies were neither neutral nor generally applicable. By its own admission, the District sought to restrict Mr. Kennedy's actions at least in part because of their religious character. ... Prohibiting a religious practice was thus the District's unquestioned "object." The District candidly acknowledged as much below, conceding that its policies were "not neutral" toward religion.

The District's challenged policies also fail the general applicability test. The District's performance evaluation after the 2015 football season advised against rehiring Mr. Kennedy on the ground that he "failed to supervise student-athletes after games." But, in fact, this was a bespoke requirement specifically addressed to Mr. Kennedy's religious exercise. The District permitted other members of the coaching staff to forgo supervising students briefly after the game to do things like visit with friends or take personal phone calls. Thus, any sort of postgame supervisory requirement was not applied in an evenhanded, across-the-board way. Again recognizing as much, the District conceded before the Ninth Circuit that its challenged directives were not "generally applicable."

**B**

When it comes to Mr. Kennedy's free speech claim, our precedents remind us that the First Amendment's protections extend to "teachers and students," neither of whom "shed their constitutional rights to freedom of speech or expression at the schoolhouse gate." *Tinker v. Des Moines Independent Community School Dist.* (1969). Of course, none of this means the speech rights of public school employees are so boundless that they may deliver any message to anyone anytime they wish. In addition to being private citizens, teachers and coaches are also government employees paid in part to speak on the government's behalf and convey its intended messages.

To account for the complexity associated with the interplay between free speech rights and government employment, this Court's decisions in *Pickering v. Board of Ed. of Township High School Dist. 205, Will Cty.* (1968), *Garcetti v. Ceballos* (2006), and related cases suggest proceeding in two steps. The first step involves a threshold inquiry into the nature of the speech at issue. If a public employee speaks "pursuant to [his or her] official duties," this Court has said the Free Speech Clause generally will not shield the individual from an employer's control and discipline because that kind of speech is—

for constitutional purposes at least—the government's own speech. *Garcetti*.

At the same time and at the other end of the spectrum, when an employee "speaks as a citizen addressing a matter of public concern," our cases indicate that the First Amendment may be implicated and courts should proceed to a second step. *Garcetti*. At this second step, our cases suggest that courts should attempt to engage in "a delicate balancing of the competing interests surrounding the speech and its consequences." *Id*. Among other things, courts at this second step have sometimes considered whether an employee's speech interests are outweighed by "the interest of the State, as an employer, in promoting the efficiency of the public services it performs through its employees." *Id*. (quoting *Pickering*).

Both sides ask us to employ at least certain aspects of this *Pickering–Garcetti* framework to resolve Mr. Kennedy's free speech claim. They share additional common ground too. They agree that Mr. Kennedy's speech implicates a matter of public concern…. At the first step of the *Pickering–Garcetti* inquiry, the parties' disagreement thus turns out to center on one question alone: Did Mr. Kennedy offer his prayers in his capacity as a private citizen, or did they amount to government speech attributable to the District?

Our cases offer some helpful guidance for resolving this question. In *Garcetti*, the Court concluded that a prosecutor's internal memorandum to a supervisor was made "pursuant to [his] official duties," and thus ineligible for First Amendment protection. [T]he Court relied on the fact that the prosecutor's speech "fulfill[ed] a responsibility to advise his supervisor about how best to proceed with a pending case." In other words, the prosecutor's memorandum was government speech because it was speech the government "itself ha[d] commissioned or created" and speech the employee was expected to deliver in the course of carrying out his job.

[H]ere, it seems clear to us that Mr. Kennedy has demonstrated that his speech was private speech, not government speech. When Mr. Kennedy uttered the three prayers that resulted in his suspension, he was not engaged in speech "ordinarily within the scope" of his duties as a coach. *Lane v. Franks* (2014). He did not speak pursuant to government policy. He was not seeking to convey a government-created message. He was not instructing players, discussing strategy, encouraging better on-field performance, or engaged in any other speech the District paid him to produce as a coach. Simply put: Mr. Kennedy's prayers did not "ow[e their] existence" to Mr. Kennedy's responsibilities as a public employee. *Garcetti*.

The timing and circumstances of Mr. Kennedy's prayers confirm the point. During the postgame period when these prayers occurred, coaches were free to attend briefly to personal matters—everything from checking sports scores on their phones to greeting friends and family in the stands. We find it unlikely that Mr. Kennedy was fulfilling a responsibility imposed by his employment by praying during a period in which the District has acknowledged that its coaching staff was free to engage in all manner of private speech.

That Mr. Kennedy offered his prayers when students were engaged in other activities like singing the school fight song further suggests that those prayers were not delivered as an address to the team, but instead in his capacity as a private citizen. Nor is it dispositive that Mr. Kennedy's prayers took place "within the office" environment—here, on the field of play. *Garcetti*. Instead, what matters is whether Mr. Kennedy offered his prayers while acting within the scope of his duties as a coach. And taken together, both the substance of Mr. Kennedy's speech and the circumstances surrounding it point to the conclusion that he did not.

In reaching its contrary conclusion, the Ninth Circuit stressed that, as a coach, Mr. Kennedy served as a role model "clothed with the mantle of one who imparts knowledge and wisdom." The court emphasized that Mr. Kennedy remained on duty after games. Before us, the District presses the same arguments. And no doubt they have a point. Teachers and coaches often serve as vital role models. But this argument commits the error of positing an "excessively broad job descriptio[n]" by treating everything teachers and coaches say in the workplace as government speech subject to government control. *Garcetti*. On this understanding, a school could fire a Muslim teacher for wearing a headscarf in the classroom or prohibit a Christian aide from praying quietly over her lunch in the cafeteria. Likewise, this argument ignores the District Court's conclusion (and the District's concession) that Mr. Kennedy's actual job description left time for a private moment after the game to call home, check a text, socialize, or engage in any manner of secular activities. Others working for the District were free to engage briefly in personal speech and activity. That Mr. Kennedy chose to use the same time to pray does not transform his speech into government speech. To hold differently would be to treat religious expression as second-class speech and eviscerate this Court's repeated promise that teachers do not "shed their constitutional rights to freedom of speech or expression at the schoolhouse gate." *Tinker*.

Of course, acknowledging that Mr. Kennedy's prayers represented his own private speech does not end the matter. So far, we have recognized only that Mr. Kennedy has carried his threshold burden. Under the *Pickering-Garcetti* framework, a second step remains where the government may seek to prove that its interests as employer outweigh even an employee's private speech on a matter of public concern.

### IV

Whether one views the case through the lens of the Free Exercise or Free Speech Clause, at this point the burden shifts to the District. Under the Free Exercise Clause, a government entity normally must satisfy at least "strict scrutiny," showing that its restrictions on the plaintiff's protected rights serve a compelling interest and are narrowly tailored to that end. A similar standard generally obtains under the Free Speech Clause. The District, however, asks us to apply to Mr. Kennedy's claims the more lenient second-step *Pickering-Garcetti* test, or alternatively intermediate scrutiny. The District cannot sustain its burden under any of them.

**A**

As we have seen, the District argues that its suspension of Mr. Kennedy was essential to avoid a violation of the Establishment Clause. On its account, Mr. Kennedy's prayers might have been protected by the Free Exercise and Free Speech Clauses. But his rights were in "direct tension" with the competing demands of the Establishment Clause. To resolve that clash, the District reasoned, Mr. Kennedy's rights had to "yield." The Ninth Circuit pursued this same line of thinking, insisting that the District's interest in avoiding an Establishment Clause violation "trump[ed]" Mr. Kennedy's rights to religious exercise and free speech.

But how could that be? It is true that this Court and others often refer to the "Establishment Clause," the "Free Exercise Clause," and the "Free Speech Clause" as separate units. But the three Clauses appear in the same sentence of the same Amendment[.] A natural reading of that [Amendment] would seem to suggest the Clauses have "complementary" purposes, not warring ones where one Clause is always sure to prevail over the others.

[T]he District offers a backup argument in this Court. It still contends that its Establishment Clause concerns trump Mr. Kennedy's free exercise and free speech rights. But the District now seeks to supply different reasoning for that result. Now, it says, it was justified in suppressing Mr. Kennedy's religious activity because otherwise it would have been guilty of coercing students to pray. And, the District says, coercing worship amounts to an Establishment Clause violation on anyone's account of the Clause's original meaning.

As it turns out, however, there is a pretty obvious reason why the Ninth Circuit did not adopt this theory in proceedings below: The evidence cannot sustain it. To be sure, this Court has long held that government may not, consistent with a historically sensitive understanding of the Establishment Clause, "make a religious observance compulsory." *Zorach v. Clauson* (1952). Government "may not coerce anyone to attend church," *id.*, nor may it force citizens to engage in "a formal religious exercise," *Lee v. Weisman* (1992). ... Members of this Court have sometimes disagreed on what exactly qualifies as impermissible coercion in light of the original meaning of the Establishment Clause. But in this case Mr. Kennedy's private religious exercise did not come close to crossing any line one might imagine separating protected private expression from impermissible government coercion.

Begin with the District's own contemporaneous description of the facts. [T]he District conceded in a public 2015 document that there was "no evidence that students [were] directly coerced to pray with Kennedy." This is consistent with Mr. Kennedy's account too. He has repeatedly stated that he "never coerced, required, or asked any student to pray," and that he never "told any student that it was important that they participate in any religious activity."

Consider, too, the actual requests Mr. Kennedy made. ... The only prayer Mr. Kennedy sought to continue was the kind he had "started out doing" at the beginning of his tenure—the prayer he gave alone. He made clear that he could pray "while the kids were doing the fight song" and "take a knee by [him]self and give thanks and continue on." Mr. Kennedy even considered it "acceptable" to say his "prayer while the players were walking to the locker room" or "bus," and then catch up with his team. In short, Mr. Kennedy did not seek to direct any prayers to students or require anyone else to participate. His plan was to wait to pray until athletes were occupied, and he "told everybody" that's what he wished "to do." It was for three prayers of this sort alone in October 2015 that the District suspended him.

Naturally, Mr. Kennedy's proposal to pray quietly by himself on the field would have meant some people would have seen his religious exercise. Those close at hand might have heard him too. But learning how to tolerate speech or prayer of all kinds is "part of learning how to live in a pluralistic society," a trait of character essential to "a tolerant citizenry." *Lee*. This Court has long recognized as well that "secondary school students are mature enough ... to understand that a school does not endorse," let alone coerce them to participate in, "speech that it merely permits on a nondiscriminatory basis." *Board of Education of the Westside Schools v. Mergens* (1990) (plurality opinion). Of course, some will take offense to certain forms of speech or prayer they are sure to encounter in a society where those activities enjoy such robust constitutional protection. But "[o]ffense ... does not equate to coercion." *Town of Greece v. Galloway* (2014) (plurality opinion).

The District responds that, as a coach, Mr. Kennedy "wielded enormous authority and influence over the students," and students might have felt compelled to pray alongside him. To support this argument, the District submits that, after Mr. Kennedy's suspension, a few parents told District employees that their sons had "participated in the team prayers only because they did not wish to separate themselves from the team."

This reply fails too. ... There is no indication in the record that anyone expressed any coercion concerns to the District about the quiet, postgame prayers that Mr. Kennedy asked to continue and that led to his suspension. Nor is there any record evidence that students felt pressured to participate in these prayers. To the contrary, and as we have seen, not a single Bremerton student joined Mr. Kennedy's quiet prayers following the three October 2015 games for which he was disciplined. On October 16, those students who joined Mr. Kennedy were "from the opposing team," and thus could not have "reasonably fear[ed]" that he would decrease their "playing time" or destroy their "opportunities" if they did not "participate." As for the other two relevant games, "no one joined" Mr. Kennedy on October 23. And only a few members of the public participated on October 26.

The absence of evidence of coercion in this record leaves the District to its final redoubt. Here, the District suggests that *any* visible religious conduct by a teacher or coach should be deemed—without more and as a matter of law—impermissibly coercive on students. In essence, the District asks us to adopt the view that the only acceptable government role models for students are those who eschew any visible religious expression. If the argument sounds familiar, it should. Really, it is just another way of repackaging the District's earlier submission that government may script everything a teacher or coach says in the workplace. The only added twist here is the District's suggestion not only that it *may* prohibit teachers from engaging in any demonstrative religious activity, but that it *must* do so in order to conform to the Constitution.

Such a rule would be a sure sign that our Establishment Clause jurisprudence had gone off the rails. In the name of protecting religious liberty, the District would have us suppress it. Rather than respect the First Amendment's double protection for religious expression, it would have us preference secular activity. Not only could schools fire teachers for praying quietly over their lunch, for wearing a yarmulke to school, or for offering a midday prayer during a break before practice. Under the District's rule, a school would be *required* to do so. It is a rule that would defy this Court's traditional understanding that permitting private speech is not the same thing as coercing others to participate in it. It is a rule, too, that would undermine a long constitutional tradition under which learning how to tolerate diverse expressive activities has always been "part of learning how to live in a pluralistic society." *Lee.* ...

[T]his case looks very different from those in which this Court has found prayer involving public school students to be problematically coercive. In *Lee*, this Court held that school officials violated the Establishment Clause by "including [a] clerical membe[r]" who publicly recited prayers "as part of [an] official school graduation ceremony" because the school had "in every practical sense compelled attendance and participation in" a "religious exercise." In *Santa Fe Independent School Dist. v. Doe* (2000), the Court held that a school district violated the Establishment Clause by broadcasting a prayer "over the public address system" before each football game. The Court observed that, while students generally were not required to attend games, attendance *was* required for "cheerleaders, members of the band, and, of course, the team members themselves." None of that is true here. The prayers for which Mr. Kennedy was disciplined were not publicly broadcast or recited to a captive audience. Students were not required or expected to participate. And, in fact, none of Mr. Kennedy's students did participate in any of the three October 2015 prayers that resulted in Mr. Kennedy's discipline.

C

In the end, ... there is no conflict between the constitutional commands before us. There is only the "mere shadow" of a conflict, a false choice premised on a misconstruction of the Establishment Clause. *School District of Abington Tp, Pa. v. Schempp* (1963) (Goldberg, J., concurring). And in no world may a government entity's concerns about phantom constitutional violations justify actual violations of an individual's First Amendment rights.

V

... Mr. Kennedy is entitled to summary judgment on his First Amendment claims. The judgment of the Court of Appeals is

*Reversed.*

[Concurring opinion of Justice THOMAS omitted.]

[Concurring opinion of Justice ALITO omitted.]

Justice SOTOMAYOR, with whom Justice BREYER and Justice KAGAN join, dissenting.

... Since *Engel v. Vitale* (1962), this Court consistently has recognized that school officials leading prayer is constitutionally impermissible. Official-led prayer strikes at the core of our constitutional protections for the religious liberty of students and their parents, as embodied in both the Establishment Clause and the Free Exercise Clause of the First Amendment.

The Court now charts a different path, yet again paying almost exclusive attention to the Free Exercise Clause's protection for individual religious exercise while giving short shrift to the Establishment Clause's prohibition on state establishment of religion. To the degree the Court portrays petitioner Joseph Kennedy's prayers as private and quiet, it misconstrues the facts. The record reveals that Kennedy had a longstanding practice of conducting demonstrative prayers on the 50-yard line of the football field. Kennedy consistently invited others to join his prayers and for years led student athletes in prayer at the same time and location. The Court ignores this history. The Court also ignores the severe disruption to school events caused by Kennedy's conduct, viewing it as irrelevant because the Bremerton School District (District) stated that it was suspending Kennedy to avoid it being viewed as endorsing religion. Under the Court's analysis, presumably this would be a different case if the District had cited Kennedy's repeated disruptions of school programming and violations of school policy regarding public access to the field as grounds for suspending him. As the District did not articulate those grounds, the Court assesses only the District's Establishment Clause concerns. It errs by assessing them divorced from the context and history of Kennedy's prayer practice.

**I**

As the majority tells it, Kennedy, a coach for the District's football program, "lost his job" for "pray[ing] quietly while his students were otherwise occupied." The record before us, however, tells a different story.

In September 2015, a coach from another school's football team informed BHS' principal that Kennedy had asked him and his team to join Kennedy in prayer. The other team's coach told the principal that he thought it was "cool" that the District "would allow [its] coaches to go ahead and invite other teams' coaches and players to pray after a game."

The District initiated an inquiry into whether its policy on Religious-Related Activities and Practices had been violated. It learned that, since his hiring in 2008, Kennedy had been kneeling on the 50-yard line to pray immediately after shaking hands with the opposing team. Kennedy recounted that he initially prayed alone and that he never asked any student to join him. Over time, however, a majority of the team came to join him, with the numbers varying from game to game. Kennedy's practice evolved into postgame talks in which Kennedy would hold aloft student helmets and deliver speeches with "overtly religious references," which Kennedy described as prayers, while the players knelt around him. The District also learned that students had prayed in the past in the locker room prior to games, before Kennedy was hired, but that Kennedy subsequently began leading those prayers too.

While the District's inquiry was pending, its athletic director attended BHS' September 11, 2015, football game and told Kennedy that he should not be conducting prayers with players. After the game, while the athletic director watched, Kennedy led a prayer out loud, holding up a player's helmet as the players kneeled around him. …

On September 17, [the] District acknowledged that Kennedy had "not actively encouraged, or required, participation" but emphasized that "school staff may not indirectly encourage students to engage in religious activity" or "endors[e]" religious activity; rather, the District explained, staff "must remain neutral" "while performing their job duties." The District instructed Kennedy that any motivational talks to students must remain secular, "so as to avoid alienation of any team member."

The District reiterated that "all District staff are free to engage in religious activity, including prayer, so long as it does not interfere with job responsibilities." To avoid endorsing student religious exercise, the District instructed that such activity must be nondemonstrative or conducted separately from students, away from student activities. The District expressed concern that Kennedy had continued his midfield prayer practice at two games after the District's athletic director and the varsity team's head coach had instructed him to stop.

Kennedy stopped participating in locker room prayers and, after a game the following day, gave a secular speech. He returned to pray in the stadium alone after his duties were over and everyone had left the stadium, to which the District had no objection. Kennedy then hired an attorney, who, on October 14, sent a letter explaining that Kennedy was "motivated by his sincerely-held religious beliefs to pray following each football game." The letter claimed that the District had required that Kennedy "flee from students if they voluntarily choose to come to a place where he is privately praying during personal time," referring to the 50-yard line of the football field immediately following the conclusion of a game. Kennedy requested that the District simply issue a "clarif[ication] that the prayer is [Kennedy's] private speech" and that the District not "interfere" with students joining Kennedy in prayer. The letter further announced that Kennedy would resume his 50-yard-line prayer practice the next day after the October 16 homecoming game.

Before the homecoming game, Kennedy made multiple media appearances to publicize his plans to pray at the 50-yard line, leading to an article in the Seattle News and a local television broadcast about the upcoming homecoming game. In the wake of this media coverage, the District began receiving a large number of emails, letters, and calls, many of them threatening.

The District responded to Kennedy's letter before the game on October 16. It emphasized that Kennedy's letter evinced "materia[l] misunderstand[ings]" of many of the facts at issue. For instance, Kennedy's letter asserted that he had not invited anyone to pray with him; the District noted that that might be true of Kennedy's September 17 prayer specifically, but that Kennedy had acknowledged inviting others to join him on many previous occasions. The District's September 17 letter had explained that Kennedy traditionally held up helmets from the BHS and opposing teams while players from each team kneeled around him. While Kennedy's letter asserted that his prayers "occurr[ed] 'on his own time,' after his duties as a District employee had ceased," the District pointed out that Kennedy "remain[ed] on duty" when his prayers occurred "immediately following completion of the football game, when students are still on the football field, in uniform, under the stadium lights, with the audience still in attendance, and while Mr. Kennedy is still in his District-issued and District-logoed attire." (emphasis deleted). The District further noted that "[d]uring the time following completion of the game, until players are released to their parents or otherwise allowed to leave the event, Mr. Kennedy, like all coaches, is clearly on duty and paid to continue supervision of students."

The District stated that it had no objection to Kennedy returning to the stadium when he was off duty to pray at the 50-yard line, nor with Kennedy praying while on duty if it did not interfere with his job duties or suggest the District's endorsement of religion. The District explained that its establishment concerns were motivated by the specific facts at issue, because engaging in prayer on the 50-yard line immediately after the game finished would appear to be an extension of Kennedy's "prior, long-standing and well-known history of leading students in prayer" on the 50-yard line after games. ...

On October 16, after playing of the game had concluded, Kennedy shook hands with the opposing team, and as advertised, knelt to pray while most BHS players were singing the school's fight song. He quickly was joined by coaches and players from the opposing team. Television news cameras surrounded the group. Members of the public rushed the field to join Kennedy, jumping fences to access the field and knocking over student band members. After the game, the District received calls from Satanists who "intended to conduct ceremonies on the field after football games if others were allowed to." To secure the field and enable subsequent games to continue safely, the District was forced to make security arrangements with the local police and to post signs near the field and place robocalls to parents reiterating that the field was not open to the public.

The District sent Kennedy another letter on October 23, explaining that his conduct at the October 16 game was inconsistent with the District's requirements for two reasons. First, it "drew [him] away from [his] work"; Kennedy had, "until recently, ... regularly c[o]me to the locker room with the team and other coaches following the game" and had "specific responsibility for the supervision of players in the locker room following games." Second, his conduct raised Establishment Clause concerns, because "any reasonable observer saw a District employee, on the field only by virtue of his employment with the District, still on duty, under the bright lights of the stadium, engaged in what was clearly, given [his] prior public conduct, overtly religious conduct."

Again, the District emphasized that it was happy to accommodate Kennedy's desire to pray on the job in a way that did not interfere with his duties or risk perceptions of endorsement. Stressing that "[d]evelopment of accommodations is an interactive process," it invited Kennedy to reach out to discuss accommodations that might be mutually satisfactory, offering proposed accommodations and inviting Kennedy to raise others. The District noted, however, that "further violations of [its] directives" would be grounds for discipline or termination.

Kennedy did not directly respond or suggest a satisfactory accommodation. Instead, his attorneys told the media that he would accept only demonstrative prayer on the 50-yard line immediately after games. During the October 23 and October 26 games, Kennedy again prayed at the 50-yard line immediately following the game, while postgame activities were still ongoing. At the October 23 game, Kennedy kneeled on the field alone with players standing nearby. At the October 26 game, Kennedy prayed surrounded by members of the public, including state representatives who attended the game to support Kennedy. The BHS players, after singing the fight song, joined Kennedy at midfield after he stood up from praying.

In an October 28 letter, the District notified Kennedy that it was placing him on paid administrative leave for violating its directives at the October 16, October 23, and October 26 games by kneeling on the field and praying immediately following the games before rejoining the players for postgame talks. The District recounted that it had offered accommodations to, and offered to engage in further discussions with, Kennedy to permit his religious exercise, and that Kennedy had failed to respond to these offers. The District stressed that it remained willing to discuss possible accommodations if Kennedy was willing.

After the issues with Kennedy arose, several parents reached out to the District saying that their children had participated in Kennedy's prayers solely to avoid separating themselves from the rest of the team. No BHS students appeared to pray on the field after Kennedy's suspension.

In Kennedy's annual review, the head coach of the varsity team recommended Kennedy not be rehired because he "failed to follow district policy," "demonstrated a lack of cooperation with administration," "contributed to negative relations between parents, students, community members, coaches, and the school district," and "failed to supervise student-athletes after games due to his interactions with media and community" members. ...

Kennedy then filed suit. ... [T]he District Court granted summary judgment to the District[, concluding] that Kennedy's 50-yard-line prayers were not entitled to protection under the Free Speech Clause because his speech was made in his capacity as a public employee, not as a private citizen. In addition, the court held that Kennedy's prayer practice violated the Establishment Clause, reasoning that "speech from the center of the football field immediately after each game ... conveys official sanction." ...

The Court of Appeals affirmed, explaining that "the facts in the record utterly belie [Kennedy's] contention that the prayer was personal and private." The court instead concluded that Kennedy's speech constituted government speech, as he "repeatedly acknowledged that—and behaved as if—he was a mentor, motivational speaker, and role model to students specifically at the conclusion of the game." (emphasis deleted). In the alternative, the court concluded that Kennedy's speech, even if in his capacity as a private citizen, was appropriately regulated by the District to avoid an Establishment Clause violation, emphasizing once more that this conclusion was tied to the specific "evolution of Kennedy's prayer practice with students" over time. ...

II

Properly understood, [t]his case is about whether a school district is required to allow one of its employees to incorporate a public, communicative display of the employee's personal religious beliefs into a school event, where that display is recognizable as part of a longstanding practice of the employee ministering religion to students as the public watched. A school district is not required to permit such conduct; in fact, the Establishment Clause prohibits it from doing so.

[The Religion Clauses, taken together,] express the view, foundational to our constitutional system, "that religious beliefs and religious expression are too precious to be either proscribed or prescribed by the State." *Lee v. Weisman* (1992). Instead, "preservation and transmission of religious beliefs and worship is a responsibility and a choice committed to the private sphere," which has the "freedom to pursue that mission." *Id.*

The Establishment Clause protects this freedom by "command[ing] a separation of church and state." *Cutter v. Wilkinson* (2005). At its core, this means forbidding "sponsorship, financial support, and active involvement of the sovereign in religious activity." *Walz v. Tax Comm'n of City of New York* (1970). In the context of public schools, it means that a State cannot use "its public school system to aid any or all religious faiths or sects in the dissemination of their doctrines and ideals." *Illinois ex rel. McCollum v. Board of Ed. of School Dist. No. 71, Champaign Cty.* (1948).

Indeed, "[t]he Court has been particularly vigilant in monitoring compliance with the Establishment Clause in elementary and secondary schools." *Edwards v. Aguillard* (1987). The reasons motivating this vigilance inhere in the nature of schools themselves and the young people they serve. Two are relevant here.

First, government neutrality toward religion is particularly important in the public school context given the role public schools play in our society. ... Families "entrust public schools with the education of their children ... on the understanding that the classroom will not purposely be used to advance religious views that may conflict with the private beliefs of the student and his or her family." *Id.* Accordingly, the Establishment Clause "proscribes public schools from 'conveying or attempting to convey a message that religion or a particular religious belief is favored or preferred'" or otherwise endorsing religious beliefs. *Lee* (Blackmun, J., concurring) (emphasis deleted).

Second, schools face a higher risk of unconstitutionally "coerc[ing] ... support or participat[ion] in religion or its exercise" than other government entities. *Id.* (opinion of the Court). The State "exerts great authority and coercive power" in schools as a general matter "through mandatory attendance requirements." *Edwards*. Moreover, the State exercises that great authority over children, who are uniquely susceptible to "subtle coercive pressure." *Lee*. Children are particularly vulnerable to coercion because of their "emulation of teachers as role models" and "susceptibility to peer pressure." *Edwards*. Accordingly, this Court has emphasized that "the State may not, consistent with the Establishment Clause, place primary and secondary school children" in the dilemma of choosing between "participating, with all that implies, or protesting" a religious exercise in a public school. *Lee*.

Given the twin Establishment Clause concerns of endorsement and coercion, it is unsurprising that the Court has consistently held integrating prayer into public school activities to be unconstitutional, including when student participation is not a formal requirement or prayer is silent. ...

[T]he Establishment Clause violation at hand is clear. This Court has held that a "[s]tate officia[l] direct[ing] the performance of a formal religious exercise" as a part of the "ceremon[y]" of a school event "conflicts with settled rules pertaining to prayer exercises for students." *Lee*. Kennedy was on the job as a school official "on government property" when he incorporated a public, demonstrative prayer into "government-sponsored school-related events" as a regularly scheduled feature of those events. *Santa Fe Independent School Dist. v. Doe* (2000).

Kennedy's tradition of a 50-yard line prayer thus strikes at the heart of the Establishment Clause's concerns about endorsement. For students and community members at the game, Coach Kennedy was the face and the voice of the District during football games. The timing and location Kennedy selected for his prayers were "clothed in the traditional indicia of school sporting events." *Santa Fe*. Kennedy spoke from the playing field, which was accessible only to students and school employees, not to the general public. Although the football game itself had ended, the football game events had not; Kennedy himself acknowledged that his responsibilities continued until the players went home. Kennedy's postgame responsibilities were what placed Kennedy on the 50-yard line in the first place; that was, after all, where he met the opposing team to shake hands after the game. Permitting a school coach to lead students and others he invited onto the field in prayer at a predictable time after each game could only be viewed as a postgame tradition occurring "with the approval of the school administration." *Id.*

Kennedy's prayer practice also implicated the coercion concerns at the center of this Court's Establishment Clause jurisprudence. This Court has previously recognized a heightened potential for coercion where school officials are involved, as their "effort[s] to monitor prayer will be perceived by the students as inducing a participation they might otherwise reject." *Lee*. The reasons for fearing this pressure are self-evident. This Court has recognized that students face immense social pressure. Students look up to their teachers and coaches as role models and seek their approval. Students also depend on this approval for tangible benefits. Players recognize that gaining the coach's approval may pay dividends small and large, from extra playing time to a stronger letter of recommendation to additional support in college athletic recruiting. In addition to these pressures to please their coaches, this Court has recognized that players face "immense social pressure" from their peers in the "extracurricular event that is American high school football." *Santa Fe*.

The record before the Court bears this out. The District Court found, in the evidentiary record, that some students reported joining Kennedy's prayer because they felt social pressure to follow their coach and teammates. Kennedy told the District that he began his prayers alone and that players followed each other over time until a majority of the team joined him, an evolution showing coercive pressure at work.

Kennedy does not defend his longstanding practice of leading the team in prayer out loud on the field as they knelt around him. Instead, he responds, and the Court accepts, that his highly visible and demonstrative prayer at the last three games before his suspension did not violate the Establishment Clause because these prayers were quiet and thus private. This Court's precedents, however, do not permit isolating government actions from their context in determining whether they violate the Establishment Clause. To the contrary, this Court has repeatedly stated that Establishment Clause inquiries are fact specific and require careful consideration of the origins and practical reality of the specific practice at issue. In *Santa Fe*, the Court specifically addressed how to determine whether the implementation of a new policy regarding prayers at football games "insulates the continuation of such prayers from constitutional scrutiny." The Court held that "inquiry into this question not only can, but must, include an examination of the circumstances surrounding" the change in policy, the "long-established tradition" before the change, and the "unique circumstances" of the school in question. *Id.* This Court's precedent thus does not permit treating Kennedy's "new" prayer practice as occurring on a blank slate, any more than those in the District's school community would have experienced Kennedy's changed practice (to the degree there was one) as erasing years of prior actions by Kennedy.

Like the policy change in *Santa Fe*, Kennedy's "changed" prayers at these last three games were a clear continuation of a "long-established tradition of sanctioning" school official involvement in student prayers. Students at the three games following Kennedy's changed practice witnessed Kennedy kneeling at the same time and place where he had led them in prayer for years. They witnessed their peers from opposing teams joining Kennedy, just as they had when Kennedy was leading joint team prayers. They witnessed members of the public and state representatives going onto the field to support Kennedy's cause and pray with him. Kennedy did nothing to stop this unauthorized access to the field, a clear dereliction of his duties. The BHS players in fact joined the crowd around Kennedy after he stood up from praying at the last game. That BHS students did not join Kennedy in these last three specific prayers did not make those events compliant with the Establishment Clause. The coercion to do so was evident. Kennedy himself apparently anticipated that his continued prayer practice would draw student participation, requesting that the District agree that it would not "interfere" with students joining him in the future.

Finally, Kennedy stresses that he never formally required students to join him in his prayers. But existing precedents do not require coercion to be explicit, particularly when children are involved. To the contrary, this Court's Establishment Clause jurisprudence establishes that "the government may no more use social pressure to enforce orthodoxy than it may use more direct means." *Santa Fe*. Thus, the Court has held that the Establishment Clause "will not permit" a school "'to exact religious conformity from a student as the price' of joining her classmates at a varsity football game." *Id*. To uphold a coach's integration of prayer into the ceremony of a football game, in the context of an established history of the coach inviting student involvement in prayer, is to exact precisely this price from students.

[Under the Court's precedents,] the District's interest in avoiding an Establishment Clause violation justified both its time and place restrictions on Kennedy's speech and his exercise of religion. ...

[T]he District's directive prohibiting Kennedy's demonstrative speech at the 50-yard line was narrowly tailored to avoid an Establishment Clause violation. The District's suspension of Kennedy followed a long history. The last three games proved that Kennedy did not intend to pray silently, but to thrust the District into incorporating a religious ceremony into its events, as he invited others to join his prayer and anticipated in his communications with the District that students would want to join as well. Notably, the District repeatedly sought to work with Kennedy to develop an accommodation to permit him to engage in religious exercise during or after his game-related responsibilities. Kennedy, however, ultimately refused to respond to the District's suggestions and declined to communicate with the District, except through media appearances. Because the District's valid Establishment Clause concerns satisfy strict scrutiny, Kennedy's free exercise claim fails as well.

\* \* \*

Today, the Court ... elevates one individual's interest in personal religious exercise, in the exact time and place of that individual's choosing, over society's interest in protecting the separation between church and state, eroding the protections for religious liberty for all. Today's decision is particularly misguided because it elevates the religious rights of a school official, who voluntarily accepted public employment and the limits that public employment entails, over those of his students, who are required to attend school and who this Court has long recognized are particularly vulnerable and deserving of protection. In doing so, the Court sets us further down a perilous path in forcing States to entangle themselves with religion, with all of our rights hanging in the balance. As much as the Court protests otherwise, today's decision is no victory for religious liberty. I respectfully dissent.

## NOTES AND QUESTIONS

**1.** After *Kennedy*, what remains of the Establishment Clause—in what circumstances might the Court actually strike down government action for violating the Clause?

**2.** The majority and the dissent in *Kennedy* have very different perspectives on the facts of this case—not just in respect to what happened, but what the facts mean. What remains of Smith, post-*Kennedy*? Is there any way a governmental entity can avoid accommodating instances of religious exercise?

**3.** In recent cases, in which the Court has elevated the role of the Free Exercise Clause and diminished the import of the Establishment Clause, one would be forgiven for thinking that the justices in the majority appear to see religious exercise as somehow imperiled, an understanding that may not match reality. As the writer Margaret Talbot observed, "[t]he America of 2022 is quite plainly not a country where citizens' ability to worship freely is in jeopardy," yet certain justices "often act as if they were alone in a broken elevator, jabbing the emergency button and hollering for help." *Amy Coney Barrett's Long Game*, The New Yorker, February 14 & 21, 2022.

# Chapter 10
# Justiciability

**Add after Note 2 on page 908:**

## California v. Texas
## 593 U.S. ___ (2021)

Justice BREYER delivered the opinion of the Court.

As originally enacted in 2010, the Patient Protection and Affordable Care Act required most Americans to obtain minimum essential health insurance coverage. The Act also imposed a monetary penalty, scaled according to income, upon individuals who failed to do so. In [the Tax Cuts and Jobs Act of 2017], Congress effectively nullified the penalty by setting its amount at $0.

Texas and 17 other States brought this lawsuit against the United States and federal officials. They were later joined by two individuals (Neill Hurley and John Nantz). The plaintiffs claim that without the penalty the Act's minimum essential coverage requirement is unconstitutional. Specifically, they say neither the Commerce Clause nor the Tax Clause (nor any other enumerated power) grants Congress the power to enact it. They also argue that the minimum essential coverage requirement is not severable from the rest of the Act. Hence, they believe the Act as a whole is invalid. We do not reach these questions of the Act's validity, however, for Texas and the other plaintiffs in this suit lack the standing necessary to raise them.

### I

We begin by describing the provision of the Act that the plaintiffs attack as unconstitutional. The Act says in relevant part:

**"(a) Requirement to maintain minimum essential coverage**

"An applicable individual shall ... ensure that the individual, and any dependent ... who is an applicable individual, is covered under minimum essential coverage ....

**"(b) Shared responsibility payment**

**"(1) In general**

"If a taxpayer who is an applicable individual ... fails to meet the requirement of subsection (a) ... there is hereby imposed on the taxpayer a penalty ... in the amount determined under subsection (c).

**"(2) Inclusion with return**

"Any penalty imposed by this section ... shall be included with a taxpayer's return ... for the taxable year ....".

The Act defines "applicable individual" to include all taxpayers who do not fall within a set of exemptions. As first enacted, the Act set forth a schedule of penalties applicable to those who failed to meet its minimum essential coverage requirement. The penalties varied with a taxpayer's income and exempted, among others, persons whose annual incomes fell below the federal income tax filing threshold.

And the Act required that those subject to a penalty include it with their annual tax return. In 2017, Congress amended the Act by setting the amount of the penalty in each category in § 5000A(c) to "$0," effective beginning tax year 2019.

Before Congress amended the Act, the Internal Revenue Service (IRS) had implemented § 5000A(b) by requiring individual taxpayers to report with their federal income tax return whether they carried minimum essential coverage (or could claim an exemption). After Congress amended the Act, the IRS made clear that the statute no longer requires taxpayers to report whether they do, or do not, maintain that coverage.

In 2018, Texas and more than a dozen other States (state plaintiffs) brought this lawsuit against the Secretary of Health and Human Services and the Commissioner of Internal Revenue, among others. They sought a declaration that § 5000A(a)'s minimum essential coverage provision is unconstitutional, a finding that the rest of the Act is not severable from § 5000A(a), and an injunction against the rest of the Act's enforcement. Hurley and Nantz (individual plaintiffs) soon joined them. Although nominally defendants to the suit, the United States took the side of the plaintiffs. Therefore California, along with 15 other States and the District of Columbia (state intervenors), intervened in order to defend the Act's constitutionality, as did the U. S. House of Representatives at the appellate stage.

After taking evidence, the District Court found that the individual plaintiffs had standing to challenge the constitutionality of the minimum essential coverage provision, § 5000A(a). ...

On appeal, a panel majority agreed with the District Court that the plaintiffs had standing and that the minimum essential coverage provision was unconstitutional. ... The state intervenors, defending the Act, asked us to review the lower court decision. We granted their petition for certiorari.

## II

We proceed no further than standing. The Constitution gives federal courts the power to adjudicate only genuine "Cases" and "Controversies." Art. III, § 2. That power includes the requirement that litigants have standing. A plaintiff has standing only if he can "allege personal injury fairly traceable to the defendant's allegedly unlawful conduct and likely to be redressed by the requested relief." *DaimlerChrysler Corp. v. Cuno* (2006) (internal quotation marks omitted). Neither the individual nor the state plaintiffs have shown that the injury they will suffer or have suffered is "fairly traceable" to the "allegedly unlawful conduct" of which they complain.

### A

We begin with the two individual plaintiffs. They claim a particularized individual harm in the form of payments they have made and will make each month to carry the minimum essential coverage that § 5000A(a) requires. The individual plaintiffs point to the statutory language, which, they say, commands them to buy health insurance. But even if we assume that this pocketbook injury satisfies the injury element of Article III standing, the plaintiffs nevertheless fail to satisfy the traceability requirement.

Their problem lies in the fact that the statutory provision, while it tells them to obtain that coverage, has no means of enforcement. With the penalty zeroed out, the IRS can no longer seek a penalty from those who fail to comply. Because of this, there is no possible Government action that is causally connected to the plaintiffs' injury —the costs of purchasing health insurance. Or to put the matter conversely, that injury is not "fairly traceable" to any "allegedly unlawful conduct" of which the plaintiffs complain. *Allen v. Wright* (1984). They have not pointed to any way in which the defendants, the Commissioner of Internal Revenue and the Secretary of Health and Human Services, will act to enforce § 5000A(a). They have not shown how any other federal employees could do so either. In a word, they have not shown that any kind of Government action or conduct has caused or will cause the injury they attribute to § 5000A(a).

The plaintiffs point to cases concerning the Act that they believe support their standing. But all of those cases concerned the Act when the provision was indisputably *enforceable*, because the penalty provision was still in effect. These cases therefore tell us nothing about how the statute is enforced, or could be enforced, today.

[O]ur cases have consistently spoken of the need to assert an injury that is the result of a statute's actual or threatened *enforcement*, whether today or in the future. In the absence of contemporary enforcement, we have said that a plaintiff claiming standing must show that the likelihood of future enforcement is "substantial." *Susan B. Anthony List v. Driehaus* (2014).

The plaintiffs point out that these and other precedents concern injuries anticipated in the future from a statute's later enforcement. Here, the plaintiffs say, they have already suffered a pocketbook injury, for they have already bought health insurance. They also emphasize the Court's statement in *Lujan v. Defenders of Wildlife* (1992) that, when a plaintiff is the "object" of a challenged Government action, "there is ordinarily little question that the action ... has caused him injury, and that a judgment preventing ... the action will redress it." But critically, unlike *Lujan*, here no unlawful Government action "fairly traceable" to § 5000A(a) caused the plaintiffs' pocketbook harm. Here, there is no action—actual or threatened—whatsoever. There is only the statute's textually unenforceable language.

To consider the matter from the point of view of another standing requirement, namely, redressability, makes clear that the statutory language alone is not sufficient. To determine whether an injury is redressable, a court will consider the relationship between "the judicial relief requested" and the "injury" suffered. *Allen*. The plaintiffs here sought injunctive relief and a declaratory judgment. The injunctive relief, however, concerned the Act's other provisions that they say are inseverable from the minimum essential coverage requirement. The relief they sought in respect to the only provision they attack as unconstitutional—the minimum essential coverage provision—is declaratory relief, namely, a judicial statement that the provision they attacked is unconstitutional.

Remedies, however, ordinarily "operate with respect to specific parties." *Murphy* v. *National Collegiate Athletic Assn.* (2018) (THOMAS, J., concurring) (internal quotation marks omitted). In the absence of any specific party, they do not simply operate "on legal rules in the abstract." *Id.* (internal quotation marks omitted).

This suit makes clear why that is so. The Declaratory Judgment Act, alone does not provide a court with jurisdiction. Instead, just like suits for every other type of remedy, declaratory-judgment actions must satisfy Article III's case-or-controversy requirement. See *MedImmune, Inc.* v. *Genentech, Inc.* (2007). At a minimum, this means that the dispute must "be 'real and substantial' and 'admit of specific relief through a decree of a conclusive character, as distinguished from an opinion advising what the law would be upon a hypothetical state of facts.'" *Id.* (alteration omitted). Thus, to satisfy Article III standing, we must look elsewhere to find a remedy that will redress the individual plaintiffs' injuries.

What is that relief? The plaintiffs did not obtain damages. Nor, as we just said, did the plaintiffs obtain an injunction in respect to the provision they attack as unconstitutional. But, more than that: How could they have sought any such injunction? The provision is unenforceable. There is no one, and nothing, to enjoin. They cannot enjoin the Secretary of Health and Human Services, because he has no power to enforce § 5000A(a) against them. And they do not claim that they might enjoin Congress. In these circumstances, injunctive relief could amount to no more than a declaration that the statutory provision they attack is unconstitutional, *i.e.*, a declaratory judgment. But once again, that is the very kind of relief that cannot alone supply jurisdiction otherwise absent.

The matter is not simply technical. To find standing here to attack an unenforceable statutory provision would allow a federal court to issue what would amount to "an advisory opinion without the possibility of any judicial relief." *Los Angeles* v. *Lyons* (1983) (Marshall, J., dissenting). It would threaten to grant unelected judges a general authority to conduct oversight of decisions of the elected branches of Government. Article III guards against federal courts assuming this kind of jurisdiction.

**B**

Next, we turn to the state plaintiffs. We conclude that Texas and the other state plaintiffs have similarly failed to show that they have alleged an "injury fairly traceable to the defendant's allegedly *unlawful* conduct." *Cuno* (internal quotation marks omitted; emphasis added). They claim two kinds of pocketbook injuries. First, they allege an indirect injury in the form of the increased use of (and therefore cost to) state-operated medical insurance programs. Second, they claim a direct injury resulting from a variety of increased administrative and related expenses required, they say, by the minimum essential coverage provision, along with other provisions of the Act that, they add, are inextricably "interwoven" with it.

First, the state plaintiffs claim that the minimum essential coverage provision has led state residents subject to it to enroll in state-operated or state-sponsored insurance programs such as Medicaid, the Children's Health Insurance Program (CHIP), and health insurance programs for state employees. The state plaintiffs say they must pay a share of the costs of serving those new enrollees. As with the individual plaintiffs, the States also have failed to show how this injury is directly traceable to any actual or possible unlawful Government conduct in enforcing § 5000A(a). That alone is enough to show that they, like the individual plaintiffs, lack Article III standing.

But setting aside that pure issue of law, we need only examine the initial factual premise of their claim to uncover another fatal weakness: The state plaintiffs have failed to show that the challenged minimum essential coverage provision, without any prospect of penalty, will harm them by leading more individuals to enroll in these programs.

We have said that, where a causal relation between injury and challenged action depends upon the decision of an independent third party (here an individual's decision to enroll in, say, Medicaid), "standing is not precluded, but it is ordinarily 'substantially more difficult' to establish," *Lujan* (quoting *Allen*). To satisfy that burden, the plaintiff must show at the least "that third parties will likely react in predictable ways." *Department of Commerce v. New York* (2019). And, "at the summary judgment stage, such a party can no longer rest on ... mere allegations, but must set forth ... specific facts" that adequately support their contention. *Clapper v. Amnesty Int'l* (2013) (internal quotation marks omitted). The state plaintiffs have not done so.

The programs to which the state plaintiffs point offer their recipients many benefits that have nothing to do with the minimum essential coverage provision of § 5000A(a). [N]either logic nor intuition suggests that the presence of the minimum essential coverage requirement would lead an individual to enroll in one of those programs that its absence would lead them to ignore. A penalty might have led some inertia-bound individuals to enroll. But without a penalty, what incentive could the provision provide?

The evidence that the state plaintiffs introduced in the District Court does not show the contrary. That evidence consists of 21 statements (from state officials) about how new enrollees will increase the costs of state health insurance programs, along with one statement taken from a 2017 Congressional Budget Office (CBO) Report.

Of the 21 statements, we have found only 4 that allege that added state costs are attributable to the minimum essential coverage requirement. And all four refer to that provision as it existed *before Congress removed the penalty* effective beginning tax year 2019, *i.e.*, while a penalty still existed to be enforced.

One other declaration refers to increased costs to the States as employers, but it is vague as to the time period at issue.

The state plaintiffs emphasize one further piece of evidence, a CBO Report released in 2017. At that time, Congress was considering whether to repeal the minimum essential coverage provision or, instead, simply set the penalty for failure to obtain coverage to $0 for all taxpayers. The state plaintiffs focus on the paragraph of the CBO Report that says that either way, the result would be "very similar," for "only a small number of people" would continue to enroll in health insurance solely out of a "willingness to comply with the law." And they argue that a "small number" is sufficient (by raising costs in furnishing Medicaid and CHIP) to provide them with standing.

In our view, however, this predictive sentence without more cannot show that the minimum essential coverage provision was the cause of added enrollment to state health plans. It does not explain, for example, who would buy insurance that they would not otherwise have bought. (For example, individuals who purchase insurance on individual exchanges—like individual plaintiffs Hurley and Nantz—do not increase the relevant costs to the States of furnishing coverage.) Nor does it explain *why* they might do so. The CBO statement does not adequately trace the necessary connection between the provision without a penalty and new enrollment in Medicaid and CHIP. We have found no other significant evidence that might keep the CBO statement company.

Unsurprisingly, the States have not demonstrated that an unenforceable mandate will cause their residents to enroll in valuable benefits programs that they would otherwise forgo. It would require far stronger evidence than the States have offered here to support their counterintuitive theory of standing, which rests on a "highly attenuated chain of possibilities." *Clapper*.

The state plaintiffs add that § 5000A(a)'s minimum essential coverage provision also causes them to incur additional costs directly. They point to the costs of providing beneficiaries of state health plans with information about their health insurance coverage, as well as the cost of furnishing the IRS with that related information.

The problem with these claims, however, is that other provisions of Act, not the minimum essential coverage provision, impose these other requirements. Nothing in the text of these form provisions suggests that they would not operate without § 5000A(a). These provisions refer to § 5000A *only* to pick up a different subsection's *definition* of "minimum essential coverage." To show that the minimum essential coverage requirement is unconstitutional would not show that enforcement of any of these other provisions violates the Constitution. The state plaintiffs do not claim the contrary. The Government's conduct in question is therefore not "fairly traceable" to enforcement of the "allegedly unlawful" provision of which the plaintiffs complain—§ 5000A(a). *Allen*.

The state plaintiffs complain of other pocketbook injuries. They say, for example, that, in order to avoid a "substantial tax penalty," they will have to "offer their full-time employees (and qualified dependents) minimum essential coverage under an eligible employer-sponsored plan." They say that the Act's insistence that they "expand

Medicaid eligibility" has led to "increas[ed] ... Medicaid expenditures." And they argue that "the [Act]'s vast and complex rules and regulations" will require additional expenditures. They seem to argue that they will have to pay more to expand coverage for employees who work 30–39 hours per week, and for those who become too old to remain in foster care.

Again, the problem for the state plaintiffs is that these other provisions also operate independently of § 5000A(a). At most, those provisions pick up only § 5000A(f)'s definition of minimum essential coverage in related subsections. No one claims these other provisions violate the Constitution. Rather, the state plaintiffs attack the constitutionality of only the minimum essential coverage provision. They have not alleged that they have suffered an "injury fairly traceable to the defendant's allegedly unlawful conduct." *Cuno.*

\* \* \*

[The plaintiffs] have failed to show that they have standing to attack as unconstitutional the Act's minimum essential coverage provision. Therefore, we reverse the Fifth Circuit's judgment in respect to standing, vacate the judgment, and remand the case with instructions to dismiss.

*It is so ordered.*

[Concurring opinion of Justice THOMAS omitted.]

[Dissenting opinion of Justice ALITO omitted.]

## NOTES AND QUESTIONS

1. Another term, another case implicating the Affordable Care Act. Justice Breyer's majority opinion fills in the details of the story since the first case challenging the Act, which we discussed at length in connection with the sections of the course addressing the Commerce Clause, the Spending Clause, and the Necessary and Proper Clause. What is the basis for the challenge to the Act made by the plaintiffs (individuals and states) in this case?

2. The Court appears to agree that the plaintiffs have suffered a cognizable injury. What is that injury? Why does the Court term this harm a "pocketbook" injury—what does that mean?

3. Setting aside the injury-in-fact requirement, on which prongs of the test for standing derived from *Lujan* does this challenge to the Act fail? Why does the Court conclude that causation is not satisfied here, given the existence of a cognizable injury? What about redressability? Is there anyone who might have standing to make this challenge after this case?

4. As noted above, standing is just one of the justiciability requirements imposed under the Constitution; even if a plaintiff has standing, a court will not proceed if the suit concerns a political question.

**Equal Protection:** Plessey v Ferguson, Brown, Korematsu → Concentration camps, Loving, Johnson v Cali → inmate seg for gang, Yick wo, Arlington heights, Cops, Rodriguez schools, Zablocki bastard kids, Cleburne disabled housing, Lee optical, NY transit methadone, Craig 21 vs 18 drinking, Michael statutory rape, US v Virginia VMI school, Richmond quotas, Grutter race law school factor, Gratz not allowed major race points, Parents Involved no bussing based on race, Plyler undocumented children

---

**Fund rights:** Education Kinda, Marriage, Voting

| Wealth: • defining trait for whole group<br>• total deprivation | Getting to Strict Scrutiny |
|---|---|
| **Class:** Suspect<br>↳ immutable characteristic<br>↳ political minority<br>↳ history of discrim | 1. Suspect class on face<br>2. Face neut by 100% impact<br>3. Face neut less than 100%<br>  A. Stat significant impact<br>  B. invidious intent<br>    1. Historical background<br>    2. Leg/Admin history<br>    3. Substantive departure |

Compelling racial int by state
1. Affirmative Action in Higher ed
2. Prevent re-seg
3. remedy state sanction Past descrim

---

• Prima facie case
• rebut by state - legit interest that discrim
  - rebut its just pretextual

time at a gathering in a house of worship to: the lesser of 10 people or 25% of maximum capacity in a red zone; the lesser of 25 people or 33% of maximum capacity in an orange zone; and 50% of maximum capacity in a yellow zone.

Both the Roman Catholic Diocese of Brooklyn and Agudath Israel of America (together with Agudath Israel of Kew Garden Hills and its employee and Agudath Israel of Madison and its rabbi) brought lawsuits against the Governor of New York. They claimed that the fixed-capacity restrictions of 10 people in red zones and 25 people in orange zones were too strict—to the point where they violated the First Amendment's protection of the free exercise of religion. Both parties asked a Federal District Court for a preliminary injunction that would prohibit the State from enforcing these red and orange zone restrictions.

After receiving evidence and hearing witness testimony, the District Court in the Diocese's case found that New York's regulations were "crafted based on science and for epidemiological purposes." It wrote that they treated "religious gatherings . . . more favorably than similar gatherings" with comparable risks, such as "public lectures, concerts or theatrical performances." The court also recognized the Diocese's argument that the regulations treated religious gatherings less favorably than what the State has called "essential businesses," including, for example, grocery stores and banks. But the court found these essential businesses to be distinguishable from religious services and declined to "second guess the State's judgment about what should qualify as an essential business." The District Court denied the motion for a preliminary injunction. The Diocese appealed, and the District Court declined to issue an emergency injunction pending that appeal. The Court of Appeals for the Second Circuit also denied the Diocese's request for an emergency injunction pending appeal, but it called for expedited briefing and scheduled a full hearing on December 18 to address the merits of the appeal. This Court, unlike the lower courts, has now decided to issue an injunction that would prohibit the State from enforcing its fixed-capacity restrictions on houses of worship in red and orange zones while the parties await the Second Circuit's decision. I cannot agree with that decision.

[T]he Court's decision runs contrary to ordinary governing law. We have previously said that an injunction is an "extraordinary remedy." *Nken v. Holder* (2009) (internal quotation marks omitted). That is especially so where, as here, the applicants seek an injunction prior to full argument and contrary to the lower courts' determination. Here, we consider severe restrictions. Those restrictions limit the number of persons who can attend a religious service to 10 and 25 congregants (irrespective of mask-wearing and social distancing). And those numbers are indeed low. But whether, in present circumstances, those low numbers violate the Constitution's Free Exercise Clause is far from clear, and, in my view, the applicants must make such a showing here to show that they are entitled to "the